My Face for the World to See

My Face
for the
World to See

Liz Renay

BARRICADE BOOKS

Fort Lee, New Jersey

Published by Barricade Books Inc.
185 Bridge Plaza North
Suite 308-A
Fort Lee, NJ 07024
www.barricadebooks.com

Reprint Edition 2002
Preface Copyright © 2002 by Lyle Stuart
Copyright © 1971 by Liz Renay
All Rights Reserved.

Library of Congress Cataloging-in-Publication Data
Renay, Liz.
    My face for the world to see / Liz Renay
        p. cm.
    ISBN: 1-56980-228-9 (pbk. : alk. paper)
    1. Renay, Liz. 2. Women ex-convicts--United States--
Biography. 3. Stripteasers--United States--Biography. 4. Mafia--
United States. I. Title.

HV6248.R395 A3 2002
364.1'34--dc21
[B]
                                                    2002016399

Manufactured in the United States of America
First Printing of Barricade Edition

CONTENTS

The men sat in the next booth at the Brown Derby. My back was to them. Suddenly I perked up as I heard my name.

"Liz Renay," one of them said. "There's a girl who had some tough breaks."

"She brought it on herself," the other voice said.

"Still . . . it's kind of sad. She wasn't just another one of those French pastries who come to Hollywood to look for fame. She had it. She has one of the most beautiful faces I ever saw. You know, she just missed being great."

I turned to get a look at the man who had just spoken. I recognized him as William Ornstein, a reporter for *Hollywood Reporter*.

Ornstein spoke again: "Yeah, that Renay really could have made it big. She was on the way to becoming a superstar. Add a few good breaks and subtract a few of the bad ones, and, you know, she could have been Marilyn Monroe."

PUBLISHER'S PREFACE

In 1971, dozens of famous movie stars, athletes and writers attended the International Book Fair in Frankfurt, Germany. So reported *Publishers Weekly*, adding, "But the star of the Frankfurt Book Fair was Liz Renay."

Indeed she was!

Bill Gaines, publisher of *MAD Magazine* and I had fun walking about twenty feet behind her as she traversed the aisles making her way through the book exhibits. People would rush over to watch her, low-cut blouse and all. She strolled, oblivious of the stares.

Only Liz could streak, stark naked, through a cheering crowd of some 5,000 fans at Hollywood and Vine and maintain her dignity. That happened as a publicity stunt after the initial publication of *My Face For The World To See*. A photo of that event is in this volume.

The late Steve Allen told me he was a judge at a Marilyn Monroe look-alike contest when Liz walked into the hall. She was late as usual, but Steve and the other judges thought Marilyn herself had come to watch the event. (Of course, she won.)

At this moment, Liz is in her Las Vegas home at work on *Sequel*. It will be a book that chronicles all the exciting things that have happened to her since this book was published.

"Exciting" could be her middle name, for not a day goes by without Liz having a new adventure. A famous billionaire casino owner wants to take her to lunch but she can't spare the time, because today Liz is preparing to be interviewed and photographed by a Mexican magazine and a Spanish magazine. This while a television crew is on its way from Canada to film a one-hour documentary on the lady whose most recent book was titled *My First 2,000 Men.*

I have often observed that any week in Liz's life is more eventful than a year in the lives of most of us poor mortals!

Lyle Stuart
Fort Lee, NJ
May, 2002

Chapter 1

BIG TOWN: NEW YORK

The room swam crazily as I downed another glass of champagne. The lights blurred and the music sounded strangely loud in my ears. "I'd better watch it," I thought. "I'm getting high again." I smiled up into the eyes of the John at my table. He was waving a twenty-dollar bill in my face. "See this, Honey? I got lotsa these, just waiting for a pretty baby like you—understand?"

Something about the music was suddenly familiar. It was my introduction. I sprang from my chair. I had to get dressed.

I flew up the stairs to the dressing room. I had to get into my costume and out the stage door before the music finished and the Master of Ceremonies announced my name. Good Lord, how could I make it? I was so high on champagne, I was all thumbs.

My heart pounded as I fumbled into the glittering gold sequin costume.

A hand touched my shoulder. "I wanta talk to you, Sweetie." I didn't look around; I knew that acid voice. It was Patty.

"Don't bother me, that's my music out there." God, couldn't she see I was frantic!

"Look, Bitch, I said I wanted to talk to you," she snarled, grabbing me and whirling me around to face her, her long

nails digging into my arm. "That's my territory you're cut-
tin' in on down there, in case you didn't know it!"

I felt hot blood rush to my face. Too many people were
putting their hands on me tonight. The last notes of my in-
tro clanged in my ears. The M.C. was announcing my act. I
had to get out there.

No time to think. I grabbed Patty by both shoulders and
flung her from me. She went bouncing down the stairs like
a bag of cantaloupes. I stepped through the stage curtain
and smiled woozily at the Johns.

Big Mike Mascarra didn't miss a beat at the cash register.
A waiter rushed up to him. "There's trouble in the dressing
room with Liz."

Big Mike smiled. "Don't worry. Whatever it is, Liz can
handle it."

I'd run into trouble in Mike's place twice before. The
last girl that started a fight with me departed with less dignity than Patty. She'd started the fracas, but in the course
of events I ripped her flimsy gown off her body.

As I concluded my wild jazz number, ending with nothing but sequins and beads and the Johns panting three deep
at the bar, I saw Patty being hustled out of the club, bag and
baggage. Big Mike had fired her on the spot. I felt a passing moment of guilt.

I hadn't meant it to go that way. I never started a fight,
but there was rebellion within me, surging so close to the
surface it could be touched off at a finger snap. Perhaps it
was the combination of Iroquois Indian blood and cheap
champagne. Or, again, the never-ending procession of men
—men—men. Men to be nice to, even if at times they
seemed loathsome.

I ambled up to the bar to cool off. The hell with the John
at my table and his stinking champagne! I needed a drink.
"Bourbon and Coke," I said. The bartender started to re-

mind me I had a champagne buyer at my table, but, seeing my defiant mood, poured the bourbon instead.

I leaned my elbow against the bar, preparing for my solitary drink and moment of relaxation. Suddenly there was a commotion at the door. An elegantly dressed gentleman was being welcomed with much ado. He was wearing a tuxedo and a snobbish air. Probably one of the crowd from the 21 Club a few doors up the street. Must have wandered into our clip joint to do a little slumming.

He sidled up to me, staring obnoxiously into my face with a silly grin. I turned back to my bourbon and Coke. This was my moment for reflection, and I'd be damned if this bore would spoil it. But that was wishful thinking. He refused to be ignored. He nudged me with his elbow.

"Say something funny. Amuse me!"

I looked at him coldly. "I'm sorry but I'm not the comedienne of this show. I'll introduce her to you." I motioned for Mary at the end of the bar. She trotted up, flashing her snaggle-toothed smile and waving her pigtails at him. From the corner of my eye I saw a look of dismay cross his face as I headed back to my table to join the ousted Patty's old flame with his champagne bottle and twenty-dollar bills.

"Who's that girl?" asked the tuxedoed snob, staring after me. "She's fascinating."

Soon the doorman called me aside. "That man at the bar is loaded," he said, "and he likes you. He wants to send you a bottle of champagne. Why don't you get him to a table and invite a bunch of the girls over to help you run up his tab? This guy's a real mark."

"I don't like him," I said. "Give him to someone else. I'm busy."

"But he wants you, Honey. Do as I tell you. You'll run up a big champagne commission on this one."

The club manager rushed over. "What'sa matter with you, Liz? Mr. Lancey's a class guy. He's the biggest spender in the joint tonight. All you gotta do is sit with him."

"Look, I told you I don't like this character. So fire me." He wouldn't call my bluff. He couldn't afford to fire me. I had the biggest following on 52nd Street. My champagne orders more than tripled those of any other girl he had. If I found someone especially annoying, why shouldn't I ignore him?

Lancey moved to the other end of the bar within earshot of my table. I watched with amused detachment as the manager approached him.

"Who does this girl think she is?" Lancey sputtered.

"Liz Renay's job is to give a performance on stage three times nightly," soothed the manager. "Who she spends time with between shows is her decision."

"If that girl doesn't join me, I'm taking my business across the street," said the stuffed tuxedo.

"Good evening, Mr. Lancey," answered the manager.

"Ha, ha, ha," laughed Patty's former John.

Lancey did not go. Instead he sent a stream of champagne bottles to my table and bribed someone for my address before he finally stepped out the door into his waiting limousine. I didn't realize it then, but Warren Lancey would play an important role in my life in years to come.

As the last stragglers wandered out the door, with a lot of phony promises and equally phony numbers tucked into their otherwise empty billfolds, I prepared to leave the club.

Anthony Coppola strode up to me. God, again! He was a friend of Big Mike's. He always seemed to be dropping in at Mike's place around closing time. He seemed to come out of the woodwork!

"Hi, Baby," he smiled. "How about joining me for a little breakfast?"

The same tired invitation.

"Thanks, but no thanks," I said, as I walked out under the canopy facing the street to hail a cab.

He was right behind me. His fingers closed hard around my arm. "Don't brush me off again, Baby! When I ask a lady to join me, it's an honor. Do you like your job?"

I stared back into his cold, shining eyes. "Not particularly," I said. "It's no bargain. Besides, if you don't leave me the hell alone, Mike won't have to fire me, I'll quit!"

The damp fingers released their grip on my arm and tough guy Anthony Coppola stepped forward to open the cab door for me like a little Sir Walter Raleigh.

"I like you," he chuckled. "You're a different kind of a broad. Some day I'm going to find out what makes you tick!"

I settled back into the cab, glad to get away from the garish glitter of old 52nd Street's strip joints. In the last few months I had become so much a part of this life. Yet, though I was of it, I was not with it. It was a compartmentalized section of my existence necessary for survival.

I tried to keep myself aloof from the smoke-filled dens as much as possible. Though sometimes the moan and wail of the saxophone got to me and my heart throbbed in rhythm with its low-down bluesy beat. Sometimes the cheap champagne colored my moods, and I looked with amusement at the whole crazy routine, playing it for laughs as well as money.

We were told to order nothing but champagne when a John offered to buy drinks. The trick was to run his tab up as fast as possible. We swallowed as little as we could get by with, dumping a glassful into the ice bucket every time the John turned his back. Sometimes we'd dump half a bottle out while he wasn't looking. Even so, just drinking a glass or two out of every magnum, it was tough not to get at least a little drunk before the night was over.

I hated this part of the routine most of all. In a way I felt sorry for the poor slobs. I developed the habit of flitting from table to table and from John to John, rarely promoting more than one bottle of champagne from each.

The sport of the game was a challenge. I enjoyed showing off a little in front of the other girls by doubling or tripling their champagne take. This made me valuable and gave me special privileges and immunities.

My taxi pulled up to the curb of the swank Gold Key Club, where I was to meet my date. Four A.M.! What a time for a date. All my dates were at 4:00 A.M. That was when 52nd Street clubs closed and the after-hour joints started swinging. The Gold Key Club was an "in" place. It was owned by gangsters. The Gold Key catered to people from all walks of life, including members of high society, who found it exciting to rub elbows with mobsters after hours. Show people, business tycoons, and racketeers rambled around the club together, listening to the song stylist, or pouring a drink from the bottle at their table, or getting corny and ordering something sensible like ham and eggs.

My dates took me here for breakfast when 52nd Street closed. Tonight I was meeting Bernard Freed, a young lawyer I'd been seeing. Bernie never came to the club where I worked. He couldn't afford the champagne routine, but he was a nice breakfast companion and a good lay, any time I happened to be in the mood for him. He met my cab, paid the driver, and quickly escorted me inside.

Vinny Maro and Tony Bender eyed us as we walked in. They were the syndicate boys who ran the Key Club. They were good friends of Anthony Coppola. They knew Coppola had eyes for me.

Tony Coppola walked in a few moments later and glared at me from across the room. When I left the table for the ladies' room, he intercepted me. "You're making a big mistake, brushing me off for a punk like that," he said.

"My after-hours time is my own," I answered.

Just then Kitty Bell came tripping down the stairs from the ladies' lounge. "Liz, there's a new magazine on the stands with a story about you! You're on the cover of *Bold* this week. Isn't that great?"

"Oh yes, Kitty, just great." I felt like laughing. What the hell was great about it? But how could Kitty know? She was too much a part of the tinseled clip-tease world. It was her only world. How could she know that just six months ago I was a $250-a-show high-fashion model, parading the runways of the Grand Ballroom at the Waldorf-Astoria or the Chez Pierre, in $1,000-a-copy Paris originals, or posing for *Vogue, Charm,* and *Harper's Bazaar* at $50 an hour? How could Kitty know why I didn't consider it an honor to have my face and half-clad figure splashed across *Bold,* a magazine I had never heard of, and for free?

What contrast from the model's world to the world of the showgirl and stripteaser! My mind wandered for a moment to the strange, make-believe world of the fashion model, where I had existed for a year before fate abruptly altered my course and plunged me into the racy world of the night people of fantastic old 52nd Street—Sucker's Shangri-la.

I felt like a flower uprooted from an artificial hothouse atmosphere and tossed onto the open ground. As a high-fashion model, I had been taught to look aloof and unobtainable, to strive for the subtle approach, to diet to unbelievable thinness and, if any curves remained, to cover them

up. I was taught to play against being a woman, conceal
any glimmer of obvious sexiness and be the essence of re-
moteness.

I learned to look down my nose in this weird little world
of color, design, and emaciated females. There was such
conformity it seemed we were all cut from the same pattern, cast from the same mold, and the same artist had lined
us up and stenciled identical faces on all of us. We had eyebrows marked the same way, eyes lined the same way, and
lips the shape currently considered smart.

We were a roomful of sisters, existing in a swirl of pretty
hats, gloves, and accessories, smoothed on by fairy design-
ers and photographers. There were red-blooded American
males in the business too, though I didn't run across many.
Most of the male models I posed with looked like
they might waltz away any minute or spread their wings
and fly out the window.

Vogue magazine presided over everything. It was the
fashion model's bible. I wondered if any fashion model had
ever heard of the pocket-sized magazine called *Bold*, where
no one cared about the clothes you wore, as long as you
didn't wear too many. On the other hand, I wondered if a
girl like Kitty Bell had ever heard of *Vogue*.

I laughed as I remembered the time two photographers
strolled into the club, caught my act, and invited me to their
table.

"It's absolutely incredible," one of them said. "You look
exactly like a high-fashion model named Liz Renay."

"Really? Oh, come now, don't tell me I looked like a fashion model up there?"

"It's true. Your face is identical. You could be twins."

Just then Kitty Bell strolled over and plopped down at
the table.

"Hey, Kitty," I said, "these guys say I look like a high-fashion model up there. What do you think about that?"

"It's a new approach, anyway!" she laughed.

We changed the subject and ordered champagne. As the evening wore on, the photographers continued to stare at me, and exchanged looks. I was glad they left before the name "Liz Renay" was announced on the loudspeaker. I don't know how they recognized me, in my gaudy costume, exaggerated hairdo, and flashy make-up. When I became a dancer on 52nd Street, I had to gain back the weight I'd knocked myself out losing to become a model. As a model, it's great to be thin. All you show is an elegant face and glamorous clothing—but 52nd Street is more concerned about the body underneath the clothes. Johns aren't excited by protruding ribs and bony knees.

As Bernie drove me home from the Gold Key Club, I almost fell asleep in the car. The mist of dawn filtered through the streets, making the gray buildings look grayer.

"The whole town is just one big smudge of wishy-washy gray," I said aloud.

"What?" asked Bernie.

"Oh, nothing," I answered, not knowing why I said it, or what I meant.

In front of the Churchill Apartment Hotel I gave Bernie a sleepy kiss. He kept his motor running while I made a safe entrance into the lobby.

I stopped by the desk to pick up my key. The desk clerk gave me a handful of telephone messages. Strange! I wasn't accustomed to having an overflow of messages like this. I had only dated two men since the recent breakup of my marriage to Lou Layer: Bernie and a handsome international playboy named Albert Sasser. I kept my address a secret from the rest of the world. I came home from work alone in a cab on the nights I didn't meet Bernie or Albert for breakfast, and no one, but no one, had ever been inside my apartment at the Churchill.

I ruffled through the messages. There was a message from the attorney handling my divorce, one from Albert saying he'd be in the club tomorrow night, one from the cab driver who had found my missing earring. All the rest were from Mr. Lancey. He must have called every fifteen minutes to have left so many messages. Damn! I cursed whoever had given him my number.

I crumpled the slips of paper into a neat ball, tossed them into the lobby wastebasket, and rang for the elevator.

Chapter 2

THE WAY IT WAS

As I reached my apartment and turned the key in the lock, I heard a stir in the bedroom nearest the door. Funny about those kids. No matter how late it was, no matter how quiet I was, when the key turned in the lock they were awake.

I pushed the door open. Two tousle-headed, sleepy-eyed angels scrambled toward me. "Mama, Mama," they cried in exuberation, "you're home!" I knelt to embrace them.

"Yes, Darlings, Mama's home." I could hardly get the words out of my mouth, I was smothered with so many kisses and hugs. Each night when I returned from work I smoothed their blond hair, pinched their pink, freckled noses, and told them how much I loved them. "Now, don't forget, we are The Three Musketeers."

"Oh yes, Mama, we're The Three Musketeers. We'll always be together till the day we die."

I walked them to their beds, tucked them in, and kissed their pretty blue eyes and rosy lips. As I looked down, I noticed a smile playing around the corners of Brenda's delicate mouth. "Mama, Mama, I forgot to tell you, I pulled my tooth last night after you left for work." She dived under her pillow to find it. "Look," she cried, holding the little particle up for me to see.

"That's wonderful. You're a brave girl. Put it back under your pillow now so the Tooth Fairy can find it."

21

"I wish I had a loose tooth," sighed Johnny.

"Don't worry, John, you can have half of whatever the Tooth Fairy leaves me," she assured him. "Us musketeers hafta stick together."

Caplop!—went something in the living room. Bam-slam-flop! It was that crazy cat the kids had brought home. "That thing must think it's a dog or a baby kangaroo, leaping around the house, jumping off furniture like it was out of its mind." I sighed. It was such an ugly-looking, half Siamese, half-alley-cat breed of a thing, but the kids adored it. What could I say?

I walked into the living room. I didn't dare fall asleep, or I might not wake up in time to play Tooth Fairy. I sank into a worn armchair by the fireplace to watch the antics of that crazy cat and reminisce while the children fell asleep. Then I'd exchange a fifty-cent piece for the tooth under Brenda's pillow, fall into my bed in the next room, and get, damn it, to sleep.

The early morning light was seeping through the front window by now. I yawned as I looked at the big clock over the mantel. It was after 6:00 A.M. It would be 7:00 before I could get to bed. Oh well, someone had to play Tooth Fairy and, in the little world I had created for my angels inside that twelfth-floor apartment, there was only me. It was my job to make the myths I invented come true for them.

As I watched the awkward cat leap from its perch, land ajar, and skitter away, I remembered another cat—the cat I loved when I was a barefoot urchin in Mesa, Arizona. His name was Fraidy Cat. I named him that because he jumped every time Mama said "scat." He was afraid of his shadow. Fraidy Cat was a constant companion, participating in my imaginary games. I couldn't teach him to speak English, so I compromised by speaking cat language. Fraidy

Cat scolded me when I did anything wrong. He shared all my secrets.

Once I caught a baby owl that fell from its nest. I taught him to sit on my shoulder. He was a wonderful pet and the hit of the neighborhood until Fraidy Cat got jealous and ate him.

I loved to play on the banks of the irrigation ditch that ran down the side of the alley in back of our house. When it was low, my sister, Evelyn, and I liked to dangle our parched, dirty feet into its cool waters. Sometimes it rose waist high and we sneaked in swimming. Once Evelyn talked me into running away from home by floating down that ditch. I was four and she was seven.

"I'm going to run away to China," she said. "Want to come?"

"I don't know. Where is it?"

"It's on the bottom of the world, silly."

"I don't want to go there. I don't know how to walk up-side down."

"Everybody walks upside down in China, silly. Besides, all you do is stand on your head. It's the easiest thing in the world!"

"But what if I do it all wrong and the Chinamen make fun of me?"

"It won't matter what they say. You can't understand them anyway, 'cause they all talk Chinaman."

"Okay, then I'll go, but how will we get there?"

"We'll just float down the irrigation ditch in a boat, stu-pid."

"What boat?"

"Oh, just any old boat. If we can't find one, we'll borrow one of Mama's washtubs."

"Mama won't like it."

"We won't tell her, silly. By the time she finds out, we'll be halfway to China!"

Soon we were on our way. We dragged Mama's big washtub to the ditch banks, pushed it into the cement head gate, got in, and gave it a shove into open stream.

"You'll never regret you decided to come with me," Evelyn yelled, as the tub sank and we found ourselves waist deep in muddy ditch water. Worst of all, we had put on our best Sunday dresses for the trip. That was only the first of my many attempts to run away. I wasn't really running away from anything—I was trying to run to something. Something grand and glorious. Something beyond the narrow world I knew.

I had seen small glimpses of that wide, wonderful world in the magazines I found in trash cans lining the back alley. Rooting through trash cans in search of buried treasure was one of my favorite pastimes as a child. Sometimes I found broken toys, but most of all I liked the magazines.

They showed pictures of fancy homes with pretty, colored floors. No one in the magazine world had bare, plank floors like the ones in our little cabin. And no one in the pictures sat on apple boxes the way we did.

One day I found the prettiest home of all. It had a swimming pool and palm trees. I ran home to show the magazine to Mama.

"Mama, Mama," I shouted over the roar of a rumbling freight train, "look at this beautiful house. Will you read me what the picture says?"

Mama straightened up from her washtub, irritably snatched the magazine, and glanced at the picture. "It says this house belongs to some fool movie star, that's all. There's nothing in this book to interest you."

"Do all movie stars have houses like this?"

"Yeah, I 'spose most of 'em do."

"Then that's what I'm gonna be when I grow up—a movie star. Then I'll buy you and Daddy a house just like this!"

Mama looked at me and burst into laughter. "People like us don't grow up to be movie stars. Besides, you have to be beautiful to be a movie star and you're the ugliest kid I 'bout ever saw."

I was stunned. It had never occurred to me that I wasn't beautiful. I didn't really know how I looked. The only mirror in the house hung out of reach, above my head. I had taken it for granted that I was pretty. I ran for an apple box and dragged it beneath the old, cracked mirror on the wall. I climbed up and peered in. The reflection of a skinny, ragged, little urchin with stringy blonde hair, buggy green eyes, and a dirty nose stared back at me. Mama sure was right—I wasn't exactly beautiful. I wanted to erase the picture and pretend it wasn't me.

When Mama saw my tears, she felt sorry. "Cheer up, being pretty isn't everything. Beauty is only skin deep, but for goodness sakes give up the silly notion of becoming a movie star. Save yourself the heartbreak, Honey."

"No, I won't. I'll make myself beautiful somehow. I'll find a way. Just you wait and see." I ran into the yard and dragged in the washtub.

"What in heaven's name are you doing now?"

"I'm starting to get beautiful," I said. I took a bath, washed the dirt from my nose, combed my hair, and put on my only clean dress.

"You're a long way from beautiful, but I'll admit you sure made an improvement," laughed Mama.

I didn't forget the dream of becoming a movie star with palm trees and swimming pool. Each day I climbed up to

look into the mirror in hopes of progress. I tried to wish myself beautiful.

One day Evelyn read me the story that went with the picture. It was all about Hollywood and how it discovers its
stars. From what I could gather, the best way to get discovered was to attract the attention of a movie producer.

My mother heated water to scrub the family wash in an
old tub she called the boil pot. The boil pot sat on four legs,
propped over a fire pit. Mama boiled white clothes in the
soapy water. On washdays when the clothes were boiling, a
trail of white, smokelike vapor escaped from the contrap-
tion and floated through the air, casting a weird shadow on
the ground below. Somehow I got the notion that this was
how desert mirages were made, and, if I'd stand in the vapor, I'd cast a mirage of myself that would float across the
desert to Hollywood.

Mama kept chasing me away from the fire pit. "Why do
you always hang around the boil pot when I'm washing?"
she demanded.

"I'm trying to help myself get discovered faster," I said.

Mama just looked at me and shook her head. It was plain
she doubted my sanity at times. Poor Mama. I did so many
things to irritate her.

Most of all I loved to draw pictures. I drew them all over
the walls, the floors, the apple boxes, the outhouse, and on
every scrap of paper in sight. I didn't just draw pictures, I
made up stories about them. They lived and breathed and
talked for me. They were alive and real. I escaped into my
fantasy world every time I had a pencil in my hand.

"Why do you stick your nose in those silly old pictures?"
Mama would scold. "Why don't you run and play like other
kids instead of sitting in a corner scribbling on a piece of
paper?"

Sometimes I was too deep in thought to notice or hear. When I failed to answer, Mama would walk over and snatch the paper from me. "Let's see what's so all-fired interesting you can't stop long enough to answer me."

Once she noticed I had drawn a picture of a huge baby and a very small mama sitting in a baby's high chair.

"How come the baby's so big?" she asked.

"Oh, that's because a growing bear bit him."

"Yeah, well how come the mama is so little?"

"Because a shrinking bear bit her."

Anything could happen in my picture stories. Nothing was impossible. I adjusted everything to suit myself. I was Lord and Master, always creating.

Mama took a dim view of my art, but Little Granny was on my side. She never ceased to encourage me, except the time I borrowed the rouge out of her purse to make a sunset. She used to tousle my hair and say, "That's all right, Honey, just keep with it, and some day you'll grow up and be a famous artist!"

Mama didn't want Granny putting fancy notions in my head. "Don't listen to those fool ideas," she warned.

Later Granny took me aside. "Your mother's a good woman and she means well, but you mustn't let her discourage you. You gotta go ahead and do what you want in life, Honey. Do anything you're big enough to do. The sky's the limit! Nobody can stop you. You can marry a king or be a movie star. Who's to say you can't? Don't listen to rules made by other people. Make your own rules. You just live once. Do what you want and be what you want!"

Granny's devil-may-care philosophy helped shape my life. When Mama complained I was getting as bad as my Granny, I considered it a compliment.

Granny was the maverick of the family. She drank beer,

and read true confessions magazines until three in the morning. She lived life with a flourish. Mama didn't approve, though she loved Granny.

Granny never let anyone forget she'd won a beauty contest as a girl. She'd say, "After all, I wasn't chosen the prettiest girl in Tennessee for nothing, you know!"

Granny pretended not to see me when I sneaked supplies out of Mama's kitchen to paint with. I raided the kitchen for anything with a vivid color. I used beet juice, mustard, clothes bluing, and cocoa, smearing the stuff on my paper to color my pictures. Mustard and clothes bluing ran together, producing a beautiful green. I used it to paint my trees. I painted roses with beet juice, and used diluted bluing for my skies, with toothpaste clouds.

My triumph came when I painted a picture of Jesus on the cross and took it to Sunday School. The teacher made a fuss about it and asked me to stand up and show it to the class, and explain how I happened to make it.

I said, "This is Jesus. He has beet-juice blood, clothes-bluing eyes, and a chocolate mustache." Everyone laughed at me, even the teacher. I took Jesus and ran out of the church in tears. I was convinced no one liked my pictures and vowed I'd never show them to anyone again. For a while I gave up drawing picture stories and concentrated on trying to be a movie star.

Evelyn told me no one could be a movie star unless they learned to perform in front of an audience. I looked around for a place to perform. Our three-room cabin faced the railroad tracks at the front and irrigation ditch at the back. Beyond the ditch was a big corn field. The outhouse stood at the back of the lot. From my position behind the outhouse, I looked out across the alley, the irrigation ditch, and the corn field. The outhouse wall became my stage. The corn field was my audience. I'd stand there doing little dances and singing songs. Sometimes I'd make a dramatic speech, and once I pulled up my dress and showed the corn field I was a girl. I pretended the rustling cornstalks were a field of people—hundreds and thousands of them, rustling their leaves in applause.

In my world everything was alive. I talked to the dishes when it was my turn to dry. At night I talked to the two coats my mother threw over my bed as covering. One was a scratchy worn-out overcoat that had belonged to Daddy. The other was soft and velvety. Someone must have given it to Mama sometime. It was tattered and worn now, but to me it was still a queenly thing. Each night I'd say, "Good night, dear sweet cuddly coat. Good night, old mean ugly scratchy coat!"

When I started to school, a whole new world opened up for me. A world of electric lights, washbasins, and toilets that flushed. I was afraid to sit on them at first, but when I got used to it I got so brave I started stealing toilet paper to put in our outhouse. I just couldn't resist, it was so much nicer than catalogs. It was a thrill to learn about electric lights and inside toilets.

I met a girl named Bessie at school and, when she invited me home, I felt like Alice in Wonderland. I couldn't believe my eyes. The floors were covered with something soft and pretty like in the magazines. I wanted to lie down on it, so I did. Bessie explained to me it was called carpeting. Then I saw the most beautiful light I had ever seen. It looked like a thousand diamonds. Bessie said it was a chandelier. We went into the bathroom, and I saw a pretty white boat.

"That's not a boat, crazy," Bessie said. "It's a bathtub." When Bessie's mother invited me to sit down on the couch, I had no idea which piece of furniture to sit on. All I saw was a room full of soft, unidentifiable blobs of color.

"Sit down on the couch," repeated Bessie's mother.

"I don't know which thing it is," I stammered. "What does it look like?"

"Over here, crazy," said Bessie. "Don't you even know what a couch is? She's the dumbest girl I ever saw, Mother."

"Now, Bessie, you mustn't talk that way about your little friend."

One day Bessie decided to come home with me. "Is this where you live?" she asked, as we stopped in front of the little white house with the tumble-down fence. When we went inside, Bessie looked around disdainfully. She pulled up an apple box to sit on, and announced she always had cookies and milk when she came home from school.

"I'm sorry, but we're out of cookies today and out of milk too," Mama said. "Would you like a piece of bread?"

"Okay, I'll have bread and butter, since you have no cookies."

"We happen to be out of butter today too," Mama said, handing Bessie a dry biscuit.

Bessie told everyone at school I lived in a shack by the railroad tracks and didn't have butter to go on my bread. I couldn't understand why Bessie made fun of the way we lived. I had always been proud of our house. My father built it with his own hands. Every nail was a labor of love. He whittled the wooden latches with his pocketknife, to fasten the canvas flaps at the windows and hold the doors shut inside the house.

Daddy met Mama when he went to her parents' farm to buy grapes and found no one at home but Mama. She was sixteen and pretty, with long, auburn curls. Daddy was twenty-two and darkly handsome. He was Mama's first beau. She fell head over heels in love with him. Mama's family didn't approve too much, but the wedding took place anyway, and Daddy took every nickel he could scrape together to build the little love nest that became my childhood home. With the small savings he had, it seemed impossible they could establish a home at all, but Daddy was not to be defeated. He took what money there was and made it do the job. He bought a little lot on the ditch banks at the outskirts of town and had enough money left to buy a bed, a stove, and a pile of lumber. A saw, a hammer, and a keg of nails were his only tools. He just kept building until he ran out of lumber, I guess.

Anyway, he took care of the essentials before he ran out. A kitchen, a bedroom, and a room to put the kids in if there should be any—and there were. Five, to be exact. First, my sister Evelyn, then me, then my brothers Gene and Jack, and my baby sister Dorothy.

The tiny house soon became a going concern. Daddy built a big wooden table and gathered up a lot of apple boxes to sit on. He fashioned cupboards, a flour bin, and a closet from planks. Mama made curtains and bed sheets of flour sacks, and raised the canvas flaps to let the sun stream in. She sang at her dishpan and when she scrubbed at the washboard, priding herself on putting out a whiter wash than the neighbors' washing machines. "All it takes is a little elbow grease," she'd declare.

In those days the most important problem we had was getting enough to eat. I can't remember a time when I didn't feel hungry while growing up. I guess that's why I was skinny and bedraggled until I hit my teens and our circumstances, along with my figure, began to improve.

I didn't wait for our circumstances to change to get some of the things I wanted out of life. Patience was never my virtue. I wanted to live—now—present tense! I wanted more than the dress on my back and the dress in the wash. I was tired of having nothing, so I began to devise ways of having something. Soon I had a back-yard beauty shop going. My price was ten cents a head and bring your own bobby pins. The word spread, and I had plenty of customers. Some pretty fancy ladies took their places on the old apple box in our back yard.

The money bought many things. I bought a set of water colors and began painting pictures of roses to sell to my back-yard beauty shop customers. I bought sewing materials and copied styles from catalogs and magazines. The girls at school saw my dresses and wanted some like them, and their mothers paid me to make them.

Daddy suggested I become a professional artist, beauty operator, or dress designer.

"Gee, Daddy," I sighed, "I don't want to do those things. I like to paint and write stories, and I have a desire for acting I can't seem to push out of my mind."

I don't know why I still thought of movies when I had never been allowed inside a movie theater. The church wouldn't hear of it.

Chapter 3

THE LITTLE WHITE CHURCH

Funny about that little church and the role it played in my life.

My first memory of it goes back to when Mama used to carry me through its doors as a sleeping child, fighting her way through the swarm of bugs under the light above the entrance. Flitting, crawling beetles and bugs and Mama swatting them off my face and picking them out of my hair is my first unpleasant memory of that little white church, but certainly not my last.

I used to hide behind my song book while the windows outside were lined with sinners who came to poke fun at us. I prayed when the others prayed, but my prayer was, "Please God, don't let them see me in here. Don't let them find out I'm a Holy Roller!"

The little white church by the railroad tracks was always good for a laugh or two. Townspeople liked to peep in and make fun of the dead-serious attitudes of the church members inside.

When I started school, I could no longer hide behind my song book. "Lizzy's a Holy Roller—Lizzy's a Holy Roller!" was the favorite chant of my playmates every time they happened to think of it. I had no defense. I just died a little every time I heard those words.

I was confused. The church taught that everything most people did was wrong, sinful, and of the Devil. I heard kids talking about the fun they had at the skating rink. I was told it was a den of iniquity I must never enter. Movies were amusement halls of the Devil. I must never go near them.

Other girls' mothers wore make-up. I was taught make-up was a sin, the artwork of Satan. Church women looked drab with their clean, scrubbed faces. I couldn't understand how lipstick could be sinful.

Cigarettes and alcohol were an abomination.

We went swimming in dirty irrigation water because swimming pools were another trap of the Devil, where men and women exposed themselves half-dressed. Exposing one's body was an abomination in the sight of God, according to the church.

Dances were high on Satan's list, too. Even the radio and the funny papers were considered worldly pleasures.

The church was my mother's life. She went there faithfully, rain or shine, trailed by my sister and me and Daddy too, any time she could talk him into it.

Daddy didn't belong to the church, though he went occasionally to please Mama, who campaigned constantly to convert him.

Times were bad. My father pounded the pavements in search of a job that didn't exist. We were hungry. So were other people. Stealing got so bad in our neighborhood the father of four children was shot to death as a prowler in his early morning attempt to steal a bottle of milk for his sick baby.

Then, one day Daddy landed a job driving an ice truck. What a time to be an iceman! Prohibition had ended, but almost every icebox was full of home brew or home-made wine. Daddy was the housewife's dream, with his flashing dark eyes and black wavy hair. Everyone offered him a taste of this and a sip of that until he was tipsy by the time he finished his route. At first he was able to hide his drinking from Mama. But soon the whole thing got out of hand, and Daddy's escapades cut quite a swath across the pious town of Mesa.

Was I ashamed of this? I should say not! I gloried in Daddy's drinking. It was a wedge I could use against the ridicule of being a Holy Roller. The next time the kids chanted "Lizzy's a Holy Roller—Lizzy's a Holy Roller," I stopped them cold. "I am not! How could I be a Holy Roller? Why my Daddy's one of the best drunkards in town!" That stumped them. For a while they stopped calling me a Holy Roller.

Then one Sunday Mama's influence won out, Daddy became converted into the church, gave up his drinking, and threw himself into his new religion with great gusto. He was more zealous than my mother. Mama said he was on fire for God. He was so happy, he wanted to convert the world. He built a big sign on top of our little frame house proclaiming: "REPENT—FOR THE KINGDOM OF HEAVEN IS AT HAND!"

It didn't take long for the kids in the neighborhood to start chanting, "Lizzy's a Holy Roller" again. Now I couldn't hold Daddy up as a champion of evil. There was no way I could deny their charges with that sign up there. The time had come to defend myself. "Holy Roller" became fighting words to me, and soon the kids learned to leave me alone.

I decided to look into the church and its beliefs. If I was going to fight for something, I'd like to understand it. Besides if it was good enough for Daddy, maybe it was good enough for me.

I began to attend meetings regularly and tried hard to accept the teachings, though I found it next to impossible to convince myself that this little handful of people was right, while the rest of the world was wrong. The preacher had a scripture to explain this phenomenon, "The path to

righteousness is straight and narrow and few there are that
travel thereon, but the path to destruction is wide and many
travel thereon."

Though logic kept fighting the thing, I finally submerged
my doubts and embraced the church wholeheartedly. By
the time I was thirteen, the church had become my life just
as it was my Mother's, Father's, and sister Evelyn's. The
three younger children didn't fully understand, but they
knelt and joined the rest of us in family prayer anyway.
We ate, slept, and breathed religion. I don't think a family
of missionaries prayed more than we did.

Meantime I was growing up and rapidly becoming whis-
tle-bait. My mother worried about me. "Do you have to
wiggle your backside like that when you walk?" she asked.
"It looks disgraceful." I was bursting through last year's
sweaters and blouses. Mama said I looked positively vulgar
the way things were beginning to bounce around. The way
she described me I felt like a cross between a Jersey cow
and a bowl full of jelly.

When I showed up for high school that year, I was met
with wolf calls and a rush of attention from freshmen to
seniors. Half the football team tried to date me. It didn't
matter any more whether I was a Holy Roller or not.

High school boys weren't the only ones that took notice.
When I paraded down the street in my tight sweaters,
swishing my long blonde hair, older men tried to pick me
up in cars. When I ignored them, they often parked, got
out, and followed me, trying to pick me up. The attention
was flattering. I was tempted from time to time, but I was
too wrapped up in church routine to consider it. I was busy
being a child of God.

The church had a special C.A. group. C.A. stood for
"Christ's Ambassadors." It was a youth group with members from fifteen to thirty-five. This group was the life-

blood of the church. The C.A. group had church picnics, social get-togethers, Bible class, and rallies at other Assembly of God churches in neighboring towns. They competed for a banner given to the church having the most members present. The C.A. group was everything to me. I excitedly attended every meeting, picnic, and rally, even though I was not old enough to officially belong to the group.

Then it happened. The C.A. leader discovered I was only thirteen! We were attending a rally at a nearby church. Competition was keen, and we needed every count to win the banner. "Stand up, Liz," she whispered. "What's wrong with you?"

"I can't. I'm not old enough!"

"How old are you?"

"Thirteen," I whispered.

The Christ Ambassador leader looked shocked. "I'll see you after the meeting." After the rally, she cornered me. "You can't be a C.A. any longer now that we know your age. I had no idea you were so young."

"Can't be a C.A.!" I echoed. "But I've got to be a C.A. It's my life. I just live from meeting to meeting."

"Sorry, you'll have to wait until you're fifteen. Come back in a couple of years and we'll be glad to have you in the group."

"Come back in a couple of years! You can't mean it! What am I going to do in the meantime? Sit in the corner?"

"If we let thirteen-year-olds in, we'd have to let twelve-year-olds in and ten-year-olds—there'd be no end to it. We've got to draw the line somewhere and stick to it," she said.

"But I'm different," I pleaded. "I'm not an average thirteen-year-old. I'm big for my age. You didn't even know I wasn't fifteen until I told you."

"That's all the more reason I can't let you belong to this group. You're a child with a woman's body. You mustn't be exposed to young, 'dating-age' males. They may forget you're a child and treat you as a woman, and you don't have a woman's mind or experience to cope with such things. You will just have to wait."

Suddenly I was angry. The church was disowning me! I had suffered the humiliation of it, fought for it, given up pleasure for it, and now it didn't want me! Well, the hell with it!

"If you think I'll go play with my dolls for two years until you let me become a C.A., you're mistaken. You can have your old C.A.'s. I'm going to the skating rink," I cried.

The Christ Ambassador leader gasped. She looked as though I'd said I was going to an opium den.

I flounced out of the church and walked a mile to the roller rink. As I neared the amusement park, my anger was replaced by apprehension as the seriousness of my decision began to register. I wondered if I was making a horrible mistake. I stood outside the gate for half an hour—torn with indecision. "Shall I enter the forbidden gates and defy my religion? I may never be the same." I shuddered.

Suddenly I made up my mind. I would see first-hand what a den of iniquity looked like. I would look at Satan's Palace! I rushed blindly in, not knowing what to expect inside the lair of the Devil. Nothing would have surprised me.

Gay, pleasant music greeted my ears. There in the brightly lit arena boys and girls skated aimlessly around in circles. They seemed carefree and happy. I recognized people I knew at school. Most of the children were from ten to twelve, some even younger.

So this was Satan's palace! In one wave of nausea, my religious belief was swept away. Every value the church had taught me was crushed under the rolling wheels of those innocent skates as I stood reeling from shock and confusion.

This place was not evil or sinful or wrong. Common sense made that obvious. "If the skating rink is not wrong, maybe movies aren't wrong either, or swimming pools. Gee, maybe it's not even wrong to kiss boys. WOW! Maybe none of the things forbidden by the church are wrong." Then the sickening realization flooded over me that I didn't know any more what was right and what was wrong.

God, how could I ever be sure? I felt bewildered, but my bewilderment was soon replaced by the heady thrill of what lay ahead. I wanted to plunge in—to try everything at once. No more little white church for me. I rushed out of the skating rink, with one thought in mind—to see the world! The real world! The world of movie theaters, bright lights, music, and dance halls. I'd try everything— do everything—see everything!

I hurried to the nearest movie theater. I could hardly wait to see the inside of another den of iniquity. The thing I had always been dying to see was a MOVIE. I bought a ticket with my collection-plate money. I could scarcely breathe, I was so excited when I was ushered down the dark aisle.

In all my life before or since, there has never been a thrill to equal the sheer ecstasy I felt upon seeing my first movie. I just stood there hypnotized by the miracle of it until the usher told me to sit down.

The breathtaking glory of technicolor burst forth on the screen accompanied by the rich tones of sound-track voices mingled with symphonic music. All so wondrously new to me. I have no idea what the title of the picture was or who the actors were. The picture was nearly over when I walked in. I only recall the beauty of the scenes and players and

the awe I experienced at the sight of pictures that moved,
lived, and breathed before my eyes.

As I drank in this wonderful new world unfurling before me, a beautiful woman with glowing bronze skin
moved sensuously across the screen in an emerald-green
evening gown. She wore a tiara of diamonds in her shining
hair. She toasted a handsome tuxedoed gentleman with a
glass of champagne, then lifted it to her rosy, smiling lips.
Suddenly the picture ended. Need there have been more?
I would have walked a hundred miles to see the magnifi-
cence of that one scene.

People were getting up. It must be time to go. I was
swept along with the crowd. People were mumbling as they
walked out. The man who had been sitting next to
me turned to his girl friend. "Boy! That sure was a lousy
picture!"

"Oh, how could you say such a thing? It was majestic,
spectacular, wonderful, the most beautiful thing in the
world," I heard myself saying.

The man shot me a puzzled look. "How in the hell would
you know? You didn't come in until the damn thing was
over!"

I walked out of the movie theater on a technicolor cloud.
Oh, what a lot of wondrous things I'd been missing all these
years. People who said movies were evil must be crazy.

"Hi, Baby, where are ya going?" murmured a voice beside me. I whirled, startled out of my daydreams, to see a
man about thirty strolling beside me. He lifted his hat to
me. I knew that bleary-eyed look. He was drunk.

"Can I buy you a drink?" he slurred. "How's about a little ole drink?"

I instinctively started to say, "No, thank you!" then
caught myself—"Why not?" Drinking was something else
I might as well try. I'd see what it was like to get tipsy.

Might as well look inside the very worst of Satan's dwelling places. The abominable beer joint. "Yes, I'll join you for a drink," I answered.

My drunken escort waltzed me into the nearest bar and seated me in a booth. A nickelodeon wailed in the corner. Couples sipped drinks quietly in surrounding booths, some looking into each other's eyes, some laughing, some holding hands across the table.

Customers sat on stools along the bar, mostly men. The air was thick with smoke. My eyes avoided a sign on the wall that said NO MINORS ALLOWED.

"What makes a lady of eighty go out on the loose?

What makes a gander meander in search of a goose?" crooned the jukebox.

"Cigarette?" asked my bleary-eyed companion.

"No, thank you—wait—I mean, yes, thank you," I blurted, taking one from the pack.

The man lit it for me and signaled the waitress. "We'd like two Singapore Slings," he said.

I felt so important sitting there smoking that cigarette. I could see my reflection in the mirrored wall as I puffed smoke with an exaggerated flourish, choking only occasionally. WOW—I sure looked grown up! No wonder they didn't know I was a minor. Maybe I was too young to be a C.A., but I wasn't too young to order a Singapore Sling.

The drinks arrived. They reminded me of a Mickey Freeze popsicle. They were three colors with an orange slice, and a maraschino cherry on top. My drink tasted like cherry pop with some exciting new flavor added. I drank mine before my companion scarcely started his. "Take it easy—don't drink them so fast," he said. "Three of these and you'll be under the table!"

"Then I'll drink three. I want to see what it's like under the table!"

When I finished the third one, I began to see what he meant. My head felt lighter, the music sounded louder, and I found myself laughing at everything anyone said or did.

This was great stuff! It made me feel carefree and gay. No wonder Daddy used to like it. I sat there enjoying the happy glow and drank another one. My words began slurring. I was beginning to sound like the man who brought me. I laughed because I wondered who was drunker, he or I. I laughed because people didn't know I was thirteen, but most of all I laughed at the thought of Mama's expression if she could see me now. It was hilarious!

My escort told me to get another song on the jukebox. I hated to admit I had never seen a jukebox before and hadn't the slightest idea how to work the thing, so I picked up a quarter and walked falteringly to the music box in the dark corner.

As I stood there looking the song selections over, trying to figure the thing out, two hands came stealthily up from behind me and closed caressingly around my breasts. At first I was startled, and then I felt a warm feeling in my entire body that I had never felt before. I liked it but I was frightened. I grabbed the hands that were fondling me and tore them away. "Don't!" I scolded. "People will see you!"

"Then let's go to my hotel room where we can be alone," he whispered in my ear in a husky voice.

"All right, but I've got to go to the ladies' room first," I lied. I hoped it had a window so I could escape. It was great going to the skating rink, it was marvelous seeing a movie, even this place was fun, but this new aspect scared the hell out of me.

The ladies' room had a window facing the alley. I climbed out into the cool, fresh air and headed for home.

Mama was frantic by the time I got there, but not half as frantic as she would have been if she'd known that I had explored a skating rink, seen a movie, gone to a bar, smoked a cigarette, drunk Singapore Slings, and let a man put his hands on my breasts in the short time since I had walked out of the church.

That night, I couldn't sleep. I kept remembering the man with his hands on me and the good feelings it had caused. In my imagination I substituted the face of the handsome actor I'd seen in the movie for the man's face. My whole body was aflame. My drunken companion had made me acutely conscious of sensuous pleasure. He had unknowingly opened a door—just a little—but it was a door that would never again be closed.

Chapter 4

GOODBYE, MAMA, I'M OFF
TO YOKOHAMA!

Pearl Harbor! The United States entered World War II.
America began to get into the spirit of the thing. Girls
just a few years older than myself were giving their "all"
for the "boys" who were fighting to save their country and
the world. I watched them with envy as they sauntered
down the streets on the arms of servicemen in uniform.

The tempo of things made it almost impossible for a
sanctimonious mother like mine to deal with the antics of
a mixed-up teen-age rebel on the rampage.

Mama tried. She would compromise. I could attend the
"All Campus" party at school if I would come home by
midnight and if I promised to tell her all about it.

"Funny thing, Mama, most of the boys I danced with
were menstruating," I said. "I could feel their Kotex pressing against me when they held me tight."

"Good Lord, boys don't menstruate," said Mama. "Child,
you don't know anything about anything. You're still a
baby. You're not ready to go out with boys. Why don't you
stay home until you get a little sense in your head—learn
what life's all about?"

I wasn't about to buy that offer. When Mama wouldn't
let me go to a dance, I'd crawl out of the window as soon
as she went to sleep. I had quickly learned that those things
the boys were pressing against me weren't Kotex. And I

44

had lots of fun pressing back, or rubbing my breasts against them, acting all the time as if I didn't know what it was all about. The boys flocked around me. There was no contest with the other girls: I had the prettiest face and the biggest boobs.

From time to time, Mama would catch me trying to sneak back into the house. My home seemed to have suddenly become a prison. I wanted to break out. I suggested to my girl friend Louise that we run away.

"Where?"

"Let's go to Reno and become show girls. We're pretty enough. And you know how the boys love to look at our bodies."

I was thirteen. Louise was sixteen and a little wiser. "We're too young to work in Reno," she said. "We'd probably have to sleep with the directors to get jobs and we're not ready to do that, are we?"

It was a plaintive question.

"We won't have to," I assured her. "We'll make it just on our beauty. We—"

"—but we don't know how to be show girls," Louise said.

"We'll learn!" My enthusiasm was growing. "We can fool them about our ages. How will they know? We're big enough."

Louise looked me over. I stood five feet seven inches in my flats, with a thirty-nine-inch bust. She glanced down at her own well-stacked body. Louise was a robust, healthy girl like me. "Yes," she said thoughtfully. "I guess we really could pass for twenty-one. Maybe we could fool them at that!"

Soon we were on our way. We hitchhiked a ride with a minister and his wife as far as Prescott. When they let us out, it was pouring rain and beginning to get dark. We decided we'd better wait till morning to catch another ride. We spent the night huddled on the floor of the ladies' room in an all-night service station.

By morning Louise's aunt and my mother had put out police bulletins with the descriptions: "Two shapely teen-aged blondes wearing sweaters and skirts."

Blissfully unaware that we were "Wanted," we stopped at a "Coney Island" hot dog stand to get a bite to eat. "You see those two sailors?" Louise said. "We'll flirt with them and they'll buy us breakfast. Okay?"

"Sure, why not. I'm starved!"

The sailors fell in line as Louise predicted. We ordered ham and eggs and, between sips of black coffee, we told them we were show girls returning to Reno.

We sure felt important when they asked us all about life in Reno and what it was like to be show girls. We invented lies about Reno living and our routines.

As we sat there enjoying the game we were playing, two uniformed policemen entered the diner. "You must be the runaway girls," said one. "That's them all right!" agreed the other.

One of the sailors spoke up. "You must be making a mistake, Officer. These are Reno show girls."

The officers laughed uproariously. "Oh, they are, are they? This one is thirteen. Now who's makin' the mistake? We probably saved you from contributing to the delinquency of two school kids playing hooky!"

Our faces were beet red as the cops led us out the door into a waiting paddy wagon. We looked like two wilted cocker spaniels the dogcatcher just bagged, as we were led from the paddy wagon to the Prescott jail.

"You and your damned big ideas!" Louise muttered.

But that was only the first of a procession of runaways,

waiting jail cells, and lecturing juvenile officers. I refused
to stay cemented to the sleepy little town of Mesa, Arizona,
and my runaway escapades drove Mama to near hysteria.

Soon, everyone in Mesa was singing "Don't Sit under
the Apple Tree" and "I Lost My Heart at the Stage Door
Canteen." And talking about gas rationing stamps and
sugar stamps and the cigarette shortage and the shortage
of bubble gum. Paulette Goddard and Veronica Lake were
our heroines. And then came Rita Hayworth and Betty
Grable.

Within weeks after the war began, Mesa was teeming
with servicemen. The town was surrounded with air force
bases, and its streets were filled with officers and enlisted
men. The navy and marine corps were also occasionally
represented.

It was very exciting for a fifteen-year-old who could pass
for twenty-one. I had no problem going to the Officers'
Clubs, the P.X.s, and the servicemen's bars.

I was able to get a part-time job as a cocktail waitress in
a local tavern that was crowded with servicemen. I took
secret delight in making others produce their identification cards to prove that they were really twenty-one.

I got the surprise of my life one night as I was leaving
the club. I came upon a couple engaging in sexual intercourse in the back seat of a parked car.

The woman's blouse was unbuttoned and her breasts
were covered by the man's hands. The couple was making
love with such wild abandon that they weren't aware of
me as I stood transfixed.

Then the headlights of an oncoming car shone into the
back seat, and I gasped as I saw the woman's face. She was
one of the C.A. leaders from the little white church.

I hurried down the street. At first I felt betrayed, but

then, as I dwelt upon the vivid scene, I realized that she
had done me a big favor. I no longer needed to feel guilty
about the things I wanted to do with the fellows. Everybody was doing it!

Servicemen weren't like our local boys. The locals were
big talkers. The servicemen believed in action. Some were
from faraway exciting places like New York and Chicago,
and I loved to talk with them about the world I longed to
explore. They, on the other hand, were more interested in
exploring me. They were obviously more interested in
making me than conversation.

They had a slang of their own that often sounded like a
foreign language to me. Once I told an Air Corps Lieutenant that I loved the pretty wings he wore on his uniform.

"Oh," he said, "you mean my leg-spreaders?"

He explained how the glamour of the silver wings cleared
the path to seduction.

On another occasion, I was on a double date with Louise.
Her date showed up wearing the Air Corps full dress hat
while mine wore the G.I. flat cap without a visor.

Louise's date said: "Hell, man, why'd you come out
wearing that damned cocksucker hat?"

"Cocksucker hat?" I said. "Why do you call it that? And
what is a cocksucker?"

I almost drowned in embarrassment in the laughter
around me. Louise then took me aside and explained what
a cocksucker was and why the hat, without a protruding
beak, was so-named.

I was pretty sure of myself. I knew just how far I'd per-
mit a roving hand to stray before I ordered a cease and
desist. What we did was called "necking" if it kept male
hands away from bare breasts. It was "petting" if it didn't.
I did some of each, depending on how much I liked my

escort. Never did anyone dream that I wasn't at least seventeen or eighteen years old.

As night after night passed, the sexual excitement became intense. Being a simple adolescent, I didn't know about self-release. Frustration kept building and, like a dope addict, I wanted more and more. I enjoyed being handled and excited.

Other girls—older girls—were sleeping around. The philosophy seemed to be that "these are our boys and they are going over there to fight for us and maybe to die, and the least we can do for them is to give them a little love."

I got away with saying no because I was the most beautiful girl in town. Soldiers, sailors, and marines seemed to enjoy just being seen with me.

Mama couldn't do a thing. She tried. Once I was quite tipsy when an army captain brought me home. She was waiting for me even though it was 3:00 A.M. She slapped his face!

Poor Mama couldn't adjust to my Mesa maladjustment. I felt compelled to go-go-go. My rebellion against the little white church was so extreme it sent the pendulum swinging the other way.

I wasn't really swinging though. I was told that I had "bedroom eyes," and I had learned to soul-kiss and tease, but I was still, as I passed my fifteenth birthday, a virgin. To me, this was my badge of virtue.

There were some tight spots. On one occasion a rather husky marine had seduced me into toplessness. Suddenly he dropped his pants. He wasn't wearing anything underneath. I watched, semi-hypnotized, as he approached me. I couldn't run and I couldn't scream. In as tough a voice as I could muster, I commanded, *"Put that thing away!"* His erection collapsed before my eyes.

Thinking back to the event, I tingled with excitement.

I was the only girl I knew who hung out with the service-men and who hadn't "gone all the way." How long could I hold out?

The answer came, inevitably. It was a night when the petting had gotten out of hand and I found myself swooning into semi-consciousness.

A young soldier named Ricky Romano held me close to him, one hand beneath my brassiere and the other caressing my private parts between my legs.

"Liz, marry me!" he pleaded. He had been proposing all evening. First at a dance. Then on the stool of an all-night diner. And now, at 4:00 A.M. on a park bench.

I was so excited I could scarcely breathe. Suddenly, the proposal seemed a perfect solution to all of my problems. I wouldn't have to face angry parents to explain my late return to the house.

"Ricky," I said. "Promise not to put it in till we're married!"

"Sure, Honey," he gasped.

"We'd better stop now," I said, not at all wanting to.

"Okay," he said, withdrawing his hands. He began to button his pants. "When will you marry me?"

"As quick as possible," I said, throwing my arms about him and giving him a two-minute kiss.

We walked the streets, hugging and kissing, until nine o'clock. Then we went to the courthouse to get married. I lied about my age and they issued a license.

Chapter 5

WAR BRIDE: CHILD BRIDE

I could hardly wait till we climbed the stairs to our room on the second floor of the Mesa Hotel. Now at last I was free to enjoy the full pleasures of sex all the way.

Ricky quickly stripped off my clothes with eager fingers. Then he was out of his. My excitement knew no bounds as he took my hand and led me to the bed.

He began furiously licking my nipples with his tongue. Then he pulled my legs apart. There was a thrust that sent tingling sensations all the way to my toes. A few more quick thrusts, some moans, and it was all over.

I couldn't believe what was happening. Was this all there was to it? Was this what all my anticipation was about? I lay burning with desire.

"Ricky," I whispered, "don't stop now. Let's do it some more. Please!"

"Sorry, Honey, I just came," he said, getting out of bed and lighting a cigarette. He paced around a while and then got back into bed.

I put my arms around him. "Please!" I pleaded again.

He rolled out of my arms, turning his back to me.

"I'm bushed," he said. And bushed he was, because within ten minutes he was fast asleep and snoring.

I took a shower to cool off. There must be more to sex than this. Was what happened to me what all the giggling and whispering among the girls referred to? It couldn't be.

When Ricky awoke, we went out for a wedding breakfast. We ordered a couple of drinks to celebrate. Ricky
celebrated his marriage and I my freedom. Yes, I was free
at last! Free from the little white church. Free from my
parents' strict discipline. Free to explore sex! Free to live!

Ricky's breakfast conversation was a mixture of strain
and leer. "Do you know," he said, "in those sweaters you
wore, your tits looked so perfect that, until I actually held
one in my hands, I thought they were falsies. They're lus-
cious!"

"Big deal," I thought.

For the next few days, we continued to live in the hotel.
I felt like a millionairess, with a maid to clean my room, a
telephone, and my own personal bathtub. I had never
taken a bath in anything but a washtub before.

I was in love. Not with my husband, but with the phone,
the bathtub, and my hotel room. This was the greatest
luxury I had ever known.

On the second day, Ricky gave me ten dollars. It was
the most money I'd ever had in my life. I rushed out and
spent it all at once on bubble bath, cologne, costume jewelry, and a five-dollar fuchsia-colored dress. I lounged in
foamy, perfumed bath water all afternoon, with the telephone near the tub, and called all my friends to tell them
the news.

I didn't know what love was like, but I knew Ricky
wasn't it.

Within days I decided to leave him. I wanted even more
freedom. Now that I was free from my parents, I wanted
freedom from Ricky too.

It took me a full week to make my move. Then, while he
was in the bathtub singing "You Are My Sunshine," I hur-
riedly wrote a trite note—the echo of something I'd read
in a paperback novel It said: "This is goodbye. It's better

for both of us this way. Please try to understand." Then I took off.

I inhaled the sweet air of freedom, forgetting that now there was a husband as well as a mother who might try to hunt me down. Married or not, runaway fifteen-year-old girls could become wards of the juvenile department.

I hitchhiked to San Diego. The truck driver who picked me up had his wife along and so wasn't in a position to make passes. I think even then I had come to learn that almost any man—no matter how decent and respectable— seemed to lose his perspective and turn on when he looked at my sensuous lips and large breasts. In time to come, when I would forget this and find myself alone with a man, the result was usually a choice between romance or a wrestling match.

Sitting in the truck, I remembered that, when Mama talked about a woman's role in bed, she made it sound as though women were supposed to endure sex but not to enjoy it. It was something they did only to please their men, not themselves.

I couldn't accept that. I was too full of warm, glowing feelings. I wanted to give myself to someone who would make love to me—who would *really* make love to me.

Even with Ricky I had pleasurable sensations. I was on the verge of fulfillment, but then it was over. It was always over almost before it began. Maybe with another man it would be different.

The bus terminal at San Diego was teeming with servicemen and their wives and families. It was so crowded you could hardly walk through. People stretched out on benches everywhere, asleep from exhaustion.

The terminal was open all night and it was warm. I had found a new home! At night I slept on a couch in the ladies' lounge and in the morning I freshened up in its washbasin. I washed my undies at night and hung them on the window to dry.

Best of all, the bus terminal provided free meals. All I had to do when I became hungry was to walk out the door of the ladies' room and stroll across the terminal toward the coffee shop. How could a pretty, buxom blonde in a hall full of sailors want for a dinner invitation? I was always picked up before I reached the door.

The approach was routine. "Hi, Honey (or Baby or Doll). Where you going?"

My answer was the same, too. "Oh, just out to get a bite to eat!"

The reply was the same. "May I join you?" Or, "Mind if I tag along?"—etc., etc.

My decision was the same. "Not at all" (as long as you pick up the check). I played this game for breakfast, lunch, and dinner. One day a sailor carried it further and took me shopping for a new dress.

I could have gone on like that indefinitely if my zealous mother-and-husband team hadn't tracked me down and had me picked up by the police department and tossed into the San Diego jail as a delinquent runaway. I was there a month before the juvenile authorities brought me back to Arizona. It was in that jail cell that I discovered I was pregnant.

Too young to really understand the significance or responsibility of pregnancy, I was overjoyed at the wonderful idea of having a baby. I didn't know quite what I'd do with it but, gee what a thrilling adventure!

The juvenile officer refused to return me to my parents. He placed me in a detention home instead.

Aunt Zina, Mama's sister, came with a court order and got me out. Zina wasn't the religious type. She liked to play cards, go to dances, and have a beer now and then. She was an attractive woman and lived in a clean, well-kept home of modest circumstances.

I was so proud of her when she appeared at the detention home. She looked like a magazine picture so smartly dressed in black, with sleek kid gloves, pillbox hat, and veil.

"She's beautiful," I decided, admiring the sweep of shining auburn hair and the smiling red lips. Zina was two years older than Mama. How I wished Mama would wear make-up and dress like that so she could look beautiful too.

Aunt Zina took me by the hand and bought me an ice cream cone. I was still a little girl in her eyes. Just a naughty child who had gotten into trouble.

When I arrived at her home, I was delighted to see she had a bathtub and telephone just like the ones in my hotel suite with Ricky. I was going to be very happy here.

Zina explained that in spite of my leaving him, when he heard I was pregnant, Ricky had applied for my government allotment and I'd be receiving $50 a month. She would take $15 as a contribution toward my share of the grocery bill, and I would have $35 a month to save or spend as I saw fit.

Thirty-five dollars a month! Wow! I was rich! What would I ever do with all that money?

When the first check came, I went out and bought presents for all the family. I appeared at my parents' home looking like Santa Claus, with a big bag under my arm. I remember the delight of my little brothers and sister as I passed out the big bag of toys one by one. They squealed with glee and tried to guess what was coming next.

I had fun with Aunt Zina. She taught me to play gin

rummy, and soon I was beating her at her own game. We laughed and joked and sewed baby clothes. And then suddenly the time had come.

My parents drove me to the hospital and warned me to get right with God, because some women die in childbirth. In spite of their frightening warnings, their concern for me was reassuring. It helped erase the memory of my bad marriage.

I named the blue-eyed baby girl Brenda. Soon after she was born, Ricky Romano and I got our divorce. The juvenile department released me from probation, and I moved back home. Mama took care of Brenda so I could work. The conflict over my interest in men was forgotten. My rebellion was over. Mama and I became close again.

I got a job in a Phoenix coffee shop. That's where I met my second husband. He was a good-looking marine who wandered into the shop to buy a cup of coffee just before closing time and started kidding with me. When he saw the place was closing, he asked if he could give me a ride home.

"Giving me a ride home is a big order," I said. "I live sixteen miles from here."

"Great, that gives me more time to talk to you."

It was swell getting a ride all the way to Mesa. The annoying part about my job was that I had to leave home at 4:00 P.M., walk a mile to the bus station, get the 5:00 P.M. bus to the coffee shop, start work at 6:00, work an eight-hour shift, catch the last bus into Phoenix, sit on the bench, and wait from 2:30 A.M. till 6:00 for the first bus back to Mesa, arrive at 6:45, start the mile-long trudge back home, arrive in time for breakfast, and fall into bed. By that time the baby would be up and crying. I'd toss around a few hours, and the first thing I knew it was time to get up and go through the whole routine again. It was exasperating. I felt like a slave on an unending treadmill.

When I told the marine that he saved me catching two buses, waiting four hours, and then walking a mile home, he was shocked. He started showing up every night around closing time to drive me home. He became a welcome sight.

Because of him, I could get some sleep, and I began to feel better. On the third night, on the drive home, he made his move. From then on, night after night, we did the friendliest thing two people could do.

At first, I let Paul have my body out of gratitude. But because he was as interested in my satisfaction as his own, I began to feel that familiar heady feeling, and this time sex turned from an act of frustration and unfulfillment to something deliciously satisfying. I was overwhelmed. It reached the point where I couldn't keep my hands off him.

This was a totally new role for me to play. I was the aggressor! I didn't want to miss a chance to be with him. On my night off, he took me dancing, but even then I was impatiently on fire until we found some lonely spot for our coupling.

Suddenly, his furlough ended and he flew back to the Marine base at Cherry Point, North Carolina.

Chapter 6

COMES LOVE, NOTHING CAN BE DONE

I found that I missed Paul, as I sat on the bench for the four-hour wait between buses, though I'm not sure which I missed most—him, or the ride home.

He started writing. I looked forward to his letters. They helped break the monotony of my dreary routine at the coffee shop and the endless hours waiting for buses.

I mentioned my birthday in one of my letters, and a package arrived containing a pretty gold watch. Shortly after, he proposed. "Come to Cherry Point and marry me," he wrote. "I'll take good care of you and your baby." The next letter contained a ticket to North Carolina—"just in case you decide to come."

One day, after an especially trying night at the coffee shop, I decided to go to Cherry Point to marry Paul Mc-Lain. In retrospect, I guess it was another escape. But it was a happy one, and we enjoyed being together, in and out of bed.

It was a brief encounter. One evening we were clinging to each other and vowing eternal love, and the next morning he was shipped overseas.

A month later, I kept trying to recall what he looked like!

Returning to Mesa, I found I was pregnant again. By then, my sister Evelyn's husband had been shipped overseas too. We decided to pool our resources and take a little house together.

With the allotment Ricky sent as child support for Brenda, Paul's allotment from the Marine Corps, and my sister's allotment, we were able to rent the house, buy the groceries, and get by nicely.

Three months slid by. My second marriage took on the unreal quality of a dream.

I became restless. I wanted to get out of the house. I wanted to meet people and do things.

I was four months pregnant by now, though it hadn't begun to show. Evelyn sensed my unhappiness. "I don't suppose it would hurt anything if you got out a little," she said. "If you want to take in a movie or something, I'll be glad to look after Brenda."

I think Evelyn knew I wasn't going to movies when I started going out, though for a while she didn't say anything. I went to late dances and clubs, where I met pilots from nearby air bases.

Sociologists would probably say that I had become one of America's "V-girls"—the "Victory Girls" of World War II. It didn't seem that way to me at the time. I had been introduced to the pleasures of the man-woman relationship and I couldn't get enough of them. I had an abundance of warm feelings for our fighting men and a sense of guilt when I refused any one of them the only thing I could contribute: myself.

I was told that I was a "dream princess"—a combination of Jean Harlow and Marlene Dietrich, with "a nicer body" than the current pinup queen, Betty Grable.

I was made love to by men in uniform in hotels, motels, automobiles, on the balcony floor of a theater, in gardens, on back porches, and on lonely moonlit country roads. If

a soldier or a sailor or a marine needed me, I was available
if I liked him. As my pregnancy became more and more
obvious and my stomach and breasts became larger, several servicemen took particularly keen delight in laying me.
I was wild and passionate.

I was also sixteen.

The memory of Paul had almost totally faded. One night,
when I got home after my usual body-to-body gymnastics,
Evelyn finally spoke up. "Liz," she said, "it's time you took
stock of yourself and faced facts. What are you becoming?
You're everybody's thrill girl. The girl who won't say no.
Your marine husband is out there fighting a war. You have
a darling daughter and another baby on the way. Don't
you think what you're doing is a little outrageous?"

"It's my body and it's my life," I said. "I'm bringing happiness to a lot of men who deserve a better break than this
war is going to give them. I suppose—"

"Do you ever think of Paul?"

"No," I said. "Look. You don't want me to lie to you and
I'm not going to lie to Paul. I'm young and healthy. I'm
lonely. I'm beautiful. Some of these young men appeal to
me. I appeal to a lot of them."

The next day I talked it over with my girlfriend Louise.
"Lou," I said, "do you think it's wrong to go out with boys
and have a ball?"

She surprised me. "That depends on how far you go,"
she said. "After all, you are married now."

"Louise," I said, "I want to live . . . to have fun. I want
to be taken places and to be kissed and hugged and—yes
—to be fucked too!"

Louise was thoughtful. "Liz, do you think you have to
go to bed with men just to hold their interest and make
them like you?"

"Maybe not," I answered, "but you must admit it gives a girl a hell of an edge. If one girl is willing to go to bed and another isn't, who do you think the boys will flock after?"

"But that isn't important," said Louise. "If a man really loves a girl, he'll be willing to wait. You told me Ricky was."

"Yes, but I'm not trying to marry these guys. I just want to have fun with them. It works out great. I have fun, they have fun, and I'm the most popular girl in town."

"But you don't have to play it that way. You were already the most popular girl in town, before you carried things that far. You could ask them to wait," she said.

"Wait for what?" I laughed. "To get married? I can't marry all of them, can I? The truth is I don't want to marry any of them, so what is it I'd be asking them to wait for? I won't ever see most of these guys again. Some will probably get killed, the rest will go back to wherever they came from. The only time for me with them is now!"

"If you feel that way about it, why get involved at all?" she asked.

"Louise," I answered, "you don't seem to understand. I am having a ball. Fun! Fun! Fun! I enjoy men. I enjoy fucking. I just can't stay home for a year to wait for a man whose face I can't even remember!"

"Then tell him so! Divorce him if you must—but level with the guy. Cut him loose. If you don't want him, maybe some other girl will!"

Louise was right, of course. I wrote Paul a letter.

Dear Paul,

I know this will come as a shock, but try to understand. You're a swell guy—that's all I remember about you. We hardly got to know each other before you went away—I can't wait for you, Paul —I don't want you to wait for me. Look me up when the war is over. Maybe we can take up where we left off. Meantime, have fun, Honey. Don't miss anything, I'm not going to. I want a divorce. Don't blame me or yourself. Just chalk it up to the war effort.

Love,
Liz

Paul was nice about it. He agreed to the divorce, saying that he would indeed look me up after the war to persuade me to marry him again.

I didn't tell him about the coming baby. The divorce went through one month after the baby was born. This one was a little boy, with big blue eyes and a mop of honey-colored hair. He was precious. I named him Johnny.

I was seventeen. I got a job in Phoenix—this time as a night-club photographer. I had never operated a camera before and didn't know how to set the gauges or judge distance. Sometimes my pictures chopped people's heads off or split them down the middle. Most of the customers were pretty nice about it, but I knew if I didn't master the technique quickly, I'd be fired.

One evening I got a boisterous, overweight gentleman about forty as a customer. He came in with a flashy-looking blonde. When I presented him with a picture that neatly sliced the top of his head off, he began to bellow and rave.

I rushed up to him. "Please, sir, don't shout. I'll gladly shoot another photograph, but if you make a big fuss you'll get me fired, and I need this job!"

He stopped and looked at me. He hadn't really seen me before. He'd been too engrossed in the blonde with him. Now he stared for a moment, then smiled. "Well, now, I wouldn't want to cause a beautiful doll like you any trouble with her boss—bring me half a dozen."

He handed me a $50 bill. "Keep the change, Beautiful."

Soon he finished his dinner and left, but I knew he'd be back as soon as he dumped the blonde. That $50 was an investment in getting to know me. He came in before closing time, smiling like a dog who'd swallowed the sirloin.

"Listen, Beautiful," he said, "I can help you. I know all about cameras. Let me take you to breakfast when you get off, and I'll teach you how to operate that thing."

I agreed. He turned out to be on the level about the camera. Within fifteen minutes I became an expert under his guidance.

Our breakfast came. "Okay, so now you can operate the camera. Next question—why do you want to?"

"Why? Well, I have a brand new baby at home that isn't paid for, a two-year-old girl that is, a divorce lawyer to pay, I need clothes, I've got bills, and I like money!"

Harold Murphy threw back his head and laughed. "You really lay it on the line, don't you, kid?"

He pulled out a $100 bill. "Put this in the kitty. It should help a little." Then, as an afterthought, "Would you like to go with me to Apache Junction to an after-hours gambling joint? If I win some loot, I'll split it with you."

"Sure," I said, wide-eyed. "What do I have to lose?"

That's how I met Harold Murphy.

The gambling trip was a success. Then I went to his home. It was a beautiful house, located in a very plush section of town. Overjoyed with my good luck, I was an easy prey for Harold. But this time, there was something different. Harold was not a fumbling, inexperienced soldier or an overeager lover. He was appreciative, gentle, kind. And, for the first time in my life, I knew the full, bountiful pleasure of loving.

I arrived home in midmorning. Before Mama could interrogate me, I spread my six $100 bills on the table.

"Mama, look!"

Mama had never seen a $100 bill before. She was fasci-
nated.

"A customer, a very nice man, took me gambling all
night. I won this money!"

Mama didn't approve of gambling, but she favored my
new economic status. It would allow me to pay off all my
debts and have some money left over.

That was only the beginning with Harold. He owned a
large ranch. He dropped off beef roasts and even brought
an electric roaster to cook them in. He took me shopping
for clothes for me and the children. He bought me a new
car and taught me to drive it. Inch by inch, he won me over
completely.

The night-club owner discovered I was under eighteen
and fired me. I think it was Harold who informed him. But
I didn't mind. I no longer needed a job. I was Harold Murphy's girl.

He rented a sumptuous love nest for me. Then, as the
relationship became more serious, he bought me a beautiful four-bedroom home on a five-acre estate near Camel
Back Mountain. It had a private drive, gardens, a horse to
ride, and a Great Dane to guard the door. I was happy
with Harold and the children. He was good to us. He took
Johnny to get his first haircut and held Brenda's hand on
her first day of school. Slowly, without realizing where
or when it happened, I fell in love with Harold.

There can be many kinds of love. I suppose it's all in
how you define it. Maybe I loved Paul and Ricky too—a
little, but not enough. I loved them lightly, the way you can
love a good ice-cream cone. Loving is a matter of degree.

Harold was my dream man, though I knew he was far
from being a physical ideal. I was almost eighteen and he
was forty when we met. He was pudgy, and his hair was
beginning to recede. I wished I could wave a magic wand

to make it grow back. I wished I knew some hocus-pocus magic to make him young and trim again. I was in love with the way he treated me and the way he made love to me—not with his appearance. If I could wave a fairy wand and bring back his youth, he'd be happier, and people would stop asking if I was his daughter. Harold loved me and my little family and gave us a good life.

He was a cattleman, with one of the biggest ranches in Arizona, and owned apartment houses, motels, and a flourishing construction company. He had never been a father, so he took my children to his heart. Brenda was only two and Johnny nine months old when he met us. He fell as much in love with the children as with me.

Weeks stretched into months and months into years. I wrote poetry, painted pictures, grew flowers, painted the flowers, completed my schooling via correspondence courses, and became immersed in study and books. My Great Dane, Ziggy, lay at my feet. The children scampered and played. Harold and I were engaged.

Four blissful years had slipped by in the Arizona sunshine, seeing Harold evenings, too inexperienced to wonder why he fled home like Cinderella at midnight and too naïve to question the endless excuses he gave as to why we weren't getting married this year. It was always next year with Harold Murphy.

One day when Johnny was nearly five, Brenda seven, and I had just turned twenty-two, I made an unhappy discovery.

It came accidentally when Harold had an acute attack of gout and was taken to the hospital. We picked a bouquet of flowers, put on our prettiest clothes, and went down to pay Daddy a surprise visit.

The children rushed into the room with the flowers. "Look what we brought you, Daddy."

A hatchet-faced woman sitting at his bedside looked astonished. "What is the meaning of this? Who are these people? Is this the juvenile you've been sponsoring?"

Harold managed a bilious-looking smile. "Oh, these are just friends of a friend of mine. The kids have a habit of calling me Daddy. It's nothing really." He looked at me pleadingly. "Please take the children and go home. This is no place for them. I don't feel well enough for so many visitors."

I stood glued to the spot. Why was he acting so strange? What was the matter? Who was this homely creature holding his hand? I resisted the truth that was forcing its way into my mind. Who was this woman? I wouldn't leave the room until I found out.

"Harold," I said evenly, "I want to talk to you alone. I'm afraid you'll have to ask your visitor to step out for a minute."

"I'm not his visitor," the woman said. "I'm his wife, and whatever you have to say can be said in my presence."

Harold looked sick. He tried to pull the covers up over his head but they wouldn't stretch. Cold beads of perspiration stood out on his forehead.

I strode past the homely woman as if she didn't exist, and faced Harold squarely. "So this is what you've been hiding from me for four years," I nearly shouted. "Four goddamned years you've been lying to me and I was fool enough to believe you."

He looked like he was going to faint. Hatchet-face's mouth flew open. "The game's up," I continued. "Right now is where you make your choice. Either she stays or I stay. Make up your mind, but understand, if I walk out of this room, I walk out of your life!"

Panic brought Harold upright in his bed. He was tortured with conflict as he glanced from face to face. Then, slowly the suggestion of a smile played around his mouth. He had thought of a solution. He looked at me steadily, his eyes reflecting his thoughts. Why should he worry about me? Hadn't I been stupid enough to believe his excuses for four years? Wouldn't I accept his lies again? Of course I would. He could dismiss me now, save face with his wife, and smooth things over later at home after he'd had time to think of a good story.

He held me in his gaze for a moment, a look of fond compassion in his eyes. Then he said, "Take the children and go home at once! I'll talk to you later."

"There will be nothing to discuss later," I answered, as I gathered the children to leave. "Goodbye, Harold."

I returned to the stately two-story dwelling that had been my home, with its rambling green lawns and apricot trees. I cried at the sight of my rose garden and grape arbors. The squash and tomato plants were in bloom now in my tiny vegetable garden. Soon the vines would be covered with ripe red tomatoes, but I'd never see them. I'd leave the way I came, with nothing.

There were many details to attend to.

I called the nice bartender who admired our Great Dane. We wouldn't be able to take Ziggy with us. God only knew where we'd be going. The bartender would give him a good home. Our family cat rubbed against my leg purring for attention. I'd have to find a home for her too.

I slid open the wardrobe closet overflowing with smart, expensive clothes. As my eyes ran along the rows of fashionable wearing apparel, they came to rest on a little group of cheap, faded dresses pushed to the back and nearly out of sight.

I burst into hysterical laughter that quickly turned to tears at the sight of them.

It would be easy to pack. Those few, worn, little dresses

were all I had brought with me. I'd walk out the way I
walked in.

The next day I met with Harold's attorney. I had the deed
to the property in my hands.

"When someone gives you a house, how do you give it
back?" I asked.

Mr. Smithson removed his glasses and stared at me. "I
don't think I follow you."

"It's very simple," I said wearily. "I just don't want this
house any more. I want to give it back to Harold Murphy."

The puzzled Smithson escorted me into his inner office
trying to convince me to change my mind as we went.
"You're making a dreadful mistake," he rattled on. I
scarcely listened. Soon he was escorting me through office
doors again—this time to the front door—still chatting
about the mistake I was making. I didn't care what he said
now. His job was done. I had a Quit Claim Deed in my
purse, which legally deeded the house back to Harold
Murphy.

I cried myself to sleep that night amidst a welter of
memories. In the morning I prepared to leave.

A white-faced, tight-lipped Harold arrived as I was load-
ing our few belongings into the waiting taxicab.

"What the hell are you doing and where the hell do you
think you're going?" he asked hoarsely.

"That is none of your concern." I reached into my purse
and produced the Quit Claim Deed to the property. I had
intended mailing it to him. "Here, you can have it all back.
It has lost its meaning for me."

Harold stared at the piece of paper for a moment, trying
to comprehend. Suddenly the significance of what was
happening became clear to him. Panic danced in his eyes.
He shoved the paper back into my hands. "You can't do
this—you can't leave me. I won't let you." His frustration

mounted. "You can't give away a $60,000 home. You're in no position to give things away! You never had a dime before you met me and you'll never have one again if you leave me!"

By now I had gotten into the cab. I slammed the door shut. "True, I never had a dime before I met you, but don't you go crystal-balling my future." I tossed the Quit Claim Deed toward him, and a gust of wind blew it into his face. My cab pulled away, leaving him in a billow of dust.

I can still see him standing there with the house deed flopping around his face. That was the last time I ever saw Harold Murphy. For months afterward, he tried to make contact with me, but I refused his phone calls and returned his letter unopened.

I went back home to Mama with the children.

"He was such a nice man," she said. "What happened?"

"He lied to me, Mama. He was married."

"Oh?" Mama's face fell. "Oh dear!"

Chapter 7

MOVIE EXTRA AND MARRIAGE THREE

I had to find work fast. I scanned the newspaper ads in search of a job. To my amazement there was an ad placed by a Hollywood movie company asking for five hundred local townspeople to work as extras in a lynch mob scene.

How exciting! I always had wanted to see a movie being shot. Imagine that—they were willing to pay $25 a day, the ad said. "Gee, I hope the job lasts a while!"

I rushed down to sign up, as thrilled as if I was the star.

I was given only three short lines: "There he is. Get him! Bring him down!" That was the end of my part—but not the end of the waves of excitement it set in motion. *Life* magazine was on hand to do a story on Frank Lovejoy and Adele Jergens, the stars of the picture.

The photographer decided to do the story on me instead, to the dismay of the movie company. I didn't realize that it was because I personified the star-struck local yokel.

The star they came to photograph ended up in only one picture—the one where he was being introduced to me. They gave me a splashy five-page story, with scads of pictures, and called me a "Young Movie Hopeful." They were right! In this brief brush with glamour I had become a movie hopeful. I remembered how I used to play actress behind the outhouse, performing for the cornstalks.

When *Life* magazine hit the stands, it brought waves of fan mail from well-wishers. Among them was a letter from Lou Layer, an Air Corps lieutenant I had met at the Mesa Dance Hall and dated occasionally before I met Harold. I hadn't seen or heard from him in over five years. He saw the magazine article and wrote me. At the time I'd known him he was stationed at an air base near my home. We lost touch when he shipped out, and I had practically forgotten him.

Now he was out of the service and working at the Pentagon in Washington, D.C. We renewed our acquaintance, and a stream of correspondence followed. He began talking of flying out to see me.

I was still carrying a big torch for Harold. I welcomed a new romance to help get my mind off him.

Lou Layer flew to Arizona and launched a two-week whirlwind courtship that literally swept me off my feet. His timing couldn't have been better. I was crushed and bewildered over my broken romance. It was easy for him to talk me into running away and marrying him.

I think I wanted to spite Harold by showing him just how fast I could replace him.

The lieutenant flew me and the kids to Washington, D.C. Soon we were settled in an apartment, where we began life as a family group. Before long, however, I grew to dislike my new husband because of his unkind attitude toward the children. They were unwanted as far as he was concerned, and he didn't let them forget it for one moment. His resentment toward them was so apparent it upset them terribly.

Our lovemaking was just as disenchanting. The things that turned him on turned me off. He was a mass of fetishes. He wanted me to wear high heels and parade around the bedroom nude except for a garter belt and black stockings. He wasn't able to get his kicks if I came to bed without the high heels! He wanted to spank me and to slap

my breasts. He enjoyed autographing them with my lipstick.

Our sex life turned into a bizarre mockery, leaving me in
a chronic state of dissatisfaction.

I couldn't help thinking of Harold. I wrote a poem to
him, which, of course, he would never see. It began:

It was a bitter quarrel, but I have won
Have sent you beaten in retreat
With heavy heart and brain that's numb
Your head is bowed in your defeat.

and, after a few verses, concluded with:

Your fond approval was part of the toll
That went with you from my door
And I'm left alone with my selfish soul
That always wanted more.

My triumph now has lost its thrill
Its significance is spent
And I'm enraged with my headstrong will
That refused to say "relent."

I cannot call back my cutting words
Or undo the harm they've done
I'm wishing now that I had lost
For then I would really have won.

I missed Harold Murphy and longed for his tenderness
and love. My love for him would haunt me for years to
come.

I persuaded Lou to leave Washington for New York,
where I could work as a model—anything to break the dull
monotony, of our lives together.

During the time I was dating Harold Murphy, I had
been selected the most photogenic beauty in Arizona in a

national beauty contest and given the title "Miss Stardust." One of the prizes was a five-year modeling contract with Harry Conover in New York.

We moved to New York, and I quickly became a successful fashion model, earning $50 an hour and $250 per show. I posed for leading fashion magazines in sable, mink, and ermine. Photographers took glamour shots of me in diamond tiaras, jade, and pearls, and I became a cover girl and television model. At the Eileen Ford Model Agency, beauty consultants made me over from head to toe. The country bumpkin from Arizona disappeared, and the image of a chic New Yorker emerged and paraded confidently down the runways of the leading hotels in Manhattan.

Success followed success until I was crowned "Most Exciting Face in New York City" in a national models contest and voted "Girl with the Most Beautiful Eyes in the World." My eyes appeared on the cover of *Esquire* peering through a pair of rose-colored glasses. How symbolic!

None of this improved my relationship with Lou Layer. My success as a model made a bad situation worse. Our joint bank account grew, and so did Lou's resentment. He seemed jealous of everything. He was even jealous of my success. He resented the children. He developed an ulcer, quit his job, and stayed home sulking. He fired the housekeeper because he resented the money she was costing and told me he would take care of the children and whatever else she'd been doing. His disposition became even more sour. Soon he began needling me with jealous accusations every time I was a few minutes late from work.

If I so much as smiled when the grocery boy made a delivery, he accused me of having a secret affair.

If I complimented Johnny on the way he combed his hair for school, I'd get an angry outburst from Lou that I never mentioned a thing about the way he looked. He imagined himself in direct competition with my seven-year-old son and reeked with hatred for him.

It became obvious our marriage couldn't be salvaged. I'd have to leave Lou. I should have done it then. I was drawing to a dead hand—his attitude continued to get worse.

One night things reached a climax when he turned his seething rage upon my helpless son. It happened while I was doing an all-night benefit for the Cerebral Palsy Drive as one of the television phone girls. I returned home long after midnight to hear Johnny sobbing in his room. I looked at Lou, sullenly sitting in a corner chair. "What's the matter with Johnny—why is he crying?"

Lou made no answer. I rushed into Johnny's room and turned on the light. His little face was distorted with pain.

"Johnny, what's wrong—what's wrong?"

His eyes searched mine for a moment, and his mouth trembled as though he was groping for words he couldn't find. I guess he knew no words to describe the hurt, so he just turned back the covers and let me look.

He was a mass of bruises from his ankle to his hip. The skin was broken and bleeding in places. His eyes and lips were swollen from crying. "He kicked me—he kicked me," he said in a hoarse whisper. Then he buried his head in the pillow as if to shut out the memory.

I pulled the covers back over his bruised little body and raged into the living room like a savage. "Why? Why did you do it, you dirty bastard?" I cried.

"The damned brat gave me a dirty look," was the sullen reply. Then—"Okay, okay, so I lost my temper and kicked the hell out of him. What do you expect? You know I can't stand the sight of those stupid kids!"

I looked at him sitting there trying to justify the cowardly thing he had done, and I despised him. I wanted to kick him the way he had kicked my defenseless seven-year-old son. I wanted to tear into him—I wanted to kill him! "You sick, sadistic son of a bitch!" I screamed.

If someone had placed a gun in my hands at that moment, I know I would have shot him with no regrets, so it was dangerous for me to stay in that house. I didn't say another word. I just walked to the bedroom, scooped the sobbing Johnny up under one arm and the sleeping Brenda under the other, and walked out into the chilly night. It was 4:00 A.M.

Lou didn't try to stop me. He just sat there staring into space expressionless, like a psycho case. I carried Johnny to the corner with Brenda following, then took a cab to the emergency hospital to check Johnny's condition. After the doctor had attended his cuts and bruises, we checked into a midtown Manhattan hotel to start a new life.

Although I had been making top money as a high-fashion model, I only had $20 in my purse when I arrived at that Manhattan hotel with two half-asleep children that morning. Lou Layer had invested most of my earnings in stocks and bonds under his name and the rest of them at the corner saloon.

The model agency only paid once a month. Lou had cashed my check a few days before, so that meant I wouldn't be getting paid for nearly thirty days.

How would we get by? How would I pay someone to care for the children while I worked? What would I do for expense money? My cab fare alone was $30 a week.

I analyzed the problem. I decided the only solution was to quit my job as a fashion model and get a night job so I could take care of the children by day and work while they slept. This would eliminate the problem of waiting a month for my modeling check, cut out the baby sitter, and elim inate the cab bill. But what could I do to earn a good living, working nights?

I decided to work as a night-club entertainer. I had never worked as an entertainer. I had no act, no costume, no music. I wanted to start at once, and I only had $20 in my purse. That did present a problem!

Once I had been to one of the clubs on 52nd Street, and it seemed to me the acts there also had the problem of no act (and very little talent). About all that seemed necessary was to be halfway pretty, have a good figure, and be able to fake a few dance steps or belt out a tune. Fifty-second Street would be a good place to start—its demands on entertainers were slight. I picked one of the clubs at random.

I called the French Quarter, bluffing my way, pretending to be an agent representing a fabulous client (ME!). "My client wants to start work in your club immediately," I concluded.

The owner, Big Mike Mascarra, answered the phone. "Look, I never heard of your client and, what's more, I never heard of you! But if she comes to see me tonight with her costumes and music, and I like the act, she can start tonight." He hung up the receiver.

Wow! I had a job! I could start tonight. Now my only problem was to make my $20 bill stretch far enough to buy us all something to eat and somehow put my act together.

I went to the grocery store across the street from the hotel. I bought a loaf of bread, butter, bologna, strawberry jam, and a half gallon of milk. This would have to do us for a while. Now, about my act! Big Mike had said to bring music arrangements and costumes. How was I going to do it? The most insignificant costume would cost at least $100. A music arrangement would probably cost $50.

I had no choice. I'd just have to carry the bluff through. I decided to throw together the most makeshift costume, pick up a piece of sheet music, and present myself looking as pretty as possible—wearing a smile.

I went to the music store and leafed through the music. I came to a sheet called "Song of the Vagabonds." I had never heard it, but it struck my fancy—I guess because my little family and I were vagabonds. I bought the music. Next, I went to the dime store. I bought a black bra and panties and yards of multicolored satin ribbons.

I sewed the colored ribbons all over the bra and panties, letting them stream to the floor. And I bought a transparent, multicolored scarf to use as a veil. The ribbons were $6, the scarf $1, and bra and panties were on sale for $1.98 per set. So my costume cost $9 and my music "arrangement" was sixty cents. I was doing fine, with change left over.

I just had time to get the thing sewed together, see that the kids finished their sandwiches and were tucked into bed, and it was time to rush to the club.

I arrived breathlessly clutching a little paper bag containing my ribbon costume and the piece of sheet music.

Big Mike liked me at once. "You're quite a looker," he said. "Prettiest girl I've seen on 52nd Street in a hell of a long time. Are you ready to start immediately?"

"Oh, yes. Will there be a rehearsal or anything?"

"Naw, we don't need no rehearsal. Just give your music to the band and your costume to the wardrobe mistress and tell the emcee how you wanta be introduced. That's all. You'll come out third on the show. The show starts in fifteen minutes."

"Yes, sir," I answered, feeling weak in the knees. God, how could I possibly go out there and improvise a dance routine to a song I'd never even heard? Why, I wouldn't know what note was coming next. I had counted on having at least one rehearsal so I could hear the music. Oh, well, I was in too far to back out now. Besides, I had to somehow make a go of this job. I needed that weekly paycheck. If the act went over, maybe I could ask Mike for an advance on my salary to tide us over till payday.

I went into the dressing room and got into my costume. The cheap bra was so brief my breasts poured over the top, showing all but the nipples. And the panties showed half my derrière. My legs showed through the strips of ribbon to good advantage.

"I do declare, that's the sexiest-looking outfit I ever laid eyes on," the wardrobe mistress chuckled. "That ought to really shake them up."

I tied the veil around my face the way a bandit would wear a kerchief, glad to hide behind something in case I should blush. My eyes peered out from above it.

There was a knock at the door. "Are you decent?" the emcee asked.

"Yes, come in," answered the wardrobe mistress.

"Holy Cow!" he said. "What do you represent?"

"Just call me 'Mystia . . . the Mystery Woman,'" I told him. The whole act was still a mystery to me, especially that damned music.

Soon the first two acts were over, and I heard the emcee call out: "And now, a newcomer to the French Quarter—a mystery woman who dances under a veil . . . straight from the mysterious land of the Far East, 'Mystia.'"

I heard the "Song of the Vagabonds" start—or at least I guessed that was what they were playing.

I threw open the curtain dramatically and stood there

perfectly still, just staring at the audience over my veil. The audience became so hushed you could hear a pin drop. Even the waiters stopped bustling about and stood transfixed waiting to see what I was going to do as I stood flattened against the velvet curtain staring them down.

They thought I was playing for drama, and that was the effect it had. The audience seemed hypnotized. They'd never dream I was just standing there until I could hear enough of the music to get the gist of it so I could start improvising a dance routine before their eyes.

I had them now, and I never lost them. I slowly went into motion, flinging the ribbons about in a profusion of color—staring at them silently over my veil. As I wound up the number in a flurry of wild whirls that made me so dizzy I nearly fell on my face, I quickly removed my veil and smiled at them. The applause was deafening. Imagine that! I was a hit! The audience loved me!

I went back to my dressing room amid whistles and wolf calls. They were still applauding when I closed the dressing room door and slipped back into the simple dress I'd worn to the club. It was the dress I'd walked out in at 4:00 that morning—my only dress. God, I'd have to send someone back to that apartment to pick up our clothes.

Big Mike met me in the hallway as I stepped out of the dressing-room door. "I don't have to tell you, you were a sensation, kid! You're hired," he said. "I'll start you at one hundred bucks a week. Now I see why your agent raved about you. Come on out front. Everyone wants to meet you. The headwaiter has a nice party he wants to introduce you to. Remember now, order only champagne."

I looked at him in puzzlement. "I don't want to meet anyone, and I don't like champagne," I said.

"Oh, come now, don't tell me you don't know the score in these places," he said, disappointment showing in his face. "Go talk to the headwaiter, he'll straighten you out on the routine here."

"Come on, kid," said the headwaiter. "I'll explain later. Right now, I've got to get you seated with these big spenders before they decide to walk out. Just order champagne. That's all. Order as much as you can."

I was introduced to the three men at the table and was seated beside the one who seemed to be playing host.

"What is your real name?" he asked. "You're beautiful!"

"My real name?" I repeated dazedly.

"Yes, what's your name other than Mystia?"

I came out of my daze. "Oh," I said. "My name is Liz, Liz Renay." I'd forgotten about Mystia, the silly tag I invented a few moments ago.

"Liz, you're a doll. What would you like to drink?"

The waiter was hovering nearby. "How about a nice bottle of champagne?" he suggested meaningfully.

That's how it all began . . . my life on 52nd Street.

After my first week there, Mike let his feature attraction go and promoted me to star billing. He said, "After all, Liz, you get more attention than any girl in the place, so you should be the star."

I was more embarrassed than flattered by the honor. They plastered pictures of me outside the club, put my name on a huge sign, and took ads in the paper.

God, I hadn't meant to shout to the world I was working in a 52nd Street strip joint. I had mixed emotions. What would the model agency think? Yet the promotion brought a substantial raise in salary.

I threw out the ribbon costume, bought a tight black satin gown with a neckline plunging nearly to my navel and a tiny black jazz costume to wear underneath. The only way I can describe the jazz costume is to say: Visualize the briefest bikini you have ever seen—and then make it briefer. If my costume had been any smaller, it wouldn't have existed.

I bought the outfit from a dancer who was leaving town.

I hired a choreographer to put a simple routine together, agreeing to pay him a little each week until we were even.

I appeared on stage in the slinky black gown with fluffy marabou feathers draped about my shoulders, a long cigarette holder in one hand, and a champagne glass in the other. I came out under low-key lighting and sang a torch song between puffs of smoke and sips of champagne. The music changed as I finished the song and champagne . . . I whirled out of my gown and went into a wild jazz number in the glittering bikini as a finale.

My popularity on 52nd Street grew by leaps and bounds. I made myself a platinum blonde and now, for the first time, people began to comment on how much I resembled Marilyn Monroe.

A short time later, 20th Century-Fox conducted a contest to find the one girl in the country who most resembled Marilyn Monroe. If you look like Marilyn, mail in your photo—the ad said. A group of fifty finalists would be selected from among the photos to be judged in a contest aboard the S.S. *Nassau* at its lower Manhattan dock. The winner would go on a cruise to the Bahamas, with champagne at the captain's table every night, and the prizes would include a $500 Savings Bond, a complete vacation wardrobe, fifteen pairs of shoes, and a Longine watch.

I mailed in my picture and contest application. To my delight, I received a telegram telling me I'd been selected as a Marilyn Monroe finalist, with instructions to come aboard the S.S. *Nassau* to be judged in the final contest.

I wondered whether to go. I really didn't feel that I looked enough like Marilyn Monroe to win the contest.

Still, I certainly could use the $500 Savings Bond and other prizes. I decided to go. What was there to lose?

Before I went to the pier, I obtained a photograph of Marilyn, held it up to my face, and looked in the mirror. I washed my face clean and then, using it as a canvas, I carefully painted Marilyn Monroe's face on mine with make-up. I marked my eyebrows and eyes like hers, put on a beauty mark where she wore hers, and painted my lips the way she did. My lips were already quite similar. I guess that's why people said I looked like her. I arranged my light blonde hair like hers and rushed to the boat. I was fifteen minutes late, and the judging had already begun.

Steve Allen, Candy Jones, and David Wayne were seated on the judges' panel.

The place was buzzing with activity when I arrived. As I burst into the room and surveyed the panel of judges, there was a dead silence as everyone stared at me. Then they started mumbling, contestants whispered in each other's ears, and the people with them chattered and buzzed. "That's really Marilyn Monroe, isn't it?" asked a voice from the crowd. The judges were discussing me, too; that was plain to see.

I think I knew from the moment I walked in that I had won the contest. I think the other contestants knew it, too. Actually, it was no contest at all. The judges were unanimous.

The next day my picture was on the front page of the *World Telegram and Sun.* I appeared as a guest on Steve Allen's show and several other television shows. *Life* magazine sent photographers to the club to do a follow-up story.

Excitement ran high at the club. A staff of nine people from the magazine set up giant floodlights to photograph my act. Just as I began my torch number, the excess strain on the power line caused the fuse to blow out, plunging the club into total darkness. They had to put in an emergency call for an electrician.

Big Mike was very proud of me and thanked me for mentioning the club on the Steve Allen show. I appeared at the Palace Theater and was awarded my prizes on stage following the newsreel of me winning the contest.

Before the boat sailed, Mike Mascarra saw to it that I was honored with a beautiful dinner party at the Gold Key Club. That's where I met Tony Coppola, Vinny Maro, and Tony Bender. My introduction to the Big-Time Underworld came over a three-tier Bon Voyage cake, champagne, and red roses.

Now Tony Coppola was pursuing me, and Big Mike considered me his private discovery.

Chapter 8

GANGLAND SAMARITAN

I was jarred awake by the telephone. It was the manager of the Churchill. "The maid tells me you're keeping a cat in the apartment," he said. "I'm afraid you'll have to get rid of it—no pets allowed here, you know."

I called the children over to my bed. Brenda was holding the beloved, bedraggled cat in her arms. "Yes, Mama?"

"The manager said we can't keep our cat, Honey. I guess we'll have to give him away," I said.

"Yes, Mama." She squeezed the cat tighter while tears welled in her eyes. "Do we really have to?"

"Gee," said Johnny, "we always have to give everything away. Can't we keep him, Mama? We have lotsa fun with him, and he doesn't eat very much."

"I'll hide him in the closet every time anyone is looking," volunteered Brenda.

My heart went out to them. Poor kids, they had been through so much and asked so little.

I remembered Fraidy Cat. He was a bedraggled old alley cat, too, but oh, how I'd loved him.

I looked at their downhearted faces as they stood there hugging and petting their cat as if for the last time.

Suddenly I made a decision. "Don't worry, Darlings," I said. "He's your cat and you can keep him. We'll just have to find a new place to live, that's all."

"Oh, boy! Oh, boy! We can keep him. We can keep

him!" they cried, jumping up and down. "Did you hear that, Cat? You can stay."

They scampered into the living room with the cat while I resumed my napping. When I awoke, I'd look for an apartment that allowed pets.

I found one before the day was over—a quaint two-bedroom apartment with a little terraced yard in back. A high board wall surrounded the tiny yard. Trees, grass, and flowers were growing in it. What a nice place for the children to romp and play with their cat!

I showed them around their new home. They loved it. "Look, it has a little fireplace," Brenda beamed.

"It's getting late," I said. "I have to get dressed for work. We can move tomorrow."

That night at work Big Mike talked to me of the new club he was opening a few blocks from 52nd Street. "I will feature you as my star attraction. We open in two weeks. Meantime, we'll start running an ad with your picture in the paper announcing the opening," he said.

"Fine," I said, hoping it meant another raise in salary.

Tony "Cappy" Coppola showed up as usual around closing time. "You're sure movin' up fast, kid," he said. "I think you can be the biggest thing in this business if you want to. Trouble is you don't show no enthusiasm. I don't think you give a damn!"

"You think right," I answered, as I strolled out into the night air to hail my cab for home.

Cappy called to me from the doorway, "Honey, you don't give a guy a chance."

Next day we got settled in the little flat with the terrace. It was wonderful there—so peaceful. The kids romped and played in the sunshine with their crazy cat. Brenda picked little bouquets of flowers and distributed them around the

house while Johnny watered the plants with a garden hose
and I slept in the front room away from their playful
squeals.

Two weeks flew by, and suddenly it was opening night
for the New French Quarter.

I sat by the mirror fixing my make-up. I wanted to
look especially nice since it was opening night for Mike's
club.

It was that special time at the cool of evening just before the sun goes down—a time when it's still light. A
gentle breeze played with the curtains. I'd call the children in soon, but they may as well enjoy the pleasant evening till the last moment.

"Look, Mommie!"

I glanced out the doorway.

Johnny was walking along a low ledge built against the
high board wall that fenced-in the yard. He had the awkward cat dangling under one arm and his portable radio
under the other. "See, no hands." He walked along the
ledge, leaning against the board wall with one shoulder
for balance.

"Play nice and be careful, Honey," I called, and went
back to my make-up. I was combing my hair, when suddenly I heard a deafening crash, splintering wood, a loud
scream, and a dull thud. I sprang to the doorway. At the
spot where little Johnny had been standing moments ago,
there was nothing but a jagged, gaping hole in the wall
with a piece of torn shirt clinging to the splintered boards.

The scream had come from Brenda. "Johnny, Johnny,"
she cried, pointing to the hole in the wall. "Johnny! Oh,
Mama, the wall broke!

"Oh, my God!" I screamed, running toward the jagged

hole. I looked down and, to my horror, there lay Johnny on the concrete.

"My God, he knocked his brains out and his eyes," I screamed. A bloody mass lay where his eyes should have been, and a pool of something awful lay around his head. His face was as white as chalk. "My God, he's knocked his brains out!" I repeated in horror.

The wall must have given way when he leaned against it, hurling his body and the splintered boards twenty feet below, where they hit the concrete.

Suddenly I was beside him, kneeling near his limp body, saying, "Oh my God, my God, my God!" like a broken phonograph record. Later, neighbors across the way told me I had slithered down the wall like a cat—high heels and all, scaling a straight-down twenty-foot wall like it was nothing.

I don't remember going down that wall. I was in a state of shock. I only know that suddenly I was down there. Brenda walked around two blocks to get to the spot.

A crowd gathered . . . neighbors from the other side of the wall . . . someone was spreading a blanket over him . . . "Don't put it over his face. He isn't really dead —I know he isn't! He just can't be!" Someone rushed to call an ambulance. When the ambulance attendants arrived, they took wet cloths and mopped the bloody masses out of his eyes, and I saw for the first time that he still had eyes. They mopped the bloody mess away from his head, too. Neighbors explained that Johnny hit the concrete with such force that blood and vomit spewed up from his mouth, falling back into his face and around his head.

When they finished washing Johnny's face, they gave him a quick once-over, and informed me he was still alive. "He's still breathing, but his pulse is fading fast," the ambulance attendant said.

They rolled his still body onto a stretcher and carried him into the waiting ambulance. Brenda and I climbed in beside him, and the ambulance roared out into the night. We may have raced past the New French Quarter with its flashy opening night banners blaring my name. I was unaware. I didn't remember the club or my opening or anything else. My only thought was of the still, white figure on the stretcher. They gave me a sedative when we arrived at the emergency ward.

As soon as they ran tests on Johnny, his name was put on the critical list, and I was told my son was in grave condition and might not live until morning.

I stood by his side in the emergency room holding his cold white hand and staring down at his chalky face with that big, ugly bruise darkening over his right temple.

He lay there as still as death, without moving an eyelash. He didn't seem to be breathing. Finally I was told I'd have to wait outside. I walked up and down, pacing the floor.

It seemed hours before one of the doctors rushed up to me. "Madam, we'll have to ask you to sign papers giving permission to operate on your son's brain. His spinal taps show blood. We may have to operate to save his life."

His words shook me out of my daze. "Operate on his brain! Oh, no—oh, my God! I've got to think this over—I've got to call someone—I can't make a decision like this alone!"

"Calm down and make a decision, lady. There may not be much time," the doctor said.

I was frantic. What should I do? I needed advice. Who should I call? I rushed blindly to the phone booth, and called my family in Arizona.

"The terrace wall broke. Johnny fell over. He's in critical condition. They want to operate on his brain. Mama, what shall I do?" I gasped.

"Pray," said my mother. "He's in the hands of God. Pray that God's will may be done."

"Mama, *you* pray," I said. "Praying's not the answer for me. I've got to make a decision!" I thanked her and hung up. Who could I turn to?

I called Bernie Freed, the young lawyer I'd been dating.

"Bernie, the wall fell with Johnny. He's in critical condition at the emergency hospital. I want your advice—"

"Well, you don't say. Sounds like you have a hell of a case against the building. Fill me in on the details—who was technically to blame?"

"My son is dying," I cried, "and all you think of is a law suit!" I banged the receiver down in his ear. I'd call Albert Sasser, my other steady boyfriend.

This was easier said than done. After a series of frantic person-to-person calls, the operator finally reached him ship-to-shore on his yacht.

"Oh, Albert, thank God I reached you!" I cried. "My son is critically injured. I'm at the emergency hospital. It happened as I was getting ready for work."

Albert sounded drunk. "Gee, that's too bad. Must have loused up your opening at the club!"

How could he take such an attitude? How could he think of the goddamned club at a time like this?

I hung up in disgust.

I started to walk out of the phone booth—then what he said registered. "The club!" That's right, I was opening there tonight. "I'd better call and tell them I'm sorry."

I dialed the number of the New French Quarter, and who should answer but Tony Coppola!

"You're sorry! You're sorry!" he yelled, "How do you think Mike feels? You damn bitch! You let him advertise your opening for two weeks—you don't show up—you don't call—and you have the goddamned gall to call up at two o'clock in the morning and say you're sorry! If Mike could get his hands on you, you'd be sorry all right!"

Suddenly I fell apart. Everything within me flooded over. Cappy screaming at me was the last straw! All I could do was cry hysterically. I just sat in the phone booth with the receiver hanging limply in my hand and cried. I could faintly hear a voice coming over the phone in my hand. "What is it, kid? What's wrong? I'm sorry. Listen to me, kid. Hey, it's not all that bad. Listen, Baby, I'm sorry. Don't cry! Please! Talk to me. Are you all right?" I wanted to answer the voice on the phone but I couldn't. All I could do was sob—big, uncontrollable, hysterical sobs.

Finally, after what seemed a long while, my hysteria played itself out, and I sat numb and spent. I lifted the receiver weakly to my ear and put the mouthpiece close to my lips.

"I'm sorry I spoiled your opening," I breathed into the instrument. "I—my son is dying in the emergency ward of the Harlem Hospital—."

I hung up and walked aimlessly out of the booth—nearly collapsing on a bench nearby. All I could do was sit there, my head in my hands.

The doctor rushed up to me. "Have you made your decision?" he asked crisply. "Will you sign the papers? We've got to proceed!"

"I know," I answered numbly. "I know, but you'll have to give me a little time!"

"We're running out of time. You've got to make up your mind!"

I sat paralyzed with indecision—unable to move, unable to function, unable to cope with the crippling decision. What if I said yes and they operated? What if Johnny died? On the other hand, what if I said no and he died when a yes answer could save his life? Oh, God, what should I do?

The door opened and Tony Coppola burst into the room, followed by Big Mike Mascarra. Suddenly Cappy was beside me holding my hands, cupping them in his. "We're with you, kid. Where's the boy? Where have they got him? Forgive me for yelling at you . . . how is he?"

I led them into the quiet operating room where little Johnny lay pale and silent with the hovering doctors. "He's in a coma," the doctor explained, "and he's sinking fast."

Another doctor advanced into the room carrying a chart in his hand. "His spinal tap still shows blood," he announced. "That indicates cerebral—"

"—What's that?"

"Bleeding of the brain," he answered quietly. "Will you sign the papers to let us operate?"

"Just a minute," cut in Tony Coppola. "Let's talk this thing over. We'll let you know in a minute." He and Big Mike quickly ushered me out the door and back to the bench where I'd been sitting.

"Why did you pick this hospital? Who is this doctor? Is he a specialist? What's his background?" Cappy's questions were coming too fast!

"I didn't pick this hospital, the ambulance did. I don't know anything about the doctor or whether or not to sign the paper," I sobbed in a rush of tears.

Cappy leaped to his feet, rushed into the phone booth, and began making calls, while Mike paced the floor.

He called Washington and spoke to someone, then made three other calls. He stood outside the phone booth nervously waiting for the parties to call him back. The phone rang every two minutes and he dived in to answer it.

Within ten minutes he rushed back to me. "All right, kid, go sign that paper. Everything's okay. This doctor's a fine surgeon. The whole staff is tops, and Harlem Hospital has a good rep."

I signed the paper. The doctor assured me he would operate only as a last resort to save the boy's life.

Cappy and Mike stayed by my side while Johnny fought for his life.

They brought hot coffee and doughnuts, which I gulped unconsciously, not tasting them. They offered me a pillar of strength to lean on when I needed it most.

Cappy took over after that and handled everything. Johnny didn't stir or move for four long days and nights. The doctors feared each day would be his last. Cappy remained at my side for hours at a time pacing the floor with me, standing vigil when I fell asleep from exhaustion, sweating things out with me all the way.

Cappy was no longer the flirtatious male on the make. He was treating me as a friend in trouble. He showed genuine concern. Occasionally he patted my hand to reassure me.

On the fourth day the doctor came to us. "The bleeding has stopped. We have no need to operate now," he said.

"Wonderful!" I cried. "No operation! Do you hear that? He'll be all right!"

The doctor shook his head sadly. "Just pray he will live till morning. Let's take this a step at a time."

"But he is better, isn't he? After all, if the bleeding has stopped, he must be better!"

"It's hard to say in a case like this. The bleeding has subsided, yet he's sinking deeper and deeper into the coma. We can scarcely find his pulse. His condition is most critical. I believe tonight will tell the tale."

Cappy and I walked the floor all night, glancing in on Johnny every few minutes to see if he was still alive.

Somehow he survived the night and so did we, without closing our eyes.

The next morning the doctor seemed encouraged. "He has a fifty-fifty chance to live," he said. "He has passed the first big crisis."

As Cappy and I sat by his bedside watching for any signs of life, Johnny suddenly opened his eyes and looked at us. His eyes were red and bloodshot. He had a dazed look, as though he wasn't really seeing. After a moment they fell shut, and he slid back into unconsciousness.

I ran down the hall. "Nurse, Nurse, Doctor, he opened his eyes. He opened his eyes!" I screamed.

I ran back into the room with two doctors and three nurses close on my heels.

As we entered the room he opened his eyes again. For a moment he rolled them around unseeingly; then he sat up, struggling to focus them. Gradually the dazed expression left, and his vision cleared. He rubbed his eyes, shook his head, and looked around the circle of strange faces. Then his eyes came to rest on me. "Mama," he cried, "what happened? Where's my cat?" Then he sank back into the pillows again, and his weary eyes fell shut.

The doctor's eyes danced.

"He's going to be all right! He made it, lady! It's a miracle, but that boy is going to live. Go home and get some rest now, so you can be back here when he really comes around. He'll have a lot of questions for you to answer."

Cappy was as overjoyed as I. He bought a bottle of champagne to celebrate, and flooded Johnny's room with toys. "Flowers are for girls," he explained. He never missed a visiting day. Johnny lay in the hospital recovering for three weeks. I didn't go back to work, but the New French Quarter mailed my check just the same. The first week I

thought it was a bookkeeping mistake and called the club
to discuss it. Big Mike got on the phone. He cleared his
throat uncomfortably. "Honey, we want you to have your
check same as if you were here as long as that boy is in the
hospital. When he gets well, then you come back to work."

That was the beginning of my long friendship with
Big Mike Mascarra and Anthony "Cappy" Coppola.

The day Johnny was released, Cappy insisted on bringing him home. He got to the hospital ahead of me.

"Okay, little man, you're going home now. And because
you've been a good boy, I'm going to buy you a going-
home present. You can have anything you want—just
name it!"

Johnny looked around the room trying to think of something he'd like to have. Cappy took him by the hand—
"Come on, little man, think of something good!"

Johnny looked down at Cappy's hand. Something spar-
kled and shone on the ring finger. "I'd like to have that
pretty ring you're wearing, if it's all right with you."

"Johnny! You can't have Cappy's ring—that belongs to
him!" I said, as I entered the room.

But Cappy was taking the diamond solitaire off his finger and slipping the glimmering blob on Johnny's biggest
finger.

"Look, I told him he could have anything he wanted
and he chose my ring. Don't think this kid don't know what
he's doin'. Most kids would ask for a choo-choo train or a
football. But not this boy—he asks for a $5,000 diamond
pinky ring. The kid's got class!"

Try as I did, I couldn't convince Cappy not to give
Johnny the ring. So my next effort was to try to instruct
Johnny on the value of the thing. "You mustn't lose it,
trade it, or give it away," I lectured. But soon after he was
back at play, he lost the ring in Central Park, in spite of all

my words of caution. I've often wondered who had the good fortune to find it.

The first night I went back to work, Cappy showed up around closing time as usual and asked if I'd go to breakfast with him. This time I didn't turn him down.

"Of course," I said, looking him directly in the eye and trying to hold back tears of gratitude. "I'd consider it an honor and a privilege to have breakfast with you."

Chapter 9

MAFIA MOLL

My friendship with Cappy progressed rapidly. We developed a fondness during Johnny's crisis that lingered on after his recovery. I saw more and more of him. He became my steady date. I suppose he grew so accustomed to taking over for me at the hospital that he continued to take over automatically.

He moved me and the children into a luxurious apartment with three bedrooms, maid's quarters, and guest rooms, all lavishly furnished.

A member of the Anastasia mob doesn't give the things Cappy gave me without getting plenty in return. He treated me with tenderness, warmth, and understanding, and I did my best to return his love.

Cappy showered me with mink, diamonds, pearls, and expensive clothing. Money was no object with him. When we went to the racetrack, he'd give me a thousand dollars to play with while he attended to more serious gambling. I still had a healthy respect for the dollar. I couldn't stand to throw it away betting on horses, since I invariably lost, but if I'd try to put a little away for a rainy day, Cappy would scold me. "I gave that to you to bet with. Now, damn it, you put that on the horses! If you're going to be my girl, you have to gamble. Live dangerously! Don't worry about money. If you need anything, ask me!"

One day he sent over a dozen cocktail rings—one more dazzling than the other. "Pick one," he said. I looked at the pile of glittering diamonds, rubies, and sapphires. They blinded me! I couldn't decide among them.

"They are all so beautiful, I don't know which to choose," I said. "Then keep 'em all," he urged. Things were always like that with Cappy. Material things held little meaning in the easy-come, easy-go world he lived in.

He sent over suits and dresses by the dozen, and mink stoles in every hue of the rainbow. When they ran out of new colors in mink stoles, he sent full-length coats. He took me to floating crap games at waterfront hideaways where hundred-dollar bills were scattered over the floor like a pile of autumn leaves.

He introduced me to hoodlums, gangsters, and underworld figures, and they treated me with respect. Frankie Carbo, Little Augie Carfano, Albert Anastasia, The Professor, Tony Rogers, Champ Segal, Vinny Maro, Jimmy Knapp, and Tony Bender were among his close associates.

They all seemed friendly and nice like Damon Runyon's *Guys and Dolls* characters.

As Cappy's paramour, I was present at many conversations involving underworld intrigues. I trained my mind to become a sieve, letting everything I heard on these occasions flow through and out without retaining any memory of names or details. Nevertheless, when I would be sitting in on a conversation that turned to murder or violence, Cappy quickly read the discomfort on my face and the language switched to Italian.

Cappy once told me this incident to illustrate the "sense of humor" that Anastasia's mob had. He recounted that a hoodlum had been ordered by the syndicate to stay out of a territory with his slot machines. When he ignored the directive, he was ordered to get out of the slot-machine racket completely. He defied the order.

Two mobsters picked him up. They tied a slot machine to each foot and dropped him in the East River.

"How horrible!" I shivered. "What the hell was so funny about that?"

"Don't you get it, Baby?" he chuckled. "He wanted slot machines so he got slot machines!"

Then there was the time Cappy sent me on a little errand. I was to meet a man at Pennsylvania Station and give him a package of hundred-dollar bills. Cappy described the man as tall, dark, and wearing a camel's-hair coat.

I was told to wear a red dress and carry a black umbrella so the man could identify me. He would approach me and ask me to join him for a drink. I was to accompany him to the cocktail lounge. When he said "Blackie sent me for a package," I was to give him the bundle of money.

Cappy wasn't sure which train the courier would arrive on, so I stood on the platform at the appointed time, eagerly watching for a tall, dark man in a camel's-hair coat.

Trains arrived, and the passengers streamed out onto the platform. Suddenly, there he was: tall, dark, and wearing a camel's-hair coat. God—he was handsome! Didn't look like a hood at all!

He smiled at me. I stood breathless, my heart pounding as I smiled back and he walked toward me.

"Hi, Baby," he said. "How about joining me for a drink?"

In the cocktail lounge we ordered cocktails. One. Two. Three. I waited. He didn't mention Blackie.

Finally I said: "Look, you're a nice drinking buddy, but don't I have something you want?"

"Hell, yes, Baby!" he smiled. "But I sure never had it put to me quite that way."

My face was scarlet as I realized that I had picked the wrong man.

I raced back to the ramp to try to locate the right party. Handsome followed me.

"Look," I said, "you're sweet. But it's time for my husband to arrive. You'd better vanish before he appears."

Handsome walked away muttering under his breath.

In the nick of time too, for another tall, dark man was getting off the train. Yes, he was wearing a camel's-hair coat. He walked briskly toward me, ignoring my welcoming smile, and walked right past me! Didn't he see my red dress and black umbrella?

I was sure this was the man. I couldn't let him get away, so I followed him.

He walked straight into the bar, and I walked in behind him and stood next to him.

Now he appeared to notice me. "Can I buy you a drink?" he said.

"Sure," I said, "but let's sit down."

"Why?"

"I'd rather."

"Well, I'd rather not!"

"Damn it! I want to sit down. It's too obvious here!"

He scowled at me. "Look, sister, I said I like it here. If you don't, then get lost!"

Who in hell did he think he was? The rude bastard!

A hand touched my shoulder. I turned to see a tall, dark man in a camel's-hair coat. He said, "Hi, Beautiful! I'm a friend of Blackie's. Care to have a drink with me?"

I walked after him to the nearest booth. Before a waitress had time to come for our order, he said quietly: "Give

me the envelope, Sugar. I got no time to waste." He took it
and was out the door and lost in the crowd before I could
erase the perplexed look from my face.

From time to time Cappy asked me to hold large sums
of money for various people. Sometimes there was as much
as $100,000 cash in my safe deposit box. I was trusted.
And trustworthy.

Nevertheless, I wasn't ecstatic about these various favors. Cappy was aware of my uneasiness. From time to time
he would say, " 'Lizabeth, I know you don't like to do
these things, and I really don't want you ever to become
involved in anything that could get you in trouble, but
there aren't many people we trust."

"Cappy," I said one day, "who did these things for you
before I came along?"

"Why, Baby?"

"Because I'd sure like to find him and give him his job
back!"

I'll never forget the time I was sent to pick up money
for a gambling debt from a doctor in Long Island and
stepped right into the middle of an abortion mill raid.

The police were everywhere. Chaos engulfed the room.
Girls were being grabbed for questioning as soon as they
stepped through the door.

I wanted to evaporate into thin air. God! I wondered if
they'd think I was in the market for an abortion. It was
clear to me that this was no time to demand $20,000 from
the good doctor or to announce I was a messenger from
the Mafia.

Before I could figure my next move or locate an escape
hatch, someone hustled me into a back room, pushed a
package into my hand, muttered, "This is the $20,000," and
shoved me out the back exit.

Whew! It was good to be in the street again! As I stuffed the twenty grand into my purse as unobtrusively as one can stuff twenty grand into a small purse in broad daylight on a crowded street, I noticed a man noticing me. I hurried to my car and sped away. Through the rear-view mirror I noted that he was following me in a taxi.

I panicked. I knew the doctor was in a hell of a jam with the Syndicate. He'd gone off the deep end trying to beat the bookies. He'd been a respectable physician. Now, because of his overwhelming gambling debts, he had become a full-time abortionist. He ran a virtual production line. He'd been knocking his debt down rapidly when the wrong cops heard about his operation.

I wondered if he'd sent the man to follow me. Maybe to rob me? That way he'd get credit for paying and still not have to part with twenty big ones. I knew he was desperate, and desperate men do desperate things.

I spent so much time ducking down one street and then another to lose my unwanted tail that, by the time I reached my rendezvous spot with Cappy, Cappy was gone. He wasn't expected back until the following day.

When I arrived at my apartment, I went downstairs to look around and be sure I hadn't been followed to my home. There he was, my shadow, standing across the street.

I was frightened. I couldn't reach Cappy. Who would believe me if I reported being robbed of the $20,000?

A shiver went through me. To what length would the man go to get the money? Would he kill me?

My children were away at school. The maid was gone for the day. I was alone in the apartment. If only I could pass that twenty grand to someone!

I went to sleep that night with the money under my

pillow. I awakened suddenly. There was a loud clatter in
the kitchen. I bolted to a sitting position in bed. Someone
was in the apartment!

I was frozen with fear. My eyes stared toward the noise,
trying to penetrate the darkness . . . trying to see anything. The noise sounded again.

What to do? I was a sitting duck. I eased out of bed as
quietly as possible, reaching for the money under the pillow as I went. I slid noiselessly underneath the bed.

I peered out from my hiding place. Maybe the house-
breaker would think I wasn't home. I tried to relax. I
stared through the darkness for what seemed like an eter-
nity.

When the misty light of dawn filtered through the black-
ness, it was obvious that there was no one in the place. No
one but me.

What had happened? It didn't make sense. If someone
had left the apartment, certainly I would have heard him
go.

Cautiously, I came out from under the bed, never taking my eyes from the empty kitchen. I dressed in a hurry
and rushed from my apartment straight to Cappy's place.

Cappy was disturbed by what I reported and offered
to have someone accompany me home. I told him the kids
and the maid would be there when I returned, so perhaps
it would be nice to send us a bodyguard.

"I'll never have you make a collection again," he said.
"You mean too much to me."

"Then you think I was in real danger?"

"I didn't say that. I just don't want you ever to be that
frightened again or to have a night like that. And besides,
you're right, if you had been robbed and told me a story
like that, I'd never have believed you!"

Cappy decided to go back to the apartment with me so

that he could take a personal look around. I began to feel sorry for the robber. Cappy was a walking arsenal. He had a shoulder holster, ankle holsters, and heaven only knows what else!

Just as we reached my apartment and I was fumbling with the key, I heard Brenda scream. It was a bloodcurdling scream—repeated again and again.

Cappy pushed me aside, unlocked the door, and flung it open.

My immediate thought was that somebody had been hiding in the closet and was now attacking Brenda. Then I saw her. She was standing on top of the bed screaming with her skirt raised. A huge rat, the size of a Chihuahua, scurried back and forth on the floor in front of her.

Cappy yelled and the rat ran. It scrambled across the room and out the terrace window.

"There's your mother-lovin' prowler, Liz," Cappy laughed.

Somehow, none of it seemed very funny to me.

The next day, Cappy presented me with a neat, pearl-handled .38 automatic. "Keep this on the night stand next to your bed," he said. "I don't want my baby to be scared of the dark!"

I took his gift and his advice. To this day I sleep with a loaded gun at my bedside, and the last thing I do each night before I go to sleep is to cock it.

Members of the mob were thoughtful enough to teach me how to use it. Luckily for the night prowlers of this world, I've never had to.

Chapter 10

SHAKEDOWN

Cappy's gun gift came in handy sooner than expected. Early one morning there was a loud, persistent knock at my door. I stumbled from my bedroom, trying to come awake as I tied my robe. Sleepy-eyed, I peered through the peephole.

I could see a man's face that I recognized from somewhere. Before I could place the face, he spoke: "Open the door, Baby. I've got something to show you. Gotta talk to you quick!"

He held up a newspaper so I could see the headline: BROOKLYN BACHELOR ARRESTED IN MILLION DOLLAR FRAUD.

"I'm Johnny Curtis," he said. "Remember me? We met at Irwin's place—at the Essex House."

I remembered. I unhooked the chain and opened the door. He rushed past me and spread the paper on the dining room table.

"We've got trouble," he said. "You've got trouble, Liz! You know Gene Campo, the gambler? He's got trouble! Your boy friend Garry Terzon's got trouble! Cappy got trouble! We all got to act fast!"

"What the hell are you talking about? What trouble?"

"Irwin Styles has just been arrested. He pulled a million-dollar swindle. This morning he got caught with his pants down. They jugged him."

"Irwin in jail? What—? How—?"

"Liz, we got no time to talk. You got to move fast. Irwin's pad was bugged by a couple of wise-guy plainclothes men. They tapped his phone, too!"

"—but what does this have to do with me?" I asked.

"Baby, we got to get those tapes fast! If they get turned in to headquarters, the shit's gonna hit the fan!"

"But—"

"Never mind 'but.' I made a deal, see. It'll cost five thou. But we got to come up with it fast! They only gave me a couple of hours. After that—it's everybody's neck!"

I shook my head in disbelief. "Johnny, you're still not reaching me. How does this affect me? How does it affect—"

"You've been hanging around Irwin's place, right? You been at his parties, right?"

"Right! But so has everybody else! Last time I was there, Jayne Mansfield and Mickey Hargitay were balling each other in his bedroom. Hell, I even met Syngman Rhee and Madame Rhee there! Everyone hangs around Irwin's place. It's like Coney Island on a hot Sunday!"

"Yeah, but your friend Gene Campo made some big layoff bets on Irwin's phone. He wouldn't want the fuzz to have that recording. And Cappy made some calls to people that—"

"—Wait! Why'd you come to me? Why not go directly to them?"

"Look, Baby, there's no time to lose! If we don't speed, we'll blow the whole thing and those tapes will be in the wrong hands! Besides, Garry Terzon's rich, right? Very rich and very married. And you've had some hot conversation with him on those tapped phones."

"How the hell do you know? What were you doing—eavesdropping?"

"Didn't have to. His end of the conversation was enough. I was there once."

I tried to think, but he wouldn't give me three seconds.

"Listen, Baby. Does Cappy know about you and the big gambler?"

"Why?"

"And do either of them know about Garry Terzon or about each other?"

I began to anger. "Wait a minute, are you a friend or a blackmailer?"

"A friend. A friend. I just want to help."

"So what's your angle?" I asked.

"I want to get those tapes. Irwin has stuff on them and so do I. None of us can afford to have those tapes go to the cops!"

"That makes sense. But why'd you come to me?"

"Baby, I don't have five grand! Irwin is in jail and can't get at his money. I don't know Cappy or Gene Campo or Terzon. I had to come to you. Now, get Terzon on the phone fast!"

"Okay," I said. "But you talk to him. You have to explain—"

"—Okay! Okay!" he said. "But hurry up! Dial!"

I did, and soon he was pouring out the whole tale of woe to Garry. Garry panicked, but he insisted on talking with me.

"Liz," he said. "Can we be sure this guy is on the level?"

"I don't know. He certainly comes on strong."

"How well do you know him?" Garry asked.

"About the way you do. Don't you remember him? He's that Rory Calhoun look-alike who was always hanging around Irwin's place."

"Oh yeah. Yeah. The handsome freeloader." There was a pause. "Well, I guess Irwin wouldn't have had him around if he wasn't okay." There was another pause. "Liz, give him the five grand. Get it anywhere you can. I'll pay it back before the day's over. I can't afford any static. I don't need any scandal."

Garry's word was gold. "Okay, Garry," I said.

I dialed Cappy. He was out of town. Gene Campo was out of town too, but I was able to reach him in Cincinnati.

"Gene," I said, "something serious has come up that I haven't time to explain. I've got to pick up five big ones immediately. I'll have them back to you by tomorrow."

"Okay, Beautiful," Gene Campo said. "Go to the Evergreen Florist Shop on Mulberry Street. Ask for Morey. I'll call him and he'll have what you want ready for you when you get there."

"Come on, Johnny, we're going to pick up the money."

I slipped into some clothes and ran a comb through my hair and we were out the door.

As I slid into his car beside him, I had an uneasy premonition. Something wasn't right.

We pulled up to the florist shop and he let me out.

"I'll drive around the block and pick you up," he said.

Morey gave me a neat packet of hundred-dollar bills. They were mint bills, fresh from the bank, with a $5,000 band around them. I tucked the money into my purse and went out to the street. Johnny's car was just pulling up to the curb. He leaned across the seat and flung the door open for me.

"Hurry, get in!" he said.

"I've got the money. I'll follow you in a cab and when they produce the tapes, I'll produce the cash."

"Don't be ridiculous! Get in!" he said.

When I hesitated, he raised his voice: "Get in, damn you! There's no time for games. We've got to make time!"

I acted against my instinct and got into the car again.

He drove like a man possessed. He was looking for something. He found it—a deserted alley. He pulled in, jammed on the brakes, and stopped the car. Then he turned to me. "Quick, Baby. Give me the dough. I can't take you with me—"

"When I see the tapes, you get the money," I said.

"Bullshit!" he spat. "You give me that money before I wring your neck! Terzon said to give it to me. It was authorized for me. I take responsibility. So get it up!"

"Sure, Johnny," I said. "I'll give you the money." I reached into my purse. "Here, Johnny," I said. I pointed my .38 automatic straight at him.

His face blanched. "Are you crazy?"

"Try me."

"Don't shoot! Please, Baby! Now take it easy—" he pleaded.

"Get out of the car!" I said in a quiet voice.

"But it's my car!"

"Out!" I said. "Fast!"

He fumbled with the door handle and almost slid into the street as the door opened. Then he ran wildly out of the alley.

I moved into the driver's seat and backed the car out. There was no sign of him. I drove a few blocks and then parked the car, leaving the keys in the ignition.

I hailed a cab and went to my bank. I put the money in my safe deposit box. Then I went to the jail to see Irwin Styles.

"I'm his sister," I lied.

"Irwin," I said, through the visitor's screen, "your friend Johnny Curtis came to see me and wanted $5,000. He said he needed it to buy some tapes from some cops. He said your place was bugged and we'd all be in trouble and—"

"Johnny Curtis!" Irwin exclaimed, as if he had just

begun to understand what I was saying. "Oh, Jesus! He's a blackmailer I had on my back and I hadn't figured out how to get rid of him." He shook his head. "I'm sorry he bothered you. There are no tapes. He's a liar."

Irwin assured me that he would be released on bail before the day was over. "It's in the works," he said.

I called Garry Terzon. "Garry," I said, "I got the five grand from Gene Campo." I gave him Gene's Cincinnati address. "You can wire it to him there. Okay?"

"Consider it done, Honey." Then he asked: "Is the matter taken care of?"

"The tapes are no problem," I reported.

"Fine," he said. "Glad to clear it up. Honey, I'll see you next week."

That night I got a call from Johnny Curtis.

"Listen," he said, "what was that all about today?"

"Are you still in town?" I asked, with mock innocence. "You're a brave man."

"Wha—what do you mean?"

"Well, you got $5,000 for some tapes and you didn't deliver any tapes."

"What the—but I didn't take the money!"

"Johnny, Sweetie, who knows that besides you and me? Your word against mine, Johnny Baby Sweetie." I added, "I sure am surprised that you are still in New York City. There are some very interested people looking for you."

There was an audible gasp and the phone clicked off.

Johnny Curtis made no further appearances at the old familiar haunts. I heard that he moved to a small town in Texas. You couldn't prove it by me. He never did send me any birthday or Christmas cards.

Nor did I ever hear from him again.

Chapter 11

KILL ME—I DARE YOU

It was exciting having a car and chauffeur waiting by my door, and a maid catering to my every whim, but living in a $700-a-month apartment and paying $50 an evening for dinner seemed ludicrous to a little girl from Arizona who grew up in a three-room cabin on a ditch bank.

The doorbell rang. Three men in white uniforms stood there. They had come to deliver the mirrored cocktail bar I had admired in the store window while Cappy and I were waiting for a cab. "Where do we put it, lady?" called one of the delivery men.

"That's a damn good question!" I said, looking around the already overdone living room. Gee, I'd really have to juggle the furniture around to find room for that mirrored monstrosity! Good Lord, just because I said it was pretty didn't mean I wanted it for a present.

There was never a dull moment with Cappy. If he wasn't sending presents, he was taking me to underworld get-togethers in back rooms of Italian restaurants, or card games, race tracks, and night clubs. He gave the children anything they asked for and, most important, he made it possible for me to stay home and take care of them. Several months rushed by. Then one night Cappy called me and said, "Elizabeth, put on your prettiest dress and come to the Villanova Restaurant. I have a surprise for you!"

I dressed, hailed a cab, and arrived in front of the quaint Italian restaurant.

I felt self-conscious as I walked in unescorted. The eyes of the men at the bar followed my every movement. I pretended not to notice, as I strode through the smoke-filled cocktail lounge to the dining room in back. This room was reserved for private parties and special guests. I wondered what sort of affair Cappy had invited me to— what surprise he had in store.

I pushed open the swinging door. There was a long table spread with a white tablecloth and lined with flowers. It was also lined with men, most of them gangsters. No women were in the room. Nearly every underworld character I'd ever met was there. This was obviously a special occasion. They had wine glasses in front of them and they clumsily got to their feet when I made my entrance. An empty chair at the head of the table was reserved for me. Cappy quickly guided me to it.

"We waited till you arrived to order dinner," he said. "Now let's have a little wine."

They all lifted their glasses to me. "Congratulations, Honey," smiled Frankie Carbo. "Yeah, congratulations," echoed several other voices. "We wish you all the best, kid."

"Congratulations? Congratulations for what?"

I turned to Cappy, searching his face for an explanation. "What's going on?"

Cappy grinned. "You're a lucky little broad. I've decided to marry you!"

I looked at him in amazement. "You've decided?" I asked in a tone so flat I scarcely recognized my voice. "Isn't that nice!"

Suddenly everyone was talking at once. "I'm renting the

Astor roof for the wedding. It's costin' ten grand, but it'll
be worth it," Frankie Carbo said. "You're going to have
one of the biggest weddings this town's seen in a long
time!"

"Yeah," said a sinister-looking character. "This thing's
really pickin' up speed—the old Cap's been getting envelopes from Vegas, Miami, and Chicago—even one from
Los Angeles. All the boys are sendin' their congrats and
their love!"

"Yeah, their love and their cash," snickered a voice
from somewhere down the table.

I sat there, glass in hand, while the voices rambled on
with plans for my wedding. They took on the unreal quality of a dream. I tried to regain control of my thoughts. "I've
decided to marry you," kept echoing in my mind.

Someone was lifting his glass to me; someone was saying a toast to me; someone was droning best wishes to me;
someone was ordering dinner for me; someone was pouring a drink for me. Suddenly, it was too much! The ab-
surdity hit me all at once.

I sprang to my feet. "Cappy," I said, "you don't tell people you're going to marry them. You ask them. A little
thing called proposing. If this is your idea of a proposal,
my answer is NO!"

I set down my glass and strode out of the room. A hush
fell over the group.

Cappy rose and was beside me before I could get to the
door. His fingers sank painfully into my arm. He held me in
a grip of iron, looking menacingly into my eyes.

"Liz," he whispered hoarsely. "You'll never make a fool
of me and live to talk about it. You'll marry me or I'll kill
you!"

"You're hurting my arm!" I said disdainfully. He released his grip.

"Come to your senses, Baby, or I'll kill you," he repeated.

A chill passed through me as I hurried into the street and hailed a cab for home . . . trying hard to dismiss his threats from my mind.

The next day I strolled out of my apartment and down the street to do a little shopping. I stopped for a paper. The man at the newsstand said, "Hear you're on the outs with Cappy. Better make peace or leave town!"

God, how did this man know what had happened between Cappy and me?

Later that day I ran into one of Cappy's cronies. "Hey, kid, you better straighten out your misunderstanding with Cappy or you're in big trouble!" he warned.

When I got to my apartment that evening and flipped on the light switch, the room remained in darkness. I flipped the button up and down, to no avail. I stumbled across the darkened room, groping for the telephone. I called the manager downstairs. "I have no lights up here!"

"That's too bad. Maybe your fuse is blown out. No one else is having trouble. I'll have it fixed right away."

I thanked him and hung up. I didn't like it. My nerves were on edge sitting there in the darkness waiting for the lights to go on.

The phone rang. It was the manager. "I can't understand it, Miss Renay. Your fuse box is jammed. Someone's been tampering with it. There's nothing I can do till I get an electrician here in the morning."

"Good heavens!" I cried. "Thank you!" I dropped the receiver into its cradle and ran out of the apartment, banging the door behind me. Maybe Cappy wasn't kidding when he'd made those threats. I began to tremble. Was someone lurking in that dark apartment waiting to kill me? Was that why they plunged the apartment into darkness? I rang frantically for the elevator. I pressed the bell again and again. Minutes flew by—cold sweat popped out on my forehead. Nothing happened—the elevator was silent.

Then I began to detect footsteps on the stairs behind me. Quietly, stealthily, someone was creeping up the stairs in back of me. The footsteps grew closer. Thud! Thud! Thud! My heart pounded with each step. Suddenly the shadow of a man loomed up on the wall in front of me. I screamed in terror and whirled to defend myself. To my astonishment, it was my neighbor from across the hall.

"What's the matter with you? Whatcha screamin' about?" he muttered.

"Oh, thank God, it's you! You scared me half to death coming up those stairs like that!"

"Had to—elevator's broke. Can't understand it! It was working an hour ago. I was on the fifth floor visiting and, when I started to come back up, no elevator. I called the manager and he says somebody's been tinkerin' around with it. Boy! We sure have some nuts in this building."

"Tinkering around with it! Oh, no! Hey, wait, don't go into your apartment. Wait, please, don't leave me here alone—let me go in there with you—let me stay with you!"

"Miss Renay, I'm surprised at you! What's come over you? You can't come with me. I'm a married man. What would my wife say? I'm old enough to be your father!"

He stepped inside, closed his door, and was gone. Once again I was totally alone in the long hallway.

The phone rang sharply. It came from my apartment. I stood glued to the spot, a battle of indecision raging within me. "I've got to answer the phone, it may be the manager. No, I can't go in there. Maybe someone's waiting to kill me. I've got to get hold of myself—I'm screaming at the sight of my own neighbor. It's my imagination. No, he jammed the fuse box and the elevator. I've got to get out of here.

No, I've got to answer that phone. Maybe the manager fixed my lights, maybe everything is okay."

Finally, I could stand it no longer. I braced myself, flung the door open, and stumbled inside, groping in the dark for the jangling instrument. I took it from the hook. A spine-chilling laugh greeted my ears. Then a voice like a madman hissed over the wire: "Next time you pick up that phone it will explode in your face because I've got it wired for sound." The bloodcurdling laugh sounded again. It was Cappy's voice. I couldn't believe my ears. I had never known this side of him.

I dropped the instrument to the floor with a crash and jumped back quickly, afraid it would blow up!

I ran from the room and started down the stairs. I had to get away fast. The lights, the elevator, and now the phone. "He must be crazy!"

I ran breathlessly down three flights of stairs in a daze before my thoughts began to take shape. "Oh, my God! I've fallen into his trap! This is the spot he maneuvered me into. He frightened me out of my apartment and eliminated the elevator so I'd run down the stairs. Someone is lurking on one of the landings between here and the ground floor—lurking there to kill me." I was frozen with indecision again—afraid to go up, afraid to go down. Finally, I made up my mind to take a chance and brave it. Maybe my killer hadn't gotten here yet and I could get out ahead of him.

I no longer dashed blindly down the stairs in a daze. I crept along the edges as noiselessly as possible, my heart skipping a beat as I neared each landing, terrified that this would prove to be the fatal one. I searched my purse for anything I could use to defend myself.

The most lethal weapon I could find was a small pair of scissors. I clutched them tightly in my hand as I crept past each new landing on the way down. Finally I reached the last landing and ran frantically out into the lobby, without slowing down or looking back. I ran into the street and hailed a cab.

It screeched to a stop and I climbed breathlessly in. "Go! Go!" I shouted to the driver. "Go!"

"Go where?" he questioned. "Where to, lady?"

"Anywhere!" I yelled. "Just go! Go, damn it! Don't sit there, go!"

He shot me a look, making it clear he regarded me as a lunatic, and sped down the street. When we got comfortably away from my apartment, I said, "Okay, driver, now take me to the most out-of-the-way hotel you know of, a place where nobody would look for me. I want to get lost for a while."

The bewildered driver shot me another peculiar glance. "Okay, lady, I think I know just the place for you if you don't mind a dump."

He wasn't kidding. It was a dump all right. It was a cinch no one would look for me there. I checked into the tiny closet of a room and hid there in mortal terror, scarcely eating, scarcely sleeping, afraid to make a move—terrified of my own shadow.

Every time the chambermaid's key turned in the lock, I jumped out of my skin. Every noise was a threat. Every footstep made my heart pound.

When I stepped out to get a cup of coffee at the corner drugstore, I noticed a rough-looking character loitering in front of the hotel with his collar pulled up and his hat pulled down. He stared at me. My hands turned to ice. My flesh crawled. I walked briskly past him. Footsteps followed me.

I darted a quick glance over my shoulder. It was the man, all right. I walked faster. The shadowy figure walked faster. Was this man sent to kill me? I could almost feel a bullet tearing into my back or the cold steel of a knife plunging between my shoulder blades.

I ducked into the drugstore and gulped a cup of black coffee.

When I stepped back into the street, the man was gone. I had only gone a few steps when to my horror I noticed another sinister-looking character following me. Was this the man? Chills ran up and down my spine as I hurried back to the hotel. Again I could feel the steel of a knife or the lead of a bullet tearing into my flesh! I practically ran into the lobby and up to my room, and bolted the door.

Every time I ventured out for a bite to eat, suspicious-looking characters followed me.

In my panic-stricken mind, it didn't occur to me that it was perfectly natural for sinister-looking characters to be loitering around a hotel of this caliber and it was all the more natural they should follow me. Why not? After all, I was a knockout. They weren't used to seeing beautiful, well-dressed women parading around their neighborhood alone.

I didn't think of that. I was too busy casting them in the role of executioner for the obvious sex angle to occur to me.

I lived this nightmare for three days and nights, sleeping only in fitful moments when I dropped off from sheer exhaustion—always aware of impending doom. As soon as I opened my eyes, the sickening realization of my predicament flooded over me. There was no escaping it—not until the third night, then nature seemed to come to my rescue. My frantic mind gave way to fatigue, and I sank into a deep, natural sleep.

I awoke in the morning feeling it was great to be alive. The sun was streaming in from the window.

I stretched and yawned lazily, still half asleep, reveling in the glorious morning unfolding around me, blissfully unaware of the madness that had tormented my mind for the last three days—oblivious to my surroundings—just enjoying life the way I usually did in the morning, too wondrously drowsy to remember the nightmare.

Then I opened my eyes to the ugly reality of my dingy room. "What am I doing here?" The dreadful picture seeped back into my consciousness and flooded my senses once more. For a brief moment despair engulfed me. The despair grew rapidly into anger—a deep, smoldering anger that exploded into blind, unreasoning rage. Suddenly I was fighting mad—too boiling mad to be afraid of anything.

"What am I doing in this stupid, dirty flophouse? The children will be back from summer camp tomorrow. What of them? Who the hell does Cappy think he is with this big-bad-wolf routine? How dare he treat me this way! No one can do this to me," I stormed. "Let him kill me! I'd rather die than live like this!"

I raced out of the cheap hotel like an Indian on the warpath, my shattered nerves giving way completely. Wild hysteria and blazing anger were a deadly combination.

I hailed a cab. I'd find that damn son of a bitch and tell him a thing or two.

I raged up the hall to his room and pounded on the door. "Open the door, you son of a bitch!" I yelled. He opened it and looked at me in shocked disbelief as though he was seeing a ghost. "Liz," he gasped.

"You said you were going to kill me—Well, Baby, here I am! It's time you do it or shut your damn mouth about it."

I pushed my way into the room and closed the door behind me.

"All right, tough guy—kill me. What are you waiting for?"

Cappy pulled out a knife and started for me. He expected me to back away. I stood my ground. He held the point of the knife to my throat. I didn't move.

He looked dumfounded. "That would be too messy," he said.

I watched him coldly as he took a gun from the dresser drawer. "This gun has a silencer," he said. "No one will know, no one will hear."

"If you're going to shoot me, go ahead," I taunted. "I've heard enough of your big talk! I'm sick to death of it!"

Cappy threw the gun on the bed and howled with laughter. "You're not afraid of God Himself, are you?"

I wasn't listening. I wasn't thinking. I looked at the gun in a hysterical daze and something inside of me seemed to snap. All that registered was that the gun was no longer in Cappy's hand. I lunged for it. I'd kill him before he had another chance to kill me. I aimed it at his head and pulled the trigger. He knocked the gun out of my hand and threw me roughly aside.

"Goddamn you." His face was white and he was almost speechless. "You could have killed me! I could be dead! Do you—do you understand what you did?" He looked shaken and sick. "You tried to kill me," he whispered, in hurt disbelief.

"You're damn right I tried to kill you. Why shouldn't I? You were going to kill me, weren't you?"

"Liz, Honey! You didn't think I would really kill you, did you? My God, I wouldn't harm a hair of your head! I just wanted to scare you a little so you'd see things my way. But, Baby, if that gun had been loaded, I'd be a dead pigeon right now."

He shook his head sadly. "You don't have to marry me.

If marriage to me is all that distasteful to you, forget I ever mentioned it."

Suddenly the reality of what Cappy was saying penetrated my mind. My hysteria subsided. Things went back into focus for the first time in three days. I shuddered at how close I came to killing a man—a man who had been kind to me, a man I had fondness for.

"Cappy," I said, "you never asked my reason for saying no. It has nothing to do with how I feel about you. It's just that—"

"I don't want to hear your reasons, Liz. From now on we'll just be friends, good friends, that's all. I will always be in your corner, but I'll never try to force things with you again."

I suddenly felt sorry. I rushed across the room to Cappy. I threw my arms around him and gave him a big kiss. "Let's go to bed," I said.

Chapter 12

CAPPY GIVES A PARTY

I didn't see as much of Cappy after that, although we had occasional dates. He remained my most ardent admirer but accepted me on my own terms and didn't try to make me his exclusive property.

Sometimes he'd come by to watch the children when they were riding horses in Central Park. It was on one of those occasions that he said, "Liz, I'm givin' a little party for ten of the boys. You know how much they like you and I'd like you to be there."

"Sure, Cappy," I said.

"Do you think you could round up ten of your girl friends from the model agency and invite them to the party? There's a C-note in it for each of them just for decoratin' the scenery."

"Cappy, those girls aren't call girls. I don't think many of them fool around—even for a hundred dollars. Some are married. Others have boy friends. You—"

"—Hey! What's the matter with you, Liz? I didn't say nothin' about them havin' to go to bed with nobody. I said decorate the scenery. Tell 'em it's sort of a modeling assignment."

"Okay, Cappy. I'll try," I promised.

It took some phone calling but I finally lined up ten of the most unattached fashion models I knew. They accepted the invitation when I assured them that they were under no obligation except to "look gorgeous" and that there was $100 in it for each of them.

When they arrived, I paid them in advance.

Cappy was one of the last to get there. The girls were standing around uneasily smiling their frozen fashion-model smiles and laughing nervously at wisecracks they didn't understand when Cappy entered and surveyed the scene.

He pulled me aside. "Liz," he said, obviously upset, "are these the dames that I paid a thousand bucks to get? I wanted pinup girls. You know, like you."

A frown creased his brow as he looked again. "Hell, Liz, these clothespins have no tits or asses or nothin'. Why are they so fuckin' skinny?"

I laughed. "You ordered them, Cappy. I told you I used to be a fashion model, not a Varga girl. You wanted fashion models and that's what I got you!"

He walked to the bar and took a stiff drink and then another. I joined him.

"Honey," I said, "I'm sorry you're disappointed."

"Jesus, Liz," he said, "you don't look like these dames. I thought they'd look like you. Like—well, like Marilyn Monroe. You know what I mean?"

I stroked his brow. "I know, Cappy."

"These dames look half starved," he said. "Maybe we ought to feed them before they start faintin' away on us!"

The rest of the group seemed to share Cappy's opinion, and the party was a quiet wake. Before the evening was over, two of the girls had left in tears, and others complained about being insulted.

"It wasn't what one of your friends asked me to do," one of them complained. "It was *how* he asked me. And he wanted me to do it under the table right in the room with everybody else standing around!"

"Who are these gentlemen, Liz?" another asked me.

"They're very important businessmen," I stammered.

"With vocabularies like that! What businesses are they in?"

I found an excuse to rush away to fill the ice bucket.

Two weeks later, Cappy decided to try again. He was having another celebration. "Liz," he said, "invite some girl friends, but no more of those skinny freaks! You must know some broads with figures."

"Cappy, why not just call some hookers? You and the boys know enough of them to hold a hooker convention!"

"Ah, Liz," he said, "we don't want no hookers. I want you to invite some nice dames. Schoolteachers. Secretaries. Nurses. You know, kind of respectable. It'll be a challenge for the boys. You know. No sure things."

I breathed a heavy sigh. "I'll see what I can do," I said.

"Good girl," he said. "Here's a thou for your trouble and another to divide among the girls."

Cappy thought I could do most anything. I don't know where he got the idea that I could summon schoolteachers. I hadn't been running a university. But somehow I continued to represent the "other world" of respectability to him.

After giving the matter some thought, I called my friend Garry Terzon, who I knew was a real swinger. I told him my problem and my proposed solution.

He laughed heartily. "Liz, I don't know why in the world I should give you my list of girls—but what the hell? Meet me in an hour. You know you can talk me into or out of anything!"

Garry's girl friends were call girls but not full-time pro-

fessional hookers, so I knew Cappy and the boys wouldn't
know them. The girls were delighted about getting paid
in advance and about my instructions that they were to
play hard to get.

"Be coy," I said. "Let these fellows think they're really
making a conquest. Let them talk you into it." I added, "By
the way, don't ask for or accept tips. It'll mean trouble if
you do—and it would give away the whole thing. You're
nice girls and you don't do it for money."

"Just for love?" one of them asked.

"Just for love," I said. "And because the boys give you
such hot pants you can't resist."

It worked. Everybody was so happy that from time to
time after that Cappy would ask me to "get some more of
those respectable girls you know."

Each such party meant a thousand dollars for me. When
I had run through Garry's list, the girls were kind enough
to suggest friends. Many a "happily married woman"
earned a hundred dollars and had some sex on the side
when her husband thought she was at a movie or a neighborhood bridge game.

Only once was there a serious screw-up. One of the girls
who had made a few appearances at my parties got ambitious. She decided she wanted my job as coordinator.

She managed to get Cappy alone. She assured him that
she could do better than I was doing. "We girls do the
work and Liz makes all the money," she complained.
"What's she got that I haven't got?"

"Brains?" Cappy suggested.

"Bull dinky!" the girl exclaimed. "She's no smarter than
I am. I don't see why everyone raves about her."

Cappy was silent.

"Listen," Miss Ambitious confided, "did you know she
was one of Garry Terzon's girls just like us?"

"Not like you, Baby. You got a big mouth! Now get the hell out of here!" Cappy twisted her arm behind her and marched her to the door. "Out! And don't ever come back!"

His loud voice attracted attention.

"What happened?" Billy Bell asked. "Why'd you dump her? She was the best-looking broad in the bunch."

"Hell," Cappy snarled. "That broad was a fuckin' stool pigeon! If there's one thing we don't need around here, it's a goddamned snitch!"

Chapter 13

I MARRY A CON MAN

Things began to move ahead in my career. I adjusted my life so that I could handle expenses without Cappy's contributions.

Warren Lancey rediscovered me. Once again he made his play for me. He tried to overwhelm me with his generosity, showering me with gifts ranging from orchid bouquets to diamond bracelets and strings of matched pearls. It was better jewelry than Cappy's—and it wasn't "hot"!

One night I was weary and cancelled a date with him with the excuse that I "had nothing to wear." Within a few days I received an assortment of Christian Dior gowns and Paris originals.

There seemed to be no way to stop him. I began to feel a little like a cricket in front of a steamroller. I tried to return some of the more expensive items but he wouldn't consider it.

Then, one morning when I stepped from my apartment building to hail a cab, a uniformed chauffeur called from a nearby limousine, "Miss Renay? Miss Liz Renay?"

"How do you know my name?" I asked. And then, "Hey —I didn't order a car!"

"No, Miss, but this car is for you."

He had gotten out by now, tipped his hat, and was glancing at a white card in his palm. "Mr. Warren Lancey ordered this car for you. I'm Morgan and I'll be your chauffeur from nine to five. Then another man will take over for the evening shift."

Everytime I thought Lancey had topped himself, he did it again. Next he threw a fabulous party and reception in my honor at the Waldorf-Astoria Hotel. He wanted to please me—and to show me off to his friends too. There were more than two hundred guests and they seemed to come from all levels of society. He flew in a marimba band from Venezuela, served pheasant under glass, and the Dom Perignon flowed from five in the afternoon until four the next morning.

It was a party that would not quickly be forgotten by anyone who attended. Silent screen star May Murray danced to the "Merry Widow Waltz" with Serge Rubenstein—and what a sight that was!

Warren thought of everything. A baby sitter whisked Johnny and Brenda away—but not before they had entertained by dancing together on the ballroom floor. They had reached the point where they were trying to sample the leftover champagne in various abandoned glasses.

"Come on, kiddies!" Warren said. "This young lady is going to take you to a Broadway show!" He produced sixth row center house seats for "Kismet" at the Ziegfeld Theatre.

Warren had a strong desire to make my children happy —as long as they were far away from where he was courting me. This climaxed in his paying their yearly tuition— several thousands of dollars—to a Tarrytown private boarding school. He bought them the required expensive wardrobes, arranged for horseback riding and piano lessons—and was quite shocked to see them back home a month later.

"Why are the children here?" he asked. "Why aren't they at school where they belong?"

"We don't belong!" Brenda said. "We belong back here with mama!"

"Yeah!" echoed Johnny. "We belong right here!"

I explained to Warren that the kids felt the place was more a jail than a school.

Warren sputtered, "But all that money I spent!"

"Warren, they were unhappy there. It's as simple as that. Maybe you can get a refund—"

"—I can't understand it," he said, sadly shaking his head. "After the favor I did them, they—"

"Please, Mr. Lancey," Brenda interrupted, "don't do us those kind of favors anymore."

Defeated in his campaign to separate me from the children, Warren decided to look upon us as a package deal.

Then he made his grandstand play.

He met me for lunch one day at Chambord. "Liz," he said, "I have a wonderful surprise for you. I've done something I know will really make you happy!" He held out a pretty gold key and gave me an eager kiss on the cheek.

"What's this?" I asked.

His faded blue eyes took on a misty quality. "I dream of you in a beautiful home in Connecticut, with a rolling green lawn, where you can paint and be happy. It's a beautiful place, for a beautiful girl like you—"

I was touched by his enthusiasm but couldn't help saying, "Do you see me there all alone?"

"Oh no," he said, a little sadly. "I see you there with the children."

"Don't you see yourself in that picture too?"

"It would be your home, Liz. It has maple trees and a maid's quarters and four big bedrooms."

"I'm beginning to see the picture myself," I said with a smile. "A bedroom for me, one for Brenda, one for Johnny —and an extra one for you. Is that it, Warren?"

"Yes, darling," he said, leaning toward me and taking my hand in his. "I'm very much married Liz, with no way out. You know that. But I want a home with you—a sort of home away from home . . ."

I found myself thinking of Harold Murphy.

"—the house is bought and paid for," he was saying. "No mortgage. And it's all yours—all but one bedroom!"

"And that bedroom?"

"You'll keep that one ready for me. You'll share it with me about once a week. Fair enough?"

I pressed the key back into his hand. "No, Warren."

"Why not, Liz?" he pleaded. "It's a beautiful house and its yours free and clear."

"Not quite free and not quite clear," I said. "I had a house like that when I was eighteen. It didn't work then and it wouldn't work now."

"What happened to the house?"

"I gave it back."

We drove to my apartment in silence.

At the door, he kissed me lightly on the cheek. "Thanks for not taking advantage of a romantic old fool," he said.

"Romantic, yes. Fool, no," I said.

His eyes glistened. I felt that he was holding back tears.

"Liz," he said, "you're very special. And you'll always be very special to me. If you ever need a friend, call me."

Then he was gone. As I undressed, I dismissed his promise. I was no prophet and couldn't know that one day I would need him badly, and when I did, he wouldn't let me down.

Soon, I was going out with a variety of men ranging from Huie Strong, the New Jersey State Racing Commissioner, to doctors, lawyers, and multimillionaire Garry Terzon. Strong was particularly helpful because he let me do anything I wanted that was within his power at the Monmouth Park Raceway. For example, any time I saw one of Cappy's friends whom the Pinkertons wouldn't allow at the track, I could arrange it so the Pinkertons would turn their backs. All I had to do was tell Huie they were personal friends of mine. The boys showed their gratitude at the rate of about $700 a week.

I got better acquainted with the fabulous con man, Irwin Styles. In return for my gracing his parties at the Essex House which were intended to promote his nefarious stock deals, his suite was always open to me to entertain my friends when I didn't want to bring them to my apartment because of the children.

I plunged back into modeling, filled weekend bookings in clubs and did small acting parts on television.

I met a very versatile young man named Bill Forrest. He was an actor, artist, writer, and producer of television shows and record albums. He was a six-foot-three Orson Welles type of man with massive shoulders and powerful build. I found him altogether fascinating. He contacted me to audition for a revue he was putting together. He wanted a Marilyn Monroe type and thought of me for the role because of the Monroe contest.

His studio and his apartment turned out to be one and the same. At first I was skeptical, but not for long. Soon his many talents overwhelmed me and I began to trust him.

I started working with Bill. The revue didn't materialize, but we did a radio show together from Fordham University. It was a beautiful show called "Vox Poetica" (meaning "poetic voice" in Latin). We recited the poetry of Rudyard Kipling, Edna St. Vincent Millay, Robert Service, Carl Sandburg, and other famous poets.

One day I told him that I couldn't keep an appointment

because Cappy and his friends wanted me to be elsewhere.

Bill Forrest said he wanted to see me for five minutes.

"Liz," he said, "what do you need with those hoods? You've got to get away from that life. You're not part of it, and it was never for you. You can go places. You've got lots to contribute."

"Bill, I do want to get away. I just don't know how."

"Marry me," he said quietly, taking my hand and gazing at me with his clear blue eyes, "I love you. You know that."

It was a little different from Cappy's "proposal." Almost at once I could see that a "legitimate" marriage might indeed lift me into another world—a relaxed world of calm and creativity.

For reasons that I couldn't understand then, Bill insisted that we go to Baltimore. I decided not to break the news to Cappy. I let him believe that Bill Forrest was just a serious working companion with whom I had to spend lots of time.

The marriage in Baltimore was my fourth. The ceremony was quiet. Just the two of us in an Episcopal church with a minister.

Bill Forrest persuaded me to put out an album of my own poetry, at my expense. It was badly done and a bad financial proposition.

Did I learn then? No. After all, he was my husband and my number one admirer. Soon he persuaded me to do another album. This time, the Greek play by Aristophanes called *Lysistrata*. It cost more to produce and thus was a bigger money fiasco than the first.

My marriage was becoming a costly adventure. As the weeks went by, my savings shrunk rapidly, wasted away on business ventures that "couldn't fail," but did.

There was one good thing, however.

Bill got me a television interview show. It was an industrial show called "Men of America." It portrayed the evolution and progress of leading corporations. Every Sunday I interviewed the Captains of Industry.

Cappy and the boys watched the show with amusement. They got a kick out of seeing me exchange banter with industrialists over the air. Cappy laughed like hell when I was scheduled to interview the president of a leading safe manufacturing company. Cappy suggested that I ask the man the best way to crack one!

The show was great fun and good experience, but all too soon it was over and I was looking for work again.

My husband seemed to think I was a walking mint. From time to time I found him examining my mink coats and my diamonds.

One morning he took me to the bank. "Now that we're married," he said, "all of our bank accounts should be joint accounts."

I agreed. Believe it or not, I was still a believer in his explanations. He was a psychopathic liar and could double-talk his way into anything. Four days later he cleaned out my account and put all the money into his.

Goodbye, $30,000.

The topper came when I went home to face him about my account having been cleaned out. As I arrived, some men were carrying my air conditioner out. He had sold everything in the house, including my typewriter, my sewing machine, Johnny's short-wave radio, and Brenda's inexpensive little cameras. The costly furnishings and my minks and all my jewelry were gone.

It took me two hours to find him. He was in a bar on Broadway.

"I've got to talk to you," I said, getting him to sit down in a booth. "Bill, I want a divorce."

He laughed. "You're not even married. You don't need a divorce."

His words went over my head.

I continued: "—And if you don't return every penny of my money and every one of my possessions, I'm going to the police now and have you arrested!"

He grabbed me, bruising my arm. "You go to the police and I'll kill you," he said.

"Don't forget who gave me that money," I warned.

"I'm not afraid of your dago friends," he sneered. I pulled my arm free, and he grabbed me by the throat and flung me to the floor. He kicked me. In an instant he ran to the bar and grabbed a whiskey bottle. I hardly realized he was gone when he was back again. I tried to shield myself as he smashed the whiskey bottle over my head. I was conscious, but I couldn't see, because blood kept running from my head into my eyes faster than I could wipe it away.

"I'll kill you! I'll kill you! You dirty bitch!" he yelled.

It took five men to grab him and throw him out. The bartender locked the door and called the police. Some women in the bar carried me to the ladies' room to wash the blood from my face. When the police came, they rushed me to an emergency hospital, where my head wound was treated. I insisted then on being taken home.

The police couldn't locate Bill until the next day. They arrested him, and he promptly paid an attorney to get my felonious assault charge reduced to simple assault. It showed me what money could do—*my* money!

A few days later, the doorbell rang. I opened it to find Cappy standing there with two companions. Someone had seen me on the street with my head bandaged. It was still bandaged.

"Who did it, Liz?" he demanded. "Who did this to you?"

"Bill Forrest," I said. Immediately I was sorry I'd spoken.

"He's a dead man," Cappy said, licking his dry lips and looking at Jimmy Knapp.

I knew Knapp's reputation. I'd heard him referred to as "trigger man."

It took me a tearful hour to talk them out of doing away with Bill Forrest. As enraged as I was at him, I didn't want to be the cause of anyone's death. I pleaded. I begged. I told Cappy that, if anything happened to Bill Forrest, I would never speak to him again.

Cappy and Jimmy agreed—but very reluctantly—to accede to my wishes.

When they left, I looked about my nearly barren apartment. One thing Forrest hadn't stolen was my painting collection. My eyes came to rest on the wistful face of a life-sized portrait I'd done of Brenda in a white party dress. She was beautiful!

I noted the other paintings—twelve in all.

The thought struck me: I could have an art exhibit! If I sold ten paintings for $200 each, that would be $2,000. Why not sell them? I could paint more.

I called art agent Paula Insel. "Are twelve paintings enough for an exhibit? —And oh, yes, two of them are not for sale."

"A dozen paintings sure aren't much of a show but, if you want to pay the gallery fees, you can display what you want. I know a small 57th Street gallery you can rent for $100 a day," she said.

"I'll take the gamble and rent it for three days. I'll put $300 price tags on the paintings. The first one I sell will pay for the gallery. How can I lose?"

As the excitement of the coming exhibit caught me in its spell, I began to think of Little Granny and the interest she took in my art. I remembered her words: "Some day you'll grow up and paint with oils and have exhibits in the biggest city in the world."

Granny's predictions were right. Here I was in New York planning my first exhibit like she'd dreamed I would. Suddenly I remembered I owed Granny a letter—several of them.

I'd sit down and write her right now. I'd tell her about the plans for my exhibit. She'd be delighted. She'd say, "Hot diggity dog, Honey, I always said you'd do it."

I leafed through the unanswered letters piling up on my desk. I felt ashamed as I sifted out three letters from Little Granny I had not yet replied to.

I read through the last one. "How's my precious jewel getting along in the Big City? Why not drop your old Granny a post card?"

I put the letter away and began my reply. "Dearest little Darling: Sorry I haven't written sooner. I have wonderful news for you."

The door burst open and Johnny staggered blindly in, his face twisted in pain. He looked flushed and feverish. He was bent double, clutching his stomach. Beads of perspiration poured down his face. He stumbled toward me, then lurched forward and crumpled to the floor at my feet, rolling over and screaming with pain.

I grabbed him up in my arms and ran frantically out the apartment door to hail a cab.

"Mommy, Mommy, I hurt. Do something, Mommy."

I rushed breathlessly past the people in the waiting room and the protesting nurse, into the doctor's office, with Johnny writhing painfully in my arms. I laid him on the table in front of the surprised doctor and half shouted, half cried, "What's wrong with my baby?"

Dr. Handler took one look at Johnny and called an ambulance to rush him to the hospital. "Acute appendicitis," he said. "I think his appendix has burst!"

We raced to the hospital. Dr. Handler called a top surgeon to perform an emergency operation.

"Please stay with me, Mommy, don't leave me," Johnny begged through his tears.

I patted his hand. "Mommy won't leave you. I'll stay right here."

He managed a boyish grin. "I'm sorry I was a sissy and cried," he said with trembling lips.

The operation was rough. When it was over, Johnny was a very sick little boy. I stayed by his bedside until he fell asleep, then tiptoed out of the hospital room and hurried home.

I was anxious to get back to Brenda. I didn't want her to worry about what had become of Johnny and me. When I got home, there she was watching TV and stroking the purring old alley cat. She was too engrossed in the program even to look up or give out with her usual "Hi, Mommy" as I came in. I decided to let her finish watching the movie before telling her about Johnny. Meantime, I'd get back to my desk and finish my letter to Little Granny.

Let's see, where did I leave off? Oh, yes, "I want you to be the first to know—I am going to have a New York Art Exhibit, just as you always—"

I was interrupted by the sharp ring of the doorbell. Buzz! Buzz! Buzz! I put the letter down and went to the door.

"Telegram for Miss Renay," said a Western Union messenger.

My heart skipped a beat as I tore open the yellow envelope. Maybe Johnny had gotten worse.

The words of the telegram leaped out at me and blurred

before my eyes. I stared at the yellow slip of paper in disbelief.

All I could say was, "No! No! It's not true. It can't be true!"

I held the wire in my hand, bold black print dancing before my eyes. GRANDMOTHER DIED LAST NIGHT, FUNERAL SERVICES WEDNESDAY.

Oh, my God! I was writing her a letter. How could she be dead? I glanced down at my unfinished letter. Words seemed to jump forward. "I'm sorry I haven't written."

Oh, why didn't I write? Oh God, I'd have to rush out there, go to her. I'd have to see that everything was done the way she'd want it. I'll fix her hair and put on her make-up. I know exactly the way she likes it—and her tombstone —I'll think of just the right words. Let's see, what would be appropriate? What would she like? "Here lies the prettiest girl in Tennessee" flitted through my mind and with it a picture of Little Granny, laughing and wrinkling her nose the way she always did. I smiled. She'd sure get a kick out of that caption. Then the impact of the truth hit me full force! Little Granny couldn't laugh any more. She couldn't wrinkle her nose at my silly nonsense. She couldn't get a kick out of anything—she was dead.

Chapter 14

MANHATTAN FAREWELL

I threw myself across the bed, sobbing. I couldn't fly to Arizona for Granny's funeral. Not with little Johnny lying in the hospital. I thought of the concerned look on his face when he said, "But you will come back every day, won't you?"

He was too little, too ill, and too dependent to be left alone while his only security flew three thousand miles across the continent. And what of Brenda? She was this moment wandering around the apartment with a stunned expression on her pensive face after hearing that her brother was in the hospital and Granny was dead. This was no time for her to be left in the hands of strangers. My children needed me. I must think of them. Granny was gone.

I went to a local florist and gave him Mama's address and a hundred dollar bill. "Send one hundred dollars' worth of pretty pink roses in a wreath." I wrote a card to be telegraphed with the flowers which read: "To the prettiest girl in Tennessee. Goodbye, Little Darling."

Next day I was startled by loud sobbing in the hallway. It came nearer and nearer my apartment. I rushed to see what was going on. It was Brenda. In her arms she carried the bloody remains of the awkward old alley cat that had become so much a part of our family. She was crying and I cried with her. "Oh God, what next?"

Brenda took to her room sobbing convulsively. I had to call a doctor to administer sedation. Too much had happened too fast in her little world. First our apartment ransacked, then the loss of Johnny as a playmate and Granny's sudden death, now her beloved cat.

I spent the next few days visiting Johnny at the hospital and cheering Brenda up. We rode the rides at Coney Island, went boating in Central Park Lake, and took in every comedy New York movie theatres had to offer.

Then suddenly it was time to bring Johnny home. This proved the best therapy of all for Brenda. She was too busy playing Big Sister to Johnny to have time to feel depressed. She invented a story about the cat getting in with a whole gang of other cats and running away from home. "Why, he became the leader of the whole gang and was having so darn much fun, I just couldn't make him come back home," she fibbed.

"Yeah, I guess you're right," said Johnny. "If he was having all that fun, I guess it wouldn't be right of us to stop him."

Once Johnny was back, he and Brenda resumed their normal play and my mind drifted once more to Little Granny. She wasn't dead to me—she would never be dead. I reread her letters in my desk, so full of cheer and inspiration.

"Honey, I have high hopes for you! You are a beauty. You have talent, you are young. Take advantage of these things, they are all too fleeting. Decide what you want and go after it. You can be a movie star if you make up your mind to be. Take a whirl at it for your old Granny. That's what I'd of done if I was born in your day and age. You

take your looks after me—I'd get as big a kick out of seeing you do something as if I did it myself!"

I read the letter over several times and made up my
mind to go to Hollywood and give movies a whirl. I'd always toyed with the idea but lacked incentive. I'll do it
now as a tribute to Granny and her unwavering faith in
me, I resolved. I'll build a whole new life out there. Cappy's
courtship had intensified again, and I thought this would
be a gracious way to say goodbye.

I sold what was left of my belongings and went ahead
with my art exhibit. I jacked the price of my paintings up
to $500 apiece. I'd need all the money I could raise. There
were two paintings in my collection I marked *Not for Sale*.
One was Brenda's portrait, the other was a painting called
"The Harem." Three harem girls lounging on satin pillows.
Trouble was, although one was a blonde, one a brunette,
and one a redhead, they were all me. I had used myself as
the model. They all had my face and body. I painted it for
fun a long time ago when Harold Murphy had jokingly said
he'd like a picture of me as a blonde, brunette, and redhead. The figures were seductively clad in harem girl costumes. The idea of a stranger owning three versions of me
in harem costumes didn't seem quite right.

When I presented the twelve paintings to the art agent,
ten marked $500 each and two marked *Not for Sale*, she
argued with me.

"Five hundred dollars each is an ambitious price for a
total unknown like yourself. You may waste the gallery
rental and not sell a thing. And take that *Not for Sale* tag
off The Harem. It's your most commercial painting."

"But I don't want to sell it."

"Okay, then put an outrageous price tag on it so no one
will buy it. That will add class to your exhibit. You can say

Paintings from $500 to $1,500. Who knows? You might get lucky and sell the damned thing."

I agreed, feeling certain no one would be foolish enough to pay $1,500 for a dingy painting I had done for laughs. I made plans to leave for California after the exhibit. I called Cappy and told him of my plans. He sounded pleased about the exhibit, downhearted about us leaving New York, and anxious to help any way he could.

"Elizabeth," he said, "your exhibit will be mobbed. I'll see to that. I'll invite every sonofabitch I know and they'll buy all the paintings, don't worry. I'll help you crash Hollywood, too, if that's what you want. Me and the boys will throw a farewell party for you and call up our friends on the Coast and tell 'em to look out after you and see you don't get hurt. We know a guy who's in with all the movie big shots. He'll introduce you around and see you get started."

Paula Insel had good contacts in art circles. She consulted the Blue Book while I consulted the telephone directory.

"If they all show up for the opening, the champagne tab will exceed the profits," she said laughing.

Soon opening night rolled around. I dressed in my most outstanding gown and hired a limousine to take me there for appearance's sake, purposely arriving thirty minutes late to make an entrance.

What met my eyes astounded me. It was a sight I'll never forget. There were society matrons, Park Avenue dowagers, and phony counts with phony monocles—all rubbing elbows with the roughest, toughest mob of underworld characters I ever saw. The society element sipped champagne delicately and oohed and aahed over the paintings, while the mobsters wandered uncomfortably around like rhinos in china closets, afraid they might break something.

Several of the party girls I'd invited to entertain Cappy's friends in the past heard the news and showed up at the exhibit. They added to the confusion by wandering through the mishmash of people and propositioning the guests.

A tough-looking thug noticed them uneasily. Then he called one of the girls aside and said, "Look, Babe, I don't care what you girls do on your own time, but this is Liz's party. She don't need your action. These ain't your contacts. Leave these squares alone—understan'?"

The girl glared at him, then walked away in a huff. The thug kept his eye on her.

She approached one of the group that had come over from Churchill's exhibit across town. Just as he was inquiring about the price of a painting he liked, she sidetracked him with a proposition to come with her to her hotel room.

The thug moved in on her, taking her roughly by the arm. "Come on, Honey, leave the gent alone. He wants to buy a painting." Then he said to the Englishman, "Don't mind my wife, mister. She has a screwy sense of humor —always tryin' to play some practical joke on somebody."

"For laughs," he threw over his shoulder as he marched her away. He maneuvered her into a corner, forcing her against the wall.

"I guess ya didn't hear me very good, Sweetheart," he said. "I told you no dice—leave them squares alone. Liz wants 'em to buy paintin's, not broads. Now you be a good girl, Honey. Pass the word to the rest of the hustlers. Okay?"

She nodded, and he released his grip on her shoulders. She rubbed them for a moment, and then slunk silently away.

She must have spread the word as she was requested to do, because within fifteen minutes there wasn't a party girl in sight. They all left in search of safer, if not greener, pastures. In a way I was sorry. I missed the sparkle and the note of gaiety they brought to the affair.

Next, two bosomy matrons cornered a rough-looking, scar-faced gentleman from Chicago.

"Isn't this flower garden too utterly divine for words?" chortled one.

"Yeah, you gotta admit them's pretty pictures!"

Just then an elderly English couple appraised my impression of Nefertiti. "My word," said the gentleman, "the realism of this thing is bastardly uncanny."

A rough-looking thug sidled up to him menacingly. "Keep your mouth shut! Stop makin' cracks about the paintin's! If you don't like the art works get the hell out of here!"

"I beg your pardon, sir!" was the startled Englishman's reply. The scar-faced gentleman cornered by the twittering matrons reached his saturation level. "I think I'll take a walk. Gotta get a bret' of fresh air," he said, strolling out the gallery door.

Paula Insel rushed forward. "Oh, there you are, Liz, darling. I must introduce you to your guests."

Suddenly there was a terrible commotion in the street. I went to the window to peer out. It was the scar-faced gentleman who had gone out for a breath of fresh air. He was cornered by two cops. A squad car was parked at the curb.

"Whacha mean, what am I doing in this neighborhood? I told you I'm looking at art pitchers. Jesus, copper, lay offa me. How the hell do I know whose exhibit I'm attendin'? It's some friend of a guy I know, that's all."

I tried to get the window open to call down to them. It wouldn't budge. I rushed out of the gallery but, as I got to the sidewalk, the officers were already hustling Scarface into the squad car.

"I tell you I'm an art lover, that's why!" he declared, as they slammed the door and pulled away.

My exhibit was something out of Damon Runyon's book. People near the windows were laughing uproariously as I walked back into the gallery. Several thugs had pained expressions as they stared after Scarface in sympathy. I called Paula to one side and asked her to get on the phone to the police station and try to straighten it out while I mingled with the guests. Soon she came back smiling. The police had agreed to let Scarface return to the exhibit on Paula's say-so—especially since the man they were looking for had just been apprehended. There had been a robbery on nearby Park Avenue. Squad cars were patrolling the area, picking up all suspicious-looking characters who had no explanation to justify their presence in the area. They hadn't believed Scarface's story about attending an art exhibit, since he didn't know whose exhibit he was attending.

As a phony count bent my ear with stories of his great accomplishments, Scarface rushed back in, smiling from ear to ear.

"Hey, you guys are okay—one phone call and they sprung me without a lawyer or bondsman. How 'ja like that?"

Paula motioned me aside. "Hey, Honey, you just sold your first painting to that millionaire over there."

"Oh, really? Which one did he buy?"

"Ha, ha, ha," laughed Paula, waving a check for $1,500 in my face. "Just guess."

"I'll be damned, not 'The Harem.' " I couldn't believe it! $1,500! Imagine that. Before the day was over I had sold five more.

"Guess what?" said Paula. "Scarface bought that dainty flower garden those old gals were yakking to him about. Now what in the world will he do with a flower garden?"

"Maybe he's a sensitive soul. Just because he has a scar on his face doesn't mean he can't like flowers."

Next day he showed up again and awkwardly asked to buy my painting of a pansy patch.

"Pansies have cute faces—remind me of little girls," he stammered.

"See, what did I tell you, Paula!"

Three of his friends showed up wanting flower paintings like Al's (which turned out to be Scarface's name). They seemed to feel cheated when Paula explained there were no more flowers and tried to interest them in other things. She sold one a nude, one an Egyptian queen, and one a tree.

The thug with the tree was most happy. "My painting has more class," he said. "Dames are a dime a dozen."

Before the day was over the last painting was snapped up, leaving only the *Not for Sale* portrait of Brenda staring wistfully from the wall. I paid the gallery fees, the agent's commission, the champagne bill, and counted the profit I could take to California.

There was a knock at the door. Two men flashed their credentials and paraded into my apartment "just for routine questioning."

"We're homicide officers," said one of them. "We're investigating the attempted murder of Frank Costello."

"Oh," I said. "I had no idea anyone tried to kill him—and what does that have to do with me?"

"Your phone number was in the suspect's billfold."

"Really? I can't imagine how it got there. I don't know anyone connected with Frank Costello."

"No? How about a guy named Tony Coppola—Cappy, for short?"

"Oh," I breathed, sinking into the nearest chair. "I do know Tony Coppola, but I didn't know he was a friend of Frank Costello's."

"Friend? Who said friend?"

The officers asked a few questions and left, saying they'd be back later. I quickly packed what was left of my belongings. I was ready to leave for the airport, bag and baggage, when another knock sounded at my door. It was Cappy. He had been released from jail.

"I was worried about you, Cappy," I said.

"Don't worry, Baby." He winked. "Things are under control."

I thought of all the prominent judges, politicians, and police officers I'd met who were friendly with the mob.

"Honey, don't leave like this. You promised I could give you a farewell party." He insisted that we check into a hotel for a couple of days before departing for California. "I gotta give you a party. You gotta have the proper send-off!"

I agreed to stay over a day, and we checked into the Plaza Hotel. The next evening I left the kids watching TV with a baby sitter while Cappy escorted me to the little party he'd planned. It was a jolly, good-natured gathering of six of "the boys." We had a gala Italian dinner with plenty of wine and good wishes. Champ Segal and Tony Rogers were mumbling something. "Yeah," said Champ. "Let's call the Mick."

"Great idea! Mickey Cohen's a great little guy! He knows a lot of good people out there."

"Yeah, he could be a big help to Liz. Show her around, introduce her to people—help her get started."

"Sure, Mickey knows everybody—movie stars, TV people, newspaper editors. If he can't help her, I don't know who the hell can!"

"If you think it's such a great idea, call him right now," Cappy cut in.

Soon Champ Segal had Mickey on the phone. "Hey, Mick, we've got somebody here we'd like you to look after. She's comin' out your way and she don't know nobody out there, see. Yeah, yeah, you're damn right she's a good friend. Did we ever ask you to watch out for a dame before? Okay then. Sure she's beautiful. What do you care? She's Tony Coppola's girl. How should I know—maybe she wants to be a movie star—"

Soon I was being introduced over the phone. "Look, Honey, tell you what I'll do. I'll meet your plane and help you get settled in Hollywood, okay? Just give me a ring before you take off and let me know what time your plane lands in Hollywood. Here's my private number. Write it down."

"Gee, that's nice of him," I said. "He doesn't even know me. It gives me a good feeling to know I won't be alone."

"What the hell, he's a damn good friend of mine. Why shouldn't he do me a favor?" said Champ.

"Yeah," said Cappy. "Well, I have a feeling this is one favor he's going to enjoy. Mickey Cohen's a ladies' man from what I hear. Wait till he gets a look at Liz."

"Yeah," said Tony, "he'll probably fall in love with you, Honey."

"He damn sure better not!" Cappy said jovially.

Everyone seemed in such a good mood.

"Hey, I think you guys are glad to get rid of me. You seem so cheerful!"

"Oh, you'll be back," said Champ.

"Hell, this isn't the end of the world or somethin', kid," exclaimed Billy Bell. "You're taking a trip to California. You're not leavin' forever!"

"Sure," said Cappy. "We're just loaning you to California to help brighten up the scenery."

"Yeah," piped Nino. "Don't stay too long. If you get lucky out there, you gotta fly back every now and then and visit us and the old Cap, okay?"

"Okay," I said. "I'll never forget any of you. You seem like a second family to me."

"We are," chorused two or three voices at once. "That's what we are to you, Liz—big brothers."

"Big brothers, hell!" Cappy laughed. "You're big wolves if you ask me!"

Soon I was on a plane bound for Hollywood, with one stopover—Mesa, Arizona, my childhood home. It had been five long years since I saw any of my family. It would be great to see them again.

Phoenix looked deserted after New York's mobbed streets—so quiet, squat, and desolate. Soon our cab was pulling up in front of my parents' white frame house with its rose bushes and honeysuckle vines.

My mother and father hurried out to meet me. The past five years had made them a little more gray and a little more tired. They were very glad to see me. They seemed even sweeter than I remembered them. Maybe they were mellowing with age. My sisters and brothers looked their five years older, though they hadn't changed too much. I was the one who had changed—*so* drastically. They talked of the town and townspeople and the church gatherings.

We lived in different worlds. I couldn't tell them about my life. They wouldn't understand. I felt waves of love for them. I wished I could visit for a month or two. I promised my family I'd never stay gone so long again. "Now I'll be in nearby California instead of New York City, and I'll be popping out to see you as often as possible."

My mother agreed to care for Brenda and Johnny while I established myself in Hollywood. The family and children waved goodbye at the railing, and I took off for California.

Chapter 15

HOLLYWOOD AND MICKEY COHEN

As the plane neared Los Angeles, I found myself wondering what Mickey Cohen was like. My eyes searched the crowd for him as I walked down the runway. There was no one to be seen that looked like a gambler or fit the description Champ Segal had given me of Mickey. Champ described him as a shorter version of George Raft. I saw no one very dashing at the airport and no one approached me, so I walked to the counter.

The man at the airlines desk looked shocked when I said, "Would you mind paging Mickey Cohen?"

"Are you serious?" he asked.

When the voice came over the loudspeaker "Paging Mr. Mickey Cohen—Mr. Mickey Cohen, come to the information desk, please," it caused a sensation. People gathered around to see if he'd show up. Paging him caused more sensation and shocked excitement than if I'd paged a movie star.

When no one answered the page, it became obvious he was not there to meet me. I felt let down and disappointed for a moment. "Oh, well, no time to worry about Mickey Cohen. I'd better get a cab to Hollywood and check into a hotel."

Champ Segal had recommended the Knickerbocker. He said it was just around the corner from Hollywood and Vine and would be an easy location for me. "Knickerbocker," I instructed the cab driver, and settled back to dream of Hollywood stardom.

At the hotel, a tall, light-skinned Negro dressed in a doorman's uniform walked briskly toward us. He helped me out of the cab and smiled a "Welcome to the Hotel Knickerbocker." His name turned out to be Earl Watson and, though I didn't know it then, he was not only the doorman, but was to act as my personal talent scout. It was through him I got my first part in a movie.

When I checked in at the desk, there was a message from Mickey saying he was sorry he was unable to pick me up at the airport but would be seeing me as soon as possible.

I hurried to my room to freshen up and unpack before he arrived. I took a quick shower and slipped into a simple black sheath. After I got the dress on, I was unable to zip up the back. Brenda had always been around to zip it for me before. There was a knock at the door. I opened it.

An immaculately dressed little man with dancing brown eyes stood smiling at me. His hair was black, faintly streaked with gray at the temples, and there was a strong scent of English lavender wafting about him. His smile broadened into a little-boy grin.

"Hi," he said, "I'm Mickey Cohen."

"I'm Liz Renay," I said. "Will you please zip up my zipper?"

He stepped inside the room, closing the door behind him.

"Why—er, yes," he faltered, a little embarrassed. His hands were soft, his nails fastidiously clean and polished. His touch was more like a caress. He wasn't at all what I expected him to be.

We sat and talked for a while. He leafed through my scrapbook. He seemed interested in what I'd been doing. We discussed my fashion-modeling career and my zany night-club routines. I found him utterly charming. I told him of my movie-actress ambitions. He offered to be of any assistance he could.

"Come on, let's take a little drive to Malibu Beach. We can stop for coffee and a bite to eat on the way," he said.

As we walked through the lobby, everyone stared at us. When we reached the front door, I saw a black Eldorado brougham with a gleaming stainless-steel top parked at the curb. I had never seen a car like it. Mickey opened the door for me. As I slid into the front seat, I noticed a woman's high-heeled shoe perched precariously on top of the back seat. When we pulled up to the Beverly Wilshire Coffee Shop, Mickey noticed the shoe. He quickly explained that a girl had thrown it at him because the only thing he was interested in doing was taking her home.

"Oh, is that what it's doing there?"

"Well, what did you think it was doin' there?"

"I thought you might have put it there for effect," I teased.

Mickey laughed heartily. "You're all right, Liz. I like you!"

We had a nice drive and an interesting conversation about our mutual friends in New York. Then he dropped me off at my hotel.

"I don't have time to walk you to your door, but please don't throw your shoe at me," he said.

Mickey knew I had no friends in Hollywood, so every evening he'd call and say, "Watcha doin' for dinner tonight, Doll? If you don't have nothin' better to do, come join me at the Villa Capri."

He was never alone. Usually he surrounded himself with eight or ten dinner guests—sometimes as many as twelve or fifteen. He always made a place for me next to his chair and treated me as the guest of honor. During my first three

weeks in Hollywood, I had lunch or dinner with him almost
every day. Mickey was always a charming gentleman and
a perfect host. He took me to night clubs. We saw every
show in town. He was bright and witty and fun to be with.

It was during one of our first lunches that he said: "What
would your friends in New York think if you and I decided
to play sweethearts?"

"Why don't you ask them?" I said.

"They already told me. They told me 'Hands Off—Keep
Off the Grass.' "

I shrugged my shoulders.

We had reached an understanding. From then on,
though he was openly affectionate to me in public, in
private, he stopped short. Due to his respect for Cappy,
our relationship remained Platonic. He was bright and
thoughtful and his flirtation with me was continuous. I had
the feeling that he genuinely cared for me. Perhaps that
was one reason he didn't want to make an ultimate move
that just might have ended in rejection and terminated the
teasing fun relationship we enjoyed together.

One day he took me to see his greenhouse, and while
he was busy on the telephone I amused myself by looking
through a stack of old newspapers I found piled on a table.
To my amazement, they were all about him. The stories
were fascinating. I'd no idea he was so notorious.

I asked Mickey about his publicity. "That's just a lot of
foolishness," he said. "Practically none of it is true—well,
not very true, anyway!"

I saw a glossy 8 by 10 photograph of Mickey standing in
front of a whole wall plastered with newspaper front pages
with his name in headlines.

"Oh, that's a *Life* magazine photo," he said. "They took
it for a story they were doing on me."

Then he said, "I used to be impressed by newspaper

headlines." His eyes took on a misty quality as he told me about his boyhood. "When I was six years old, I used to sell newspapers on the streets of Chicago. Every day I looked to see who was on the front page. I thought to be on the front page was about the greatest thing a person could do. Being in headlines made them big and important. King for a day." He smiled sadly. "You know somethin', I was more interested in what was on the front page than the people who bought the papers from me. I never got past the front page. If somethin' wasn't important enough to be on the front page, I wasn't interested. Each day I'd grab a paper to see who or what made headlines, and I'd say, "Some day my name will be headlines and my picture will be on the front page!"

"Well, Mickey, you sure got what you wanted," I said, looking at the pile of headlines.

"Oh, that was only kid stuff. Just a game I was playin'. It has nothin' to do with now."

Mickey and I became very close during my first three weeks in Hollywood. He confided in me about a lot of things. I asked him about the hand-washing complex he was said to have.

"I'll tell you, Doll, that goes back to my newsboy days. There was a water fountain near the corner where I sold my papers. One day I started to hand a lady her change and she said, "My, what dirty hands you have, little boy. Why don't you go wash them?" I was so embarrassed I hung my head and ran to the fountain to wash. Before I knew it, my hands were black again. I ran back to the fountain every few minutes. When I'd give someone their change, I'd notice my hands were black again. I didn't understand newspaper print was rubbing off on them. I couldn't figure out how they kept gettin' black, so I ran back and forth every five minutes to wash 'em. It became a habit, I guess, and the feeling just stayed with me."

The more I got to know Mickey and understand him the more warmth I felt toward him. He seemed never to have grown up. I had the feeling life was just a game to him—basically, he never outgrew the desire to play cops and robbers.

Chapter 16

GLAMOUR-TOWN DREAM!

I sat in the Knickerbocker Coffee Shop having lunch and taking stock of my situation. I'd been in Hollywood three weeks without seeing the inside of a movie studio.

Mickey Cohen was fun, and he was showing me a good time, but I hadn't come to Hollywood for that. I had to get a job and an apartment, and send for my children before my money ran out.

I walked to the front of the hotel. Earl, the doorman, rushed up with his cheery smile. "Cab, Miss Renay?" he asked.

"Earl, how does one go about finding a good theatrical agent? I don't know where to begin. Do you know of any?"

Earl was thoughtful. "You might try calling Screen Actors Guild. They'd send you a list. Then you could see a few and make up your mind. Of course, it's hard to get a good agent unless you have a lot of screen credits."

"Screen credits! I've never even seen a movie studio. I don't know what they look like!"

Earl's eyes brightened. "Would you like to visit a movie studio?" he beamed.

"Why, certainly," I said, thinking he meant a guided tour. "How do I arrange to do it?"

"Well," said Earl, lowering his voice to a near whisper. "I just parked Stan Berg's car a moment ago. He's in the cocktail lounge right now, and guess what! He's on his way to Warner Brothers. He's going there to see a buddy of his. He and his buddy go fishin' together, and guess who his buddy is! The head talent scout of Warner Brothers Studios!"

"Wow!" I exclaimed, feeling a tingle of excitement.

Earl continued: "That's the only way to go to a movie studio—first class. Go with someone who knows the right people and can do you some good. Want me to ask Mr. Berg if he'll take you with him? See, I know Stan Berg and I know he loves to meet pretty girls. He'd be delighted to have your company." Then: "Here he comes now! Mr. Berg! Here's someone I want you to meet!"

Stan Berg was tall, attractive, and sun-tanned, with sandy brown hair and twinkling, gray eyes.

"Well, who do we have here?" he asked. "Marilyn Monroe?"

"This is Miss Renay," said Earl. "She's here from New York and never saw a movie studio. She'd love to ride out to Warner Brothers with you."

"Sure," Stan said. "How lucky can I get? Wait'll old Solly sees her, he'll flip! Welcome aboard, Miss, uh—what'd you say your name was?"

"Liz Renay."

"Okay, Liz, I'll take you to Warner Brothers with me and introduce you to Solly Biano, head of new talent out there. But let's have a drink first."

"I could use a drink. The idea of seeing a movie studio and meeting a talent scout makes me nervous."

As soon as we were seated in the dimly lit lounge with cocktails in front of us, Stan asked, "How long have you been here, Liz?"

"Three weeks."

"Have you seen any agents or met anyone in the film industry?"

"Yes, Mickey introduced me to several people. But, so far, nothing."

"Who's Mickey?"

"Mickey Cohen, a gambler I know who has a lot of connections."

Stan Berg paled. "Gambler!" he sputtered. "That's really cleaning things up! That guy is poison in this town. Look, kid, take my advice and stay away from him. All that joker can do you is harm—believe me!"

"Don't tell me Mickey isn't a nice guy. I know him and he's been great with me."

"Look, Honey, he may seem nice to you, but this town feels very unnice about him. Being identified with him won't help your career."

"What career? I don't have one yet."

Stan grabbed my arm. "I'm going to take you to Warner Brothers right now and introduce you to Solly Biano, the casting director. He's a pal of mine. I know a few people in the movie industry. I'll introduce you to them and see that you get off to the right start—if you don't go getting yourself all fouled up with hoodlums."

"Don't call Mickey Cohen a hoodlum!"

"Why not? Look, maybe he's got his good points, but he's a hoodlum and a publicity hound. That's a bad combination. There's nothing he wouldn't do to get his name in the paper."

"That isn't true! You just don't know him—"

"—Okay, okay, so he's Prince Charming. Anything you say. Let's get to Warner Brothers before the studio closes."

Banks of ivy lined the drive to Burbank. I got goose pimples as the massive Warner Brothers studio loomed into view, with buildings nestled like huge quonset huts at the foot of a purple mountain. This was it! This was my dream world. Soon I would be inside a studio shaking hands with people who made movies. It was a fairy tale come true!

A studio guard admitted us and we drove through the gate. Soon we were hurrying down a long, shining corridor to an office with a sign on the door, SOLLY BIANO.

A secretary led us into the inner office, and there stood a well-groomed Italian gentleman of about forty, with charcoal-gray hair, cropped in a boyish crew cut.

He spotted Stan Berg and came across the room to greet him.

"Why, Stan! You old son-of-a-bitch! How've you been?" he asked, slapping Stan on the back and shaking his hand.

"Slow down, Solly. I want you to meet a friend of mine. Her name is Liz Renay."

Then, for the first time, Solly turned the focus of his attention on me. His eyes widened as though he had discovered something wonderful.

"She's beautiful! Magnificent! Just what we're looking for!"

He grabbed me by the hand and dashed out of the room with me, leaving Stan Berg with his mouth open.

He rushed across the hall, pulling me after him, and we burst into an office with a sign reading EDDIE RYAN, T.V. DEPT.

"Eddie, look at this girl!" he said.

Eddie Ryan stood up and stared at me the way Solly Biano had stared. "You're just what we're looking for. Be here at 9:30 tomorrow morning."

"But—but—but— This is all happening so fast," I stammered. "I don't understand. Look, I don't even have an agent. I'm not an actress. I—"

"Do you have a Guild card?" Eddie asked.

"What's a Guild card? I just came out here to see what a movie studio looks like. I plan to get an agent and everything—but, so far—"

"No matter," said Eddie. "Alice, call S.A.G. and get this young lady into the Guild. Arrange for her to pick up her card at once. She's going to play Jessica in the next Sugarfoot epic."

Alice led me into an inner office and took down the necessary information for a Class A membership in Screen Actors Guild, while Solly hurried back to report the news to Stan Berg.

As soon as Alice finished with me, Stan sped with me to the Guild building in time to file my membership before the union closed.

Stan Berg was nearly as excited as I. "Hey, kid, this is not the way these things happen! It's impossible to get into Screen Actors Guild unless you have a part in a movie. I don't know how in the hell they worked it out!"

"Oh, but I do have a part in a movie. I start tomorrow in the Sugarfoot series. I thought Solly told you!"

"Well I'll be damned!"

As we neared the S.A.G. building, the events of the afternoon seemed like a page out of *Alice in Wonderland*. Was crashing the movies this easy? Could a girl walk into the first movie studio she saw and walk out with a part? That wasn't the way I heard it!

"You take the cake, Baby," said Stan, as we pulled in front of the Screen Actors Guild building. "I'll buy a bottle of champagne. Gotta help you celebrate."

I signed a contract for the role the next morning. Four days later we were shooting.

I had come to Hollywood prepared to struggle and fight for a long time. Yet here I was with a Warner Brothers film contract in my purse and a Screen Actors Guild card in my wallet before I'd even had time to find an agent. It all seemed too easy.

The whirl of studio parties was very exciting. Every party brought its share of invitations from producers, directors, and screen stars.

I dated a number of famous screen stars including Burt Lancaster, Ray Danton, George Raft, Frank Sinatra, and Marlon Brando.

Just for fun I kept a private journal on the actors as lovers, with a sliding scale of one to ten. Lancaster rated ten stars. Jerry Lewis only got one.

Two experiences come to mind. I was on the set of a film and I'd had too much beer. Just after the shooting ended for the night, I slipped and slid into the mud. The star of the picture picked me up and carried me to his car.

He later told me that he had asked me where I wanted to go. "I want to go to a movie studio," I had said.

Sure enough, he drove up to the gates of a major studio. It was closed but, upon his arrival, guards tipped their hats in deference and the studio gate was unlocked.

He took me to his private studio. There was champagne in the refrigerator and a leopard-skin rug on the floor. It was a wonderful night.

By contrast, a famous movie star and television comedian wanted me to parade around in nothing but high heels and black silk stockings while he played with himself. He somehow fancied that, while getting his kicks this way, he was still being true to his wife!

I developed a philosophy of love. It was apparent that eight out of ten men (the other two were probably gay) would make a play for me on any pretext at all. I did nothing special to encourage this. But unless I wore a mask and dressed in a potato sack, the men were there.

I couldn't date them all. But I could pick and choose the most interesting men around, and try the ones I liked. I felt

like I was in a giant supermarket where I could select anything at all that was on the shelves. The anything at all included some of the most glamorous men in the world.

I also realized that, to get where I wanted to get, I would
have to go the casting couch way. It was a nice coincidence
when someone I wanted to go to bed with anyway was in a
position to help me.

My social life became a kaleidoscope of meetings with
colorful men in colorful places.

With Burt Lancaster, it was steins of beer from Malibu
Beach, California, to "Germantown" (Yorkville in New
York City) during his filming of *Elmer Gantry*. With
Marlon Brando, it was exotic rum drinks in Polynesian hideaways, ending in his chaotic apartment. With Frank Sinatra, it was a flight to Atlantic City for a champagne party
in his private suite.

When Mickey Cohen phoned, I was busy. He seemed to
understand, though he didn't sound happy about it.

"I promised the boys I'd keep an eye on you," he re-
mined me. "If there's anything you need or if you have any
trouble—"

"Thanks, Mickey," I said. "We'll get together again as
soon as I'm caught up."

There seemed to be no catching up. I had to report to
the studio at 6:00 each morning for make-up and wardrobe call. By the time we finished shooting and I got
home and unwound, it was 7:00 or 8:00 P.M. About all I
wanted was a quiet dinner before retiring. I declined complicated or lengthy invitations.

I enjoyed playing Jessica. She was a combination chorus
girl and school teacher in the Sugarfoot series. The story
took place in the days of the Old West.

One day, when I was being dressed and made up, I
caught a sudden, fleeting glance at the reflection of my bon-

net-framed face in the dressing-room mirror. The reflection startled me. It looked like a colored enlargement of the tintype portrait of my grandmother when she was voted the prettiest girl in Tennessee. The resemblance was so striking it seemed uncanny. There I stood, dressed the way she dressed as a girl—frilly bonnet, skirt falling to my feet, folds of lace petticoats with lacy pantaloons underneath.

"Little Granny isn't dead, after all," I marveled. "She lives on in me."

I walked across the Warner Brothers lot to the sound stage, casting a long shadow in front of me—the silhouette of a bonneted girl from the Old West, lifting her skirts daintily so as not to soil them in the dirt.

Suddenly I felt very close to Little Granny. Perhaps she was near. Maybe that was why everything was falling into place so neatly. Maybe she was up there pulling a few strings to help me. Maybe somewhere up there, she knew.

The Sugarfoot film went great, and the weeks to follow were sheer fantasy. I could do no wrong.

The Warner Brothers studio took me to its heart and under its protective wing. Solly Biano put me into the studio drama classes. Raoul Walsh and Paul Gregory scheduled a color screen test for the female lead in one of their highest-budgeted pictures of the year. I was overjoyed.

"Hey, that's good news," said the blond young man sitting next to me in drama class.

He looked familiar. He should have—his name was Tab Hunter. Tab and I became friendly. He was sweet and accommodating about driving me around the sprawling Warner Brothers lot.

James Garner and Cliff Robertson chatted with me during commissary time or when I ran into them on the lot. They gave me helpful pointers on acting.

While preparations were being made for my screen test

at Warner Brothers, an avalanche of lucky breaks came spilling into my lap. If Little Granny wasn't up there pulling strings, then who was? I couldn't just get this lucky!

I was signed to do an important TV role on CBS's Climax Show opposite Ray Danton and Hoagie Carmichael. A producer from NBC-TV called and invited me to appear on the Groucho Marx Show and sing a song. I appeared on the show, singing, "I'm in the Mood for Love" and reciting one of my original poems entitled, "Your Eyes." Groucho wiggled his eyebrows, rolled his eyes, and made a funny quip, and the program was a scream from that point on. The director said it was a rip-roaring show and Groucho was never funnier! He invited me to come to NBC and do advance publicity for the show. He said they'd do follow-up publicity later.

As if this wasn't enough, I got lucky on the show. I answered the jackpot question and won $2,000, besides being paid $155 for singing the song. Groucho asked what I intended to do with the money I won. I answered that I'd use it to further my career in Hollywood.

I had the dice. I was hot! I couldn't lose! When I went to Warner Brothers' cashier window to pick up my check, I couldn't find my Social Security card or remember the number. Even this silly incident turned into a lucky break. When I walked into the Social Security office to track down my number, the publicity department pounced on me, as Warner Brothers had done. They photographed me for newspaper and magazine stories across the country and put me on radio explaining what an actress should do if she lost her Social Security card.

TV columnist Eve Starr dedicated an entire column to me, headlined STARLET SKYROCKETS TO FAME! She noticed the brown and golden flecks in my green eyes and named me "The Girl with the Polka-Dot Eyes." The name was picked up by other columnists.

NBC photographed me with Groucho and took pictures of me singing into the mike and presenting Groucho with a copy of my poem, "Your Eyes."

The producer of "Climax" called and offered me the lead in a future Climax production.

Warner Brothers called me in for my technicolor screen test. I went through it like someone sleepwalking, unable to believe all this was happening so quickly, so effortlessly.

I'd only been in Hollywood two and a half months and I was already up for parts in seven top TV shows; I had received a major screen test and made a Warner Brothers film; I had appeared on CBS and NBC television and radio; and I had received considerable newspaper publicity.

Then the most exciting thing of all happened. It happened as I was lunching in the commissary at Paramount Studios. During the last few excitement-packed weeks, I had made many friends in Hollywood—actors, actresses, producers, directors, and columnists. I was having lunch with a young actress named Rita Sands, and one of the music directors from Paramount Studios, Leo Shukin.

Nick Savano, a Hollywood agent from the office of Goldstein & Tobias, and several people from Paramount's music department were at the table. It was a long table. I was seated at the extreme end with Leo Shukin to my right and Rita to my left. We had been served lunch when a slightly stooped, balding, little man walked in, followed by an entourage of people. Among them was actor Yul Brynner.

The hostess seated them at a table directly in line with my view. The little man took the seat facing me. Almost immediately his eyes caught mine and remained fastened there as if he couldn't tear them away. His steadfast, piercing gaze made me uncomfortable. I looked to my right and chatted with Leo. I turned to my left and chatted with Rita. I looked down at my plate, but always when I looked up, there he was, his eyes burning into mine.

Finally the other people at his table began to stare too, quickly appraising me, then turning away, but the little old man just kept looking. He said something to Yul Brynner. Yul looked at me for a moment, nodded, and went back to his lunch. This was becoming embarrassing.

I nudged Leo. "Leo, there is a little old man staring at me so much that he's making me nervous."

Leo looked up, his eyes registering disbelief as he recognized my admirer. "That little man staring at you happens to be Cecil B. DeMille!" he said.

The waitress moved away from the DeMille table and walked toward ours. "You're wanted on the telephone, Mr. Shukin."

"Excuse me," said Leo, rising. "I'll be right back."

In a few minutes he returned, trembling with excitement. "That was no phone call! De Mille told that waitress to call me out there to inquire about you! He wants your name, phone number, agent's number—everything!"

"Give him my name. I'll be your agent!" cut in Nick Savano of Goldstein & Tobias. "I'll handle this. Let him contact me!"

Suddenly, everyone was talking at once. Leo Shukin was jotting down my phone number and other information a mile a minute.

Nick Savano was trying to sign me on the spot.

"He said you have the most exciting face he's seen in twenty years—a combination of beauty and authority," exclaimed Leo. "Can you imagine a compliment like that from a man like Cecil B. DeMille!"

"Yeah, I've never seen him get excited about anybody," said Nick.

Rita's voice cut through the maze. "Oh, Liz, isn't it wonderful! You've been discovered! He can make a star out of you overnight!"

I looked up. The little man was smiling now and he nodded his head to me as if to say, "Hi, Beautiful!"

I smiled back, beaming my appreciation for the compliment. Mama didn't think I was beautiful, but Cecil B. DeMille did.

Chapter 17

SATIN AND SABERS

When my cab pulled up in front of the apartment, I was shocked to see a handsome young marine sitting next to Brenda in the garden patio under the palm trees. I was even more surprised to see him holding her hand and looking into her eyes.

What the hell was going on? What was he doing here? Couldn't he see my Brenda was only a baby? She had just turned fourteen not long ago.

I hurried toward them. The marine was very young. He couldn't have been more than nineteen.

They were laughing and giggling. Gee, they looked happy. I took another look at Brenda, trying to be objective.

She was blonde and beautiful, with a wistful, angelic face and cool, green eyes. In spite of the air of sweet young innocence about her, she could easily be taken for sixteen. My baby was growing up!

They rose and walked toward me, hand in hand.

"Who is this young man, Brenda? I don't understand."

"My name is Leo Landry," he said. "I'm very happy to meet you, Mom."

Mom! Why was he calling me Mom?

"Oh, Mama, I'm sorry I didn't tell you about Leo until now, but I just couldn't. You always think of me as such a baby. I knew you wouldn't understand."

"Understand what?"

"Well, to start at the beginning, I guess you might say —Leo is my piano lesson!"

"Your piano lesson? Make sense! What on earth are you talking about?"

"Well, Mom, Leo and I have been seeing each other for three months. When Grandma sent Johnny and me out from Arizona on the Greyhound bus, I sat in the seat next to Leo. We got acquainted on the trip and Leo wanted to see me again. I knew you'd say no, Mama, because I'm only fourteen—well, I'm fourteen and a half now—but I knew you wouldn't want me to start dating yet. Still, I just had to see Leo, so I devised those piano lessons."

"You mean Leo has been meeting you at your piano lessons?"

"No, Mama, he's been meeting me instead of my piano lessons. There were no piano lessons."

"Brenda, how could you deceive me like that? I can't believe it."

"Mama, it's not as bad as it sounds. Besides, I saved all the money you gave me for the lessons so I could give it back to you. Mama, remember last weekend when I begged you to let me go visit Grandma and you gave me a round-trip ticket?"

"Yes, of course. Don't tell me you didn't go to Grandma's! You left Friday night and didn't come back until Sunday afternoon. My God!"

"Mama, I cashed the ticket in and put the money in the drawer with the piano-lesson money. It's all waiting for you."

"God, Honey, I don't care about the money. All I care about is you. Where were you from Friday night till Sunday afternoon if you weren't visiting Grandma?"

"She was with me!" spoke up the handsome marine. "We eloped to Mexico and got married!"

"Married! Oh my God," I said, sitting down in a chair. "Brenda is only fourteen! She isn't old enough to be married. I want her to finish school. This is a terrible mistake —I think we'd better all go into the house and talk this over."

"If you mean, let's talk about getting the marriage annulled, forget it, Mama. I'm married and that's that. I could be pregnant. It's too late to think about annulments."

"We want to ask your help," said Leo. "We want you on our side, Mom, not against us. Brenda and I are very much in love. It's not a fly-by-night affair. We've been seeing each other for three months. I'll admit fourteen is awfully young, but Brenda tells me you were only sixteen when you married her father."

"Yes—and look how that turned out! I was a silly, irresponsible kid. I didn't know what I was doing. As a result, I was married twice, divorced twice, and had two children before I was eighteen and before I even knew the meaning of love. Do you think I want to see the same thing happen to Brenda?"

"It won't. Brenda does know the meaning of love, and she isn't a silly, irresponsible kid, like you say you were. She's very mature for her age. You did a good job bringing her up. To tell you the truth, I didn't dream she was so young until a few days ago. She told me she was eighteen, and that was easier to believe than her true age."

"Oh, Mama, please understand and don't be mad. I love you so very much. I want you to approve of our marriage and accept Leo as your son-in-law. Please don't fight us!"

"We were sorry you weren't with us when we got married in Mexico, but we are anxious to make it all up to you. We have to get married over again anyway, because the Marine Corps doesn't honor Mexican marriages. We want to do it right next Sunday. I want to invite all my buddies from Camp Pendleton," he rushed on.

"Yes, Mama, and I want you to be my matron of honor, and I want a pretty white wedding dress with roses and lace and a white veil. Most of all, I want you and Johnny there."

"We need your help, Mom," said the handsome marine. "You have to go with us to get the license and sign a paper of consent and written confirmation that Brenda is over sixteen so we won't run into any problems. We want it done legal and right."

"I don't see how my lying about my daughter's age makes anything so right and legal—"

"Look, Mom, once we're married in the United States, it's recognized and binding and Leo can put in for my allotment. I want a beautiful wedding. That Mexican Justice of the Peace ceremony was so ugly, I'd like to erase it from my mind."

"Okay, kids, let's go. Since you're already married, I guess I may as well go along with it and give you all the help I can—because God knows I'm certainly on your side. I wish you all the happiness in the world."

I took Brenda and Leo to the courthouse to get the license, and gave my consent to their marriage, hoping I was doing the right thing. Brenda promised she'd continue her schooling via correspondence courses, as I had done. I consoled myself with the fact that Leo Landry was such a wholesome young man. He was French and very dashing. Brenda could have done worse.

When we returned from the courthouse, I got busy mak-

ing plans for the wedding, while Leo rushed back to Camp
Pendleton to alert his buddies to put in for weekend
passes.

I rented the Carolina Pines banquet room, ordered the
wedding cake, champagne, and refreshments. Rita Sands
wrote wedding invitations while Brenda and I went shopping for her wedding gown.

We found a dress of satin and lace with a long train,
and I ordered her bridal bouquet. I went through motions numbly, like someone made of wood. I couldn't believe this was happening. My fourteen-year-old baby
getting married! It seemed like a bad joke.

Soon the night arrived. Leo and his buddies polished
their brass and got their formal marine blues ready while
I got Brenda dressed. I applied her make-up and fixed
her hair. She looked like a blonde angel.

This was silly. How could my baby be getting married
when she didn't even know how to dress herself?

The wedding was a formal, military affair. Leo's buddies formed an arch of gleaming, crossed sabers for the
couple to walk under.

George Raft was supposed to give the bride away, but
he was detained on business in Cuba. Mickey Cohen volunteered.

Mickey said the crossed sabers gave him the willies.
He wrote a $500 check to Leo as a wedding present. The
kids got checks from several others, and enough pots and
pans and dishes to cook for a regiment. My gift was three
months' rent receipts to a one-bedroom apartment across
the street from me, so that if Brenda needed help she
wouldn't have far to go. I had a hunch she'd better stay
close to Mama for the first two or three months or she
might get lonesome while Leo was doing his duty at Camp
Pendleton.

Mickey Cohen took us to see the Slate Brothers Show after the wedding.

"Mickey, don't you think this show is a little risqué for Brenda's ears?" I asked.

"No, I don't," he replied. "If that baby's old enough to marry a marine, she's old enough to learn the facts of life!"

We drove the kids to their apartment and applauded when Leo carried his bride over the threshold. Then Mickey dropped me across the street.

"Well, Lizzy," he said, "you just lost your little girl. Don't believe that malarky about gaining a son—once the kids get married, they're gone. Oh—they're still around, but it's not the same. You don't own them any more."

"I don't want to own them, I never did—I just want to see them happy."

"Say, Liz, how about you? Do you think you'll ever get married again?"

"Gee, Mickey, I haven't thought much about it lately. Why do you ask?"

"Well, I think you're a real fine lady. I admire you a lot, and I just want to call it to your attention that, in case you do decide to get married, Jewish men make the best husbands."

We laughed. Mickey gave my hand a squeeze, kissed me lovingly on the mouth, and soon his big Eldorado zoomed out of sight.

Mickey was a strange, unpredictable little guy—but in my presence he was always a gentleman. He was right about my losing my little girl, for soon Leo took her to New Orleans to live.

Chapter 18

"ANASTASIA MURDER SQUAD"

As I glanced out the taxi window on the way to the movie studio, a headline caught my eye. It blared: ALBERT ANASTASIA MURDERED IN BARBER CHAIR!

"My God, that was Cappy's friend, his pal! Cappy must be all broken up over this."

When I got home my phone was ringing. It was Cappy, almost too choked up to talk.

"Lizbeth," he said, "the police are looking for me. They'll be picking me up for questioning. I wanted to talk to you now. I may not be able to much longer. Guess where I was when they killed Albert? I was on my way to Fort Lee to pick up those goddamned movie stills you sent me. Albert was getting a haircut. Who the hell would think he wasn't safe at 10:00 A.M. in a barber shop? Who'd believe a thing like this could happen?"

"Cappy," I cut in, "if you had been there, you might be dead, too. You're lucky you weren't there!"

"Like hell I'd be dead. I'da filled those two dirty rats so full of lead they'da looked like Swiss cheese the minute they walked through that door. Albert would be alive this minute if I'da been there!"

Suddenly his voice lowered. "Liz, Baby, I gotta lam outa here. Somebody's comin'!" The connection was broken, leaving only a dial tone as I sat holding the phone.

I had no sooner hung up the receiver than it rang sharply

174

again. This time it was Mickey Cohen. "Hi, Doll. Did you hear the news about your boyfriend's boss getting knocked off?"

"Boss! Is that what he was? I thought he was just a friend."

"Oh, come on, you couldn't be that naïve! Cappy was Anastasia's right-hand man and personal bodyguard. You musta known that!"

"All I know is Cappy's in a lot of trouble now. I just spoke to him!"

"You bet he's in trouble. He's lucky to be alive. But I didn't call you about this. I need you to do a favor for me, Doll. Will you?"

"Why, uh yes, of course, if I can. What is it?"

"Good, I'll be right over. This is something I'd rather discuss in person," he said, breaking the connection.

I sat and waited for Mickey to arrive. In the past ten weeks I'd been so taken up in the magic of my budding movie career, I'd scarcely seen Mickey. I felt a little guilty. After all, he had been very nice to me when I arrived in Hollywood before I had made other friends, and it certainly was nice of him to give the kids a $500 wedding gift. Well, I'd show my appreciation now by doing this favor, whatever it was. That would sort of make it up to him.

Mickey arrived looking like an ad for a men's fashion magazine in his immaculate custom-made suit.

He whistled as he surveyed me in the outfit I'd worn to the studio. "How about letting me take you to dinner for our little discussion?"

"Sure," I said, glad for the opportunity to compensate for my neglect.

Soon we arrived at the beautiful Sportsmen's Lodge in San Fernando Valley and ordered dinner. I told Mickey of the good fortune I had encountered and explained the reason I had seemed to disappear for the last couple of months.

Mickey was delighted. "Why shouldn't you make it big? Just tell me one girl in Hollywood that's got half of what you've got—unless," he added sheepishly, "maybe Lana Turner."

Mickey leaned forward confidentially. "Liz, you still have a New York bank account, don't you?"

"Why, yes, but there's not much in it. I've only a couple of hundred dollars there."

"That's okay, just so you have an account," he said. "Look, Liz, I hate to bother you with a thing like this, but I need you to write me a check for $2,000 tonight. Mark the check 'for personal loan' to be paid back within thirty days, okay?"

"But, Mickey, I told you I have only $200 in my account. You're asking for one zero too many."

He laughed. "Look, Doll, I'll see the two grand is there to cover the check before it gets there! Don't worry."

"Then why do you need me to give you the check in the first place? I don't understand."

"It's not necessary you understand. All you gotta do is mark it 'for personal loan' as I asked. I need to pay someone a couple of grand tonight. I want to pay them with a check. Your New York bank account is a natural. It gives me four or five days' time to get the money there to cover it."

"All right, I'll give you the check, but if you don't have the money there it will bounce sky-high!"

"Don't worry, Baby." He smiled, patting my hand. "The money will be there. Thanks for the favor. I may need you to do it again next week for a larger amount."

Mickey drove me home and walked me to the door.

Then he suddenly kissed me full on the mouth. "Good night, Angel," he whispered.

Next day Warner Brothers called me to come in for an interview with Mervyn LeRoy about a part in *The F.B.I. Story*. I was to play the notorious "lady in red" who betrayed John Dillinger. I took Rita Sands along to read opposite me in the scenes. "Boy, you have a lot of things pending," she sighed.

The following day the studio called to say the results of my screen test were "sensational," and they wanted me to read for the part of Aldo Ray's wife in *The Naked and the Dead*. Things were piling up so fast I couldn't think.

A few days later I got a call from the vice president of my bank in New York. Mickey Cohen didn't get the money there in time to cover the check I had written. "The money arrived three hours after we returned the check for insufficient funds," he informed me.

I called Mickey. He was frantic. I canceled my appointments at the studio and spent the afternoon making long-distance calls back and forth to New York straightening out the bouncing check.

I persuaded an officer from the bank to call the man Mickey had given the check to and assure him that the bank had made an error in returning the check and advise him to send it right back for immediate payment, because the bank was holding the money to cover it.

I instructed the bank to charge any phone calls regarding the check to my Hollywood number.

Mickey thanked me heartily, apologized for embarrassing me, and said he'd reimburse me for the phone calls. He gave me a kiss on the cheek and departed.

Next day I received an excited call from Nick Savano asking me to come to his office at once. DeMille had contacted him. "Good God, girl, DeMille wants you to play

Esther in his next Biblical extravaganza! Do you realize
what that means? You, an unknown, starring in a multi-
million-dollar DeMille extravaganza? If you'll pardon my
saying so, I just don't understand it! Don't get me wrong.
You're a great-looking chick—but, Esther?"

"Look, if you're interested in handling me, you better
knock off that attitude. For God's sake, don't say that to
DeMille."

"You think I'm crazy? Don't be ridiculous! I told him I
thought you'd be perfect for Joan of Arc. Matter of fact, I
discussed your saintly qualities and angelic face with him
for half an hour. You know what he kept saying? 'Authority,
this girl possesses great authority!' "

I picked up a paper from the corner newsstand. Cappy's
face stared up belligerently! The caption was *KEY WIT-
NESS IN ANASTASIA MURDER INVESTIGATION.*

Headlines on another paper screamed *ANASTASIA
GUARD KEY TO MURDER MYSTERY.* A picture of
Cappy shielding his face from photographers' flash bulbs
filled the front page. In the days to follow, the papers were
full of the Albert Anastasia murder suspects, theories, arrests, and underworld reactions.

None of this seemed to have any personal meaning to me.

Soon Mickey Cohen called again. "Look, Doll," he said.
"I need another check right away. This time for $3,500."

"Mickey, dear, maybe you'd better try someone else—
someone who has money in the bank."

"Listen, Honey, if you're worried because the money
didn't get there last time and you're afraid it won't again,
I'll tell you what I'll do. You give me the check now, and in
a couple of days we'll wire the money to your account
from here. That way there can be no slip-up. Just give me
a couple of days, Doll."

I was glad I could still be of help after the other foul-up.

I wrote the $3,500 check, marking it "As Loan," the way he requested.

There were more pictures of Cappy and stories about him. The papers said he was being held on bond. I wondered why he didn't put up bail and get out of jail. Could it be he felt safer there?

I mailed some cheer-up cards to him in care of the jail and a letter to his sister's address.

Four days went by. I called Mickey and said, "Look, Mickey, I don't want to be a party pooper, but let me remind you that check will bounce if we don't get the money there now!"

"I know, Doll. Don't worry about a thing. I'll call you first thing in the morning. Bye bye, Angel!"

I stayed home from the studio and waited all day for his call, afraid to leave the telephone. When I hadn't heard from him by six that evening, I dialed his number in Westwood.

I was surprised to hear his voice and even more surprised at his nonchalant attitude.

"Oh, hello, Doll," he said. "How's everything going?"

I was exasperated. "Why haven't you called me? I waited all day for your call."

"I didn't have the forty cents change!" came the teasing voice on the other end of the line.

I just couldn't believe his lack of concern. "If he wants to play games, we'll play games," I told myself. "If my check bounces, I'll let it. It's his problem, not mine."

The situation suddenly appealed to my sense of humor, and I called a cab and went to Western Union. "I'd like to send a money order for forty cents," I said.

"Oh, you can't do that," said the man behind the counter. "It would cost you a dollar and fifty cents just to wire the forty cents."

"That's all right with me and, as for the message, just put—'Now what's your excuse? Love, Liz.'"

Mickey got a big kick out of the wire. Next morning his attorney, Eddie Gritz, was knocking on my door before I was awake.

"I have the cash," he called through the door. "I'm here to take you to Western Union to wire it to your bank."

I quickly dressed and we drove to Western Union. A naïve-looking young man came forward to the counter. He acted as if this was his first job and we were his first customers.

When I wrote the amount $3,500, he immediately inserted a decimal point after the thirty-five, making it read $35.

"The way you had it written, it said thirty-five hundred dollars," he giggled.

"That's exactly what I wanted it to say," I answered wearily.

"You mean to say you're wiring $3,500?" he exclaimed. He began figuring for what seemed a half hour. Eddie and I fidgeted nervously. "That will be $16 altogether," he said after long deliberation. We gave him the $3,500, paid him the $16 fee, and left.

We joined Mickey for lunch, reporting that all was well, the money was on its way.

"Good," he said. "It should be there before the bank opens."

Next day I received another call from the same vice president who had helped me straighten out the previous mess. "Liz Renay, what on earth are you doing?" he asked. "A check came in yesterday morning for $3,500. After we returned it for insufficient funds, a night letter arrived with $3,500 to be deposited to your account. What is this anyway?"

"Night letter!" I cried. "Oh, that silly fool at Western Union! No one said anything about sending it as a night letter. I guess the poor dope took it upon himself to save us money."

I called Mickey and told him what had happened.

"Oh my God, Liz! This is awful. You've got to help me! I can't afford to have that check bounce—this, of all checks!"

"Okay, take it easy. I'll do what I can."

Again I pleaded with the bank officer to call the party in Hollywood and assure him it was a bank error and advise him to send the check back for immediate payment.

When it was done, I called Mickey. He thanked me profusely. I glowed with satisfaction that once again I had pleased the little man and had been of service to him in my small way.

The next two weeks flew by in a dizzy whirl. George Raft escorted me to all the "in" places. My Sugarfoot TV segment was shown on television. Soon my Groucho Marx show would be on coast-to-coast TV. I moved from the Knickerbocker Hotel to a lovely three-bedroom apartment.

Nick Savano called to say he had received a call from Cecil B. DeMille in New York. "DeMille says he'll be in touch as soon as he gets back from New York. He wants to arrange for you to come to his office to discuss his plans for you," he said.

It appeared that a golden future lay ahead for me in Hollywood. I had found my home town.

I decided to take a quick trip to New York to wind up the loose ends I'd left behind. One thing I needed to do was see attorney Leo Gitlin to straighten out my affairs and work out my income tax return.

That evening I told Rita my plans to go to New York.

"That's a wonderful idea! I've got enough money saved to go with you. There's an agent I'd like to see about a Broadway show."

"Great! We'll have a ball! We'll leave right away and be back in a few days."

A housekeeper moved in to look after Johnny, and Rita and I packed for New York.

As I rushed out with my suitcase, I noticed some mail in the mailbox. I grabbed it, and tossed it into my purse unopened.

"Hurry, we'll miss the plane!" called Rita.

I dashed for the cab. What the hell, I could read my mail on the plane.

In a few short hours we stepped off the plane into a howling snowstorm in New York City. Wind whipped our skirts about our legs and blew flurries of snow flakes into our hair. We hailed a cab and hurried to the Plaza Hotel. After we'd unpacked and put on our warmest sweaters, I got busy on the telephone.

I called Leo Gitlin and arranged to meet him downstairs in the Oak Room the next day. "We'll have lunch and discuss putting my affairs in order," I said.

"Fine," Leo agreed. "Let's meet at eleven and get a head start on the lunch hour."

Next I called Irving Zussman, a press agent I had met during the Marilyn Monroe contest. Irving seemed to know everything that was going on with everyone, everywhere in town. I called him to get the latest scoop. He recognized my voice immediately.

"Liz, Baby Doll, when did you get into town?"

"Just this minute, Irving."

"I guess you heard about your friend Cappy."

"You mean about his being arrested in the Anastasia murder investigation?"

"No, I meant the latest news! He's dying! He collapsed in jail with a heart attack and was taken to the hospital. I understand he's on the critical list. It was in yesterday's papers."

"Oh, my God, how awful!"

"Rita, Cappy had a heart attack!" I dialed information. "I'd like the number of Phyllis Pusso in Fort Lee, New Jersey."

The operator gave me the number and I dialed it.

"Who in heaven's name is Phyllis Pusso?" asked Rita.

"I'm calling Cappy's home in New Jersey to offer my sympathy to his family and see if there's anything I can do to help," I answered.

Cappy's sister's voice came over the phone. "This is Liz Renay," I said. "I'm calling to let you know how sorry I am about Cappy. I heard—"

"Liz Renay—Liz Renay!" she exclaimed. "Just a minute, I'll let you talk to Cappy!"

"Oh my God, Elizabeth," said Cappy. "I can't believe it. You're here. The very day I get out, you're here to see me. This is too much to hope for!"

"I—I thought you were in the hospital, Cappy. Irving said—the papers said—" My words trailed off in bewilderment.

"Oh, you know those stupid newspapers! They'll print anything. When I was being released from jail, I fainted and someone shouted, 'He's having a heart attack.' I was taken to the hospital and there's your story. I was there for a few hours' observation and here I am. And who is it calling me but my Elizabeth!"

"Cappy," I said, "I'm glad you're all right. Why did you faint when they took you out of jail?"

"I don't know, Baby. I guess I couldn't stand the fresh air!"

"Well, I'm glad I got to talk to you, Cappy, and here's wishing you all the luck in the world."

"Wait! You're not sayin' goodbye, are you? Where ya' callin' from?"

"From the Plaza Hotel, Cappy. You can call me here any time you like. I'll be here a few more days."

"Call you, hell! I'm on my way over there right now. Meet me in the Oak Room." He hung up the phone.

I told Rita: "Tony Coppola is on his way over here. I hadn't intended to see him. He's in such hot water."

Rita was familiar with Cappy's story.

"Look, Liz, since he's on his way over and you have to see him anyway, let's give the guy a break and make him happy. Let's have a party for him."

The idea struck my fancy. "Yeah, a coming-out party," I laughed.

We started calling friends and told them to meet us at El Morocco in an hour. Then we went downstairs to wait for Cappy in the Oak Room.

In a few minutes he arrived, looking pale and tired. It was obvious he wasn't feeling nearly as well as he pretended.

He was unshaven and needed a manicure. The murder, the subsequent grilling, and the weeks of solitary confinement had taken their toll.

He smiled a wan smile. "You'll never know what it means having you here at a time like this, Lisabeth."

I introduced him to Rita, and she told him about the party we'd planned at El Morocco. It was then I noticed he was wearing his house slippers. Oh, well, if he didn't mind wearing bedroom slippers to El Morocco, why should I care?

We hailed a cab and soon pulled up in the slushy snow

in front of El Morocco. Tom Vaughn was waiting at the curb. Our friends inside must have cast votes, and Tom won the dubious honor of standing in the icy wind to greet us.

Tom was tall, blond, and attractive in a sophisticated, conservative way. The Manhattan executive, personified.

"Greetings, salutations, and the rest of the rubbish!" he said, as he opened the cab door with a mock bow.

"Hi, Thomas!" I smiled, stepping out into the slush and the chill. As Cappy climbed shakily out of the cab, Tom got a look at him for the first time. Rita scrambled out prettily, but Tom's eyes were still glued to Cappy.

I followed his stare as Cappy walked toward the club entrance with Rita close on his heels. I tried to look at Cappy through Tom's midtown Manhattan eyes. What was he looking at? Was it that Cappy needed a shave and haircut? Had Tom noticed the long fingernails from the weeks of solitary?

Tom's whisper broke my contemplation. "Liz, who's your friend in the bedroom slippers?"

"Howard Hughes—who else?"

We joined the three other couples at the long table and celebrated wildly. Cappy was king tonight. The hell with anyone who didn't like it! We ordered champagne and more champagne, and, as Cappy and I danced at the elegant El Morocco, bedroom slippers and all, we brushed against the Duke and Duchess of Windsor.

We laughed and danced and drank until the place closed. We said good night to our friends, and Cappy escorted us to our hotel, then took the cab home to New Jersey.

We had a hard time waking up the next morning, with our champagne hangovers!

"Come on, Liz. We've got to get up. We've got to meet your attorney in the Oak Room. Remember?" nudged Rita.

I forced myself awake. We got dressed and reached the Oak Room in time for our 11:00 A.M. appointment with Leo.

Leo Gitlin was on the button. There was another attorney with him, a Mr. Lord, from Philadelphia. I introduced them to Rita, and we proceeded to order lunch. Leo requested a phone at our table for incoming calls he expected.

During lunch, Mr. Lord remarked that Rita and I could pass for sisters. Leo disagreed, saying he saw no resemblance whatever. Mr. Lord then pointed out that we were the same height and about the same weight, we had the same color hair, and both of us were wearing black wool suits and black cashmere coats.

"Now if that doesn't qualify them to look like sisters, I'd like to know why not!" he grinned.

As soon as we finished lunch, Rita excused herself.

"Liz, I'd like to run over and see that Broadway agent I told you about. I'll go now while you and Leo work out the details of your affairs. I'll be back within the hour," she said.

We agreed that was a good plan, and Mr. Lord escorted Rita to the front door and saw her into a cab.

When he returned, Leo and I had a pile of canceled checks and receipts spread out in front of us. As we sat sipping coffee and sorting papers, the phone on our table began to ring.

Leo picked it up and, with a surprised look, handed the receiver to me. Who could possibly be calling me? No one knew I was here in the Oak Room.

Rita's breathless voice poured out of the receiver. "Oh, Liz, get out of there. Right now! I'm not kidding—leave!

Run! Hide! Get away! Hurry, they're after you! They're going to arrest you! Get out of there fast!"

"Rita, calm down, get hold of yourself! Who's going to arrest me? What are you talking about?"

"The police. They followed my cab for five blocks. They forced it to the curb and pulled me out. They said, 'You're coming with us, Miss Renay.' When I showed them my identification and proved I wasn't you, they dropped me and headed back to get you. They are running back to the hotel on foot. They'll be there any minute— Get out! Get out!"

"Rita, Honey, you're all upset for nothing. I'm not guilty of anything! I have nothing to fear from the police. It's a mistake. We'll straighten it out! Come on back to the hotel and don't worry about a thing."

As I hung up the receiver, I noticed the alert, inquisitive look on both attorneys' faces. "What's up?" they asked.

"The police mistook Rita for me and picked her up. She showed her I.D. and they let her go. Now they're on their way here to get me. But why?" I added, almost to myself. "I've done nothing."

"Come on, let's get out of here right now! We can discuss what you haven't done later!"

Leo stuffed the papers into his briefcase, and we all made a rush for the front entrance. Leo spotted two plain-clothes men guarding the door and stopped short, holding out his arm to stop me. "Turn back," he said. "Front door's blocked."

We sped toward the side entrance, to find it blocked by two more plainclothes men. Then Leo noticed the stairs. "Come on, we'll ditch them by going up the stairs. We'll disappear into the hotel and hide for a while until we figure this thing out!"

We walked briskly to the staircase and were on the first

landing when we heard a loud voice from the foot of the stairs. "Hold it! Don't move! We've got you covered."

It was the detectives who'd been guarding the front door.

"We're taking you to headquarters with us, Miss Renay," the tall one said.

"You can't do that!" asserted Leo Gitlin. "I'm Miss Renay's attorney. You can't go around picking people up unless you have a warrant for their arrest."

"Whatever you say," the tall man answered. "If you want her arrested, we're prepared to arrest her. We thought maybe it wouldn't be necessary."

"Who are you? What department are you from?" sputtered Leo.

"Homicide. We're with the special squad investigating the Albert Anastasia murder!"

"Murder!" exclaimed Leo. "Well, if you're taking Miss Renay, I insist on going with her."

"You insist!" the short one laughed. "Don't worry, you're coming anyway. You and the other gentleman there and that briefcase you were stuffing papers into. It's all coming—so don't bother to insist!"

"Sorry," said the tall one. "The district attorney will want to question all of you."

With that, they began hustling us toward the front door, pushing and prodding us along. Leo and Mr. Lord moved awkwardly in front of me, unsure of their position, baffled looks on their faces.

It was then I caught sight of another little man with a baffled look on his face as we were marched across the lobby to the police car outside. The little man stood there staring at me the way he had stared on that other occasion, only this time his mouth stood ajar and he looked aghast as the procession filed past him.

Then Cecil B. DeMille shook his head sadly and walked back into the Oak Room.

"Oh God, Cecil, you of all people. Why did you have to be here today?" I said softly as I was shoved into the police car.

"What's that?" asked Leo, nervously.

"Nothing, forget it." I settled back in the cab wondering why Leo Gitlin, Mr. Lord, and Rita Sands were all so upset. This was a murder investigation. I hadn't murdered anyone! What did I have to fear? I was more upset over the fact that DeMille had witnessed the incident. My God—what would he think? Would this be "Goodbye, Esther"?

Little did I realize that the chain of events then being set in motion would eventually make a shambles of my life, smash to bits my budding career, and leave only a pile of jigsaw puzzle pieces in its wake.

I was led into one room, and the attorneys were taken to another. An officer grabbed my purse roughly from my hands and dumped its contents onto the desk in front of me.

There it was, everything from lipstick to Tampax, strewn out in front of us, staring us in the face.

The assistant district attorney poked about in the conglomeration asking, what's this and what's that?

He picked up my reducing pills and, in a highly official tone, told one of the officers to have them analyzed. He handed my address book to another assistant and told him to have it photostated.

It seemed silly, pointless, and unnecessary. I was becoming more annoyed by the minute.

"Hey, listen, fellows, are you for real? Or are you playing Sherlock Holmes?" I asked, as one of them tore open a Tampax to see if something was hidden inside.

It seemed to me a comic-strip situation, only Dick Tracy made more sense. What the hell were they looking for in a Tampax?

The assistant D.A. picked up the stack of letters I had grabbed from my mailbox on the way to the Hollywood airport. I'd forgotten all about them—they were still unopened.

There were three white envelopes, personal letters from friends, no doubt. The other was a long, brown envelope. Probably my monthly bank statement and last month's canceled checks.

The D.A. was opening the brown envelope. "What's this?" he demanded, holding up a couple of checks.

I was irritated. "Haven't you seen canceled checks before? They come back from the bank. They make good receipts."

He turned to me, dangling the two canceled checks in my face. "What about these two?" he asked, accusingly.

"Oh, for crying out loud, how should I know? You've got them in your hand. You tell me!"

"I'd like to know one thing," he said, acidly. "What possible reason could you have for giving Mickey Cohen $5,500?"

Oh God! Those damn checks I gave Mickey! They had come back in my envelope of canceled checks. If only I had destroyed them. If only I'd opened those letters. How could I explain them?

"Look at the date on this one!" said a detective. "The day after the Anastasia rub-out."

"You don't say! Take these out and photostat them," said the D.A., handing them to a police officer.

"Well, Miss Renay, what do you have to say about those checks?"

I felt ill. "Nothing," I said weakly, "nothing at all."

"Oh, I see," said the D.A. "You plan to play it cute." He paused. He was writing something. "Well, here's a subpoena for you. Maybe you prefer to tell the Grand Jury about those checks under oath!"

I took the piece of paper and walked woodenly out of the room. Leo Gitlin and Lord were gone. I took a cab back to the Plaza. As I walked into the lobby, someone called, "Liz, here we are, over here!" I looked around. Leo, Rita, and Lord were waiting for me.

"At least they let you go!" said Rita. "What happened?" We went into the dining room and ordered dinner.

"Let's go back to Hollywood tomorrow," Rita suggested. "I don't like the looks of all this."

"I'm afraid that won't be possible for me, Rita," I said, laying the subpoena on the table.

"Oh, no," said Leo. "They didn't!"

While we all nervously choked down our food, I told them what had happened at the district attorney's office. The subpoena was for the day after tomorrow. That would give me a day and a night to think. I'd need every minute of it.

I called Mickey in Hollywood and told him briefly what had happened. I didn't ask him what I should say or do, remembering his words of caution concerning his phone. "Never say anything on my phone that you wouldn't say directly to the police department," he once warned. "My phone is bugged."

I tried to tell him things with double talk, but had no way of being sure he got the message. He wasn't able to say much either, so the call accomplished little.

I didn't dare contact Cappy again. Seeing him was the reason I was picked up to begin with. Perhaps a tail had followed him to my hotel, or maybe his phone was tapped like Mickey's and they had overheard our conversation.

I decided my best bet would be to visit Champ Segal. He was a friend of both Mickey and Cappy. After all, he was the one who put me in touch with Mickey to begin with. He'd know how to advise me.

I took a cab to Champ's luxurious Park Avenue apartment. He was disturbed when I told him the news.

"This is bad—real bad," he said. "Be goddamned careful what you say up there. You could get Mickey in a real jam! Better say you loaned him the money and he still owes it to you. That's the simplest way. Then nobody's in trouble," he said, shaking his head and rubbing his chin. "You're a good kid, Liz. I know you don't want to foul Mickey up. He treated you right, didn't he?"

"Yes, of course he did. No, of course I don't want to foul him up."

My mind was spinning when I walked from the plush apartment lobby onto the snow-banked streets and hailed a cab to Leo Gitlin's office. I found Leo staring aimlessly at the growing pile of unanswered mail on his desk.

"Hi, Honey," he said. "I just can't work. I'm worried about you and the mess you've gotten into."

"That's what I've come to discuss with you."

"I'll accompany you there tomorrow, my dear, but no one can go with you into the jury room, you understand. I'll have to wait outside the door."

"I know, Leo. That's why I want to discuss it now. Listen, I can't tell the truth up there tomorrow. I might get Mickey Cohen in trouble if I do."

"You can't worry about him. You've got to think of yourself."

"I'm sorry, Leo, but I consider him a friend and I don't want to do anything to hurt him.

"Another thing, Leo. What if I don't know all the true facts involved? What if this is more complicated than

iz streaking at the Hollywood Boulevard and Vine Street intersection where she displayed her famous body for some 5,000 male spectators.

Liz at 13 (with a schoolmate). That sultry Renay look had already begun to develop, as evidenced in this adult photo.

As one of Eileen Ford's star models.

At times, that regal look was reminiscent of
Marie Antoinette!

And always, the promise of pneumatic bliss!

A natural beauty being natural.

This see-through negligee reveals that Marilyn Monroe look-alike backside.

As a burlesque star, she worked to packed houses.

Totie Fields, lady comic views some of Liz Renay
features.

Portrait of a painter with her as hanging out!

film *Deadwood 76*.

Liz holding a lion cub. Pussy with a pussy?

Addressing the Los Angeles press club. Liz has been making news for half-a-century.

Cleaning up the act.

Liz and her daughter Brenda.
They were sometimes mistaken
for sisters.

Letting them all hang out.

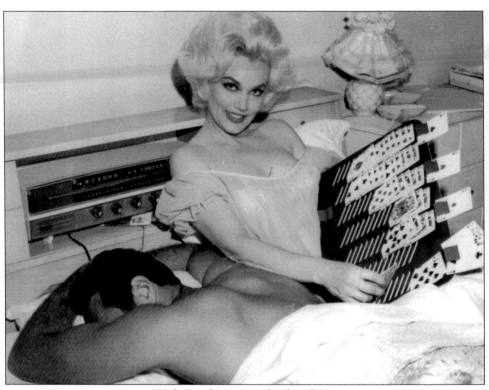

With Read Morgan, husband #5.

William M. Gaines was publisher of *MAD Magazine*. This photo was taken at the Stuart Place in Jamaica, West Indies.

Close friend Sylvester Stallone.

Liz in her own words: "Life for me begins with every sunrise. Each day is a new day. Beautiful, promising, exciting, delicious. I live every hour and love every minute."

what meets the eye? What if I could step on toes I don't even know about? Champ Segal seemed awfully insistent that I just call it a loan and let it go at that. Besides, he's right. That's the simplest thing to do!"

"No, Honey," Leo said. "The simplest thing to do under oath before a Grand Jury is to tell the truth. Otherwise—"

"Listen, Leo. If I go up there and say I loaned him the money, it ends there. Open and shut, no loose ends. That'll be the end of the confounded thing."

"Except for one thing," said Leo. "They'll want to know where you got the money to cover those checks. You can be sure, they're already checking your bank. They will uncover that the money was sent from California to cover the checks. You will have to tell them where you got the cash—don't forget that."

"Well, they can't prove anything. I'll say I won it in Las Vegas."

"They'd never believe you. If you're going to lie at all, then you'd better give them a pat story. My advice is to tell the truth, but if you can't take my advice, then prepare a damned good story. Dig up someone who is willing to stand behind you and swear he gave you the money to cover the loans you made to Mickey with the understanding that, when Mickey pays you back, you, in turn, will pay him back. Be sure this person is able to show he has that kind of available cash or you're right back where you started from," he said, rubbing his hands together thoughtfully. "What about that playboy you used to date—that fellow Terzon—will he do it?"

"It's a good suggestion. I'll call him and ask. See you tomorrow at the Grand Jury." I walked out into the fluttering snow flakes.

"Good God, if it isn't Liz Renay!" called a familiar voice.

It was Irwin Styles. "What are you doing back in New York? Let's go in here for coffee and doughnuts and a hello!" he said, tugging at my arm and motioning toward a nearby coffee shop. What a happy coincidence running into a friend of Garry's! I told Irwin about my predicament over crunchy doughnuts and several cups of hot coffee.

Irwin, my smooth con man acquaintance, had a unique talent with doubletalk. He could get messages across loud and clear without committing himself to concrete statements. He was an expert in the art of subterfuge.

"Irwin, I'd like you to do me a favor. Call Garry Terzon and get the point across to him about the favor I need and see what his reaction is."

"I'm glad to do it for you, Liz, but don't you think it would be better if you made the call yourself in view of—"

"Look, Irwin, I go before that Grand Jury tomorrow. There's no time to lose. I've got to know this thing's set. I can't call Garry Terzon. He's married, and his wife is jealous and possessive. It's better if a man calls."

"Why didn't you say so, Lizzy? It's as good as done. Let's grab a cab to my hotel. We can make the call in comfort from my suite at the Essex House."

Chapter 19

LANCEY TO THE RESCUE

I called Rita and invited her to join me at Irwin's suite for dinner. She could get there by the time we finished our phone call.

Soon Irwin had Garry on the phone explaining my plight in such masterful doubletalk that even Garry's wife wouldn't be able to detect a thing if she was eavesdropping on another extension (the way I was, at the moment). Irwin said everything without saying anything and Garry agreed, although I can't say he showed much enthusiasm. When Irwin finished, Garry asked if he could talk to me. "May I discuss it with your partner?" he said, indicating he couldn't talk freely.

I came on the line immediately. "Did you get the picture?" I asked.

"Yes, I got it, but I don't like it."

"All I want to know is whether I can count on you all the way and for certain, Garry. If not, for God's sake, say so now! Tomorrow's the day."

"Of course, you can count on me. Have I ever let you down?"

"Thanks, Garry. I'll consider it a closed issue then. Goodbye." I hung up the phone, mission accomplished. It reminded me of a foreign-intrigue TV script.

Irwin, Rita, and I ordered a bottle of champagne and got a little tipsy celebrating solving the first phase of my prob-

195

lem. Then Irwin called his attorney, Louis Kay, and asked
him to join us for dinner. Kay seemed set on attaching himself to me and the case. He asked if I'd mind if he accompanied me to the Grand Jury hearing, without charge.
"There's going to be big interest in this case," he said.
"Big publicity."

I told him I already had an attorney going with me, but
if he wanted to tag along, fine.

"I think this whole thing is getting to be fun with you,"
said Rita. "Sort of a game."

The next day I got dressed to kill and put on my pretty
black fox jacket. Leo and Irwin's attorney, Louis Kay, accompanied me to answer my Grand Jury subpoena. To
our utter astonishment, no Grand Jury was in session that
day—just District Attorney Hogan seated alone at his desk.

"I decided to give it one more try," he said. "I'm going to
question you privately and, if you tell me the truth and
are cooperative, maybe we won't have to bring you before the Grand Jury after all."

He proceeded to grill me for an hour and a half, alter-
nating between the angry and the sympathetic approach.

I gave him the Garry Terzon story I had invented, but
he obviously didn't buy it. Finally, he rose to his feet and
said, "It's no use. We are getting nowhere. You'll have to
face the Grand Jury."

He handed me another subpoena, this time dated two
weeks ahead. Dammit, why in blazes hadn't he put me
before the Grand Jury today, instead of holding me over
for two weeks. Now I'd have to stay in New York. How
could I do it? I had made only temporary arrangements
with the housekeeper who was looking after Johnny in
Hollywood. I'd have to fly back to Hollywood, make other
arrangements for Johnny, then fly back to New York again

in time for my subpoena date. Did District Attorney Hogan think airplanes were free? Or that I was made of money?

I got into the elevator fuming and fussing to Leo and Louis Kay as we descended. Then the elevator opened, and so did my mouth at the sight before me. A regiment of newspaper photographers, reporters, and TV newsreel cameramen crowded around the elevator, mobbing my path. They milled outside like a herd of cattle, bumping together as they attempted to focus their cameras.

They all spotted me at once as the elevator door opened. "Oh," I cried. "Oh!" As I pursed my lips to say, "Oh," a hundred flash bulbs went off in my face. They blinded me. Reporters pushed and shoved to get at me. I could scarcely get out of the elevator, they were crowding me so.

I forced my way through the sea of exploding flash bulbs and questioning reporters. I was carried along by their pushing and shoving. They ran after me in the street with their endless questions, until I finally escaped in a cab.

By the time I got back to my hotel that evening, my face stared back at me from the front page of every newspaper in the city. My silly face, lips pursed as if I was throwing a kiss to the world, filled the entire front page of the *Daily Mirror* under the bold caption, ACTRESS GRILLED IN ANASTASIA MURDER.

The news quickly spread across the nation. *LIZ RENAY, MYSTERY WOMAN IN ANASTASIA CASE. LIZ RENAY, NEW DARLING OF THE UNDERWORLD, LIZ RENAY, MICKEY COHEN'S GIRL FRIEND.* Everywhere I went, everything I did made headlines.

Rita and I packed our things and flew back to Hollywood. Reporters crowded around us at the airport, and newsreel cameramen followed us to the ramp as we boarded our plane, then they hurried to phone in the story, *LIZ RENAY FLIES BACK TO HOLLYWOOD.*

When our plane landed in California, the Hollywood press and TV newsreels took it up. Newsmen huddled in raincoats in the drizzling dawn, waiting at the ramp. The moment I stepped through the airplane door, cameras began rolling and flash bulbs bursting.

Reporters ran after me, following me with running questions through the airport to the luggage department and into the street. Rita followed along after me, trying not to lose pace or be separated by the throng. Then we drove away in a taxi, and they hurried to phone in their stories, *LIZ RENAY ARRIVES BACK FROM MURDER INVESTIGATION.*

I arranged for my aunt to stay with Johnny till the mess was over. Soon it was time to fly back to answer the Grand Jury subpoena in New York. Mickey sent his attorney, Eddie Gritz, to New York with me to confer with Leo Gitlin.

The press and newsreels followed my every action. Some of the stories were becoming exaggerated and distorted. The image of a twentieth-century Gun Moll was slowly emerging from the patchwork pattern of combined news media.

Eddie Gritz and I boarded the plane for New York, pushing our way through a sea of chattering reporters. Soon headlines screamed, *MICKEY SENDS HIS MOUTHPIECE TO NEW YORK WITH LIZ RENAY.*

We landed in New York amid a flurry of pictures, newsreels, and publicity. *LIZ RENAY HERE TO FACE GRAND JURY*, shouted headlines.

We arrived a few days ahead of schedule. I called Cappy and arranged to meet him for a chat and a cup of coffee. We met in a quiet, out-of-the-way place. I wore a dark, unrevealing coat and dark glasses but, in spite of my attempted discretion, we were recognized by a lone reporter, who quickly multiplied into a trailing entourage of reporters. We couldn't shake them. Because I refused to talk to them as they snapped our pictures, the caption under the pictures read, *LIZ RENAY SNUBS PRESS.* Bold headlines across the picture of my innocent cup of coffee with Cappy sizzled with the words, *GANGLAND LIZ IN SECRET HUDDLE WITH ANASTASIA GUARD.*

The next day Rita and I were spotted by reporters again, and they jogged along the sidewalk beside us, carrying on a running interview until we reached Leo Gitlin's office. The interview went like this:

"Do you go out with Mickey Cohen?"

"Yes, sometimes."

"Is there anyone else you're dating you'd like to mention?"

"No."

"Isn't it true you used to date Cappy Coppola and he proposed marriage once?"

"Yes, but we were never engaged."

"No? And now you don't date him any longer?"

"I live in Hollywood now. He lives in New York."

"I understand you're now Mickey Cohen's girl!"

"Well, I—I'm just a good friend, that's all!"

"Thank you, Miss Renay."

Next day the papers shrieked, *LIZ RENAY JILTED CAPPY FOR MICKEY COHEN. LIZ RENAY, MICKEY'S NEW LOVE. LIZ RENAY COHEN'S STEADY GIRL. MICKEY'S THE ONLY MAN I DATE, SAYS LIZ,* and on and on.

Mickey was interviewed on the Coast. A picture of him holding a photo of me followed with a quote from Mickey: *IF LIZ SAYS WE'RE ENGAGED, THEN WE'RE ENGAGED.*

I was scheduled to appear before the Grand Jury the next day. So much was happening so fast that the full impact didn't have time to register. Things were totally unreal—too fantastic to be true.

I dressed that morning in a plain, off-white, knit suit. I hurried to Leo Gitlin's office. *Life* magazine and a dozen reporters and photographers were crowded into his office awaiting my arrival.

As we left Leo's office amid flash bulbs and questions, I noticed, to my consternation, that a whole entourage of attorneys had attached themselves to me and were trailing along on all sides. My attorney, Leo Gitlin, the only one I had retained, was on one side of me. Irwin Styles's attorney, Louis Kay, was on the other. Eddie Gritz, Mickey's attorney, and Joseph Aronson, Cappy's attorney, crowded in on each side of him. Bringing up the rear was an unidentified attorney. I didn't know who he belonged to. I'd never heard of him. He kept explaining he was a friend of a friend I'd never heard of either. There they were, offering me their services without charge. Some attorneys seemed to crave publicity. They had much in common with actors.

As I paraded down the street, flanked by five attorneys and trailed by magazine, newspaper, and TV cameras, I felt foolish. "Wow!" I said to Leo Gitlin, above the din of surrounding voices. "I wouldn't need this many attorneys if I shot Anastasia myself."

Suddenly, the procession halted. We were in front of the Grand Jury door. I strolled inside, leaving the battery of obliging attorneys chattering outside to each other.

I was seated on the witness stand facing the Grand Jury. The district attorney showed me Rogue's Gallery photos of underworld characters, most of whom I didn't know, had never seen or heard of! He asked what seemed to be pointless questions about things I knew nothing of. Then, after a long time, Albert Anastasia, Tony Coppola, Mickey Cohen, and those damned checks came up for discussion.

I repeated my well-rehearsed story. "Oh, yes, I know Mickey Cohen. He's a very nice person as far as I can see. Yes, I gave him $5,500 as a loan. Why? Because he was short of cash. Yes, of course, he intends to pay it back. Where did I get the money? I borrowed it from a wealthy boy friend, Garry Terzon, with the understanding I'd return it as soon as it was returned to me by Mickey. A very simple little transaction, you see."

The jury and prosecution seemed to accept the story, scarcely questioning my answers. Then the district attorney said, "You are excused. You may step down now, Miss Renay."

I burst through the door into the arms of Leo Gitlin, dancing around in a circle with him. "That's that," I said. "I'm glad it's over!"

Flash bulbs popped around me, and I patiently answered questions for the press. I gave Leo Gitlin a little hug and a fond farewell, and Eddie Gritz and I took off in a cab to pack our bags and head back to Hollywood.

Life magazine photographers were waiting at the hotel to take up where they had left off before the Grand Jury appearance. We ducked into the elevator before they spotted us. Eddie got off at his floor. "I'll meet you in the lobby in an hour," he said. "Good," I answered. "That will give me time to dress and pack."

I took a warm bubble bath and slipped into a cool pink nightie to wear while packing my bag. Just as I finished, there was a knock at the door. I opened it, still wearing the pink nightie.

There stood the *Life* magazine photographer and writer

we had ducked downstairs. The photographer grinned. "You've come a long way since I first discovered you in Arizona," he said.

Then, for the first time, I recognized him, Peter Stackpole, the photographer who had shot the story that caused so many changes in my life when I was working as a movie extra in *The Sound of Fury* in Arizona.

"That was a long time ago, Peter," I smiled.

"Hey, you look marvelous in that nightgown," he said. "How about letting us grab a shot for the story?"

"Sure, why not? You're practically an old friend."

When Peter and his aide had finished and left, I changed into a simple knit suit, picked up my suitcase, caught the elevator, and strode out into the lobby to make contact with Eddie Gritz.

"Liz Renay," called a feminine voice. I whirled to see Paula Insel, the art agent, walking across the lobby to meet me.

"I'm so glad you're in New York, Liz," she smiled. "I've been trying to reach you in Hollywood."

"Paula, dear, it's nice to see you, but I'm leaving this minute—I'm on my way to the airport now."

"Nonsense, you can't leave town. Your art exhibit is scheduled for day after tomorrow. Remember? I've been calling everywhere trying to reach you. I didn't know whether to cancel it, or what."

"I'll be damned, I'd completely forgotten we reserved that gallery date." It had been several months and so much has happened, I haven't even thought about an art exhibit.

"But you must hold the exhibit! You reserved the gallery for three days and you'll be charged for it anyway and, Liz, you just can't do this to me. I've invited the art critics and lots of patrons. You'll make me look bad!"

"Look, Paula," I said. "You don't understand our problem. An exhibit's impossible! We don't have any paintings. I haven't so much as looked at a tube of paint since I left New York."

"That *is* a problem," agreed Paula, shaking her head. Then her eyes brightened. "Liz, I've got an idea. Would you be willing to knock out some fast abstracts? You know—quick, splashy, colorful things that take no time to paint?"

"I don't see what you're getting at, Paula."

"Well, Liz, I could deliver a set of paints, a can of Japan Quick Dry and a dozen canvases to your hotel in the morning. If you could knock out a bunch of modern abstracts, we could have an exhibit after all—an abstract exhibit!"

"You've gotta be kidding, Paula. I spend an average of a month or longer on a painting. It would take me a day or two to paint a decent abstract. You're suggesting I paint twelve of them in one day. Why, that's less than an hour per painting."

"I think you can do it," Paula said. "I really think you can do it. Look, Liz, all I'm asking you to do is gamble one little day. One day's effort—if it doesn't work, you've only lost one day's time, right? If it does work, we save your exhibit. What do you have to lose?"

"Are you sure that Japan Quick Dry will work? Are you sure the paintings will be dry?"

"Yes, it'll work if you use plenty of it and don't paint too thick and gobby. And then we'll spray them with Retouch Varnish, and they will be dry to the touch. If we sell them, I'll make the buyers wait two weeks for delivery. When they get the paintings, they will be dry all right. Hey, I'll tell you what I'll do. I'll go back to my studio and send over the supplies right away so you can get started tonight."

She hurried away before I could argue the point.

I walked to the newsstand and bought a dozen papers to spread over the hotel floor to protect the carpet from paint.

Eddie Gritz came up behind me just as I was paying the newsstand attendant. "Good God, you must really dig looking at your face on the front page," he said, "because I know you couldn't dig that story!"

"Shut up, I bought these papers for an artistic endeavor. I was just talked into painting twelve paintings in the next twelve hours!"

"What are you talking about, Liz? Have you lost your mind? If we don't hurry, we'll miss our plane."

"Cancel my reservation, Eddie, I'm staying over. My goddamned art agent just talked me into having an art exhibit day after tomorrow with one day to prepare!"

"There's nothing screwier than a dame!" said Eddie disgustedly. "I'll have to cancel mine too. If you stay, I stay! My instructions were to accompany you to New York and return with you to Hollywood."

"Suit yourself. Care to have a cup of coffee with me?"

"Sure," said Eddie, motioning for a bellboy. "Will you please take Miss Renay's bag back up to her room? And put this one in mine."

I carried the newspapers into the coffee shop to read. My picture was on the front page of every paper in town again. *LIZ RENAY HIP-HIPS HER WAY TO GRAND JURY*, one exclaimed. *LIZ RENAY, MOST STUNNING PULSE-STOPPER TO APPEAR BEFORE A GRAND JURY IN RECENT YEARS. LIZ RENAY GETS SPOT-LIGHT INSTEAD OF LIMELIGHT.* There were stories and pictures throughout the papers. "I'll bet those photographers would be surprised if they knew I planned to use their literary masterpieces as floor coverings for paint drippings."

By the time Eddie and I finished our coffee, the art supplies arrived. "I'll talk to you later," said Eddie. "Boy, I got to see this before I believe it!"

I was thankful that most of the canvases Paula sent were not very large. I spread out the papers, and went to work. I scarcely had time to think, I painted so fast. I just sort of hitched my paint brush to my subconscious mind and let it do the work, allowing my imagination to run wild.

I doodled in paint, painting anything that came to mind at the moment, expressing any fleeting mood or passing fancy.

I turned on the TV. Jungle drums were beating. I painted something wild and primitive. I switched channels —violins were playing. I painted something soft and pastel with a touch of fantasy, and on and on, into the night and into the morning. By 11:00 A.M. I had done it! I hadn't slept all night—I was exhausted, but I was finished! I cleaned the paint off my hands, the brushes, and the furniture, and stood back to survey my work.

Paintings lined the walls on all sides of the room. I counted them—there were ten (only ten, instead of twelve). Dammit, Paula hadn't sent enough canvases. Suddenly, the beauty and impact of what I had created struck me, ka-wham! This was the best abstract work I had ever done! It had more freedom, more abandon, more flair, more color, more imagination! It was wild!

Suddenly, I was very, very tired. I called Paula. "Paula, I just finished those damned canvases you sent over. I've had it! I'm dead! I'm going to sleep now. You forgot two canvases, but if you mention me painting two more, I'll cut off your tongue."

Paula was exuberant. "Darling, I knew you could do it! Don't worry, I only sent ten because I got permission from two of your customers from the last exhibit to let us borrow their paintings to show. We'll put *Not for Sale* signs on them. I'll be right over."

"Good, get the damn smelly things out of here so I can sleep in peace. I'll leave the door unlocked and don't you dare wake me."

I didn't hear Paula come in or take the paintings. I slept all day long and right through the next night. When I awoke the next morning, I wasn't sure I hadn't dreamed the whole crazy thing.

The phone rang and Paula's voice removed all doubt. "Oh, Liz, darling, the paintings are beautiful, wonderful, magnificent! Wake up, today's the day. Your exhibit opens at 12:00 noon. I've ordered champagne, caviar, and groovy hors d'oeuvres."

I pulled myself together, showered, and dressed. When I arrived at the gallery, the press was swarming all over the place photographing the paintings. Magazines were shooting stories. Three of the abstracts sold the first hour.

The exhibit was a huge success. When I got home, my hotel had become a madhouse. Papers as far away as London were calling me for feature stories. The news of my exhibit made newspapers all over the world, with photographs of me and my paintings.

Only, the captions were the wrong captions. One shouted, GANGLAND LIZ DISPLAYS HER PAINT-INGS. Another read, LIZ RENAY DISPLAYS ANOTHER TALENT. INSTEAD OF THE ROGUES' GALLERY, IT'S THE ART GALLERY! Only one New York paper was kind enough to run a lovely article on the second day with the caption, ARTIST RENAY'S ONE-MAN SHOW SELLS SEVEN OUT OF TWELVE PAINTINGS.

All of the papers were good to me. Aside from the sensa-

tional captions, the stories were not critical of my artistic
ability.

Before the exhibit finished its third and last day, all the
paintings but one had been sold. Paula had fallen in love
with it, so I gave it to her as a present.

The next day Eddie and I boarded a plane for Hollywood, with the usual exploding flash bulbs. I was growing
accustomed to the press by now. Reporters no longer
seemed annoying. Not only was I beginning to take them
for granted, but I found myself enjoying all the attention.

When our plane landed, it was met by Mickey's pal
from Chicago, Itchy Mandell, in Mickey's bullet-proof
black Eldorado Cadillac. The newspapers were Johnny-
on-the-spot and didn't overlook a thing. *MICKEY'S LIZ
RETURNS HOME*, they prattled. *MET BY HIS SQUIRE,
ITCHY MANDELL AND HIS MOUTHPIECE, EDDIE
GRITZ*. One paper wrote a humorous parody on the situation, with a caricature portraying me as queen of the underworld being escorted from the airport by knights in
armor.

Itchy drove me directly to Mickey Cohen's apartment.
Mickey rushed over and kissed me on both cheeks. "Poor
angel," he said, "our friendship sure has caused you a lot
of trouble."

He said there was much to talk about but he had to
rush away at the moment. He asked if he could take me to
dinner that night. I agreed.

He picked me up about 8:00 P.M. and we went to La
Rue's Restaurant.

As soon as we walked in the door, newsreel cameras
began to grind, flash bulbs exploded, and floodlights filled
the room. The place lit up like the Fourth of July. Newsreel men, newspapermen, and *Life* magazine reporters
asked questions all at once.

We had dinner in the glare of TV floodlights and the click and grind of movie cameras.

When we left the restaurant, the men from *Life* magazine followed us to the Slate Brothers Club on La Cienega. They sat and watched the Don Rickles Show with us, snapping pictures all the while.

Then they followed us into an ice cream parlor that Mickey owned, and snapped a picture of Mickey and me dipping straws into the same strawberry soda.

Tom Duggan interviewed me on television, and I made several appearances on Paul Coates' TV show, not as an actress or entertainer but as a bizarre character out of the headlines—a sensational new gun moll. —Something unique!

Life magazine hit the stands. That made it complete. If anyone in America had missed reading about the gangster's moll, Liz Renay, the *Life* story took care of it.

The New York Grand Jury was only the beginning. When I got back to Hollywood, I was subpoenaed in Mickey's income tax evasion case, then the Treasury Department called me down, and the FBI brought me in for questioning.

Always it was with a flurry of newspaper front pages, national newsreels, radio broadcasts, and TV interviews. Back and forth went the subpoenas, back and forth I went, coast to coast, like a yo-yo, answering them. I received subpoenas every time I stepped off a plane on either end of the continent. I received them on the lots of movie studios. Thirteen subpoenas altogether, and thirteen barrages of publicity to cover them, coming and going. I began to feel a sense of celebrity. People stopped me on the street and asked for my autograph. It was hard not to confuse this Mardi Gras of publicity with fame.

But, infamy was the apt word. The night my hilarious

Groucho Marx Show was scheduled to be shown, it was pulled off the air, and an NBC spokesman made a comment that was sent out by the wire services and appeared in newspapers across the nation and in show business trade papers such as *Variety* and the *Hollywood Reporter*. He said my show was taken off the air due to my present notoriety and that NBC felt it would be in questionable taste to show it. He went on further to point out that it was costing NBC $20,000 to kill the show.

This obviously put pressure on CBS, which followed suit by canceling my forthcoming role in "Climax." Its producer admitted to me I had been put on the studio blacklist.

Warner Brothers dropped me from drama class, discarded my screen test, and washed its hands of me.

Solly Biano told me quite frankly that I was dead at Warner Brothers and that no other major studio would touch me. "No studio can combat that damned gangster publicity," he said, "not if their P.R. department worked night and day."

The notoriety kept growing. It had developed into an uncontrollable avalanche. Even that silly incident of my wiring Mickey forty cents was played up. A photograph of the telegram appeared next to a picture of me, with a story about Liz Renay's droll sense of humor.

This thing had become a towering black Frankenstein monster. I was the notorious Liz Renay, Gangster's Moll— Underworld's New Darling!

Then, to my surprise, I got a break. An independent producer called me for a part in a television film. I was overjoyed. I rushed to the studio to sign the contract the next day. I was sent at once for wardrobe fittings. "We will start shooting next Wednesday," said the producer. "You just got in under the wire on this one!"

As I left the wardrobe department, I noticed a tall man sauntering toward me. He must be an actor, he sure looked familiar. He drew closer, withdrawing a white slip of paper from his pocket.

My God, it was that damned subpoena server. No wonder he looked familiar! I hurried toward the studio gate in an effort to evade him, but the tall man with the long stride soon overtook me.

He smiled as he flashed his official identification.

"Good afternoon, Miss Renay," he said, tipping his hat.

"Oh, hell, put your I.D. away and spare me the routine. Just give me the damned subpoena, okay?"

"I'm sorry to serve you here. It's just my job, you know. Nothing personal, Miss Renay."

"Sure," I said. "Nothing personal in the way I dislike seeing you, either. Just part of an attitude I'm getting."

A cab pulled up—must be mine. I rushed to meet it.

"So long, Liz," called the Fed. "See you in court."

I slammed the door, gave the driver my address, and settled back to look at the subpoena.

Holy Cow! The date was for next Wednesday. How could I be in federal court Wednesday? That was the day the film started shooting. I couldn't be both places at once.

One thing for sure—the choice was no contest. I'd damned sure rather shoot a TV film than answer questions for another Grand Jury!

I must get a postponement on the jury appearance. They weren't going to louse up the first break I'd had since the notoriety fouled up my career. This show could be important.

I called the U.S. attorney asking permission to delay my next jury appearance for a few days.

He refused flatly. I argued the point and finally asked my attorney to call and reason with him.

The answer was, "No dice. We will not change it for one day, never mind two or three."

I called the federal office in a fury. "What are you trying to do, wreck my career?" I cried. "How much can a few days matter?"

"We are trying to conduct an investigation. Or hadn't that occurred to you?" was the cool answer. I took a cab to the production office. "I'm sorry, but you'll have to count me out," I said. "I have a Grand Jury subpoena the U.S. attorney refuses to postpone."

"*You're* sorry!" said the irate producer. "This gives us no time to look for a suitable replacement. The wardrobe is being prepared to fit you and we're ready to start shooting. You're putting me in a hell of a spot. Can't you appreciate my problem?"

"Yes, I can appreciate your problem. In fact, I appreciate it so damned much, I'd like to trade problems with you!" I said.

My phone nearly jangled itself off the hook during the next few days with calls from newspapers, newsreels, TV interview shows, and national magazines. I appeared on Tom Duggan's TV interview show again. John Willys did a special filmed interview with me for his TV news show. Paul Coates opened his TV show about me with the quip, "And now for another chapter in the life and loves of Liz Renay—" I was interviewed on all the news shows and by all the newspapers.

Then, suddenly, all was silent. Dead silent. The phone stopped ringing, the press stopped hounding me. Everything seemed to stop at once, as if the merry-go-round ran down.

Brenda was in New Orleans with her husband. Johnny had gone to Arizona to stay with my family until my ordeal was over. Suddenly I was alone with nothing but smashed hopes, shattered dreams, and that overwhelming silence.

A week went by—two weeks—three weeks. The silence was deafening. I was engulfed in a blanket of smothering nothingness, cut off from the mainstream, caught in a static backwash of inactivity.

I called Solly Biano at Warner Brothers. "Solly, what am I going to do?"

"I'm afraid it's all over for you, kid. I shouldn't even tell you this but your screen test came out great."

"What happened to it? What will they do with it?"

"Nothing! Maybe burn it. You're too hot. Honey, you've had it."

"Oh, Solly, you can't mean that?" I said in disbelief. "How can my career be over when it just began?"

"I don't know, Honey. All I know is that for now, you're forget-its-ville."

In the weeks that followed, I saw what he meant. I was dead all right. As dead as yesterday's headline. My name had become as poisonous in Hollywood as Mickey Cohen's.

Producers and directors who had been rushing me before were now consistently out when I called.

The red velvet carpet that Hollywood unrolled before me when I arrived in town was abruptly yanked from under my feet, leaving me alone stumbling around in a vacuum.

The party was over.

Chapter 20

THE UNITED STATES OF AMERICA —VERSUS LIZ RENAY

Three long torturous months had gone by since Hollywood slammed its golden door in my face. I sank into a deep depression and finally took to bed with the flu. It was a welcome escape for me. Retreating under the covers was a good way to avoid seeing people, though a few faithful friends refused to let me withdraw. Rita Sands kept coming by in an effort to cheer me up.

"You've got to pull yourself together, Liz," she said, in a worried tone.

John Russell, my partner on the ill-fated Groucho Marx Show, dropped by, offering to do what he could do to help. Barbara, a friend from Warner Brothers studio, came by with hot soup, which she nearly forced down my throat, but to no avail. I only wished they'd go away and leave me alone.

"Why did things go so wrong just as I got lucky? Why couldn't they go right just this once?" Bitter tears stung my eyes. Strains of a church hymn wafted into the window from a neighbor's radio. Then a minister began his sermon.

"The Lord giveth and the Lord taketh away. Blessed be the name of the Lord."

I sat upright in bed and listened. I began to think. What had I lost? What had been taken away from me in that flood of distorted publicity? Was it something I'd worked for, sweated for, strained for? No, it was something Lady Luck had dropped into my lap. Something I'd accepted in wide-eyed wonderment. Then why was I so bitter at losing it? I was no worse off than before I started. I had no career when I came to Hollywood and I had none now. Why not pretend I just arrived and start all over again? The hell with the sob-sister routine! I bounced out of bed, pulled back the draperies, let the sun stream in, and, for the first time, I noticed spring had arrived.

I crossed the room and dialed Rita Sands' number. "How would you like to do a night-club act with me?" I said. "Sort of a sister act?"

"Liz, I'd be delighted! I'll be right over. I'm so happy to see you're getting back to your old self again!"

I couldn't wait to get started. "We'll do a two-girl comedy act like Betty and Jane Kean," I said. "We'll call it Rita and Liz."

I stitched up seams while Rita sewed on sequins. We worked through most of the night finishing our costumes. We rehearsed a few songs, and then sat down and thought of every funny joke either of us had ever heard, jotting them down on paper.

After striking out all but the funniest gags, we began weaving them into twenty minutes of fast-moving situation comedy. Bursts of laughter rang out through the apartment as we worked.

"If the audience likes it half as much as we do, we've got it made!" Rita said.

I went to an agent, and he got us a booking at Hollywood's Capri Club, with opening night just a week away.

We rehearsed until we knew the act frontwards, backwards, and sideways, and could do it standing on our heads. Then opening night arrived.

We donned our gleaming sequin costumes and went to the club. Soon we were standing backstage listening to our introduction. Then we were tripping across the stage, costumes a-glitter under the glare of the spotlight. We were on!

"Hello, Swingers," I began, as the sharp round of applause subsided. I ran through the snappy little introduction we had written for the act, and gave Rita the cue for her opening line.

Dead silence.

Rita stood frozen to the spot, not opening her mouth, an odd expression on her face. I managed to cover that first line. Then I went into my second, throwing Rita her next cue and a little nudge with it. She stood there like a sphinx, not changing expression.

Could she have suddenly gone deaf? I ad-libbed some ridiculous answer that brought a groan rather than a laugh from the audience. I threw cue after cue. Dead silence.

Suddenly Rita came to life. She couldn't remember anything in its place, but since she didn't want to stand like a ninny, she recited any line of the material that came to her mind. While I was busy telling a story, she'd blurt out the punch line. My frantic reactions brought howls of laughter from the audience. They seemed to think it was part of the act.

Finally, the band took pity on us and went into our closing duet. I was relieved to hear strains of that zany little ditty. It would take us off the stage. I wasn't surprised to find myself doing a solo, in place of the duet, with a statue at my side. The only surprise was the applause we received. The audience actually liked it. That was the only time anyone would ever see *that* act! We couldn't have repeated it if we tried. Soon we were back in the safety of the dressing room, with Rita in tears.

"Oh, Liz, I let you down. I ruined everything! I'm sorry! I don't know what happened. I was so scared, I couldn't talk!"

"I noticed that," I said dryly.

We sat looking at each other for a moment, and then we both burst into hysterical laughter—laughing until tears filled our eyes.

"Don't worry, the audience thought it was all part of the act," I said. "Makes you wonder, doesn't it? Anyway, we made a good try. Let's have a drink."

We got into our street clothes and went out into the club, and got loaded. It was then I noticed a distinguished-looking gentleman in a dark suit sitting at a front table. He was a big man with broad shoulders and dark wavy hair, graying at the temples. He was attractive in a rugged sort of way and appeared to be in his late thirties. He sat absently tossing a champagne cork into the air. The bartender followed my gaze.

"That's Joe Collins," he said. "He's big-time. He's a builder." I saw Mr. Collins watching me out of the corner of his eye.

The next day I salvaged what I could of the comedy material, prepared it for a single delivery, and forced myself to learn it. Rita worked on songs all day. We decided I would do the comedy patter alone, and Rita would fill in a singing spot with some songs she knew well enough to feel secure with.

That night when we went to work I was astonished to see my name in lights across the front of the club as the headliner. The club's owner had discovered I was the notorious Liz Renay and wanted to take full advantage of it. He showed me a big ad he'd taken in the papers. Newspaper columnists and reporters were there.

"Be grateful they weren't here last night," I remarked to Rita.

I came out with a song, went into my comedy patter, and ended the act in a jazz dance number. It wasn't much of a routine, but it was funny and pleasant and the audience liked it. Most important of all, I was back in action again.

Action breeds action. Soon things were happening. Tom Duggan and Paul Coates invited me to appear on their shows—this time not as a notorious character, but as a night-club entertainer. The club phone jangled with all sorts of offers. Rita lost her opening-night jitters and filled the singing spot beautifully. Joe Collins took a strong interest in me and came to the club every night to chat with me between shows. Soon we were going together.

An independent movie producer called and offered me the starring role in a movie opposite Gerald Mohr. I remembered Gerald Mohr from the Foreign Intrigue TV series. I was exuberant!

I said goodbye to Rita, Joe Collins, and the night-club owner, and flew to Roswell, New Mexico, aboard the film company's private plane. I had to pinch myself all the way to our location site. The movie company checked me into the town's nicest hotel.

After we had been on location three days and I lay relaxing in my room after a hard day's shooting, the phone rang. "You have a visitor," the desk clerk said. "A Mr. Collins."

Well, this was a surprise! It was great seeing Joe again. I took him to the set the next day and he seemed to get a big kick out of watching me do my scenes. I played the part of a night-club singer. I wore shimmering gold lamé capri pants with a low-cut top to match. The costume had a half-skirt of gold and black satin streaming down behind. The director instructed me to work with this skirt during my song by waving the folds of satin around in a teasing, sexy way as I toyed with the customers during my song.

The director put Joe in the picture as part of the night-club audience. I sang my song directly to him. He sat at the front table, the way he did when I appeared at the Capri Club in Hollywood. Gee—what fun! When the scene ended and the prop men were busy setting up for the next one, I sat down with Joe at his table. "Joe, why did you fly here to see me?" I asked.

"Maybe because I'm in love with you, you little character!"

Joe was big and strong, and I felt protected in his presence. I needed someone to lean on.

The next day a story broke in the local newspaper insinuating that Mickey Cohen was financing the film. The producer was furious. "How in the hell did they get a stupid idea like that?" he said. "I wonder if Mickey spread the rumor himself."

"Don't be ridiculous," I said, but secretly wondering myself.

When the shooting was finished, I flew back to Hollywood with Joe Collins. Rita met us at the airport.

I returned to work at the Capri Club, but I didn't stay long. Joe Collins insisted that I quit work.

"Club work is not for you," he said. "I'll handle all your expenses until your movie career gets back on its feet if you'll just do as I tell you."

For appearances' sake, I took a separate apartment next to his. We shared the same terrace. The physical attraction between us was intense. We didn't seem to be able to get enough of each other.

One Sunday Joe and I flew to Arizona to visit my family and to bring Johnny back to Hollywood.

"I want to invite your entire family to dinner," Joe said.

I called Mama and told her to round up the whole group and meet us at Maricopa Inn. When they started parading in, Joe's eyes widened. He counted eighteen people, including the children.

The hostess pulled six tables together to accommodate the group. It looked like a banquet. She seated Joe at the head of the table.

"I feel like Jesus Christ at the Last Supper," he laughed. His remark went over like a lead balloon with my religious family.

When I returned to Hollywood, two federal men served me with a subpoena to appear as a witness in Mickey Cohen's income tax case. The subpoena servers were accompanied by the press and newsreels, and I was back on the front pages again.

I appeared at several Grand Jury sessions probing Mickey's finances. Over and over again I was asked the details of the checks I had given him.

Why couldn't they just forget the damned checks and leave me alone? Newsreel cameras and press photographers followed my every move. I was back on all the news interview shows. During one Grand Jury session I had to leave the jury room for the ladies' room. Newsreel cameramen hurried along behind me, following me right up to the door. They focused on the ladies' room sign before they realized what it was.

"Good God, I can't even take a pee without you," I said.

Subpoenaed along with me was Billy Graham, the well-known evangelist. The newspaper caption read GRAHAM AND RENAY GET SUBPOENA. Billy Graham had given Mickey Cohen a larger check than I had, and in much the same way. I wondered how he would explain it.

I flew to Arizona to visit my family and was amazed by my mother's attitude. She was more concerned over Billy Graham's subpoena than mine.

"Gee whiz, Mom, it seems you'd be more worried about your own daughter's problem than about Billy Graham. You don't even know him!"

"Yes, but he's a man of God. This may ruin his whole career."

"What about me and my career?"

"Your career isn't important. All you are doing is acting!"

"So how sure are you that Billy's not doing the same thing?"

"Billy's career is the work of God and a benefit to humanity. I don't know what he has to do with Cohen—it must be a mistake. Your career is sinful and worldly and you'd be better off without it."

"Okay, Mama, you worry about what happens to Billy Graham. I'll be concerned about me. Old slick Billy will talk his way out of it. He makes his living talking."

"I'll pray for him."

"Okay, Mom, pray for him. Squeeze a little one in for me too, if you can spare it." I gave Mama a hug to erase the hurt look in her eyes. "Forget it, Mom, I was only kidding. If it makes you feel better, I'll say a prayer for Billy, too."

"Your prayers won't go any higher than the ceiling as long as you live the sinful life you do," she said.

Soon I was back in Hollywood facing the federal Grand Jury, the FBI, the Treasury Department, the Internal Revenue Service, and the Department of Justice. I knew little of the subjects I was being questioned about, and the question-and-answer sessions dragged on for tedious hours, so I began making a game of the whole sorry business, playing it for laughs whenever I could. If the papers persisted in casting me as the femme fatale, darling of the underworld, then I'd play the game too, and give them something to write about. I was full of surprises. Sometimes I'd show up for a tax hearing wearing dark glasses, a Greta Garbo hat, and suede trench coat. The next time I might appear at FBI headquarters in stretch pants, so tight I could barely walk, topped with a sweater that looked like it was sprayed on. To add to the confusion, next time I'd show up swathed in mink, wearing a Christian Dior gown, hat, gloves, and accessories, à la *Vogue* magazine.

My appearance was only the beginning of the games I played with the prosecuting attorneys. Once the U.S. attorney asked me to describe someone, and I said, "He's nondescript."

"Nondescript is no description," he hurled back. I smiled and said, "On the contrary, nondescript is my description."

He kept pushing me for a definition of nondescript, refusing to accept it as my description of the man in question. His remarks became sharp, demanding, and rude.

"Describe what you mean by nondescript," he snapped.

"Well, let's see," I pondered. "For instance, you're very nondescript." Muffled laughter swept through the room, and the prosecuting attorney's face turned crimson.

Another day the prosecution decided to confiscate my address book as I sat on the witness stand and the jury was preparing to leave the box.

I started to hand it over, then voiced a protest. "I need my address book. It will interfere with my career if you take it."

"We will return it to you tomorrow," replied the U.S. attorney.

"But I need it now. I'm appearing on television tonight, and my book contains names of producers, directors, and friends I want to alert."

The U.S. attorney went into a huddle with the other

members of the prosecution staff. Then he stood up and motioned for the jury to be seated. "I'm sorry," he said, "but I'll have to ask you all to remain in the jury box while we allow Miss Renay to copy telephone numbers from her address book."

He handed me a pen and a large sheet of paper. "Please do this as quickly as possible."

I sat in the witness chair and started to copy every number from my book. I wasn't sure when, if ever, it would be back in my possession.

After several minutes, I noticed a man get up and walk from the jury box to the prosecution's table. He seemed to be requesting something. I continued my hurried scribbling. Soon the U.S. attorney tapped me on the shoulder. "Miss Renay."

I looked up. "What is it?"

"The foreman on the jury wants to inquire about your TV show."

"Yes?"

"The jury would like to know what time and what channel."

The world was still full of surprises.

Joe Collins was waiting to take me home. "How'd it go?"

"Funny thing about that jury—I actually think they're on my side. They seem spellbound when I enter the room. They laugh at my little jokes and hang onto every word I say, and today they wanted to see me on television."

Joe cautioned: "You are the eternal optimist. You think everyone loves you and no one wants to harm you. Don't be surprised if those little people behind those friendly faces are preparing your indictment this very minute. Sure, they hang on every word. They are looking for you to trip yourself up so they can convict you of perjury."

It happened one afternoon as I returned to my lovely terraced apartment with my agent's representative, Sandra Lane. Sandra worked as a sub-agent for Lou Markman on Sunset Boulevard. Lou handled the deal for the movie in Roswell. He was anxious to take a crack at helping me buck the invisible blacklist. He assigned Sandra Lane to take me on interviews and drive me to appointments.

Sandra, a fun-loving girl, took a big personal interest in my career. She involved herself in almost every phase of my life. She drove me out to confer with Mickey Cohen about the jury sessions. She scolded Joe Collins when he arrived late or wasn't as attentive as she thought he should be. She filled Rita Sands in on all the latest news and answered my private phone if it rang while I was in the bathtub. Sandra was well aware of the whole dismal picture concerning subpoenas and Grand Juries. She was called in and questioned once or twice herself—just because she knew me.

Sandra and I were laughing and joking about the way we outsmarted a wolfish producer as we strolled past the swimming pool and up the sunlit walk to my apartment. Suddenly Sandra stopped in the middle of a laugh and froze dead in her tracks. I looked up and came face to face with a U.S. marshal and a policewoman. I felt a sudden chill at the sight of the policewoman. What was she doing here? There had never been a policewoman along before. There was a serious, solemn look about them, a little different from before. I think I knew the answer even before the marshal spoke.

"You're under arrest, Miss Renay," the federal marshal announced, in a crisp, clear voice. He handed me a piece of paper headed by the words, "The United States of America versus Liz Renay."

My eyes blurred as I tried to read the words. Jesus Christ, how did I ever manage to get into a spot like this?

I stood transfixed, while the policewoman took my purse and searched it. She gave me the once-over. Was she looking for a gun? It would have been impossible to conceal a weapon on my person, sheathed in the sheer, sleeveless chiffon dress I was wearing.

While the policewoman patted my body suspiciously, feeling my bumps, the marshal's voice droned on in a meaningless stream of words—words that didn't register. I was too busy rereading the paper he had handed me. I was under indictment by the United States government, facing a federal penitentiary, and on my way to jail. I was so stunned I had to be led to the police car. My mind had stopped working. My heart stood still.

"Are you coming willingly, or do we have to handcuff you?"

"Yes—I mean, no—I mean—oh, do whatever you like. What's the difference?" I said, in a voice I hardly recognized.

Sandra's voice called from the spot where she'd frozen. "Don't worry, Honey. I'll call Joe! He'll get you out. Damn that Grand Jury!"

Someone pushed me into the police car. The door closed. I was seated between the policewoman and the federal marshal. We were moving now. The marshal's voice droned on, mingled with the droning of the motor. I lay back against the seat, eyes closed. I had come to Hollywood to land a contract with a movie studio. My contract turned out to be an indictment, and my studio the Hollywood jail.

What was it the marshal was saying? He repeated, "Young lady, you have been indicted on five counts of perjury. Each count carries the possibility of one to five years. This is a serious matter. Do you realize you are facing twenty-five years?"

I bolted upright! "Twenty-five years! What are you saying?" My voice was so loud I startled myself as well as my captors. "You gotta be kidding. They can't give me twenty-five years for telling a few white lies. Twenty-five years is forever!"

I knew they weren't kidding. If only they were—if only this was a sick, practical joke—if only it was a bad dream and I'd wake up soon—if only . . .

I settled back against the cushions and closed my eyes again. White lies, just a few harmless white lies told to help a friend. But were they white lies? Is there such a thing? Mama didn't think so. Neither did the church. Funny I should think of that darn church at a time like this. I could picture the white-haired preacher leaning forward over the scarred pulpit as he cried, "The devil is a liar and the father of liars. All liars shall have their part in the lake of fire!"

Maybe the preacher was right. Maybe this was my lake of fire. Soon we had pulled up to the federal marshal's office. While I was being fingerprinted, the door burst open and in rushed an aggressive-looking man who introduced himself as a federal bondsman. He chatted with the U.S. marshal briefly, produced some papers, then walked briskly toward me.

"Come on, Honey, Mr. Collins is waiting in the car outside. We've come to take you home."

"My God, I just got here. How could you do this so fast?"

"Mr. Collins wasn't far from my office when he got Miss Lane's call. He relayed the call to me, and I prepared the bond while he was driving to my office. I'm only minutes from here, you know."

I walked to the door in a daze. Things were happening too fast. I felt like a bouncing ball. First I was free—then on my way to jail—then suddenly free again, and all in less than an hour's time. I wasn't geared for so fast a pace.

Joe's sleek black Cadillac was parked in front with the door open for me. The bondsman ushered me to it.

"Well, how's my baby? What have they been doing to you?" Joe asked, smiling, obviously proud of the speed with which he was able to rescue me. I was grateful, as well as dumfounded, as I slid in beside him and rested my weary head on his shoulder.

"Chinatown is near here, Darling. Your buddy Sandra is driving there now to meet us. We can all have dinner and talk. Glad we could intercept you before they took you to jail."

We pulled up in front of the Ming Tree Restaurant in Old Chinatown. An exuberant Sandra sprang from her car and ran toward us.

"Oh, Liz, you poor dear. I told you we'd get you out. And to think you thought the damned Grand Jury liked you. They were just a bunch of sheep."

Joe ordered mountains of food, but I couldn't eat. "Now, tell me what this is all about," he said, over the steaming Chinese cuisine.

Sandra told him. Five counts of perjury. Possible prison sentence of twenty-five years.

Joe winced. "I had no idea it was this serious. No idea."

As soon as I got home, I took a hot shower, swallowed some sleeping pills, and slid under the covers. I couldn't wait to blot the whole mess out of my mind with soothing, beautiful sleep. I snuggled under the soft comforter, and soon was in dreamland. I was awakened by the sharp, insistent ringing of my bedside phone.

"Hello," I said. "Hello, hello," but the phone kept right on ringing. That was strange. I held the receiver to my ear, or I thought I did. I aroused enough to observe I was only holding an imaginary receiver to my ear while the real one remained frantically ringing on the hook. I managed to find it, bleary-eyed from the sleeping pills with a mouth tasting like fuzzy cotton.

"Hello," I said, out of the fog.

"Liz, what in the hell are you doing home?" asked Mickey Cohen, in astonishment.

"Sleeping," I yawned. "Trying to get some rest."

"How'd you get home? I don't understand! We're waiting here at the jail, me and the bail bondsman and the press. We rushed here as soon as I got word you'd been arrested. We've been waiting here for three hours for them to bring you over. What the hell happened?" Mickey sounded disappointed that someone beat him to the rescue. He loved playing knight on a white charger to damsels in distress. He felt it his personal duty to rescue me, since my problem grew out of my association with him. At the moment, I was too sleepy to concern myself with anything so involved.

"Mickey, Honey, you don't have any objection if I just go back to sleep, do you?" I yawned.

"Not if you'd fill a guy in on what's going on around here first!"

"Okay, Mickey, I never got to jail because a federal bondsman intercepted me at the marshal's office five minutes after I was picked up. I went to Chinatown, had dinner, came home, took some sleeping pills, and went to sleep. It's as simple as that. Now may I say good night?"

"I'll be damned if you don't beat all!" he muttered. "What'll I tell the press?"

I sighed, "I'm sure you'll think of something."

Chapter 21

A MATTER OF LOYALTY

Next day over brunch we discussed my problem. "Joe," the attorney said, "Liz has nothing to worry about. They indicted her to scare her into talking. All she has to do is tell what she knows about Mickey and they'll drop the matter. They don't want Liz—they want Mickey!"

Soon Joe was convinced my problem wasn't as serious as he'd thought. He was also convinced I should tell what, if anything, I knew about Mickey, answer the questions, and get out of the mess as easily as possible. "Think of yourself," he said. "The hell with Mickey Cohen and the rest of them. Let them worry about their own damned problems!"

Our friendly brunch ended in violent discord and bitter disagreement, with Joe banging his fist on the table and issuing an ultimatum. If I didn't take his advice and follow his instructions, he would wash his hands of the matter completely. "I won't be a party to helping Mickey Cohen, directly or indirectly," he said. "Either you do as I tell you or you're on your own. Don't have Sandra call me the next time they arrest you. I won't be there!"

"Joe, you can't ask me to hurt Mickey deliberately," I answered. "He has always been a friend to me."

Joe turned on me angrily. "What's the matter, Honey, are you in love with the guy? What's he ever done for you that makes you willing to slip your neck into a noose for him?"

"Please, Joe, you don't understand. I don't like to hurt people! Not Mickey, not anyone! I wouldn't want to hurt a stranger on the street. You can't ask me to be instrumental in sending a friend to prison."

"Why not, if that's where he belongs? Prisons were built for guys like Mickey."

In the week that followed, I thought constantly of Mickey Cohen, his predicament, his trial, and my involvement in it. Almost every day I received calls about the seriousness of his position. Bookmakers, gamblers, friends, and other savvy people said Mickey would be shown no mercy. "They plan to throw the book at him, put him away for as long as possible. He's being railroaded into prison," was the general opinion. "The prosecution will stop at nothing to get a conviction," they said. "This has become a political issue with big pressure from Attorney General Kennedy's office."

As the days went by, I turned the issue over and over in my mind, always coming up with a single answer. There was no other. The sharp ring of my telephone jarred me out of my contemplation.

It was Joe. "Honey," he said, "I just finished having lunch with an FBI agent who is a personal friend of mine. He's closely connected with the Cohen case. This thing is more serious than we imagined. They plan to railroad Mickey. They'll put him in prison and throw the key away. They've got the deck stacked and they're holding all the cards. The poor slob doesn't stand a chance. He'll probably get twenty years before they're through with him!"

"Poor Mickey," I sighed. "This confirms what the others are saying. How could they? It's not fair. All they have against him is a simple case of income tax evasion."

"Listen to what I tell you, Sweetheart. I got it straight from the shoulder! He's going away, come hell or high water, no matter what you do, so you may as well save yourself. Don't stick your neck out for nothing."

"Joe, how can you take that attitude? You tell me the cards are stacked, he's being railroaded, they'll lock him up for twenty years, and you actually think I should help them!"

"Liz, come off it. Forget about this damned guy. He's finished. You're on the losing side, Baby."

"Losing side? And what, may I ask, is the winning side?"

"The side of law and order, of course. It's your duty as a citizen to uphold federal authorities."

"My duty as a citizen? And how about my duty as a human being? What about my duty to my own conscience?"

"Now, wait a minute, Liz. If we put this thing on a right and wrong basis, you haven't a leg to stand on. Do you consider telling lies right? I shouldn't think there'd be a doubt in your mind as to the right and the wrong of this issue. Obviously, the only right thing to do is tell the truth."

"In most cases, yes, but in this case, I don't agree with you. I don't believe in what these men are doing. I think they are wrong. I won't be a party to helping them do something unfair. The hell with this good-citizen bullshit! Mickey Cohen is a citizen, too, like anyone else, and deserves the same justice and rights as you, me, or the president. If any other citizen was up for income tax evasion, they'd probably get a year or two, and the judge would suspend the sentence. They'd go free. Yet you say Mickey will go to prison for twenty years. How in the hell can you say that's right?"

"Because Mickey's a gangster and deserves to go to jail!"

"Oh, are you going to play God and decide who deserves what?"

"No, I'll let the Internal Revenue Service play God. Them and Robert Kennedy."

"Well, they'll have to do it with no help from me."

"Liz, you're being ridiculous. Haven't you been hurt enough? This mess has destroyed your career. People have branded you a gangster's moll. What do you think they'll say if you try to help him now?"

"I don't give a damn what they say. If they want to call me a gangster's moll, let them! I have to be guided by my own conscience."

Joe was silent for a moment. "You really believe in what you're doing, don't you?"

"Emphatically."

"Liz, I want to help you. You can't fight City Hall. You can't win."

"There is no way to win," I answered.

"Look, Baby, let's not talk about it any more. I don't want to quarrel with you. I love you. Let's have dinner and forget this stupid mess, what say?"

I promised to try and hung up the receiver.

It immediately rang again, causing me to jump. Must get hold of myself.

"Hello there," said a voice with a phony British accent I'd recognize anywhere. "You'll never in the world guess who this is!"

"Well, I'll be damned, Warren Lancey! Where in hell did you drop from?"

"Aren't you the clever one! How in the name of God did you guess it was I?"

"It wasn't hard, believe me. Your voice is one of a kind."

"My word, I don't know whether to be flattered or insulted—but, never mind—when can I see you, now that

I've located your whereabouts? Would you be so good as
to join me for a cocktail?"

"Why not? I could use a little fresh air. I'll stroll down to
the Roosevelt Hotel. Could you meet me in the Cinegrill
in half an hour?" I said.

What a surprise! I was glad for the diversion—anything to get my mind off Mickey and the indictment for a
while. It would be fun to sit and chat with a voice from
my less troubled past. A nice society snob who had probably never heard of Mickey Cohen. Warren was waiting
for me when I reached the Cinegrill cocktail lounge.

He strode forward to meet me with a big smile,
squeezed my hand, kissed me lightly on the cheek, and led
me to a table. "I came as soon as I read about your predicament in the newspapers. My, it's a ghastly mess you've
gotten yourself into, poor dear."

"Oh, so you know!"

"My dear girl, I never forgot you. I guess I was half in
love with you—call it what you may. You have been an
obsession with me since I first laid eyes on you in that
dreadful club. I have followed your dubious—shall we say
—career via the newspapers since you left New York and,
I might add, followed it with great alarm! I had hoped
it would never come to this, but I suppose it was inevitable with the questionable company you keep."

Good God, would he never shut up? His pious lecture
was all I needed!

"Cheers," I said, downing the drink that had been set
in front of me. He had even remembered my favorite cocktail.

"Don't gulp your drink, my dear. You must learn to sip
it in a ladylike manner. It's gauche to 'down the hatch.'"

Wow! Warren was too much! He sure rubbed my fur
the wrong way at times. Oh well, I'd be nice, have a few

cocktails, and then excuse myself. At least I could spend an hour being irritated by something other than my indictment.

We chatted aimlessly. I made small talk and concentrated on not listening while he prattled on about the error of my ways.

Then, after I felt I had spent sufficient time not to be considered rude, I rose from the table. Warren sprang to his feet. I extended my hand to him. "It's been very nice seeing you again. I'm happy you called," I said, perjuring myself anew as I prepared to leave.

"Sit down, sit down, my dear girl. You don't understand at all. You surely don't think I came all the way out here to find you just to have a friendly cocktail, do you?"

"No? What was it you had in mind?" I asked, amused.

"My dear Elizabeth, I came to California to rescue you from your nasty dilemma. I have already engaged the best law firm in the state of California—the Lloyd Wright office. One of the chaps with that firm is a former U.S. Attorney. He has many good connections and unlimited knowledge in these matters. The Lloyd Wright office will smooth this messy matter out for you in no time at all."

I sat down, shocked. I knew hiring the Lloyd Wright firm would be an expense of at least $5,000. This was incredible! I thought back to the last time I'd seen Warren. The time I'd turned down the home in Connecticut that he wanted to give me. I remembered his parting words, "If you ever need a friend, call me."

And now, after all these years, he was here. And I hadn't called him, he'd called me.

I looked at his faded blue eyes with new interest. Why? What feeling could he still have that would move him to fly three thousand miles to rescue me? Here was a man who obviously disapproved of Mickey as much as Joe Collins did. Yet here he was, eager to help, and with no questions asked. Why couldn't Joe be as concerned with my welfare?

"Warren," I said, "let's go to the Wright office right now. I sure do need a good lawyer."

We left the Cinegrill, and I stopped by the apartment and scrawled a note to Joe. I pinned it to my door. He'd find it when he came to pick me up for dinner. "Dear Joe—A friend arrived from New York to help with my defense. He's hiring the Lloyd Wright office. We're on our way now. I'll be having dinner with him. See you tomorrow.—Liz."

This would make Joe furious, I knew, but maybe it would teach him not to withdraw his assistance when I needed it, just because I refused to let him edit my thinking.

After I pinned the note to my apartment door and got back into Warren Lancey's car, he began driving in the wrong direction. "Hey, Warren, where is the Wright office?"

"It's the other way but, don't worry, I have no intention of kidnaping you, Liz. It's just that we must go by Tamar Electronics and pick up Holt."

"Who in the hell is Holt, and where does he fit in?"

"You see, Liz, I want to help you, but I must remain as far in the background as possible—I have a family to consider, you know. Jerry Holt is a good friend. He's one of the Wright office's most honored clients. They handle about $15,000,000 in government contracts for him every year. He more or less twisted their arm to persuade them to take your case."

"But why shouldn't they want to take my case? Do I have B.O., or something?"

"No, B.A.—Bad Associations," he answered smugly,

proud of his play on words. "You see, the Wright office has celebrity clients such as Bing Crosby. They must guard the prestige of their office by careful selection of their clientele. However, they have agreed to take your case, and now they'll do everything in their power to win it, rest assured."

Soon we pulled up in front of Tamar Electronics. A guard raised the gate. An elegantly dressed man of about forty-five stepped forward. He had dark wavy hair, beginning to gray at the temples, and a wry smile. This was Jerry Holt. He walked briskly to my side of the car, opened the door, and said, "Hi, I'm Jerry. Slide over so I can climb in and we'll scoot across the street to the cocktail lounge."

"Nice to meet you, Jerry," I smiled. "Thanks for twisting whoever's arm you twisted."

"Don't mention it, Honey. Always glad to do what I can for a damsel in distress. Besides, Warren and I are buddies from way back."

We had a few drinks and discussed the visible pros and cons of my case, then Warren excused himself. "Jerry will take you to the Wright office. No need for me to tag along. I'm at the Beverly Hills Hotel. Call me there as soon as you leave the lawyer's office."

"Better still," said Jerry, "I'll drop Liz off at the Polo Lounge. Meet us there and we'll all have a drink."

"Good enough," said Warren.

Jerry and I finished our drinks and left for the Wright office.

Soon we were in the Polo Lounge with Warren, and I was feeling much relieved.

"How'd things go?"

"I can't tell you how much I appreciate what you're doing, Warren. I was very impressed with Earl Wright and

Augustus Mack. I'm sure they'll do what they can to get
me out of this mess."

Jerry finished his drink and departed. Warren and I
went out on the town, drinking, dancing and celebrating.
Then we returned to his hotel room, where I gave him his
reward. He got dressed just in time to catch the midnight
flight back to New York. I saw him off at the airport. It
was 1:30 A.M.

When I got home I observed that Joe's car was not in his
garage, and his apartment was dark and silent. My heart
sank a little. Well, what had I expected when I stood him
up to go to bed with Warren Lancey and then rubbed it
in with that note? I suppose I couldn't have expected to
find him sitting on the curb waiting for me to come home.

I climbed into a warm bath. I was startled from my soothing reverie by a noisy commotion in the courtyard. What
could be going on at this hour? I jumped out of the foamy
water into a terry cloth robe and rushed to the window.

It was Joe, drunk and hilarious, scarcely able to walk.
There was a brunette girl with him who seemed nearly
as intoxicated, helping him to his apartment.

As they came closer, I recognized the girl. It was Meg,
the little mouse from his office, Joe's Girl Friday.

At first I was relieved. Who could possibly be jealous of
Meg? She wasn't pretty or even attractive. I had seen her
in Joe's office many times without seeing her at all.

My relief was soon replaced by anger as I watched Joe
lose his balance and slip to the flagstones, giggling as Meg
fell on top of him and began smothering him with kisses.
My God, how long had this been going on?

Soon they gathered themselves together, and both stumbled drunkenly into Joe's apartment.

I paced the floor. What does a girl do in a situation like

this? The thing between Joe and me had become quite serious. We had been discussing marriage.

I thought of my rendezvous with Lancey. I decided to do nothing, slipped into a shortie gown, bolted my door, and went to sleep.

Chapter 22

SILVER SCREEN PREMIÈRE

When I awoke the next day, the sun was streaming through the window and the hands of my bedstand clock read 10:00 A.M.

"Dammit," I cried. "I missed spying on Joe!" He would have left for the office by now and I'd have no way of knowing if that damned Meg spent the night with him.

I dialed his apartment phone number. No answer.

As soon as I put down the receiver, the phone rang. Must be Joe now.

"Good morning, Sunshine," said Sandra's cheery voice. "I've got good news for you. Are you ready for it?"

"Yeah, hell yes. I could stand a little good news right now. What is it? Are we being invaded by Mars?"

"Look, smart ass, the première of your movie *A Date with Death* is scheduled for tomorrow night. I thought you might like to know. It opens on Hollywood Boulevard, right near you."

"Really? Wonderful! You know, I didn't even see the rushes! Hope I was good! I'll call Joe now. We'll meet you and your date at the theater at seven-thirty. After the show we can all go out on the town, okay?"

"It's a deal!" Sandra hung up.

I dialed Joe's office number. Meg's saccharine voice cooed over the wire. "Mr. J. H. Collins's office. May I help ˎ please?"

My temper flared at the sound of her voice. "This is Liz Renay and there's nothing you can do for me, Baby, except to connect me with my fiancé."

"Oh? And who might I ask is that?"

"Joe Collins, Birdbrain! Even you should be able to figure that out!"

She was unperturbed. "I'm sorry, but Mr. Collins is not accepting personal calls today."

I felt like barging into Joe's office and wrapping the telephone around Meg's neck—but the hell with it! If Joe wanted to play this kind of game, I'd play it right back with him. I'd go to the première with someone else. If anyone made contact again, it would have to be Joe.

The phone rang. It was Jerry Holt. "Hello," he said. "An interesting new aspect just came up in your case. The Wright office called and asked me to bring you to the office for consultation. Since you authorized them to discuss your case with me, they filled me in on the new development and I have a couple of ideas on it. I'll meet with you tomorrow and discuss my ideas and then we'll make an appointment to see the lawyers."

"Great! Jerry, can we make it around six? They are showing my movie tomorrow night—it's the première, and it starts at eight. Would you like to come?"

"How exciting! Of course I'd like to come!"

The next call was from Sandra. "Liz, Honey, is everything set with Joe?"

"No, I'm not going with Joe. I'm going with a fellow named Jerry Holt, but we'll still meet you as planned."

"Well, of all the crazy things! This will break poor Joe's heart!"

"Sandra, if you must know, I'm having problems with Joe. He spent the night with his secretary. Today, when I tried to call him, she refused to put me through."

There was a long silence on the other end of the phone. "I just can't believe it. It doesn't make sense. Meg's the plainest thing in Joe's office. There must be a mistake. Maybe I can help straighten out the misunderstanding."

"Forget it, Sandra, there is no misunderstanding. I saw him take her up to his apartment last night and I got the message this morning. If there's any straightening out, Joe will have to do it."

Soon my doorbell rang and a messenger presented me with a dozen red roses. While he was there, another messenger brought five pounds of chocolates in an elaborate red velvet box, dripping with satin ribbons.

Was this Joe's way of fixing things? That situation would need more fixing than roses and candy.

I tore open the envelopes and looked at the cards. They weren't from Joe. Both cards read—"To your success tonight. Jerry Holt."

That night Jerry and I had a leisurely dinner at La Rue's. We sat at the same table where I had had dinner with Mickey Cohen under the glare of TV floodlights and a thousand flash bulbs.

La Rue's seemed quietly different tonight. "Liz," said Jerry, leaning forward and taking my hands, "you met me for dinner to discuss your case. Let's have dinner first, see your movie, and then discuss your case after that."

We were met at the theater by Sandra Lane and a young writer friend of hers. She soon tugged me aside to talk in privacy.

"Liz, why didn't you tell me Jerry Holt was so important? He's a multimillionaire. He's on the cover of *Business Week* this week. He's Man of the Year and all that jazz."

"Look, Sandra. Jerry is not my lover, he's merely a friend of a friend."

Sandra looked crestfallen. "Dammit, I wish he was your lover. That's what you need, Liz—a millionaire. That would solve all your problems."

The theater was crowded. The picture began. Events moved rapidly leading to my initial appearance. Soon the moment arrived. I caught my breath as my celluloid image moved across the screen toward Gerald Mohr and then into a full close-up. The image's lips parted, it lowered its lashes, and opened its eyes. God, it had big eyes! It stared up into Gerald Mohr's face. It was holding an unlit cigarette in its hand. "Got a light?" it asked.

The image took the light, inhaled leisurely, and blew a puff of smoke into Gerald Mohr's face.

Someone behind us said: "What a babe!"

Another voice in the dark: "She's really got it!"

Jerry leaned toward me, patted my hand, and whispered, "And to think I was worried about you!"

"Liz," said Sandra. "You're great!"

"Good God, I haven't done anything yet except take a drag of a cigarette. How can you tell?"

"Quiet," whispered the man behind me. "We'd like to enjoy the picture."

I thought about how surprised he'd be if he knew the girl he was trying to shush was the same girl he was ogling on the screen.

I felt so proud. Then a horrible thought struck my mind. This was it! I'd just shot the works. Those few moments that flitted by so briefly represented all the best stuff, for the beginning of the picture had been shot last—and the last part, first! The opening scene represented the last day's shooting. I had been nervous and uncomfortable during the early shooting. It was only as the picture progressed that I relaxed and became natural in the part. Just as

I got really comfortable in the role, the movie was over. Too bad it hadn't been a rehearsal for a Broadway show, instead of a feature film.

I was sure that, from now on, my performance would only get worse. Sadly, my predictions proved to be true. Jerry squirmed in his seat. Sandra cleared her throat. Then it was time for me to appear as a nightclub entertainer and sing the title song of the picture, wearing the tight gold lamé pants suit. I remembered the director asking me to toy with customers in flirtatious gestures.

Surely, this number would come off all right. After all, a professional recording star had sung the song. All I had to do was fit lip sync to her voice. How could anything go wrong?

I watched, Sandra watched, Jerry watched, and the whole damned theater watched as the celluloid image of something resembling a creature from outer space swaggered across the screen onto the night-club floor wearing what seemed to be a shiny, metal space suit with a capelike swatch of material trailing behind.

"They've gotta be kidding with that outfit," whispered the man behind me. "It would take a can opener to get that thing off," said another.

I shuddered at the sound of the voices, the looks of the image, and the knowledge that it was me. I wanted to sink down under the seats and slither silently away as I watched my image parade flamboyantly back and forth wearing a schoolgirl grin and waving that damn cape around like a female bullfighter.

The director had said to look sexy. My God, I looked about as sexy as Dracula's daughter. Swish—swish—swish—went that silly half-skirt, punctuating every line of music with the irritating regularity of a nursery rhyme. I seemed to open and close my mouth like a goldfish, always about half a beat off on the timing. The long-shot view was as close as they dared come. Thank God, for small favors.

Jerry fidgeted uncomfortably. Sandra groaned, her escort sighed, someone in the audience snickered—and I wanted to evaporate!

Toward the end there were a few shots that had been filmed during the first week's shooting. I had forgotten them, but there they were.

The man behind me whispered, "I can't understand this dame. Sometimes she looks great—sometimes awful!"

Sandra nudged her escort. "You see, I told you it was that damned director's fault. I told you she was star material." I was thankful when the end came and I could walk meekly out of the theater.

Jerry and I excused ourselves from Sandra and her escort and left for a coffee shop near my apartment. We ordered coffee and pie, and Jerry tried to get my mind off the film fiasco by talking about my legal problem.

"Liz, your old boy friend, Garry Terzon, is being extradited from New York and he'll be appearing as the star witness against you."

"But why? What does he have to do with Mickey Cohen?"

"The poor bastard is drowning in trouble because he tried to furnish you an alibi. The feds have torn his office apart and have gone over his books for the past fifteen years. And the way I understand it, they found a few things they weren't looking for. Now they'll try to use him against you by pushing whatever advantage they have. Can you trust him not to turn on you to protect himself?"

"God, I don't know what his reactions will be under that kind of pressure. The poor son-of-a-bitch. I wish to hell I hadn't involved him."

Jerry leaned forward. "I've got an idea how we can put

him on such a spot he wouldn't dare go against you. That's what I wanted to discuss privately before we see the lawyers."

"No dice, Jerry. I don't play that way. Don't even tell me about it."

Jerry looked at me strangely, almost as if I had slapped him in the face.

I leaned forward and kissed him. "But thanks for the beautiful roses and the lovely box of candy, and thank you for escorting me to that torture chamber."

"Torture chamber? Oh, you mean *A Date with Death!*"

"Yes, *A Date with Death,* the death of my career," I said.

"It wasn't that bad," he lied.

"It was worse and you know it. You were a doll to suffer through it. Jerry, I appreciate what you and Warren are doing. As for Garry Terzon, he got into this mess helping me. I have to do what I can to get him off the hook now."

"Liz, don't forget that he's being called as the star witness against you. That means he has already given them information that conflicts with your testimony."

"So who could blame him after what they put him through?"

Jerry said goodnight at my apartment door. I noticed a light in Joe's place. Everything in me wanted to go knock on his door and patch up our quarrel, but I couldn't assume he was alone and, if so, that he wanted to see me. I'd have to wait for him to make the first move.

The fiasco of my movie performance and the knowledge that I had gotten Garry Terzon into my trouble weighed heavy on my mind. I wanted to rest my head against Joe's comforting shoulder, but perhaps Meg or someone else was occupying it.

As I sat alone, I remembered the letter I'd taken from

my mailbox as I left with Jerry for the theater. I had dropped it into my purse on my way out. I fumbled in my bag and found it. —Nothing important, just a letter from Dr. Levine, probably a bill for my last biyearly physical. I tore open the envelope with casual disinterest. And then the words seemed to sway before my eyes.

Dear Miss Renay,
    Your cancer test did not come back negative. This is a matter of urgent concern. Please come into my office immediately.
                                        Sincerely,
                                        Dr. E. J. Levine

I sat, stunned and unfeeling. What could happen next? I faced a twenty-five-year prison sentence, my boy friend was cheating with his secretary, my one and only movie lead turned out to be a bomb, my alibi would appear as a witness against me, and now cancer! "Dear God, don't you have a few more little goodies you'd like to drop in my lap!"

When Sandra called the next morning, I told her about the letter. "Oh, no," she almost wept. "Haven't you got enough problems without this?"

She arranged to pick me up at the Lloyd Wright office and take me to Dr. Levine's office from there.

The next day when I was getting dressed for the lawyer's office and my appointment with the doctor, another phenomenon occurred. As I combed my hair, a big bunch of hair lifted right off my head and remained in the comb. I didn't feel a thing. It was as though the hair roots had just let go, allowing the hair to float gently away with the ease of a slow-motion movie.

I picked up my hand mirror to see the back of my head.

"Oh, no!" I cried at the sight of a slick round bald spot,

the size of a silver dollar, on the top of my head. "What the hell has happened to my hair?" I wondered if cancer caused hair to fall out.

I dressed quickly, put on a pillbox hat to cover the awful spot, and called a cab to take me to the Wright office.

The lawyers decided the best thing I could do, considering extenuating circumstances, was to change my plea from innocent to guilty on one count if, by doing so, the government would agree to drop the other four. This would eliminate Garry Terzon as a witness against me. They wouldn't need a witness if I pleaded guilty.

"On a first offense you're almost sure to get a suspended sentence," soothed the lawyers.

I wasn't so sure about that, but I felt a wave of relief as I stepped out of the Wright office to wait for Sandra. The most important thing to me about changing my plea was that it cut my possible sentence time from twenty-five years to five years. The thought of twenty-five years was so staggering, I couldn't relate to it, even in my imagination. Five years I could at least cope with mentally.

Sandra arrived with a pained, sympathetic look on her face. "Liz, darling, how do you feel?" she asked.

"Sandra, I'm not dying. Nothing has changed since you saw me last."

"Oh, but think how awful it will be if you have cancer and they send you to prison for twenty-five years. You'd die there with no proper medical care," she wailed.

"Sandra, stop that crap! It's not established that I have cancer. Besides they have prison hospitals and, for your information, if I do go to prison, the most I can get will be five years."

"How do you figure that?"

"I'm going to plead guilty and take my chances, in order to get four counts struck from the record."

"Oh, Liz, they'll never give you a fair shake. They'll throw the book at you the same as Mickey, since you tried to help him."

"I'll have to chance that. It's worth it, to eliminate the possibility of twenty-five years."

"But Liz, if you plead guilty, you'll have to change your story as well as your plea, and tell the truth. You know you can't do that."

"Look, Sandra, when I plead guilty to one count, and get the other four dropped, they stay dropped, you understand, no matter what I do later. So I'll tell them a new story, and they'll be stuck with it."

"Yeah, it sounds logical," Sandra agreed, brightening up a little.

Soon we were in Dr. Levine's office, where I submitted to a biopsy to determine whether I actually had cancer or if something else had caused my pap smear to register questionable.

When I finished the test, I removed the cute pillbox hat from my head.

"Dr. Levine, what does this mean?" I pointed to the ugly bald spot, while Sandra gasped.

Dr. Levine examined the spot. "That's alopecia," he exclaimed. "Alopecia is brought about by severe shock, extreme anxiety, or prolonged mental anguish. What happens in the case of severe anxiety is that the hair roots let go and the hair falls out, abruptly, overnight."

"Will it ever grow back?" asked Sandra, in dismay.

"Stop getting so excited before you get alopecia, yourself," I said. "Sit down and relax."

"Yes, it will grow back as soon as Miss Renay is no longer subjected to the stress that brought it on."

"Oh, is that right? Well, it happened right after I got your letter telling me I might have cancer," I said, and burst into laughter. Suddenly, the whole thing seemed funny to me. I sat there and laughed and laughed until tears ran down my cheeks.

"Let her laugh," said the doctor. "It's emotional release. It will do her good. Meantime, see that she takes these tranquilizers three times a day." He was writing out a prescription. Suddenly, nothing was funny any more. Tears were still running down my face, but now I was crying instead of laughing. Why the hell was I crying? I must be flipping.

"Nervous reaction," mumbled Dr. Levine. "Here, Liz, take this." He was shoving a pill and cup of water toward me. I took it, but the tears wouldn't stop.

Joe burst into the room and took me in his arms. I sat there, still crying pointless, meaningless tears. I just couldn't stop.

"My darling, my baby. Oh, God! Sandra called me and I came as soon as I could. Nothing's going to happen to you. I'll see to it. We'll get a specialist. We'll get everything you need. I'll take care of you. Oh, will you ever forgive me?"

I managed to stop crying, but now Sandra was crying and tears glistened in Joe's eyes. Good God, did I actually have cancer? Was I dying and didn't know it?

Suddenly I was very tired. Sandra drove home while I rested my head against Joe's shoulder and slept.

Chapter 23

SHOULDER HOLSTERS AND HULLABALOO

The next day Augustus Mack called and said it was set for me to change my plea officially from innocent to guilty. The prosecution agreed to drop four counts if I'd plead guilty to one.

A huge picture of my face flashed across the front pages again with the caption: *LIZ RENAY TO TELL THE TRUTH.*

The headline didn't really bother me. I was too relieved by the news I'd received from Dr. Levine. I did not have cancer. The false alarm turned out to be just another symptom brought on by nerves. The scare was over.

Late the next afternoon as I waited in my apartment for Joe to take me to dinner, I noticed two men sitting in a car across the street from my apartment. I absently wondered about them.

Soon Joe's Cadillac pulled up in the side driveway behind our apartments. He always came in that way, leaving his car in the alley with the motor running while he dashed in to pick me up.

I slipped my stole around my shoulders, picked up my evening bag, and headed for the door. I turned my ankle and fell out the door. It was almost as though someone shoved me out the door into Joe's arms. Joe half carried me along the flagstone terrace, then picked me up bodily and put me into the car.

He slid under the wheel beside me and slowly backed out the driveway, into the street. My ankle was not sprained, and the pain soon subsided.

The two men in the car parked across the street pulled out immediately and fell in behind us. Joe became curious and watched them in the mirror. The car stayed on our tail not more than a car's length behind. Joe made a quick turn at the next block. The car followed. Joe made a series of turns up one street and down the other and around in circles. The car could not be shaken.

"I don't get it," he said. "That car is following us, and making no effort to hide it. They want to stay as close to us as possible. They couldn't care less that we're on to their game."

"I noticed them sitting in front of the apartment this afternoon. Maybe they were watching my apartment."

"Good God, Liz, do you think they're mobsters? Could they be unhappy about you changing your plea?"

"Why should anyone care if I change my plea? After all, it's my neck. Pleading guilty doesn't change anything."

"Yeah, but do they know that?"

"How should I know what those men know? I don't even know who they are!"

"Well, they're damn sure not detectives, or they wouldn't follow so close and make things so obvious. You know what I'm afraid of? I'm afraid they're staying close because they plan to shoot into the car."

A wide expanse of pavement lay ahead of us. The restaurant loomed up ahead. Joe seized the opportunity. He jammed his foot on the gas and zoomed ahead abruptly, leaving the pursuing car temporarily behind. He swerved to a screeching halt in front of the small neighborhood diner. He jumped out of the car, pulling me after him as he ran for the restaurant door.

We burst inside and slid into the first available booth, with Joe facing the door where he could watch for the car and its two occupants. I sat facing Joe, with my back uncomfortably to the door.

"Why are we just sitting here?" I asked. "Let's make a run for it—go out the back way—call the cops—do something!"

"Ssssh," said Joe. "I think we're safe here until we can figure things out. They wouldn't follow us into a public place like this. Oh my God, there they are, pulling up across the street."

Joe leaned forward tensely, his face white, beads of perspiration standing out on his forehead.

"One of them just got out of the car and is heading this way," he gasped. "My God, here he comes through the door. Sit still, Liz. Don't move. If he tries anything, I'll tackle him."

"Tackle him?" I repeated in disbelief. "Are you crazy?"

The man walked briskly past our booth. Joe stared at him with the glassy eyes of a man in a hypnotic trance, unable to move a muscle.

The man stopped and slid into the empty booth next to us. He sat calmly facing me. This time Joe's back was toward the danger. He mopped the sweat from his face with his napkin and leaned toward me. "Where is he? What's he doing?"

I stealthily slipped my hand into the purse on my lap, withdrawing a pencil. "He's sitting in the booth behind you," I wrote on my napkin. "He's facing me."

"God," whispered Joe, leaning still closer. "Keep your eyes glued to him. If he makes one move to get up or do anything, let me know and I'll tackle him. I was good at football. It's our only chance."

A waiter approached our table. Joe grabbed the napkin

and pencil out of my hand and began scribbling a hurried note. "Act as though nothing's wrong. Go into the back and call the police. Man in booth next to us is a gangster out to kill us. Get help!" he wrote.

"May I take your order?" asked the waiter.

"Yes, we'll have two steak sandwiches and two cups of coffee," Joe said rather loudly, as he shoved the napkin into the waiter's hand, then put his finger to his lip to signify silence.

"Yes," said the waiter. "Will that be all?" His eyes scanned the note nervously. He disappeared quickly, without bothering to take an order from the mystery man in the next booth.

"He'll do it—he'll call the police. Everything will be all right," whispered Joe. "Meantime, keep your eyes open. If he moves a muscle, let me know."

As I sat staring at the rugged features of the stranger opposite me, he began making gestures and pointing toward his chest. Suddenly he took hold of his suit lapel and pulled his coat back, revealing a black leather shoulder holster and gun. He gestured again, patting the gun and then quickly closing his coat. I hoped the approaching waiter caught sight of it.

The man smiled toward the waiter. "Bring me a cup of coffee," he said.

"Yes, sir," answered the trembling waiter and scurried back to the kitchen, giving me the high sign he had taken care of the request on the napkin.

My eyes were as big as saucers as the man sipped his coffee, slowly and deliberately. My sandwich lay in front of me, untouched.

"Act natural. Eat your food," whispered Joe.

I leaned forward, lowering my head so that Joe blocked me from the man's view. "He just flashed a gun at me, Joe!"

Joe's eyes narrowed. "What do you mean flashed a gun at you?"

"He pulled his coat back like this and flashed a shoulder holster and gun at me like this."

"Why the hell would he do that? It doesn't make sense. Are you sure you're not imagining things?"

"Really, he flashed a gun at me. I swear it! I don't care how silly it sounds!"

"Okay, okay. Just keep your eyes glued to him and let me know the next time he makes a false move."

The man finished his coffee, put a quarter on the table, and slowly got to his feet. I turned to stone as he walked briskly past our table. I couldn't talk. He walked to the door, opened it, and stepped out.

Joe sprang to his feet. "Why the hell didn't you tell me he got up? It's a wonder you didn't get us both killed!" He ran for the front door and began bolting it, while the owner hustled all the customers out the back way. "No check. Please, just leave. There may be trouble," he said. "The police are on the way."

When the last customer was out, he bolted the back door and quickly pulled down the blinds.

Joe peered through a crack in the blind and watched the car across the street. "Oh God," he cried, "they've got this place surrounded. Another car full of them just pulled alongside the first car. They must be making plans. The new car is pulling up the street and parking. Sonofabitch! Here come two more in another car. They're stopping to talk to the first car. This thing is big. They're really out to get somebody. Where the hell are those goddamned police? You can never find a policeman when you need one. What's taking them so damned long?"

Joe rushed to the phone and began calling everyone from the homicide squad to the FBI.

Soon there was a pounding at the door. "Open up, it's the police!" called a voice.

"Yeah?" Joe yelled through the door. "How do we know you're the police? Stick your credentials under the door."

Police identification was shoved under the door. Joe looked at it, and unbolted the lock. Two plainclothes men stepped inside, bolting the door behind them. "What's this all about?" one of them demanded.

"The place is surrounded by armed gangsters!" exclaimed Joe. "Carloads of them! This is Liz Renay. You've read about her in the papers. She is changing her plea from innocent to guilty tomorrow in Mickey Cohen's case. We think those men might be out to kill her."

"Are you Liz Renay?" asked one of the officers.

I nodded.

"Why didn't you say so? You should have called the FBI. Where are these gangsters you're talking about?"

"The car that was following us is parked across the street, down a half block, and the other two cars are circling the place. They must have gone around back," Joe answered.

"Yes," I filled in. "One of the men in the car across the street followed us in here. He was carrying a gun in a holster. I saw it."

"Yeah?" said the police officer. "You don't say." He rubbed his chin thoughtfully. "Are you sure that's them in that car across the street?"

"Oh, yes," said Joe. "I'd recognize that man anywhere!"

"Good," said the officer. "Then you'll be of help. If these men aren't after you, you have nothing to fear, right? How about walking down the street past their car? Take a good look to be sure it's the right men. We'll be right behind you, covering you all the way. If you see it's the wrong men, turn and walk back toward us. If you recognize them, keep walking and we'll close in and make the arrest."

"That's fine with me," said Joe. "Those men have no reason to shoot me. They're after Liz Renay. Let's go."

The owner anxiously unbolted the door and we stepped outside. One of the officers turned to me. "Get back inside, girl," he muttered. "You can't go with us. Do you want to get yourself killed?"

"All right," I said, and turned to open the door. It was bolted again from the inside. "Let me in," I yelled, rattling the latch.

"Go away," shouted the owner. "Haven't you caused me enough trouble? You're out, stay out. None of you are coming back in here. I don't want no trouble!"

I whirled around and found myself standing alone in the street. Joe was rushing across the road in a near run. The two police officers were trotting across the street behind him with guns drawn. I ran after the officers. "Wait for me!"

"Go back—go back. You can't go with us."

"I've got to go with you. You can't leave me alone in the street!"

"Get back. It's too dangerous. You can't go with us. We won't let you!"

"Oh yeah? Try and stop me. I'm staying close to you. You have guns. If it's dangerous with you, it's more dangerous without you!"

I ran alongside the officers as they ran after Joe. They kept pushing me back, insisting I stay away from them. It didn't make sense for me to stay alone and unarmed in the street if carloads of gangsters circled the block to gun me down. Couldn't they understand I was safer with them?

Wait a minute! Were they afraid that I'd be shot at
and they'd be hit by accident? Did they want me as far
away as possible in case a hail of machine-gun fire was
aimed in my direction?

I guess I couldn't blame them. We were across the street
now. I ducked into the first doorway I came to, flattened myself against the wall, and tried to hide. If someone was going to shoot me, no use taking a couple of young officers
in their prime with me.

As I stood in that doorway, I marveled at the calm I
felt. I wasn't really afraid. Somehow, I couldn't believe
anyone would want to kill me. I hadn't harmed anyone.
Every underworld character I'd come in contact with had
helped me, protected me, and taken me to his heart.
Why would any of them want to harm me now? Deep
down, I knew they wouldn't.

Joe was nearing the car. I watched from my hiding
place. He was walking alongside the car now. He glanced
quickly at the men inside. Would he walk by, indicating it
was the right car? I soon had my answer. Joe not only
walked by, but was making come-on motions with his
hands, like a cop directing traffic.

The officers converged on both sides of the car with
guns drawn. It was plain to see they had the situation well
in hand.

Joe stood still for a moment watching the officers, and
then he ran back past the car and down the sidewalk, div-
ing into the doorway, surprised to find I had beaten him
there.

"You all right, Honey?" he asked, giving me a little
squeeze. "It's all over now. Everything's going to be all
right. We can stay here and watch them arrest the sons of
bitches and then maybe we can get to the bottom of this."

We watched for what seemed half an hour—but no one

arrested anyone. The officers seemed to be showing the men in the car their credentials.

"Look, I think I know the answer, Joe."

Soon the plainclothes men sauntered back toward us with sheepish looks on their faces.

"Well," demanded Joe, "what gives? Who are those men?"

"We can't tell you that. I can't give you any information about who's following you other than to assure you they will not harm you. They are interested only in your welfare, Miss Renay, and your protection."

"Oh, I see. What you're telling us is that they're federal agents and you're outranked. Is that it?" asked Joe.

"Yes, we're outranked, all right," said the young officer.

"Well, answer me one question," said Joe. "Why did that man flash his gun at Liz in the restaurant?"

The officer smiled. "He was convinced you were a hoodlum. He was letting Miss Renay know she had protection. He would have sprung into action if she had given him the slightest signal. They were assigned to watch her apartment, guard her, and to follow within shooting distance any time she left her premises. When you pulled your Cadillac in at the back entrance and carried Miss Renay to your car, he figured you must be a gangster forcibly taking her out of her apartment at gunpoint, probably to kill her."

"Jesus Christ! I couldn't help it if Liz turned her damned ankle and I had to carry her to the car. All I wanted to do was take her to dinner. If I tackled that guy in the restaurant, what do you suppose he would have done, shot me?"

"What would you do if someone you believed to be a dangerous gangster suddenly tackled you?"

"I could be dead!" Joe was appalled.

We crossed the street to Joe's car and got in. As we

pulled away from the curb, the federal car pulled out and followed us. Joe stopped the car right in the middle of the street and got out.

"Why take two cars?" he yelled. "Make it easy on yourselves. Come on and join us. We'll all go together."

Chapter 24

THE JUDGE WITH A SENSE OF JUSTICE

The next day Augustus Mack escorted me to federal court. I officially changed my plea from innocent to guilty on one count, and the four remaining counts were dropped.

My face sprawled across the front pages again, and bold, black headlines announced: *LIZ RENAY TO TELL THE TRUTH! BEAUTY BACK BEFORE GRAND JURY.* Thursday, July 16, was set as the date I was to appear before a Federal Grand Jury to correct my testimony, and the following day I would go before Judge Martin for sentencing.

"Liz, you've got to win the sympathy and protection of that judge," counseled Sandra. "Get him in your corner."

"How?"

"Look, Judge Martin is from Memphis, Tennessee. That's a real break for you, Honey. If the political machine had a fix in with the regular judge, they just blew it when he took ill and had to be replaced by a visiting judge. They wouldn't dare try to influence Martin. This is a real advantage."

"What are you talking about?"

"Honey, a judge from this area would probably be all wound up in the political machine that's out to get Mickey Cohen. You'll have a better chance with an unbiased visiting judge."

"Yeah, I guess you're right."

"Liz, promise me I can select the wardrobe you wear to court. I think I know what would soften a kind, old southern gentleman from Memphis."

"Select my clothes if it makes you feel better, but I think you're attaching too much importance to this change in judges. How do you know he's a kind old gentleman? I understand he recently gave a postal clerk three years for opening a letter. First offense."

Soon I was back before the Federal Grand Jury. I straightened out the lie about Garry Terzon lending me the money, thus absolving him from any connection with the case. I straightened out as many other details as possible, sticking to my old story only where absolutely necessary, smoothing the mess out the best I could.

I was awakened the next morning at sunrise by Sandra's insistent banging on my door.

"Wake up," she called. "Today's the big day!"

I walked to the door, pulled it open with a yawn, and rubbed my eyes at the sight that greeted them.

There stood Sandra with her arms full of organdy ruffles and lace and a giant picture hat. She walked into the apartment and began spreading the apparel out for me to view.

There was a blue silk dress, embellished with rows of white organdy ruffles around a wide sweetheart neckline. It nipped in at the waist, then flared into a rippling circular skirt. The wide-brimmed picture hat was circled with white velvet ribbon, with a huge red rose in the center. There was a purse to match, and a frothy lace petticoat.

"Well, my sweet Alice Blue Gown," I laughed, dancing around the room with it.

"Don't laugh, you'll be glad to look like a southern belle in distress when you're standing in front of the man from Memphis—just you wait and see."

"Sandra, you've got to be kidding. I can't wear that get-up
to court. Believe me, people aren't that gullible—especially federal judges."

"It's your only weapon, Liz. Why not try it? What do you
have to lose?"

"My mind! Or at least that's what everyone will think
I lost if I show up looking like Scarlett O'Hara in *Gone
With the Wind*."

Sandra scolded and complained all during breakfast,
but I didn't relent. I slipped into a simple gray, pin-checked
ensemble and began writing a list of details for her to attend to if worst came to worst.

Soon Earl Wright and Augustus Mack joined us, and
we proceeded to federal court.

The courthouse steps were mobbed with press photographers, newsreel cameramen, reporters, and curiosity
seekers. The newspaper reporters seemed sympathetic.

"We're all rootin' for you, Liz! We're on your side,
Honey!"

Soon I was ushered through the heavy swinging doors
of the packed courtroom.

Newspaper reporters crowded around the edges of the
room, ready to make a beeline to the phones.

The judge's gavel silenced the din of chattering voices,
and the trial began—my trial!

I looked up into the eyes of the white-haired man who
sat in quiet-robed dignity behind the oak-paneled bench
resembling a pulpit. He reminded me of a kindly reverend
about to begin his Sunday sermon.

For a brief moment, his steady gray eyes stared into
mine, as though he was studying me. I felt conspicuous in
my tight-fitting checked sheath. I would have been grateful now for Sandra's organdy ruffles and picture hat.

Judge Martin asked the probation officer to read his find-
ings.

The probation officer began, "Your Honor, the defendant has pleaded guilty to Count III of a five-count indictment charging perjury. In Count III she is alleged to have
testified falsely under oath before a Federal Grand Jury.
The matter pending before said Grand Jury pertained to
violations of Federal laws by one Michael 'Mickey' Cohen.
Defendant is alleged to have given false testimony regarding certain conversations and arrangements for certain
money and funds . . .

"Defendant admits she perjured herself in her testimony.
She states that at the time she did not realize it was of great
significance and did not feel she was doing any great harm
to anyone.

"Defendant states Cohen told her he wanted a check
written on defendant's bank account in New York City.
She made out the checks to Cohen in the total amount of
$5,500.

"The two cancelled checks were on defendant's person
at the time she was picked up and questioned in New
York City in connection with a much publicized murder
in that area.

"She could not contact Cohen at the time, did not know
what the situation was and felt the matter of the checks
possibly could do harm to Cohen. Defendant states she
consulted her attorney in New York, who allegedly advised
her against any false testimony, but suggested that if she
were going to state other than the truth to the Jury, to use
the story she later used regarding the checks.

"Defendant claims she phoned Garry Terzon in Pitts-
burgh and he gave her to understand he would go along
with her story if questioned. Defendant insists the story
was not suggested to her by Mickey Cohen."

The probation officer then summarized my personal history.

He talked about my three marriages. He talked about sixteen-year-old Brenda and fourteen-year-old Johnny. He made the point that I'd brought them up without any help from their fathers.

His report was obviously favorable. He spoke of my exhibits and my talent as an artist. He spoke of my singing, dancing and acting, and of my poetry-show in New York.

He concluded, "The defendant gives the impression of being an intelligent and capable person—though her personal history has not been one of stability, especially in the several marriages, though two of these were at a very early age.

"From the viewpoint of the Probation Office, based on her lack of prior record and the potential she has for making a good, legitimate living, she would be amenable to probationary supervision. Whether probationer can or would effect changes that seem advisable remains to be seen."

My attorney, Augustus Mack, said in part, "Your Honor, the facts are so simple, one wonders how they became so involved. She had nothing personal to gain whatever, it was just like making an accommodation endorsement on a note and then having the note go sour.

"The explanation is something like the little boy who was walking along the street, and another chap in the neighborhood threw a rock and it went through the window of a house. The little boy saw it as he was walking along the street. It frightened him and he started to run.

"The owner of the house came out and caught him and said, 'Why did you throw a rock through my window?'

"The little fellow was so scared, he said, 'I don't know.'

"I think there was a chain of unfortunate circumstances that started when Miss Renay thought she was doing somebody a favor, and she didn't want to get them in any trouble, and instead of saying: 'I don't know where the money came from,' which is the truth, she said that she borrowed the money and made up a story about it and then one thing led to another.

"Analyzing it, your Honor, I think it has its basis in excitement or getting panicky, and having some unfortunate advice when she sought it.

"I think it was entirely without any ill intent, your Honor, and is a situation that just happened . . ."

He concluded with, "I want to say that in the brief time I have known Miss Renay, I have come to respect and like her. She has a lot of good stuff in her. And I would say that she is a good girl. She is a talented girl."

When he moved to sit down, Judge Martin said, "Before you sit down, Mr. Mack, I should like to ask this question of you. Is it your understanding from the Probation Officer's Report that she is at the present time what is commonly called a 'Kept Woman'?"

Augustus Mack smiled. "No, your Honor," he said. "Completely to the contrary. I investigated that and I am completely sold on the fact that she is not. I am also completely sold on the fact that she is what I would term a moral girl."

Judge Martin replied: "I thought his report brought out that she was presently being supplied with means of livelihood, including her apartment, by some male friend."

Augustus Mack said: "I think that is right."

Judge Martin observed: "The conduct morally of a defendant is on the mercy of the Court, so to speak. It is an important matter dealing with whether or not it is a case for suspended sentence or prosecution. That is why I asked you the question. I wouldn't be so personal unless it did involve this lady's liberty."

Then Judge Martin asked the district attorney for his recommendation.

The U.S. district attorney was out for blood. "Your Honor," he said, "it is the Government's position that any time a witness appears before a Federal Grand Jury and commits perjury, that that perjury should be punished by a penitentiary sentence.

"The Government feels a penitentiary sentence in a case in which perjury is committed before a Federal Grand Jury tends to uphold the dignity of the Grand Jury.

"The Government has a second reason for believing that a penitentiary sentence should be imposed in this case. The defendant here gave this testimony before the Federal Grand Jury because she feared it might harm one Mickey Cohen, and Mickey Cohen is a person who is an ex-convict and who enjoys the reputation, as he himself put it, of not being exactly an angel . . .

"Furthermore, it is the Government's position that no amount of talent on the part of this defendant excuses perjury before a Federal Grand Jury.

"The Government further believes that a penitentiary sentence is appropriate in this case because of the deterrent effect it will have on other witnesses who appear before the Federal Grand Jury.

"In this particular investigation, the Government has called approximately twenty witnesses. These witnesses have been reluctant and they have given conflicting stories. We think that a penitentiary sentence in this case would persuade those people who we believe may have given false testimony to come in and give us truthful testimony, and we believe that it would have a very healthy effect on those witnesses who are yet to be called."

The Judge listened attentively, seeming to reflect on what he had just heard. Then he asked me: "Miss Renay, was there any relationship of close friendship between you and Mickey Cohen?"

"Yes, your Honor, but not of a romantic nature," I replied. I explained how I had met Mickey, and how he had introduced me to many people and tried to help me.

The Judge said: "I have to be direct in my next question. I am searching for the truth. Are you now being kept by some man?"

I explained: "Your Honor, sometimes you can't answer a question with 'Yes' or 'No' and really make it a truthful answer." I went on to describe my relationship with Joe Collins. I pointed out that we had apartments in the same building but that they were separate apartments.

Judge Martin followed with a little speech of his own.

"I wouldn't need to be told by anyone that perjury is a serious crime," he said. "The penalty for perjury, I think, is five years under the statute. There are crimes that have longer terms, like armed robbery of a bank or kidnapping.

"I think I have earned a reputation in criminal courts," he continued, "that I am a stern judge, and I have a very low probation record as a District Judge . . .

"There is something that I have to come back to, and that is your present moral conduct. I am not quite satisfied with your explanation of your relationship or how you are presently being supported."

At this point, Augustus Mack stood up. "If your Honor please," he said, "I understand that Mr. Collins is present in the courtroom and if the Court wishes to hear from him, he is available."

The Judge said: "Bring him up if he wants to make a statement about it."

Joe Collins took the stand and was sworn in.

The Judge thanked him for being a voluntary witness. Then he got right to the point. "Are you keeping Miss Renay?"

Joe was beautiful. "I don't consider it so, your Honor," he said smoothly. "I am in the process of finalizing a divorce and I am intending to marry Miss Renay if it is agreeable to her at the time my divorce is final.

"She has had very little opportunity to work these last few months and I have tried to help out to the best of my ability. I try to do the best I can.

"Her daughter's husband works for me. He is a young boy who just got out of the Marines and he is doing a fine job. I have tried to advance her monies to take care of her son and to provide living expenses for her. If this is a crime, I am—"

Judge Martin interrupted: "—It is not a crime. It is a matter of morals that I am concerned with."

Joe nodded and continued: "Let me put it this way. I never met Mickey Cohen in my life and I don't know anyone else that has a record that I know of. Miss Renay has not associated with any of these people. She and I have been going together every day for about twelve months. And, as I say, my divorce was filed several months ago. I fully intend to marry Miss Renay.

"I don't know who else she could get to take care of her son and herself at this time, your Honor. With all this pending, she had no chance to work. She has done the best she can. That is all I can tell you."

Judge Martin said: "Mr. Collins, what business are you in?"

"I'm a building contractor," Joe said.

"Have you been a building contractor for quite a while?"

"I've been a contractor for about ten years. Since I got out of the service."

"You made a public statement here that you intend to marry the lady if she would accept you?"

Joe looked directly at me. There were kisses in his eyes. "She has already accepted me, your Honor." Then he added: "Provided she doesn't change her mind!"

Judge Martin smiled. "Well," he said, "I suppose it is a woman's privilege to change her mind. But she has indicated she is not going to."

The Judge said that he was sorry that, as a Federal Judge, he couldn't perform the ceremony! He thanked Joe and dismissed him.

Judge Martin then reviewed the facts in the case.

He paused, and my heart began to skip beats, for I knew he was coming to the bottom line. He had seemed sympathetic but "seemed" might not be enough to keep me from behind prison bars! I listened attentively as he spoke again. I tried to anticipate what his decision would be.

"We don't recognize any established religion in the United States," he said. "We have freedom of worship. Thomas Jefferson, author of the Declaration of Independence, wrote an epitaph for his own tombstone: 'Here lies Thomas Jefferson, author of the Declaration of American Independence, of the Statute of Virginia for religious freedom and father of the University of Virginia.'

"He didn't even mention the fact that he had been President of the United States, but he did stress three things: political independence, religious freedom and education.

"Now, while we do not have any established religion and we hope we will never have it forced upon our people, one of the principles of every religion is the doctrine of repentance. This principle has been carried into the law of the United States by the setting up of a system of suspension of sentence in cases where, within the judgment of the Court, it is deemed better for society, as well as the offending individual, to have a suspended sentence rather than go to prison.

"This defendant, Liz Renay, has had bad associations; likewise she has had some pretty tough luck. She is an intelligent person as appears from her talk here in the courtroom. In my opinion, she can be rehabilitated.

"Mr. Collins seems to be a worthy man. He is a good-looking man, I will say that, and if he matches up with her, as he says he wants to, I think they will go the straight path together. I have real confidence in giving a suspended sentence to Miss Renay.

"I want you to realize, Ma'am, that this is entirely impersonal. I never saw you before you came into the courtroom. You never saw me until then and probably will never see me again. I am merely acting for Uncle Sam in carrying out his will. It is the advice of an old judge who has served now for twenty-four years that you remember the old saying that evil communications corrupt good manners. You have had some unworthy associates. Cut them out for keeps and you will work out all right.

"It is the sentence of the Court in this case of United States versus Liz Renay that on her observance of the laws of the United States and of any state that she may be in, her term of imprisonment is suspended and probated for a period of three years on condition of good behavior.

"I say to the United States Attorney that I think you have performed your duty fully. The fact that I am not agreeing with you does not mean that I am criticizing you or the other District Attorneys. Unhappily for the judge, he has final responsibility."

The U.S. Attorney scowled. He and the men standing around him were obviously upset and disappointed.

The kindly old gentleman from Memphis had spoken. The prosecution looked crestfallen. Augustus Mack wiped tears from his eyes. There were cries of joy from friends and well-wishers. Sandra's joyous whoopee was loud enough to bring a contempt of court charge. Newsmen swarmed around me like a buzzing hive of bees. I felt numb.

"Men!" I breathed. Men, how vast a part they play in my life. Some men get me into trouble, other men get me out. Good men like Joe Collins, Augustus Mack, and this gentle, white-haired man wearing a judge's robe.

I felt like crying. I was crying. Gee, I hadn't noticed till now. "Congratulations," people from the crowd shouted. "Congratulations!" said a number of reporters.

"Thank God for a fair judge!" I breathed.

When I got home that evening and watched the newsreels and saw the papers, I couldn't believe my eyes. There was a picture of Joe Collins and me and a beautiful story about Joe's dramatic courtroom proposal and Judge Martin's regret that he couldn't perform the ceremony.

Headline captions read: *LIZ RENAY WINS PAROLE!*

The papers handled it so that it seemed I had won the Sweepstakes and was on my way to the altar, rather than that I had been given a three-year suspended sentence for perjury.

"All's well that ends well," said Joe, over dinner. "Let this be a lesson to you. You're out of trouble. For Christ's sake, stay out!"

Chapter 25

GOODBYE, JOE

Life resumed in an almost normal manner. Leo continued to work for Joe's construction company. He and Brenda seemed happy in their little apartment by the sea. Joe was busy setting up an investment company called Pacific Trust Deed Association. I helped him with the art work, planned his advertising campaign, designed the emblem for his company, and made window displays for opening day. Meanwhile, I started work on a night-club act. I was working with a recording artist from Warner Brothers and a rock-and-roll group called Stan Gunn and the Hep-Cats. I hired a writer to write comedy skits and parody songs.

My opening number was "I Didn't Know the Gun Was Loaded." This number was a blast—it would literally start the show off with a bang! I'd walk out in a cute cow-girl outfit with two pearl-handled revolvers in my holsters and start shooting up the place, just for openers. "I Didn't Know the Gun Was Loaded!" Blam! Wham! Pow! The guns would shoot blanks, but .22 blanks are louder than bullets and make as much smoke. If Mickey Cohen and his boys showed up opening night, they'd probably dive under the tables from force of habit.

I finished rehearsal early the next day and asked my writer to drive me to the Hollywood Gun Shop. I bought two pearl-handled revolvers. "Boy, you have to sign your

271

life away to get those things, don't you?" my writer com-
mented, as I scribbled my name, address, and other answers on the paper.

"We have to keep a record of all sales on firearms for
the police department," answered the gun salesman.

When I got home, Joe was just pulling into the driveway.

"Come on, Honey, let's go to dinner. I'm starved."

"Gee, like this? Oh, all right, as long as you don't take
me to Chasen's in my leotard."

"How about Chinese food?"

"You've got yourself a deal."

We pulled up at the Ming Tree. Joe bubbled with enthusiasm about his new venture.

"Honey, you've just got to come down to the new office
tomorrow. I've reserved a desk for you. You can sit undis-
turbed and do the art work for the brochures we're planning. You'll love the place! I want you to be there for the
opening."

"Wonderful!" I answered with mixed emotions. What
excuse could I give the eight people who planned to re-
hearse with me in the morning?

I slipped into a phone booth on the way to the ladies'
room and relayed my problem to Sandra.

"Sandra, you've got to help me. I can't be at rehearsal
tomorrow, and I don't want Joe to hear me calling all those
people to cancel or he'll feel bad."

"*He'll* feel bad! How the hell do you think I feel about
you skipping rehearsal! How many more do you plan to
skip? Tell that damn Joe to hire an artist. If he wants to
monopolize your evenings, fine, but when he cuts into
career time, he's got me to reckon with."

"Sandra, will you call everyone and see that they don't
make a wasted trip to my house in the morning?"

"Of course, I'll call them. You don't think I'd let you blow the whole act, do you?"

I returned to the table, feeling somewhat relieved.

Next day I was up, dressed, and breakfasting with Joe by 8:00 A.M.

Joe's new office was a dream. Huge plate-glass windows faced Wilshire Boulevard. High above the street my signs beckoned to investors, offering 10 percent interest on their money.

We stepped inside. The place was enormous, with rows and rows of desks neatly enclosed in glass half-walls, with open passageways. The salesmen and executives were all in easy view, each with his own private nook to function from.

Many people were at work, but the place was silent as a tomb. People moved about with the quiet caution of bank employees.

There was a display of free gifts for the first one hundred investors, placed between the door and the front counter —a portable TV, a set of dishes, and smaller prizes for smaller investors.

A secretary sauntered up to the counter and back again. It was Meg. We exchanged icy glances.

Joe escorted me to my little cubbyhole with its gray metal desk. "Here is the material to be printed in the brochure. Think of a good illustration for the front, and work out the art work and photography, okay? If you can finish by lunch, we'll knock off for an hour or two."

Joe returned to his desk and I began studying the brochure. Soon I was lost in my own little world of imagination, creation, and design. I busily sketched idea after idea, oblivious of the people in the other cubbyholes honeycombing the office.

Most of the investors were men but occasionally a female investor's heels clicked down the long hall and turned into a cubbyhole to exchange her cash for a piece of paper marked "Second Trust Deed" and a free prize from the door.

That was about the only noise to be heard, as investors passed through the doors, exchanging cash for paper. In and out they went, quickly and quietly. There were twelve to fifteen of them in the office in various stages of this ultra-smooth process when, suddenly, the calm was shattered by the appearance of two men. They strode in through the front door and announced loudly, "We're from the sheriff's office! We're looking for Liz Renay."

Whispers from the shocked investors buzzed through the office.

"Liz Renay! Did you hear that? They're looking for Liz Renay!"

"Liz Renay? Isn't she Mickey Cohen's girl friend?"

"This place must be run by gangsters!"

"I'm taking my money out of here fast!"

"Me, too! I'm not about to invest my money with Mickey Cohen!"

Joe rushed forward. "I own this company. There is a misunderstanding here. Can I help you?"

"Yeah, maybe you can, buddy. You can tell me why Liz Renay purchased two .22 revolvers at the Hollywood Gun Shop yesterday," said one of the police officers.

Joe looked sick. "Liz Renay—out buying guns? It doesn't make sense. Why would she buy guns? Are you sure about this?"

"Quite sure. Where is she?"

One by one, the worried investors filed out of the place, as Joe tried to placate the police officers.

"My God," I thought, "I've certainly managed to louse

up Joe's opening day!" I came forward. "I'm Liz Renay."

"Liz, darling, tell these men you didn't buy any guns, will you?"

"But I did! I bought two revolvers at the Hollywood Gun Shop yesterday."

"Oh, no!"

"This is ridiculous, Joe. I bought them to use as props for my night-club act in Las Vegas."

"Yeah," said the officer. "A likely story! Suppose you tell that to the sheriff."

"Just a minute," I said. "Suppose I didn't buy them for my night-club act? So what? It's not against the law to pick up a couple of guns, is it?"

"It is for you, young lady! You're a convicted felon, on probation. You're not allowed to buy a gun."

"If you came here to arrest me, forget it. I didn't purchase guns at all. I purchased props! When I ordered those guns, I ordered them converted to shoot blanks before delivery. I don't even have them yet, but when they're delivered tomorrow, they'll be harmless."

"Not so fast, young lady. You could have them changed back, for all we know."

"And that's an example of how much you know. Converting a gun to shoot blanks ruins it, and it can't be made to shoot bullets again."

"How do we know what you're saying is true?"

"Call the gun shop. Ask them. They'll tell you it's a hell of a waste of good guns, like they told me."

"We'll take your word for it till we check it out. But, if you're lying, we'll be back for you!"

The officers walked out, and the chattering office staff rushed up to get the latest scoop.

"Come on, Liz, we're going to lunch!" said Joe, moving away from the curious group.

"Mind if I join you?" a voice asked. It was Meg.

Joe tried to pretend he hadn't heard.

"Joe, dear," she repeated loudly. "I'll come along. I have business to discuss with you over lunch."

I suddenly lost my appetite. "I have no intention of having lunch with that creature," I said.

"But, Liz, this is opening day. Meg happens to be my secretary, and I'm sure she has important things to discuss or she wouldn't suggest it."

"Then discuss them, Baby, but not on my time. Just put me in a cab."

Joe looked helpless. "Meg," he said, "I'm afraid you won't be able to join us. Take your lunch hour now and I'll talk with you when I get back."

We drove to a quiet restaurant in Beverly Hills. Joe broke the silence.

"Liz, do you think the police will harass you forever?"

"I'm more interested to know if you intend to have Meg hanging around forever. She bothers me more than the police!"

"Meg's my secretary. Period. So let's skip the subject. But those damn police—they're beginning to get in my hair!"

"And how do you think Meg affects me?"

"Forget Meg. I don't even know she's alive. She looks more like a boy than a girl, and I wouldn't want her if she was the last woman alive."

"Oh, is that why you invited her to spend the night at your apartment?"

"I was drunk. Don't bring that damn incident up again or you'll get *me* mad. If you hadn't been out half the night with that deadhead Lancey, I wouldn't have been with her. I guess we can blame the whole thing on Mickey Cohen!"

"Yes, that's convenient. You'd like to blame everything on Mickey, wouldn't you, Joe?"

"Look, Honey, let's not quarrel over that pipsqueak. He's not worth it. I haven't said a word about all this bullshit costing me twenty potential investors today and I don't plan to, but—"

"Then why did you? It was your idea for me to come down there in the first place. I should be rehearsing."

"Oh, and that's another thing I've been meaning to talk to you about, Liz. We're getting married soon, and I want you to give up this night-club thing. If you're going to be my wife, I want you home with me at night, not entertaining a bunch of drunks."

"If I hadn't been entertaining a bunch of drunks, I wouldn't have met you."

"Thanks a lot! Anyway, do me a favor and drop this night-club bullshit, will you?"

"Oh, Joe, how can you ask such a thing of me? What if I asked you to drop your mortgage company?"

"Then we'd both starve! Honey, it would be rough enough if you weren't blacklisted but, with that crap to contend with, you may as well give up."

"No, I won't give up! I'll never give up! I'll clear this mess up, somehow. You'll see!"

During the next few days, to keep occupied, I started painting again. One day as I sat painting Cleopatra in all her splendor, Sandra called and asked me to meet her. She was with a combination vocal coach, writer, and choreographer, who was interested in whipping up a nightclub act for me on a percentage basis.

We agreed to meet in a little bar called the Rocket Room. It was right next to Joe's office. We could drop in and ask Joe if he'd like to join us for the discussion. Maybe he wouldn't object this time. The cab dropped me in front of Joe's office and I went in to ask him.

"Mr. Collins isn't in this afternoon," an executive informed me. "He's tied up on an urgent business matter outside the office."

I thanked the man and left, glad to get out of there without running into Meg again. She wasn't at her desk.

I walked next door to the Rocket Room. As I stepped from the brilliant sunlight into the dimly lit cocktail lounge, I was temporarily blinded. I could make out shadowy figures huddled together at cozy tables illuminated by the flicker of candlelight. I stumbled and groped my way toward the tables, while my vision gradually cleared.

Slowly, two of the shadowy shapes sitting at the table closest to me came into focus.

"Joe!" I cried. Joe whirled, startled by my voice. I didn't notice the person seated next to him until I saw the panic in his eyes. I turned my gaze from his guilty face into the burning eyes of Meg Caldwell. She smiled coyly.

"It's a small world, isn't it?" she cooed.

Joe regained his composure. "Well, Sweetheart, what are you doing here?" he asked, managing a weak, phony grin.

A lump was rising in my throat.

"I'm meeting someone."

"Well, what a coincidence! So are we. Meg and I were waiting here for some business associates. Meg's got to go with me to their office to take some dictation."

Meg giggled, nearly choking on her drink.

"Dictation? Oh sure! You don't have to explain what you're doing here. It's pretty obvious."

"That's right, Joe, why explain?" slurred Meg drunkenly, throwing her arms around his neck.

"Goddamn it, you keep out of this!" Joe snapped, shoving her roughly from him.

"It doesn't matter, Joe. I couldn't care less about anything Meg has to say." I turned to walk toward the door.

"Wait a minute!" Joe cried, springing to his feet. "Just who in the hell were you meeting here? Is that why you're walking out? Are you afraid for me to see who you were meeting?" He grabbed my arm, roughly spinning me around to face him.

"You've got to believe me! This is not what it appears to be," he pleaded.

"I know." I smiled. "Your office told me you were out on urgent business."

I tried to pull away. Joe held me tightly in his grip. "Who the hell are you meeting here?" he demanded.

"Us," answered a familiar voice, as Sandra and the choreographer walked into the room.

Joe released his grip on my arm.

"Come on, Sandra, let's get the hell out of here. Joe has urgent business to take care of. Besides, it's too crowded in here for me."

Sandra and her friend followed me out the door, with bewildered looks on their faces. Joe was close behind. He followed us to Sandra's car.

"Please, Darling, I can explain everything," he pleaded.

As we drove away, Sandra asked, "Liz, what in the hell's wrong between you and Joe?"

"I guess I've been too busy with my own interests to notice what was going on," I said.

We went to Sandra's apartment to discuss the act. We ran through a few numbers with the choreographer. He tried to explain his ideas but I couldn't concentrate.

"Liz, I'm going to take you right back to Joe's office. You've got to hear his side of the story."

We returned to her car.

"Please, Sandra, just take me home."

"Nonsense, I'll do nothing of the kind. We're going to see Joe."

She headed for Joe's place.

Suddenly Sandra stepped on the gas and sped up, passing right by Joe's office—but not before I caught a glimpse of Joe pulling up in his car with his arm around Meg. Her hair was all rumpled.

"Now, for God's sake, will you take me home?" I said quietly.

An hour later, my bell rang. I opened the door. Joe rushed in, throwing his arms around me.

"Darling, I can't stand to quarrel with you. You've got to believe there's nothing between Meg and me. She's my secretary. A guy can have a close relationship with his secretary. It doesn't mean anything. A secretary is something you hire and fire. I don't think of Meg as a woman— just an office machine—a walking file cabinet—can't you see what I mean?"

"Of course, I can. Machine, my ass! What kind of machine—a sex machine?"

"Liz, what can I say to convince you?"

"Just one thing, Joe. Say you'll get rid of her! You say that she's something you hire and fire, so fire her. If you don't, I'm leaving!"

"Wait—just a minute!" Joe said angrily. "I love you, but you can't lead me around by the nose and make me jump through hoops. We may as well get that straight right now! Nobody tells me who to hire or fire. Nobody gives me an ultimatum."

"Joe, it's that girl or me. She goes or I go."

"You have no right to insist that I fire Meg. She's my

girl Friday, my right hand. She knows more about the business than I do."

"Then your answer is no?"

"It certainly is, and you're not leaving either. I won't let you. I love you."

I didn't argue. We went to a movie that night and then to a dance. I didn't bring the subject up again. But I knew I was going to leave Joe.

The next day I called the movers to take everything from my apartment and put it in storage. I arranged to move to a hotel. I guess Joe sensed something was wrong. For the first time in a long time, he came home on his lunch hour. When he saw the moving van in front of the building, he rushed into the courtyard and started racing up the stairway to my apartment. Halfway up, he collapsed and crumpled to the concrete with a heart attack.

The landlady called an ambulance and they rushed him to the hospital on a stretcher. I continued packing boxes in my bedroom, unaware of what was happening outside my door.

Sandra helped, sniffing back a tear now and then. "Are you sure you're doing the right thing, Honey? He was awfully good to you. Look at the way he stuck his neck out for you on the witness stand. I know you love him."

"If he's cheating now, what will he do after we're married? I love him but I can't cope with cheating. I want Joe all to myself. With me it's got to be everything or nothing."

"Then don't be surprised if you end up with nothing!" she sighed. "The last time I noticed, you were no angel yourself. You have to learn to take it if you're going to dish it out."

By six o'clock that evening the last of the boxes and the last piece of furniture were loaded on the van. We locked the apartment, gave the key to the landlady, and started driving toward the hotel where I had taken a room.

A car careened wildly around the corner and speeded after us. It was driven by someone in a white coat. Two men were in the car.

"Sandra, guess what? We're being followed by a man in white," I exclaimed.

Sandra turned the corner. The car skidded around the corner right behind us, close enough for me to see the driver's face.

"My God, Sandra, that's Joe driving the car. He's wearing a white outfit like a doctor wears."

"Joe?" cried Sandra, stepping on the gas. "He must be furious—we'll try to lose him."

Sandra drove like a maniac—up one street and down another, through alleys, stop signs, around the blocks, with Joe's car right on her tail. Suddenly we found ourselves in a dead-end street. We couldn't go another inch. Joe pulled his car across the road behind us. We were trapped.

He leaped from the car like an angry bull, rushed forward, pulled our car door open, and yanked the protesting Sandra from behind the wheel, ripping her blouse in the process.

"I ought to slap the hell out of you, you damn bitch!" he said. "Why did you run from me and make me chase you all over town?"

I scrambled out of the car and jumped between them. "You leave Sandra alone. Just because I left you, don't take it out on her. What the hell are you doing dressed like that?"

"Go on home, Sandra, Liz is coming with me!" cried Joe, his voice quivering with anger. Then he wavered, staggered, and fell in a crumpled heap on the ground.

The other man leaped from Joe's car and ran forward

in a panic. It was Frank Mueller, Joe's office manager. He
knelt, cradling Joe's head in his lap.

"My God, don't stand there. Go call an ambulance before this man dies!" he shouted. "He wouldn't listen—I
begged him not to leave the hospital, but he wouldn't listen, he just wouldn't listen!"

I looked at Joe's big hulk of a body lying there in that
white gown. He was still wearing the hospital's identification band on his wrist. There was something touching
about his face so pale and still. He looked so innocent in
the sterile hospital gown, with his rumpled hair. Soon I
was kneeling beside him, begging him to open his eyes,
promising anything if he'd just wake up and live.

Soon the ambulance arrived. Sandra and I rode to the
hospital with Joe. He was still unconscious when we arrived
so I signed him in. A worried-looking Frank Mueller arrived with Joe's attorney.

"Liz, I don't know what to make of Joe's behavior," he
said. "He was brought here because he had a slight heart
attack. As soon as he came to, he rushed out of the hospital to your place. He said you were leaving and he must
stop you. They made him sign a paper absolving them of
any responsibility for his life before they'd allow him to
go. He knew he was taking his life in his hands, but he
didn't care. He must love you more than his own life."

I paced the floor until the heart specialist, Dr. Covel,
emerged. "You can go home now, Miss Renay," he said.
"If Mr. Collins doesn't have any more upsets, I think he
will be all right. He won't be up and around for a while,
but he'll recover."

I was so grateful that I wanted to hug the doctor. I spent
every day at the hospital until Joe was well enough to be
brought home. Then I cared for him in his apartment from
early morning until he fell asleep at night, when I'd take

a cab to my hotel and grab a little sleep until time to return in the morning to fix his breakfast.

Joe and I became very close during his illness. We had long talks. Talk was the only activity Joe was capable of during his three-and-a-half-month convalescent period. I read to him, cooked for him, and gave him his medicine. There was only me in his strange new world of tranquilizers and back rubs—no contacts with the outside except via the telephone. We had nothing to debate, nothing to disagree about, nothing to argue over. There were no quarrels, no passions—just a quiet, half-dozing recuperating invalid with a boyish grin.

Sometimes I sat and watched him sleep, feeling almost maternal. I tried not to think of my decision to leave Joe. He needed me now. I didn't kid myself that this was the real Joe. I knew he was only resting because his wings were clipped. Soon he'd be well again—what then?

As I looked at his helpless, sleeping face, I remembered the sparrow I once caught with a broken wing. I brought it into the warm house and cared for it. It was content until its wing began to mend. I knew one day it would fly away. One day it did. I knew Joe would be ready to try his wings again soon and, in my heart, I knew our relationship would end. I wanted something from Joe he was unable to give, in spite of his love for me.

Soon the day came when Dr. Covel said Joe could get up and go to his office for two or three hours. He'd be able to get back into the swing of things, little by little. I helped him get ready and he slowly made his way to the waiting taxicab and drove away.

Joe didn't return in two hours as he said he would. Five hours went by. Then I received a phone call from an embarrassed Frank Mueller.

"Liz, Joe got up too soon, I guess. He's had a bit of a set-back. He sort of collapsed again, and he can't be moved for a few days. He'll have to stay where he is."

"Oh, gee, what a shame. I was afraid he was getting up too soon. Is he back in the hospital?"

"No, as I was saying, the doctor feels it's best not to move him for a few days. He'll have to stay right where he is."

"But that's silly. How can he stay in the office?"

"Oh, he's not at the office. He stopped off for a few minutes at a friend's house on the way home and that's where he collapsed. Dr. Covel just left there and said Joe isn't to be moved for three or four days. He has ordered a full-time nurse sent over."

"But where is he—will he be all right?"

"Oh, yes, I'm sure he'll be all right. The only thing he's worried about is you and how you're going to take it. He wants me to bring you by to see him so he can explain things personally."

"Explain what things?"

"It's just that—well, he collapsed at Meg's apartment. Oh, don't worry, he can explain everything. It's not the way it looks. You see—"

I hung up the phone in disgust. The very first day out of bed—I didn't care to hear his explanations.

I decided to leave Hollywood and go to New York out of his reach. That way he wouldn't soft-soap me into re-considering. Let Meg take care of him. Let her have him. I was through. My phone rang continuously as I packed my things to go. Finally, as I was ready to walk out the door, I picked up the receiver in exasperation.

Joe's pleading voice came over the wire. "Liz, darling, please come over here, I beg you. I'll put Meg on to talk to you if you like—anything you say—Meg says you can stay here with me until I can be moved—anything, Liz— anything to convince you."

"Why are you trying so hard to convince me? Convince me of what? Look, Honey—you stay right there with Meg. Marry her for all I care—this is goodbye."

I slammed down the receiver, dashed out, and hailed a cab for the airport. Soon I was winging my way to New York. I checked into an inexpensive hotel and contacted a music arranger. I could go to work on a night-club routine. There was no one to stop me now.

I rehearsed, but my heart wasn't in it. All I thought of was Joe, night and day. It was maddening.

Then one day about three weeks later, Joe called. I couldn't believe my ears. How did he find me?

"I had a hell of a time tracking you down," he said, "but I thought I should call and tell you the news. I'm married!"

"You're married? Joe, I don't believe it! You met someone and got married in the last three weeks?"

"No, I took your advice and married Meg," he answered.

I was stunned. "But Joe, how could you? You said she looked like a boy and you wouldn't have her if she was the last woman on earth!"

"You left me there, Liz—she took care of me and, well —I married her. That's all there is to it!"

"Joe, just because we broke up is no reason to marry someone you don't love."

"Of course, I love her. I married her, didn't I? That should prove I love her."

"Yes, it should, but does it?"

"I married her. That speaks for itself."

"Well, pardon me for asking!"

"Liz, I just want you to know I am out of your life for- ever. You'll never see me again. You and I are no good for each other. We live in two different worlds. I love you, but I made my decision and I'm sticking with it."

"Okay, Joe! You two deserve each other. Meg can have you with my blessings." I hung up the receiver and burst into tears. I felt like someone had just dropped an atom bomb on my head. I wanted to call back and say, "Joe, I love you. We belong together. We've made a horrible mistake. Can't we start over?" But I couldn't. I had to be strong.

I cried myself to sleep. I walked around in a zombie-like trance, unaware of anything going on around me. The realization that Joe and Meg were together even at this moment hung like a lead weight over me.

"Oh, Joe! Why?"

Chapter 26

BUCKING THE BLACKLIST

The phone rang. A male voice identified its owner as the attorney for Bill Forrest.

"I have news about Bill Forrest," he said. "He—"

"—For all I care he can drop dead!" I interjected.

"He just did," the attorney said.

The attorney explained that shortly after my fracas with him, Bill had flown to Tokyo and that's where he died. He was directing a movie called *Katakai*. He was also living it up. After spending all night with some beach girls, he died of a heart attack.

The attorney had known of our marriage. He told me my "secret mate" had left an estate of about $250,000!

It was August, 1960. More than a year had passed since I had been placed on probation. I'd tried to live an exemplary life.

Now I was back in the headlines again.

As miserably as he had treated me, I felt bad about Bill Forrest's death. As psychopathic as he seemed to be, he had considerable artistic talent. I wept for that. His body was flown to New York and I attended the funeral in tears.

For a while, it seemed that poetic justice was returning the things Bill had stolen from me. As his wife, I was in line for his estate.

But during our last bitter quarrel, he had said something about my not needing a divorce because I wasn't married. Now it turned out that Bill was already married and thus was a bigamist on top of everything else.

My claim to the $250,000 melted.

Broke again.

Then Sandra Lane got a booking for me at the Showboat in Las Vegas. She reminded me to register with the Vegas police department as a convicted felon. They could revoke my parole if I didn't. I took no chances. I went down for the routine fingerprints and registration, but I didn't tell them where I was working. It was none of their damn business as far as I was concerned. I used the name "Brandy Marlo" and remained incognito.

I lost some of my salary challenging the crap tables and roulette wheels—but returned to Hollywood with enough cash to carry me through at least a month's work on my book.

How would I live when the month ended? Where could I get money for expenses until I finished the book?

I hit on a plan. I'd borrow from my friends. Not a lot from anyone, but a little bit from each so it wouldn't inconvenience any of them.

I sat down and figured exactly what my monthly nut required—rent, food, utilities, telephone, laundry and cleaning, carfare, Johnny's school, clothes, and miscellaneous. My expenses ran about $500 a month. I added another $100 as a margin for the unexpected. Okay, so I needed $600 a month. It isn't everyone who has an extra $600 lying around the house every month. But what about $50 or $100? Not a friend on my list would even feel a loan as small as that. I made a list of people who had been calling to offer their assistance since the trouble began. I hadn't needed them before, but I could sure use them now.

George Jessel had called. "Liz, I know you're in trouble and things are rough. Just let me know if there's anything I can do to help. If you need money, I'll be only too happy to help you out."

Leo Gitlin had called from New York. "Liz, don't be too bashful to ask for help if you need it. I'll be glad to see you through until this mess clears up. If you want anything, you've got my number."

Garry Terzon had called. "Liz, you were an angel to spare me the aggravation of that Grand Jury. Don't think I don't know you risked your own neck to do it! Let me make it up to you. If you need a favor, say so, okay?"

Even my family doctor called and offered assistance. "Miss Renay, this might seem a bit out of order, but I've known you for a long time and, well—I don't know how to put it, but do you need money?"

There were thirteen on the list of people who had gone out of their way to offer help. I only needed $600 a month. With thirteen people I'd only have to borrow $100 every second month, or borrow $50 from each of them every month.

It was a simple plan. It would solve my problems and not present any to others. I set aside a small notebook to keep an account of each and every loan. I sent out telegrams to six people, requesting a loan of $100 from each. I could do this systematically, every month. If I did a night-club booking, I would skip a month or two. I wouldn't have to leave my apartment. I could call the wires out over the phone.

I wired my New York attorney: DEAR LEO, PLEASE SEND ME $100. WILL PAY YOU AS SOON AS POSSIBLE. I MAY ASK THIS OF YOU FROM TIME TO TIME UNTIL MY POSITION CHANGES. LOVE, LIZ.

Next, my agent—and on down the list. I went into my study and got busy writing. I worked until 3:00 A.M. I was awakened next morning by a Western Union messenger delivering the first money order. They continued to arrive all day as I worked on my book. By evening all were accounted for. I took a break and strolled down to the Western Union office to cash them. Six hundred dollars—it was nice to have friends I could count on in an emergency.

I listed every loan on my probation report, as required by regulations.

My probation officer, Alice Allison, seemed nice enough, but I always got the impression she was trying to catch me off guard, doing something I shouldn't be. If she only knew the celibate life I was leading at the moment!

One morning in the wee hours I was surprised by a call from a priest friend I'd met during the time I worked on the Vox Poetica radio show from Fordham University. Father Penachio and another priest had just arrived with a five-hour layover until catching their next train. They apologized for calling at 4:00 A.M. and asked if they could rest at my place.

"Of course! I'll pick you up at the station. And I'll fix you breakfast."

The priests were dressed warmly in topcoats as protection against the chilly 4:00 A.M. mist. It was sprinkling lightly. I didn't recognize them at first. They didn't look much like priests in those topcoats. Then I saw Father Penachio's broad smile.

"Good morning, Father. Come in out of the dampness!"

Immediately after I picked them up, I noticed someone following us. Wouldn't the federal heat ever stop and let me live in peace? Did the powers that be really think I'd be foolish enough to make a false move so they could revoke my probation?

In my apartment, we chatted briefly and then I set the alarm for 6:30. That way they could enjoy a two-hour nap.

I could prepare breakfast while they shaved and showered. We'd visit over coffee and they'd still have plenty
of time to catch their train. I emerged from the kitchen
next morning with a big tray of ham and eggs and butter-
scotch coffee cake. The priests stepped out of the bathroom in their dark suits with collars shining. They sure
looked more priestly after a little freshening up.

As we sat around the living-room coffee table discussing
New York and my old radio program, I heard high-heeled
shoes clicking up the walk to my door. Then a sharp, au-
thoritative knock sounded. My God, who could that be
at 8:00 A.M.? The knock sounded once more, louder and
more insistent. Father Penachio went to the door. When
he saw the neatly dressed gray-haired lady, he said, "How
do you do. I'm Father Penachio—and you must be Liz's
mother. Did I guess it?"

"No, I'm not her mother," said Alice Allison, striding
into the room.

"No? Don't tell me, let me guess. You're an aunt?
Right?"

"No. I'm not an aunt."

"Do sit down and have some coffee. I give up, who are
you?" asked Father Penachio, with a smile.

"I'm Alice Allison, and if you must know, I'm Liz's probation officer."

"Probation officer!" gulped Father Penachio. "Now if
that doesn't shut my mouth!"

"Who are you and what are you doing here?" asked Mrs.
Allison, eyeing the two immaculately dressed Catholic Fathers with the breakfast tray spread out before them.

"Just a minute," I cut in. "You may be my probation officer, but you're not theirs. They needn't answer your questions."

"Okay, then I'm asking you. Who are these gentlemen and what are they doing here at this hour?"

"I thought it was obvious. They are priests and they're having breakfast. Did the cop tailing me fail to notice my house guests were men of the cloth? Sorry for your wild-goose chase."

"Would you like some coffee cake?" asked Father Penachio, passing the plate of nut-encrusted goodies.

"No, thanks, I'll be going. This was just a routine check. I happened to be in the neighborhood."

"At 8:00 A.M.? Really, Miss Allison! You *are* an early bird! If the Fathers didn't have to catch a train, we'd still be asleep."

"Catch a train? But they just got here," she exclaimed.

"And how do you know that? But that's a silly question, isn't it, Mrs. Allison?"

I went back to my writing. One day my phone rang. It was Sandra. "Liz, darling, I just arranged a booking for you in a Santa Barbara supper club. They want you to emcee the show and do comedy patter. I think it will be a good experience and it's only three weeks away."

"Sandra, I'm writing. I don't want to stop, I don't want to go to Santa Barbara, and I don't want to be an emcee. So that's the end of that!"

"I'm afraid not. I already signed the contract for you and agreed to have you there for three weeks. It's right on the beach and it will do you good. You need a break from that darn book. You're becoming a hermit. There's a yacht club and some handsome sun-tanned Romeos down there —some rich ones, too. I think you're about due for a good romance. Know what? You're in a rut."

"Sandra, I can't do it. I won't stop."

"Liz, the change will do you good. You won't be using

your real name. We can hide from the world for three
weeks. No newspapers, no parole officers, no cops, no nothing—just a pleasant job and lots of sand and surf. I bought
us bikinis for sun-bathing. You and I will have a ball—
wait and see!"

I tore myself away from my half-finished book, closed
my apartment, packed a bag, and soon Sandra and I were
driving along the ocean side on our way to Santa Barbara.

"What name am I going to use?"

"Gee, Liz, I haven't thought of one yet. Anything's all
right. Pick a simple name like Mary Jones or Sally Smith,
or something. I don't want anyone to find you here. Don't
use a name that sounds like Liz Renay."

"What do you think of Alice Allison for a name?"

"It sounds all right, but haven't I heard that name somewhere before?"

"Yes, that's my probation officer's name."

"Well shut my mouth!" Sandra laughed. "Only you
would think of posing as your own probation officer."

When I saw the name Alice Allison on the marquee outside the club, I laughed louder than Sandra. The irony of
it all. Right now, Alice was probably racking her brain
wondering where I had disappeared to.

The first night when a voice announced, "Presenting
the lovely Miss Alice Allison," I could scarcely keep a
straight face on stage, the whole thing struck me so funny.
For two weeks Sandra and I had a ball. We went on yacht
parties, sun-bathed nude in hidden coves, discovered private beaches and had fun with their sun-drenched owners,
while exploring Santa Barbara.

On the third week, our luck ran out. Using Alice Allison as a stage name backfired. The subpoena servers
searching for Liz Renay spotted it. Since I wasn't allowed

to leave the state, they presumed I was somewhere in California and probably working in a club. With these deductions, they put special emphasis on night clubs in their search. They couldn't find a Liz Renay. Then, as I learned later, one of them saw the ad in the Santa Barbara paper. It read, "Come see Alice Allison."

"Alice Allison! Holy Cow, I'll bet that's Liz Renay."

"What makes you think so?" asked his colleague.

"Because Alice Allison is Liz Renay's parole officer, and Liz is just the girl who would do something like this."

Soon federal agents converged on the club and started asking questions about Alice Allison.

"Is she pretty?"

"Hell, yes!"

"What does she do?"

"Who listens? It's how she looks that counts!"

"Sounds like Liz, all right."

Sandra rushed into my dressing room. "Grab your powder puff and douche bag—let's get the hell out of here. We've been exposed!"

"So, what do we care?"

"Honey, it's the feds I'm talking about! They're outside with a subpoena or warrant, or something, and asking about you!"

"Christ, why didn't you say so! Never mind the powder puff, let's go." We made it back to Hollywood before they caught up with us and served the subpoena.

Holy Cow! I had to go before the Grand Jury the next morning. My eyes couldn't believe the words I read. This time they were subpoenaing my book. I was ordered to bring the synopses, chapters, and all notes pertaining to my book.

Soon I was walking down the long shiny hall leading

to the jury room, my arms full of manuscript. The usual newsreel cameras, blinding floodlights, and scurrying newspaper photographers trailed behind.

I decorated the nation's front pages again, this time holding the unfinished book. *LIZ RENAY'S LIFE PRE-VIEWED BY GRAND JURY*, read the captions.

When it was over, I went back to work on the book. I sent wires again to my friends for the monthly loans and they came through immediately, as before. I spent the month with my nose to the typewriter. At times when I was "all written out," I'd paint a little for diversion.

Then Sandra arranged another booking—this time in Hollywood in a place called "Tin Pan Alley," under my own name, with much advance publicity. The opening night audience was sprinkled with celebrities and the house was packed. I spotted George Raft at a front table and Fabian in the back.

"This is great," said Sandra. "You've got 'em packed in three-deep at the bar, and every table is filled. I guess I made the right deal, after all."

"What do you mean, the right deal?"

"Well, I figured you'd pack the place, so I made a deal for you to take 25 percent of the gross, instead of salary," she said proudly. "You get $100 a week as a token salary to cover expenses, but the percentage is the big thing."

"I don't know about that, Sandra. How will we know if they're giving us a fair count on what they take in? How can we be sure what my 25 percent amounts to?"

"Don't worry, I'm sure they'll give you a fair shake. We can estimate what the place is doing. They can't fake it much."

"It's too indefinite. I'd rather have a salary I could count on."

The booking went well until pay day. Sandra and the

owner argued violently over my percentage. Since they couldn't come to terms, the matter was left pending and I received only my $100. The next week the same thing happened. Sandra, more angry than ever, refused to accept the club owner's figure, so I again received only the $100 token salary. By the third week, the feud progressed so far that Sandra withdrew me from the club and filed a claim with the union.

I left, feeling depressed and confused. How could we hope to collect a claim that was never clearly defined?

I buried myself in my creative work again. Sandra called with another booking, this time in the cocktail lounge of one of the better bowling alleys. I would open there New Year's Eve.

Sandra was disappointed at my lack of enthusiasm, and she complained about my unappreciative attitude.

"I'm sorry," I said, "but it's not my idea of a fun place to spend New Year's Eve. I'm tired of joints, fighting with gin-mill owners, filing claims with unions, and all of the rest of the crap that goes with it. It's degrading!"

"Degrading, is it!" stormed Sandra. "It's a good, honest job. It's not half as degrading as borrowing money from your friends!"

"I'm sick of that, too, but it won't be much longer. If I can just get this damned book finished, I'll have no problems. This book is the answer."

"Answer to what?"

"Everything! I'll get a big advance and pay all my debts. I'll get royalties and maybe I'll make a sale to movies. Meantime, I'll clear up the bullshit to where I can go back to work at the studios—don't you see?"

"Oh, yes, I see—and what if the whole thing's a flop and you don't make a dime and all you have left is a manuscript and a pile of debts?"

"I can't think like that, Sandra. This book has got to be the answer."

"People write books every day—hundreds of them that are never published, Liz. Or hadn't you heard?"

The next day the sanctuary of my studio was violated by a visit from Alice Allison.

"As your parole officer, I must tell you that the probation office is unhappy about your not holding a regular job," she said. "We would like you to get one right away. As it stands, you have no visible means of support."

"But what does that matter? I've painted over thirty paintings. I'm sure I can sell some of them. And I'm writing a book."

"We don't approve of your borrowing money from friends, as you state on your report. This is no way to live, and no good can come of it. You must break this pattern and get a regular job."

"Well, if you insist, I guess I can go back to night clubs, damn it."

"No, I'm not suggesting night clubs. I think they're a bad influence. That's where you met those gangsters in the first place, wasn't it? There are plenty of respectable nine-to-five jobs a girl can get to support herself if she makes the effort, Liz."

"Gee, Mrs. Allison, you sound more like my mother every day. If you don't approve of night clubs, what job do you suggest for me? Tell me—suggest something. How about modeling? Do you think that would be respectable enough?"

"It's certainly not what I had in mind, but it's better than working in bars. I think it would be fine as long as the work is steady."

"Okay, I'll see if I can line up some modeling assignments."

"You'll feel better when you start standing on your own two feet again, Liz. Wait and see," she said, as I let her out the door.

I wished the probation office, Sandra, and everybody else would leave me alone. All I wanted to do was write. Maybe it was an escape from reality. Maybe I was retreating into a fantasy world the way I did with my picture stories as a child.

I liked the safe, serene world of pencils and paper. The world outside was harder to understand. It seemed to push and pull me like a puppet on a string. Why couldn't I do something right just once in my life—something that everyone would approve of, rather than belittle? Just once, maybe I'd make a decision that wouldn't bring criticism down upon my head.

Why did so many people make it their business to run my life? Why couldn't I do as I pleased with my life—my body, my mind? After all, they belonged to me, didn't they?

I called Sandra. "Guess what Alice Allison suggested I do?"

"Do tell me. I can hardly wait!"

"She says the probation office does not condone borrowing money from friends. She says my book is a pastime, not an occupation. She suggests I get a nine-to-five job. She'd rather I'd teach a Sunday School class, but she agrees that modeling will do if it's regular. She says I have no visible means of support. Hell, I don't even have an invisible means!"

"Don't joke. This is serious. You've got to do what she says or she'll make trouble for you. Look, Honey, you have already done half your probation. It would be dumb to foul up now with only eighteen months to go. Why don't you take a regular job for a while just to please her?"

So it was that Sandra took me job hunting next morning. We put applications on file with all the leading employment agencies. We went on interviews and filed applications.

Soon we were flooded with phone calls wanting to know if I was the notorious Liz Renay of the headlines—the one involved with gangsters. But, none wanting to hire me.

Finally, it happened. One of the offices where I had applied for a job called me and told me to report for work the following Monday. It was for a daytime hostess job in a Beverly Hills restaurant. That should keep Alice Allison happy. I whistled on my way to work that sunny Monday morning. I felt great as I strolled along the sidewalk in my crisp shirtwaist dress, ready to begin my role playing hostess.

I knew something was wrong the minute I entered the restaurant. It was too quiet, and the vibrations were all wrong. The manager walked toward me with a worried look on his tightlipped face.

"Miss Renay, I'm sorry—you understand, don't you— we just can't employ you under the circumstances—the publicity—you know—the notoriety. Pardon my being blunt, but in your case one doesn't know what may happen next, and with your suspended sentence this very moment —you just aren't a reliable employment risk—with our training program we can't afford—"

"I understand what you're trying to say," I cut in.

I was furious. "Sandra, it's become a challenge. I'm going to get a steady job if it kills me—anywhere—doing anything—just so it's a job."

"Okay, Liz, I know one place that won't look down their nose about your suspended sentence or publicity. There's a real slum of a street in Los Angeles near the Statler Hotel where customers are the roughest crowd you ever laid eyes on. This street is peppered with a lot of little bars. They're always advertising for barmaids to run the joints during daytime hours."

"What's a barmaid?"

"The female equivalent of a bartender. All you'd have to do is learn to mix a few drinks. Most people order beer in those joints, or whiskey straight, nothing fancy. These are little hole-in-the-wall spots with nothing but a jukebox and a pinball machine. It'll be a snap. There aren't more than twenty-five bar stools. They use two girls to a bar."

"Any special reason for your brilliant recommendation that I work in a dive?"

"That's simple. Everyone else is scared to hire you. These people won't be. They'll put you on a pedestal and treat you like a queen. To them, Mickey Cohen's a big hero—a little tin god."

"What makes you think Alice Allison will approve of a God-awful place like that?"

"Let's face it, Honey, what can she say? She told you to get a regular, steady, daytime job, didn't she? Well, technically this fills the bill. As long as you are working regular hours at a steady job, she can't say anything. Look at it this way—even if she disapproves so much she makes you quit, she can't say you didn't try, and your probation report will show that at least you made the effort."

"Okay, I'll do it. I hope she does make me quit. Then maybe I can write my book in peace."

"Yeah, this job will make borrowing money from friends look like taking up a church collection," Sandra chuckled.

That day I looked for work as a barmaid. At the first place I applied, I got a job. When I walked into the dark smoke-filled bar, the customers nearly choked on their beer. They whistled and yelled, and the owner was impressed.

"Wonderful!" he shouted above the voices of the eager customers. "You got yourself a job, Blondie. You can start tomorrow."

"Fine, what shall I wear?"

"Wear slacks and sweater, the tighter, the better. What's your name, Blondie?"

"Liz Renay."

"Liz Renay? You gotta be kidding! You ain't Liz Renay. She'd never work in a spot like this—that girl's loaded."

"Yeah, she's Mickey Cohen's girl friend."

"If you're Liz Renay, why don't ya ask Mickey for money?"

"Look," I said, "I'm not that Liz Renay. I just happen to have the same name. My name's Elizabeth Renay—no connection."

"Okay," said the owner. "Boy, If I had a name like that, I'd change it. Can't do you no good."

"Why?" I asked.

"For the same reason I'd change my name if it was Al Capone or John Dillinger. Anyway, you be here at 10:30 in the morning with your Social Security card, ready to start. And don't forget the tight sweater!"

I thanked him and left. My skin crawled. There was something about the place that made me want to scratch. Wait till Alice Allison got a load of this job.

The next day I put on a pair of tight red capris and a white angora sweater and set off to work at my new job. I got there before opening time. There wasn't a customer in the place. The owner was chatting with a well-dressed gentleman of about fifty-five.

"Hi, Blondie, come say hello to the sanitation commissioner," he said.

I strolled up, smiling. The smile froze on my face as I

noticed the way the gray-haired man was staring at me and nodding.

"This is our new barmaid," said the owner. "Ain't she a knockout?"

"You're Liz Renay," the commissioner said. "I knew you as soon as you walked in the door. What are you doing in a place like this?"

"Wait a minute. You mean to say Blondie here really is Liz Renay? *The* Liz Renay?"

"Look, I'm here because I want a job. I want to earn a living. What the hell difference does it make if my name is Liz Renay or Sadie Glutz?"

"It makes a damn big difference to me, Blondie. You're a good-looking dame and I'd love to hire you, but I don't want no trouble. You're in a lotta hot water, see. All I gotta do is put you behind my bar and cops will be swarmin' all over my joint. I got enough trouble with cops as it is. No offense, Honey, but no job."

I looked at him for a long moment before his words really sank in. Could it be true? I was being turned down for a job in a dive like this? My face flushed with anger. I stepped out into the street, hot tears stinging my eyes. I didn't want to go into another bar in this crummy area to use a phone, but I'd have to call a cab to get out of the Godforsaken place. About a block away I found a coffee shop with a telephone.

As I entered the coffee shop, a hand touched my elbow. "Mind if I join you for a cup of coffee?" said a voice from behind me.

I turned and found myself staring into the cool, gray eyes of the Sanitation Commissioner. "I'd like to talk to you," he said.

"Okay, why not?" I answered, as I slid into a booth. We

ordered coffee and doughnuts, and then he leaned forward and reached for my hand. I quickly withdrew it.

"Liz, you're a beautiful woman. It's a damned shame you got all messed up the way you did. I'm sorry I put the squelch on your job, but that rat race is not for you, anyway. You need a job with a little more class. I'd like to help you if you'd let me."

"Oh, and how's that?"

"I know a lot of club owners. I could recommend you to one and not tell them you're Liz Renay."

"What about my Social Security card?"

"You'll have to get one under a different name. Use your maiden name or something. What the hell. Meantime, how about dinner tonight? I really want to help you, Honey, but how about us getting to know each other a little better first?"

I burst into laughter. "You really think I've hit the skids, don't you? You think I'm so desperate for a job that I'll do anything, right? Well, I've got news for you. I don't need this crap! I've got friends who will lend me the money I need. If you think I'm going to play fun-in-bed games with you just to land a skid-row job, you're wack-a-ding-ho!"

I called Sandra when I got home. "You can forget about those goddamned dives. They don't want me, either. They have too much heat. They're afraid I'll bring the police department down on their heads."

"It's okay, Honey. That's out, anyway. I was about to call you. I've got you an audition in a cute little club in Beverly Hills as a singer. The lady who owns the club knows you're Liz Renay and doesn't give a damn. She admires you and thinks you deserve a break. You won't be the feature. You'll be one of the regulars on the show. That way, you can stay indefinitely."

"But Sandra, you forget one thing. It's one thing to toss

off a little special material in my act or run through a comedy parody or two, but to get up there and sing straight numbers—you really have to be a singer, which we both know I'm not."

"Look, Baby, it's a job! So you're no Eydie Gorme. So you'll just have to fake it!"

"But—but—"

"Don't worry, Liz, you'll knock 'em dead. If you step out on that stage in a wild-looking gown, nobody'll give a damn if your singing's not the greatest. You can sell a song, Honey—I know you can."

"Sandra, you're giving me a hell of a handicap to overcome but I'll try."

When I stepped under the spotlight, I was happy to see that the room was sprinkled with familiar faces. Actors, actresses, and studio people made up much of the audience. A sigh of relief swept over me. Show people were kind and generous to beginners.

I began my first song with confidence. I had fun with it. I know my performance was mediocre, but what the hell! I was among friends.

"Yea! More! Great!" yelled actor Charlie Bronson, from a front table. Soon his whole group joined in. "Wonderful! Terrific!"

Next I chose a funny parody from my comedy routine. It brought the house down. From that point on, I could do no wrong. They didn't want to let me off the stage.

The owner was impressed. "You're going to do fine here, Honey," she said. "You can start Monday."

I went home on a high-flying cloud. I could hardly wait for the weekend to go by so Monday would roll around. What fun doing songs for the show crowd—and getting paid for it! Alice Allison would stop nagging, Sandra would be happy, and I'd have a ball.

Monday morning the telephone woke me. I grabbed it happily.

It was the club owner's voice. "Liz, dear," she said, "I hate to tell you this, but I'm not going to be able to use you in my club after all. Sheriff Pritchard of Beverly Hills paid me a visit over the weekend. To put it bluntly, he doesn't want you in Beverly Hills."

"But what does he have to say about where I work?"

"Well, Honey, it's like this. He says any club that hires you will have Mickey Cohen and every hoodlum from Los Angeles hanging around. He warned me that, if I value my license, I'd better cancel your booking and keep that riff-raff out of Beverly Hills."

"Well, I'll be goddamned. The probation department insists I get a job, and the police department refuses to let me work. Well, the hell with it! If you want to let him intimidate, you go ahead. As for me, I'm going to call Pritchard and give him a piece of my mind!"

"I'd rather you didn't."

"I'm sorry, but I've got to tell that son of a bitch to go to hell. This has got to stop some place!"

I got Sheriff Pritchard on the phone right away. "Hello, Killjoy, this is Liz Renay. Thanks a lot for lousing up the job."

"I don't know what you're talking about. All I did was offer the club owner some good advice," he answered self-righteously.

"Why don't you leave the advice to Ann Landers and go catch criminals? Isn't that what you're getting paid for?"

"I don't have to listen to your insults, Renay!"

"That's right. You can hang up and avoid this problem the way you're avoiding other problems by shoving it back to Chief Parker's territory in Los Angeles. It sure makes your job easier, doesn't it?"

"How I do my job is none of your concern."

"When you refuse me the right to work in Beverly Hills, that concerns me plenty."

"Look, I didn't force that club owner not to use you. I only advised."

"Oh, don't tell me we're back to the Ann Landers bit! You should be real proud of yourself!"

I hung up the phone before he had a chance to reply. Then I jumped out of bed, dressed, and started out in search of a job again.

I came home feeling jubilant—like skipping and running and jumping for joy!

I dialed Sandra's number. "Hey, Sandra, guess what? I've got a job. I start tomorrow. Wait till Alice Allison hears about this one—she'll flip."

"Yeah, what is it this time? Selling narcotics to school kids?"

"Sandra, be serious—I'm not kidding. I got a swell job in a doctor's office. I'll be working as a receptionist and telephone girl. Also, he said I can assist him."

"You're not a nurse. Assist him with what?"

"I don't know. He said he'd explain everything to me tomorrow. I can't wait to let Allison know."

"Before you tell Allison, work there a few days—see how you like it. Just in case something goes wrong."

"Oh, all right, but nothing can go wrong this time. You see, this doctor knows I'm Liz Renay and doesn't care one bit. He wants to help me."

"Where'd you meet him? How did this job come about?"

"You'd never guess how it all happened! I was out backtracking on some of the jobs I applied for. I wanted to find out if all the turn-downs were really on account of Mickey Cohen."

"You already knew that. I don't get it."

"I wasn't completely sure about some of them. I wanted to double check. I kept thinking—if just one will hire me, just one, that's really all I need. Anyway, I was sitting in the outer office of one place waiting to go in and this doctor was also waiting. We got into a conversation and, first thing you know, I was telling him my problem with the Mickey Cohen notoriety. He suddenly leaned forward and said, 'Look, Liz, you can start to work tomorrow for me. You'll be my receptionist and assistant!' Imagine that!"

"I hope it's all right, Liz. You're a beautiful girl and he may have hired you just as an excuse to be near you."

"Oh, Sandra, don't make intrigue out of everything."

I looked through my wardrobe and found the plain, white linen sheath that reminded everyone of a nurse's uniform. I put it on and practically floated to work the next morning in a rosy cloud of anticipation.

Dr. Ettington's office was small, and it was immediately apparent that we were all alone. He was quick to explain. "I gave my nurse the morning off so I'd have the opportunity for a long talk with you, Miss Renay."

"Well, here I am, ready and willing to learn," I said.

"Yes," he cleared his throat. "Yes, well, first of all I want you to know I don't mind you being Liz Renay nor do I object to your underworld connections. In fact, that's part of the reason I hired you."

"Part of the reason you hired me?"

"Listen, Renay, you and I will be a hell of a team. We can do fabulously together—wait and see."

"Dr. Ettington. I don't know what you have in mind, but all I need is a job so that I can list it on my monthly report to make my probation officer happy."

"Monthly report? Probation officer? Now, just a minute —that's one thing we can't have. You can't say you're working for me, understand? I don't want it to appear on my books, or anything. I'll have to pay you under the table, but don't worry, you'll make plenty."

"You don't seem to understand my problem, Doctor." I said. "I'm on probation. I have to have a visible means of support."

"Look, Renay, we'll think of some way to get around that. Meantime, listen to my idea. I specialize in abortions. I'm willing to cut you in for 25 percent of all the clients you steer my way through your connections. You know the underworld. Think of all the Las Vegas show girls, call girls, and prostitutes needing abortions. All you've got to do is pass the word around for them to send the girls to you. We'll have all we can handle! We can do eight to ten a morning at $500 a crack. Do you understand what that kind of money means?"

My heart sank. "Doctor, all I wanted was a receptionist job. I don't want to get into abortions."

"Nonsense, of course you do! Just wait till you pass the word around."

I flew to the elevator. I couldn't wait to get back to the sanity of my apartment.

The next week I had more offers—lots of them. Offers to be kept—propositions and chances to get chased around offices—but no one offered me what I wanted—a plain, ordinary job, with no strings attached.

Chapter 27

DISTURBING THE PEACE—
AND A PEACEKEEPER

The outlook was grim. Then, to top everything, one day when I was passing through another large city, I was picked up for questioning. Although it was very obvious to the assistant district attorney that I knew nothing about what they were interested in, the probing persisted.

The two of us sat alone in his office. "Listen," I said, "I'd very much appreciate it if you would let me go. You know I have nothing to do with this case."

"Yes, I can well understand why you'd prefer not to be connected, considering all the publicity it may involve," he said, gazing at my cleavage.

Publicity was just what I was afraid of. I hadn't been able to get probation office permission to leave California, so I had sneaked off without it. It could mean serious trouble if it came to light.

"I could probably fix this, Miss Renay," he continued, "if I had a strong enough motive to do so."

"Like what?"

"Like you'd have to go to bed with me."

I excused myself and hastened to the district attorney's private office, very much annoyed.

"I understand you wanted to see me, Miss Renay," the D.A. said.

"Yes, I thought you'd be interested in knowing that your

310

assistant, Mr. Joseph Whalen, said that he could fix it so I'd be released, if I'd go to bed with him. Is that true?"

"He couldn't fix it, Liz," the D.A. said, leaning forward over his desk. "It's me you'll have to go to bed with. I'm the one who can fix it."

He was right. He could fix it and he did.

Back in Los Angeles, I remained jobless.

I was ready to give up hope when a knock sounded at the door. It was Brenda and Leo.

"Hey, Mums!" called Leo. "My boss is dying to meet you. He wants you to pose for a swimming pool ad. He says he has a great job for you that could last a year."

"Yes," echoed Brenda. "He uses the name Phil Starr, though that's not his real name. He's a big fan of yours. He remembers you from your play *Good Night, Ladies*."

"Great! If this job works out, it will solve my problem. When did you start working for a swimming pool company, Leo?"

"When the job with Joe Collins ran out, this job came along. I'm on the crew that digs the holes for pools. It's very similar to the construction work I did for Joe."

Brenda, Leo, and I met Phil Starr for dinner that evening.

He discussed the plans he had for expanding his company. He said he needed to bring in more capital and launch an extensive advertising campaign with good publicity shots to show prospective investors. He said he wanted a shot of me wearing the bath-towel costume I wore on stage in *Good Night, Ladies*. He thought it would be more exciting than an ordinary swim-suit shot.

"What we need is something a little different," he smiled.

Soon the subject of money came up, which was of paramount importance to me. Starr suggested a fee of $50, and my heart sank. When I was a New York fashion model, an assignment like this brought at least $250.

My disappointment must have been showing because Starr quickly explained that these first shots were only tests to see how I looked in the bath towel. He said that later, when I posed for magazine ads, I could make as much as $200 for an afternoon's shooting and, if they decided to use me for television commercials, I could make hundreds of dollars.

"If everything goes the way I plan it," he said, "you'll be the symbol of California Pools coast to coast. We'll make you the 'California Pools Girl' and put you on a retainer."

"Well, that sounds good," I said.

A few days later I met Phil Starr for dinner. I pressed him to hurry with the arrangements.

"I'll introduce you to my partner," he said. "He helps plan our advertising. He'll love you. He'll be all for the idea."

When I met Starr next, he was with his partner.

"I think Miss Renay is lovely, and the idea sounds fine," the partner said.

Soon Phil Starr called me.

"Liz," he said, "I'll pick you up in an hour and take you to the pool at Travel Lodge. I'll have old Zade meet us there to grab some quick test shots of you in the bath towel. Okay?"

I glanced at my watch. It was 2:00 P.M. I hadn't had lunch. "Gee, Phil, I'm starved! Will we have time for a fast sandwich before the pictures?"

"Of course, Honey," he said. "We'll have a bite to eat with Williams. Then we'll take care of business."

Phil picked me up and we drove to the Wild Goose Tavern, where we met his partner.

I ordered a steak sandwich. The two men ordered a

procession of drinks. They seemed intent on drinking the tavern dry.

At first I tried to get Phil to stop drinking and get on with our project. I finally began to feel like a nagging wife, and he obviously was beginning to think of me as one, so I decided to play it cool, relax, and drop the subject. If he wanted to goof the afternoon off drinking, who was I to stop him? Better to go along with things and not make him angry. I needed this assignment too badly.

Finally, in defense against sheer boredom, I joined the men by ordering a drink myself. And another and another.

When it was 7:00 o'clock and we were all half smashed, Starr went to the phone and when he returned, said he had called the photographer and told him to meet us at the Travel Lodge to take the pictures.

"But Phil," I protested, "I'm half looped. Besides, it will soon be dark. The sun will be down. How can we get good pictures?"

"Don't worry about it, Baby," he slurred. "These are only test shots, and the Travel Lodge pool is lit up like a Christmas tree. We can do pictures just fine."

His partner left us, saying he had to be home for dinner.

Soon we were careening down the road to the Travel Lodge.

"Take it easy!" I said, as we nearly sideswiped another car.

We came to a screeching halt in front of the Travel Lodge, and Phil lumbered out to register. Soon he was unlocking the door to Room 8.

When we got inside the door, he began to undress. Off came the pants, the belt buckle clanging as it hit the floor. He flung his coat on a chair, yanked off his tie, and was stripping off his shirt, when I said, "Mr. Starr, what the hell are you doing?"

"Don't give me that corny stuff, Baby," he said thickly. "You came to the motel with me. You ain't no kid. You know the score. We'll take the pictures. But let's have a little fun first!"

Goddamn it, why did some men have to be such animals? I looked at Phil standing drunkenly before me in nothing but his shorts. I felt ill. I felt more ill when he staggered toward me, his hot whiskey breath in my face.

He was short and stocky, with a pot belly and graying hair. If he looked like Clark Gable, he'd be no bargain in that drunken state. But Gable, Phil Starr was not! I decided to pass, regardless of the consequences. The next problem was how to placate him—not make him angry.

The best approach seemed to be to stall him somehow. He was so drunk that maybe I'd get lucky and he'd pass out, fall asleep or something.

I said, "Sure, Phil, we'll have fun. Only let's take the pictures first before you mess up my hairdo. Okay? Now be a nice guy and call and find out what's holding up the photographer."

It worked. Phil staggered across the room to the telephone. "Get in that damn towel then," he tossed over his shoulder, "and make it snappy."

He dialed a number. I slipped out of the dress I was wearing and into the bath towel he wanted. Just as I was trying to get the darned thing fastened, there was a knock at the door. I panicked. I dived under the covers of the bed as Phil staggered to the door.

"Phil!" I yelled. "You're not dressed! Hold it a minute!"

"It's just the photographer," he said, and pulled open the door.

I wrapped up in the bedspread and sat like a chenille mummy in the middle of the bed as two well-dressed young men burst into the room.

I was embarrassed with Phil parading around in his shorts. I could imagine what the photographers must be thinking.

"Do either of you have a safety pin?" I asked. "My towel is falling off!"

They looked blank. "Your what?"

"Oh, never mind. Look, fellows, Phil's a bit under the weather. Let's get on with the pictures."

"What pictures?" asked one of the young men.

"You are the photographers, aren't you?"

"No, lady, we're the vice squad," he said, producing credentials. "What's your name, miss?"

Oh my God, no! Not the vice squad! There stood Phil in his shorts.

As I sat wrapped in my bedspread cocoon, I wondered what the next move was. What could I do? How could I get out of this? If only I could turn back the clock from the time I left for the Wild Goose Tavern. How could I get away before they discovered I was Liz Renay? How could I run in this bath towel? The window—the bathroom window. That was the answer. I'd ask to get dressed, go in to get my clothes, and escape through the bathroom window. They would have to let me go get my clothes.

I stood up, letting the bedspread fall away, revealing the bath towel with its snaps popping.

"Mind if I put my clothes on?" I said.

"Guess you'll have to. You can't go to headquarters wearing a towel."

"Headquarters? Hold on! You've no charge against me," I said. I started for the bathroom.

One of the officers stepped in front of me, blocking the door. "Oh, no, you don't," he said. "We'll give you your clothes and you can dress in that closet there. It doesn't have windows."

He handed me my things. "What's your name, lady?"

"Sally Jones."

"That's unlikely. You'd better tell us the truth, lady, because we'll find out," the officer said, as he grabbed my purse and dumped everything out on the bed.

"Oh God," I thought, "there went the ball game!" My purse was full of Liz Renay identification—my Screen Actors Guild card, for openers. This would bring the probation department down on my head. Why had I listened to Alice Allison? Why hadn't I stayed home and written my book? Why hadn't I continued borrowing from friends? So what, if the probation department didn't like it! They couldn't revoke my probation for that. But, with this stupid situation, God knows what they'd do. Maybe they'd charge me with indecent exposure. If so, I could beat the charge. After all, I wore the same costume on the legitimate stage. God, what a mess! If only I could turn time back just one day, twelve little hours, and start over again!

When I was dressed, I stepped from the closet and saw that Phil Starr had managed to get into his clothes too.

The two officers were examining the contents of my purse. They were engrossed with the list I'd written while I was waiting for Phil. I explained the items to them. After all, there was nothing on the list to hide. They tried to twist my notations around and put words in my mouth, but I was quick to correct them.

Then they picked up my identification cards. I expected startled reactions—maybe even looks of delight when they realized what a notorious fish they had in their net.

They glanced at the I.D. matter of factly, registering no surprise at all. "Well, what do you know? Liz Renay. So your name wasn't Sally Jones after all," one of them said. "How about that!"

Why weren't they surprised? Were they following me, just waiting for a chance like this? Or did Phil set me up? Was he working with the police department? Why did he go to the door in his shorts and where was the goddamned photographer we were supposed to be meeting?

"We're taking you downtown, Miss Renay. You're under arrest."

"Under arrest for what?"

"Your name is Liz Renay. Miss Liz Renay, as I recall. You're registered here as Mr. and Mrs. Grant. Single persons can't go to a motel and register as man and wife, you know. It's against the law. There's a law on the books called resorting."

"Resorting. I never heard of it. I didn't register here as anything. This is not my room. I don't know whose name it's under."

"Whether you heard of resorting or not doesn't make it any less legal. You don't hear about it because it probably hasn't been used in twenty years, but it's still a law. It's a morals law. Resorting means checking into a motel for immoral purposes."

"Wait a minute now. There wasn't a damn thing immoral about my purpose. This was strictly business. I came here to do a modeling assignment."

"In a bath towel?"

"You're damned right!"

"Okay, Liz, you can tell that to the judge."

Phil Starr and the officers held several whispered conferences, and then we were hustled off to the police station.

We were questioned again at the station. Phil spent his time whispering to one of the officers in a corner. Finally, the officer stepped away from the huddle.

"Mr. Starr has agreed to plead guilty to resorting. That way, he will be able to pay a ten-dollar fine and go home. Would you like to do likewise?"

"Hell, no! I won't plead guilty. Why should I plead guilty? I'm not guilty and neither is he!"

I turned to Phil. "Phil, are you crazy? Why are you pleading guilty? We're not guilty of anything!"

Phil hung his head. He couldn't look at me. "It's better for me like this. I can't fight it. I'm a married man with a family. I'm a businessman. Can't afford the publicity. This way, I pay the fine, go home, and forget it. No one will know."

"Don't do it! Please, Phil, don't do it! Don't you see how you're jeopardizing me?"

"Sorry, Liz, it's the only thing I can do. I gotta think of my wife and family."

"Damn it, if you'd thought of them, you'd have kept your stupid pants on and we wouldn't be in this mess."

"Sorry, I guess I drank too much."

"Look, Phil, the least you could do is fight this thing. It is your fault, you know."

"I know and I guess I'm a heel, but I'll have to do what's best for me," he said, with lowered eyes. Then he was gone.

I was escorted to the Lincoln Heights Jail, where I was fingerprinted and searched. I was allowed one phone call. I called a bail bondsman I knew through Mickey Cohen.

Soon I was breathing free air again, but it would only be a matter of days before the case would come up before a city judge.

I went home with my mind in a whirl. I called Brenda and Leo. "Leo, how long have you worked for Phil Starr?" I asked.

"Oh, about three weeks. Why?"

"I just wondered. How did you happen to go to work for him?"

"As a matter of fact, it all started over a conversation about you. One day I was showing your picture around and talking about what a fantastic mother-in-law I had. No one would believe me. They thought I was pulling their leg. Then this guy, Phil, walks up and starts saying what a Liz Renay fan he is and starts asking all kinds of questions about you."

"What kind of questions?"

"Oh, what you were doing and if you were appearing in any more plays or night clubs at the moment. He raved about *Good Night, Ladies* and the costume you wore and said he'd like to see you if you were appearing anywhere. Then he asked me if I'd like to go to work for him."

"Is that all?"

"Yes, as far as I remember. Why? Is anything wrong?"

"Yes, plenty's wrong. I'll tell you about it when I see you."

The next day I went to see Mickey Cohen. "Mickey, the goddamnedest thing happened to me last night."

"Yes, Honey, I heard about it. Someone ought to break that creep's neck."

"Mickey, I don't know what to make of it. The man took me to the Travel Lodge and said his photographer would meet us there. He said he'd pay me $50 to pose in a bath towel in front of the swimming pool. He sells pools. Then he jumps out of his clothes. There's a knock at the door—he's there in his shorts—I tell him not to answer the door—he rushes and opens it, anyway. We're expecting a photographer, and who walks in but the damned vice squad? Doesn't that sound like a setup to you?"

"Honey, I've been trying to figure it out ever since the bail bondsman called me. Obviously, the vice squad was following you, but where this Phil Starr character fits in, I don't know."

"Mickey, could you check out Phil Starr for me? I'd like to know everything I can about this guy. Will you do that for me?"

"Of course I will, Doll. I'll get you a complete rundown in a couple of days."

I had to think fast. When I returned home, a card was thumbtacked to my door. It read, "Robert Hermann, Attorney at Law." He was a friend of Joe Collins. I turned the card over. A message was scrawled on the back. "If you need any help, just call me." I'd take him up on his offer. Maybe he could figure this mess out.

When I stepped inside my apartment, I heard the shower running. Who was it? What in heaven's name was going on now? I hurried to the bathroom. As I reached for the door, a youthful voice stopped me. "Don't come in, Mom," he called. "I'm taking a shower."

Good heavens, Johnny was home. I hadn't expected him for another week. What an awful time for him to arrive! Maybe I could hide it from him. I'd have him in school within the week. If only the timing worked in my favor, maybe Robert Hermann could get a postponement and push the matter ahead on the calendar a little.

The doorbell rang. It was Brenda and Leo. Leo had heard the details on the job. The pool company was buzzing with it.

"Boy, is Phil Starr taking it on the chin," he said. "His men are really giving him a bad time over this. He feels like a heel. I swear I thought he was going to break down and cry while he was talking about it today. He can't even look at me."

"Leo, do you think it's at all possible he could have set me up for the police?"

"Not a chance. There are guys there that have known him for fifteen years. He's just a chaser out for a good time, that's all. He sure didn't plan this, I'll guarantee you that. It's causing him too much hell. His wife is threatening to leave him. His son isn't speaking to him, and his men are ribbin' the hell out of him. On top of that, he's been receiving threatening calls. Because of your background, he's convinced the threats are real. He's the most frightened and miserable guy alive."

I picked up the phone and called Mickey Cohen. "Forget about checking on Phil Starr. Leo works there and from what he tells me, I think Starr is a blundering stumble-bum, but not a police informer. By the way, if you're the one making the threatening phone calls to him, stop it, for heaven's sake!"

Then, quickly, the day arrived. Robert Hermann escorted me to the Los Angeles courtroom. I was greeted by the city attorney, Ed Davenport. He was surprisingly young and handsome. "Liz," he said, "I am embarrassed for my department. The resorting law went out along with high-button shoes, as far as I'm concerned. It's like the law that states you can't hitch a horse on Main Street on Sunday. I don't doubt you'd win your case if you fought it, but your attorney tells me how much you dread the unfavorable publicity. If you agree to plead guilty, we'll drop the resorting charge and reduce it to a simple 'disturbing-the-peace' charge. Then you can pay a fine and forget it."

Was it going to be this simple? I had my doubts. "Why reduce it to disturbing the peace? Why not drop it altogether? I'm not guilty. Why should I plead guilty to anything?"

"Only for expediency, Dear. Ask your attorney. He'll explain it to you. You see, I'm not in a position to just drop the matter. It's already before the judge. It will be easier all the way around to reduce it to a lesser charge so it can be disposed of. Disturbing the peace isn't even a law, it's just a city ordinance. It's about as serious as a parking ticket. Surely you couldn't object to pleading guilty to that."

"How about my probation? Can it be revoked on a minor misdemeanor like disturbing the peace?"

"I never heard of a federal case being revoked on a city ordinance. If they revoked a convict's probation every time someone gave him a parking ticket or something, the jails couldn't hold the population."

"Look, we have to be certain. Is it possible for Liz's probation to be revoked on disturbing the peace?" cut in Robert Hermann.

"Such a thing has never happened in the history of the federal probation office. Why don't you call your probation officer and discuss the matter with him?" Davenport suggested.

"That's exactly what I'll do," I answered. I wished Alice Allison hadn't resigned just when I needed her most. I soon had my new probation officer, Mr. George, on the phone. He listened sympathetically, then said, "No, Liz, no one's going to revoke your probation on a disturbing-the-peace charge. You've nothing to worry about."

"Okay—as long as I have your word on it," I replied, with a sigh of relief. I told Robert Hermann that we had the probation department's green light.

"Well, that's a relief," he smiled.

Soon I stepped before the judge, pleaded guilty to disturbing the peace and quiet of the neighborhood, was promptly fined $75 and allowed to go home.

Whew! Was it really over?

Chapter 28

A VOICE ON THE PHONE

The telephone woke me next morning. It was a man who said he worked in the office of Ed Davenport, the city attorney. He was speaking scarcely above a whisper. "Take down this number," he said. "Then go to a phone booth and call me and give me the number of the booth you're calling from. I'll go out and call you there from a pay phone. Get a piece of paper, quick!"

I fumbled in the drawer of my night stand. "Okay, I'm ready."

He repeated the number. "Hurry, Liz, what I have to say is urgent."

I threw on some clothes and rushed to the nearest phone booth. I relayed the number to the strange voice and waited for him to call me back. I wondered what all the intrigue was about. I soon had my answer.

"Liz, I shouldn't be calling you like this, but I just had to. I feel Ed Davenport's partly responsible, since he's the one who advised you to plead guilty to disturbing the peace."

"My God, what is it now? What does Ed Davenport have to do with this?"

"Honey, you're going to jail. You're going away for three years, and those guys are going to make you do every day of it. I'm telling you straight. This will give you a chance to prepare—break up your apartment—send

323

your children away. They'll be picking you up in three days."

"Goddamn it, who are you? What do you mean—I'm going to jail?"

"You don't know me, Liz, but I'm a fan of yours and a friend. United States Attorney Laughlin Waters was so upset when Judge Martin overruled his recommendations in your case and suspended your sentence that he swore he'd revoke it if it was the last thing he did. His office needs a conviction badly in the Mickey Cohen case. They've spent tax money on that investigation for three years without a conviction to show for it. Now you're going to be it. The police have followed you ever since you went on probation trying to catch you in anything you did. They've got you now and they won't let go."

"But Ed Davenport said they wouldn't revoke me and my probation officer, practically guaranteed it."

"Honey, you don't know what you're up against. Laughlin Waters stormed into Davenport's office and practically tore it apart. He said, 'Now I've got her where I want her and I'll see to it she does every minute of that three years!' "

"Well, the judge will have something to say about that. The Waters office tried to send me to prison when I pleaded guilty to perjury, and they couldn't do it. What makes him think he can do it on a disturbing-the-peace charge? He can't get a federal judge to go along with a stupid thing like that."

"Last time you had a visiting judge, Honey. That was different. This time you'll have Judge Hall. Laughlin Waters has Judge Hall in his hip pocket. You don't stand a chance."

"Who are you, anyway?" I asked.

"Let's just say I work in Ed Davenport's office," he said.

"Thanks for the warning, whoever you are." I hung up.

I decided I wasn't giving up yet. I'd call some people and see if I couldn't change the picture. Maybe the judge could be paid off.

I got my answer quickly from the first person I called.

"Not with all the tea in China, Honey. This originates from Robert Kennedy's office."

"Robert Kennedy doesn't know I exist. Why would he fix things against me?"

"Because you're part of the Mickey Cohen case. He's out to get Mickey Cohen and anyone connected with him and will stop at nothing. Kennedy is a zealot out to make a big name for himself. Too bad Davenport suggested you plead guilty to that trumped-up charge. But who could believe they'd be willing to put a thing like this on the records of the federal probation office?"

I hung up the phone feeling sick. How could this be happening? Could Robert Kennedy be so base that he'd smash my life, and send me to prison for three years on a phony disturbing-the-peace charge?

I sent a wire to Walter Winchell. It read:

DEAR WALTER: I'VE BEEN TOLD I WILL BE PICKED UP IN THREE DAYS AND SENT TO PRISON FOR THREE YEARS, DUE TO A PHONY DISTURBING PEACE CHARGE. IS THIS POSSIBLE? CAN YOU HELP ME? WHAT SHALL I DO?   LIZ RENAY

He published the telegram in his column, along with a plea to Governor Brown.

I was in a daze. Should I take the word of my anonymous tipster and break up my apartment? How could I believe him? No, I'd go on as though nothing was wrong and hope for the best.

The next day, Brenda arrived at my apartment, bag and baggage.

"I've left Leo," she announced.

"But, Honey, what happened? Why?"

"It just hasn't worked out, Mom. I guess we were both so young when we got married—and, well, I've been growing up, and Leo seems to stand still. We just don't fit together any more."

"Please think it over carefully, darling. Don't do anything hastily that you'll regret. This is a serious step."

"There's nothing hasty about two years. That's how long I've been thinking it over."

What could I say to Brenda? How could I tell her they might be coming to take me to prison for three years day after tomorrow? How could I tell Johnny?

That evening I cooked the children's favorite dishes and built a fire in the fireplace. It was the last week in March, and the weather was cool and windy. We sat by the cozy fire and talked of pleasant things. We laughed and enjoyed one another. Brenda lay on the floor with her blonde head in my lap. She looked like a little girl. To me, she was still a baby—just a little girl weary from playing a woman's game.

"Oh, Mama, I feel so safe and secure—just like I did when I was a kid. I think this is the happiest I've been since the day I left home—since my wedding day."

I held back my tears. How ironic that we should be together like this on the eve of disaster!

Children, I thought wistfully, tonight is what memories are made of. These are the times we must store in our minds and imaginations to remember when times are not so happy.

"Oh, Mama, I'm so glad to be home," sighed Brenda, stretching like a lazy cat.

"Me, too," smiled Johnny.

God, they were making it hard for me! Tomorrow I'd

have to tell them. Tonight was too lovely to mar. We sat on the floor talking till midnight.

Brenda and Johnny woke me in the morning with a breakfast tray. Breakfast in bed—a nice send-off, I thought to myself, then angrily brushed the thought from my mind. I must stop thinking like that. Perhaps the nightmare would vanish. Brenda helped me tidy up the kitchen, and we all gathered in the living room to watch TV. It was 2:30 P.M.

A knock sounded at the door.

"I'll go, Mom," said Johnny, springing to his feet and bounding eagerly to the door.

"Is your mother home, son?" said a male voice.

"Yes, she is," answered Johnny.

The man identified himself as a federal marshal. There was a policewoman with him. "Won't you come in?" I said.

"You're under arrest and will be held without bail for revocation of your probation for disturbing the peace and quiet of the neighborhood," he read, not believing his own words.

Johnny's face blanched. "How are we disturbing the peace? All we're doing is watching television. Oh, Mom, what does he mean?"

Brenda sank weakly into the nearest chair. She looked as though she'd faint. Suddenly, she buried her head against the side of the chair. I could see her shoulders moving as she silently wept.

"You kids be good till I straighten this out. Take care of each other and keep the doors locked at night. I'll send someone over to look after you real soon. I'll work things out. You won't be deserted. Please don't worry."

I looked at Johnny. A big tear glistened on one cheek. The marshal's face was pale.

"You're allowed one call, Miss Renay," said the police-woman, as she dabbed at her eyes with a handkerchief.

I called Sandra. "Sandra, dear, my children are feeling very low. Will you please do what you can to cheer them up? Call some of my friends and ask them to drop in as often as they can. I'll appreciate it greatly. I wish you'd take them out to dinner tonight and maybe a show."

"I don't understand. What's wrong with the kids? What's wrong with you?"

"Sandra, this is the only phone call I'm allowed. I'll have to count on you. Call Robert Hermann and tell him to meet me at the jail. I'm being held without bail on a dis-turbing the peace charge. They plan to revoke my pro-bation."

I hung up the phone.

The marshal and policewoman and I descended the short flight of steps from my apartment with my children's sobs filling my ears.

"A thing like this is sure hard to figure out," said the marshal between clenched teeth. "I'm sorry, Miss Renay, truly sorry." The policewoman choked, blowing her nose.

My hands were ice-cold and a strange numbness set-tled over me as the marshal's car headed downtown.

Chapter 29

THE HONORABLE JUDGE HALL

Soon we were at the Los Angeles county jail. I was fingerprinted, stripped of all my belongings, and led to the shower room. Before I could begin my shower, a policewoman burst in.

"Not so fast, we have to delouse you."

"Delouse me? There must be some mistake. I don't have lice."

"If you don't you soon will. We delouse everybody when they come in and once a week after. There's no way to keep lice down. Close your eyes."

Holy Cow, there went my champagne blonde hair toner! Next, she handed me a bowl full of something.

"Pour this over your privates," she said. "It will kill the crabs."

"Crabs? Oh, this is ridiculous! I've never had crabs."

"It's part of the procedure, Dearie. You pour it or I will."

I grabbed the bowl into the shower with me and dumped the stuff down the drain.

"You'll be thankful I gave you this, Girlie. It not only kills the crabs you got, it prevents you from catchin' any more—sort of immunizes you."

I stuck my head out from behind the shower curtain, extending the bowl. "May I have a little more? I spilled most of mine."

"Sure—anything to keep the pesky crabs down. But

watch it, be more careful next time. This stuff costs money, you know."

Soon I was led down the long corridor to the cell blocks. Nothing I'd seen or heard about jails prepared me for what I saw. Every bunk was filled. Bodies sprawled all over the floor on filthy canvas mats, and lay on the floor under the bunks. Every time someone moved, dust arose. The filth turned my stomach.

"A place like this shouldn't be allowed to exist," I said to no one in particular. "It's a disgrace to human dignity."

A matron shoved me into a cell. Both bunks were already filled. The officer peered through the cage at me and pointed to a filthy canvas pad on the floor in front of a cruddy commode.

"That's your bed, Princess."

I patted the soggy cotton pad to brush away the surface dirt. Dust billowed out like a cloud. The girl above me started to cough.

"For Christ sakes, I wish these new broads would stop stirring up the dirt every time they come in," she complained.

I settled down on the foul-smelling pile and tried to force myself to sleep amidst the stench and the thrashing bodies. Every time someone turned over, a wave of coughs and sneezes was set off by the dust.

Glaring light from the corridor shone squarely into my eyes, but that was better than putting my face next to the smelly commode. I closed my eyes and tried to sleep. I felt a soft swish of fur across my face. I screamed—and my scream was echoed by a dozen screams as the rodent darted between the canvas pads and across the sleeping bodies.

When I awoke next morning, I felt something slick against my cheek. I lifted my head from the dirty canvas pad. A giant cockroach was smashed against the padding.

"Good Lord," I winced. "I smashed the thing in my sleep and I've been lying on it all night." I put my hand to my cheek. It was sticky with cockroach ooze. I pulled my hand back in horror and rushed to the corroded wash basin to clean it. Cockroaches skittered all over the place. I found one in my oatmeal the next morning. The girls accused the jailers of serving us dog food as a main course. I hopefully doubted this, but couldn't stand to try it with that image in mind. The soup was a tasteless mixture of canned tomatoes, cornstarch, and water.

Brenda, Johnny, and Sandra visited me often, as did my new lawyer, Robert Hermann. They all had to peer through a heavy mesh screen. We could scarcely make each other out. I begged them not to come. I didn't like them to see me looking like a wild woman with my stringy DDT hair, no make-up, and in a shapeless jail uniform, peering through the screen like a caged animal. I was relieved when the matron came to take me before Judge Hall. She returned my clothing and make-up and escorted me to a special room, where I could get dressed for court. What a relief!

Every head turned, every eye stared as the county jail matron led me into the crowded courtroom and seated me on the front bench next to my lawyer. The whole affair seemed ludicrous—a silly pretense. Whoever heard of being in federal court on a disturbing the peace charge?

A sweet young voice floated up to me out of the gloom behind. "Mom, we're here. We want you to know we're here with you."

No mistaking that light, breathy, teen-aged voice. It was Brenda. I turned to pat her hand and saw Johnny seated beside her. A wave of pride swept through me as I looked at them: proud and erect as little tin soldiers. Brenda looked blonde and beautiful in her pretty blue and white dress. Johnny had become quite the young man; he had grown into a Ricky Nelson type, with clear, blue eyes and sandy brown hair.

"I hope we can take you home with us, Mom," he whispered.

"Yes," said Brenda, "we came to take you home. Sandra drove us down."

Sandra's voice piped up from somewhere behind me. "Liz," she whispered, "what am I to do about the party? Tomorrow is your birthday, and we have thirty-five guests coming."

Sandra fretted about everything. She didn't know where her job as manager ended. Truly, it never did, for where the manager ended, the friend began. I smiled back at the little group. "Don't worry, darlings, things always seem to work out."

But would they? I wondered what Judge Hall would be like. I had heard rumors that he was a woman chaser, that he drank heavily, that he let his friends off drunken-driving charges—frequently. I had heard him called an egotist, braggart, and hypocrite. But I wouldn't judge him on hearsay. I only hoped that he would be equally fair with me.

I thought back to Judge Martin, remembering him almost fondly. Fair, open-minded, erudite, and sincere, he would have won my admiration however he had ruled.

This, however, was a different scene. I was in court on a phony disturbing-the-peace charge. I couldn't understand how a federal judge could waste his time on such an insignificant case.

A hush came over the room as Judge Hall entered the room. He was a plump, self-satisfied-looking man, with bulging eyes, several chins, and a hangman's expression on his face. He plopped into his seat.

I glanced behind me for encouragement. Sandra Lane smiled hopefully at me.

The clerk called "Case Number 27,478, United States vs. Liz Renay."

Judge Hall scowled. He asked if I had anything to say.

"Yes, your Honor," I said. "I pled guilty to a disturbing-the-peace charge and paid a fine . . . Before I pled guilty I called my probation officer and asked him how he thought this would affect my probation and he said that he didn't think my probation on a federal case would be revoked for a misdemeanor like this.

"Your Honor, while I have been on probation for eighteen months I have made a lot of mistakes, not intentional mistakes, but I could have done things more wisely than I have.

"I have tried during these eighteen months to resurrect my shattered career. It has been a difficult job. I have done during this period four rather successful night-club engagements, I have nearly completed a book, and enough paintings to have an exhibit. Outside of that, everything I have tried has backfired, due to this terrible publicity I've had.

"I would have been wiser to have taken a steady job to support myself and my children. However, I have a number of good friends who believe in me and have been willing to help me by lending me money."

Judge Hall interjected: "These are men friends?"

"Men, yes, most of them."

"And they loan you a hundred dollars or so?"

"Larger amounts than that sometimes," I said.

"Sometimes?"

"Whatever I happen to need. I have discussed with my probation officer that I have been borrowing money from friends to hold me until my career gradually rights itself."

Judge Hall asked another question. "I don't quite understand this borrowing," he said. "You were arrested and
charged with resorting with a man. According to the
police report you were in a motel room and you were not
married to him. Is it after such an occasion as that that
these people loan you money?"

"I never borrowed any money from that fellow and
never intended to," I explained.

"I mean other friends. I think you stated that you borrowed from quite a few people."

"That is true."

"About $50 or $100, usually after an act of sexual intercourse, is that right?"

I shuddered as I felt the implications of the judge's statement. He had already in his own mind and without a scrap
of evidence, decided that I was a prostitute—a $50 hooker.
He persisted: "Is that a fact?"

"No!" I declared.

Judge Hall bore in: "Well, is it a fact that that is the way
that you borrow from friends?"

"No. The people I borrow money from aren't even in
this town, do not reside in this city . . ."

"What happened to this marriage that you told Judge
Martin was going to take place . . . ?"

"I had every intention of marrying Mr. Collins at that
time. Circumstances caused the marriage not to come
about."

"What circumstances? Is he still supporting you?"

"No."

"Is he still paying your rent?"

"Mr. Collins is now married to another girl and I am not
in touch with him," I said.

"You haven't answered my question. You said he was

married to another girl. He can be married to another girl and still be contributing to you."

"He isn't."

This didn't satisfy the judge. He seemed to consider it an affront to the court that I hadn't married Joe. He asked about Joe's divorce decree.

"There is a period of waiting of one year in California," I explained.

Judge Hall shook his head. "Not when it is a final decree, and I cannot only say that as having experience as a lawyer, but from having had four divorces myself, so I know a little bit about the divorce law."

A wave of laughter swept through the courtroom. Some of the spectators were surprised at a federal judge making a joke of his divorces in open court.

My attorney, Robert Herrmann made his plea. "Your Honor," he said, "Miss Renay's past history is completely devoid of arrests, with the exception of the perjury conviction. . . . Other than that one conviction, Miss Renay has absolutely no history of trouble with the law. Her history for the past seven or eight years has been followed assiduously by the newspapers. There is Miss Renay's public image, which I believe to be a fiction and a myth, due to her unfortunate association with Mr. Cohen. Her entrance into the show business world was as a moderator for a Fordham University program in New York, a type of discussion program of intellectuals and artists. Because of her natural attributes, her normal place was before the public.

"She came to Hollywood three or four years ago, embarked upon a career, was given screen tests and—"

The judge cut in: "When she came to Hollywood she was met by Mr. Cohen."

After that, he scarcely seemed to listen. Nevertheless, Hermann continued, trying vainly to capture the judge's ear and reach his heart.

Ignoring my attorney, Judge Hall spoke to me. "If you had so little to do with Mickey Cohen, why did you give him checks for $5,000?"

"This seemed at the time a simple favor I was doing," I said.

"You considered it a simple favor to give Mickey Cohen $5,000?" He snorted.

"I did not give him anything. I merely allowed him to use my New York bank."

"You gave him a check."

"Yes, and someone deposited money to cover those checks in my account. It was just a matter of allowing him the convenience of using my bank."

"I don't understand . . ."

I was overcome with frustration when Bob Herrmann spoke up again. In a loud, clear voice, he said, "Your Honor, the Mickey Cohen thing ruined Miss Renay's career in Hollywood. It came to a screeching halt. But be that as it may, her entire past history does not indicate she is of a criminal nature or a menace to society that would dictate that she not be released, subject to court conditions."

The attitude of the judge changed ninety degrees when the U.S. Attorney stood up.

"Just a few points, your Honor," he said. "The mutual friend in New York who put Miss Renay in contact with Mr. Cohen was a gentleman by the name of Champ Segal, who has quite a reputation in New York. The other one was a gentleman by the name of Tony Coppola. Miss Renay went with Mr. Coppola a number of times and was called his girl friend. Tony Coppola was the bodyguard of Albert Anastasia, who was murdered in a New York barber chair . . . Tony Coppola has just pleaded guilty in New York to income tax evasion . . ."

"I think I would like to have testimony about whether she is living a life of sin," the Judge said. He turned to me again: "Have you had an income of $1,600 or $1,700 a month as reported to the probation officer?"

"I have reported my income exactly as it has been," I replied.

The Judge asked: "What does it amount to, Mr. Probation Officer?"

The Probation Officer tried to explain. He said: "Some months the average amounts to $600 and $700 and expenditures probably around close to $1,000, some months the income is over $1,000 but it is always $700, $800, $900."

Bob Hermann seized upon a pause to clarify what had just been said. "There is no disagreement there, your Honor. We agree that she has received the sums as reported. But may I ask, is this proof of her living in sin?"

"Let us put it a little bit more bluntly—whether or not she is living as a prostitute," the Judge said.

Bob Hermann couldn't completely conceal his shock at the judge's attitude. "Your Honor, there has been no evidence to suggest that at all. Most of these parties are from out of the state. . . ."

On and on it went. When the judge couldn't make me out a prostitute, he suggested that I was setting up men for Mickey Cohen to shake down. It was pointed out that I'd had very little recent contact with Cohen.

Hermann was now so obviously shocked at the judge's attitude that he found himself lecturing the judge. "Your Honor, we can't take these things out of context, crucify her, find her guilty by association . . . We are not trying Mr. Cohen, we are trying Miss Renay. If the City Attorney's

Office and the presiding judge saw fit to fine Miss Renay seventy-five dollars and this should be accompanied by a prison sentence which is completely unrelated to the conduct for which she was originally charged, then I feel frankly that Miss Renay's ends of justice are not being served."

Judge Hall scowled. "The terms of her probation," he said, "were that she should not disobey the law. It doesn't have to be the same kind of an offense as before at all."

At ten minutes to twelve, the Judge announced that he had a civic luncheon to attend and declared a two-hour recess.

I watched with much apprehension as my prosecutor and the judge left to lunch together.

After the recess, the trial droned on. The arresting officer took the stand. His testimony fell apart. Then the judge wanted to know what I meant by the item on a list of things to do that said: "Must do at once—get apartment to function in."

"I paint and I have a lot of studio equipment," I said. "I have it moved into my bedroom now because my son, Johnny, is occupying my studio. I wanted to get a three-bedroom apartment so that I could continue with my work and not be cramped."

"Was Mr. Scher in his shorts when the officers opened the door?" the judge asked at one point.

"Yes, he was," I admitted.

"You were undressed?"

"I was in the same costume in which I paraded all over the legitimate stage in the play *Good Night, Ladies,* I had put that towel on to show him how I looked in it. This had been discussed with a lot of people, including his partner, my children, friends and everyone else."

"To show him how you looked in a towel?"

"Yes, I was to pose for pictures. I had met one of the owners of California Pools, with Scher—or Mr. Starr, as I knew him—in regard to this job. I met him in a public place and we discussed this, before I left to go put on the towel. . . . Some of the people present in the court-room today knew I was going there for that reason. The fact that Mr. Scher decided to dive out of his clothes and get all sorts of bright ideas was certainly not my fault."

Judge: "Did you ever engage in sexual intercourse for money?"

"No."

"Did you ever engage in sexual intercourse with anybody and receive a gift of $100 or $50 or any sum of money from them for it?"

"No."

For no apparent reason, the judge again began to harp on the Joe Collins thing, saying that I had shown bad faith in not marrying Joe Collins!

I was moved to speak up. "Your Honor," I said, "I don't think it has any bearing at all on anything."

"That is up to me to determine. It is my job to decide what is material and what is not, and it is not yours."

Another hour passed as the same material was examined again and again. Then my attorney spoke up: "I would like to renew my motion at this time for a continuance. Miss Renay is before this court for purposes of revocation of probation from a perjury charge on a disturbing-the-peace charge. We have had innuendoes as to the nature of how Miss Renay earns her living . . . We have had state-ments made by police officers which they have them-selves contradicted and I think in all justice to Miss Renay, she should be given an opportunity."

The motion was denied.

There was then a proposal to hear Starr/Scher in

chambers to avoid embarrassment for him. I objected.
"Why should he be protected?" I said. "Your Honor, he
was not concerned about protecting me. I have been the
victim of wild, unfounded accusations all day in this court!"

The judge said: "The court can receive Mr. Scher's
testimony in chambers. On these probation hearings the
court is allowed to get information from any source that it
desires. I will hear his testimony in chambers and if I con-
clude thereafter that it should not be confidential, I will
make the appropriate order."

The testimony in the judge's chamber revealed nothing
new. Nor could Scher explain his conduct or why he had
pled guilty. He said that the plea "was a matter of convenience."

Robert Hermann was allowed one final plea on my be-
half. But even as he spoke so eloquently, I could see that
his words were having no bearing on the judge's stone-
faced mood.

"The question before us now," Herrmann said, "is
whether this one act of disturbing the peace should go
contrary to the original judge's decision to place Miss
Renay on probation. She has nothing in her past history to
suggest that she would be a menace to society.

"I would be very much chagrined to realize that it is
possible for a woman to be imprisoned for having a relationship with a man, and no proof that she has accepted
money. In fact, the proof has been the opposite. The record states that she did not receive money.

"This woman has raised two fine children, and other
than this peccadillo there is nothing to suggest that she
is a menace to society.

"Surely justice cannot be harmed or injured by keeping
her under observation. We have one incident of disturbing the peace, and if her entire life is ruined for this one

incident justice would not be served. Probation under whatever terms your Honor may impose would better serve the purpose. Your Honor, I again request that the probationer be returned to her children."

And then, my unbelieving ears heard Judge Hall proclaim, ". . . It is the judgment of the court that the defendant's probation be, and is hereby, revoked and she is forthwith committed to the custody of the marshal.

"She is committed to the custody of the marshal to serve her original sentence as pronounced by Judge Martin.

"Court is adjourned."

Chapter 30

NEXT STOP, PRISON!

I stood in stunned amazement. This couldn't be happening to me. I couldn't be sent to prison for three years because someone said I disturbed the peace and quiet of the neighborhood. My mind refused to accept what I had just heard. No! No! I would wake up any minute. It was impossible—insane!

Who was this farce in judge's robes—who used a federal courtroom for his sadism? "This is a disgrace!" I heard myself crying out suddenly. "You can't smash my life just because of Bobby Kennedy's damn political machine!"

A federal marshal grabbed my arm and began leading me from the courtroom. As we reached the door, hysterical sobs struck my ears. "My God, the children!"

Suddenly, Brenda's arms were around my neck. Tears splashed against my face as she clung to me, kissing my cheeks and sobbing convulsively. "Oh no, Mama, no, no, no, they can't take you away. They can't put you in prison. You haven't done anything."

Johnny battled his way through the crowd and the police officers, tears streaming down his cheeks. As his hand reached out to me, he was jerked roughly aside by a police officer. I heard him hoarsely whisper, "Oh God, three years."

Then they were tearing Brenda from me. She wouldn't let go. I heard the sleeve of her dress rip from her arm.

342

"Take your goddamned hands off of her," I shouted. "Leave her the hell alone!"

She fought to hang on to me. They tore us apart. I was swept swiftly forward in a sea of curiosity seekers and police officers. The gap between us widened quickly as Brenda was shunted back and I was dragged down the corridor by the police. "Don't worry, darlings," I yelled back over the herd of bobbing faces. "Everything will be all right. I'll be out in no time. Be good—don't cry."

I was so worried about the children and trying to comfort them, the full significance of what happened still hadn't registered.

On my birthday, the next day, Sandra came to see me. Brenda and Johnny brought birthday cards, but I wasn't there to receive them. I'd been whisked away early at dawn.

I spent my thirty-fourth birthday being hustled off to the Terminal Island Federal Prison.

I drank in the sights and sounds of the free world as we drove along. I wanted to enjoy them one more time before they shut me away for three years.

I looked at the ocean, the boats, the convertibles full of fun-loving young people out for a good time, the restaurants, the cabarets, even the hot-dog stands, the trees, the flowers. I remembered other trees and other flowers—strange, disconnected things—my childhood home—the cozy warmth of it, the kerosene lamps, the old tamarack tree, our pet alley cat. Yes, my long-forgotten childhood seemed more real to me than the unbelievable last few days. I remembered the way my mother sang to me by the fire and told me I was the only little chicken left in the nest, while my father worked in the cotton fields and my big sister trudged down the railroad tracks to school.

Life was so simple in that little cottage, so uncompli-

cated. Now I was on my way to prison. How? Why? My
mind was like a movie camera running backward out of
control. I thought of so many things—anything and everything to keep my mind off the one thing I couldn't bear
to think about, my children. What would become of them
now? My dear, sweet children, the loves of my life.

My family would be shocked, my friends would be
saddened. But the ones with the knives in their hearts were
my children. They would miss me the most because they
loved me the most. What was it the song said—"You always hurt the one you love . . ."?

I saw a sailboat. People on board were having a picnic
—whooping it up, drinking beer from mugs. What fun they
were having! Dammit, that was my world out there. How
dare they shut me away from it? I was still young and
beautiful—in my prime. Time was fleeting. Time was precious. I wanted to live, to love, to experience life.

I was jerked forward as the marshal's car came to an
abrupt stop. We were there!

A prison guard let me in at the big iron gate. It clanged
shut behind me with a resounding thud. This was it,
the end of the line.

"Is this all there is to it?" Somehow, I'd expected it to be
bigger. I could survey the whole institution at a glance.
The six buildings and sprawling fenced-in grounds looked
squat and uninteresting. How could I spend three years
in this small, boring place? How could I contain myself,
my hopes, my dreams, within the boundaries of these four
little walls?

The police captain led me toward one of the smallest
buildings in the group. It was low and drab. The police
captain didn't stop. She kept leading me farther down the
polished corridor until we stopped abruptly in front of a
small barred door. She unlocked it.

"Go inside," she ordered. I stepped through the door and it clanged shut behind me. There was a sharp click as the automatic lock fell in place. This was it—my home for the next three years—a seven-foot-wide prison cell. I stared at the gray, foreboding walls and they stared back defiantly. I felt trapped. "I won't be able to stand it," I thought. "I'll go nuts locked up in a hole like this."

The next day a prison guard stuck a letter under my door. It had been forwarded from the county jail. It was from Brenda.

"Oh, Mom," it read, "I still can't believe it's true. We've got to get you out of there. That trial was a nightmare. You looked so stunned when that awful man read the sentence. I thought I hadn't heard right, that I misunderstood. Then they were taking you away to prison. I wanted to tell you how much I love you. I wanted to kiss you goodbye, Mother, then everything seemed to go black. All I could feel were hands grabbing me, pulling me away from you. I said, 'I want to kiss my mother goodbye.' I couldn't free myself from all those hands grabbing at me, and the voices belonging to the hands screaming in my ears. They kept yelling, 'Let go of her! Don't go near the prisoner! Get away from her!' Seemed like a million voices shouting—a million hands tugging. I was hot and sticky. I was cold and clammy. I wanted to die. Then I heard your voice, Mom. You were brushing my hair from my eyes. You kept saying everything was all right, not to cry. You were wiping tears from my eyes and sweat from my face. You tilted my chin up and kissed me. You said, 'Be a good baby.' Then we were walking down that long corridor. I was sobbing against your shoulder and all those flashbulbs were going off, and then I was swept away by a sea of people—where did they come from? I saw Johnny pushed and pulled along, his eyes full of tears. Today is your birth-

day, Mother. If only there was something we could say or
do. Your apartment seems like a morgue. I'll try to get
ready to go to the jail now, if I can stop crying. Love,
Brenda."

I paced the floor. I couldn't sleep, couldn't eat, couldn't
think.

Attorneys filed motions for modification of sentence.
When these were denied, they filed a motion charging unfair revocation. I tried everything possible to escape that
cell. Nothing worked.

I devised a makeshift calendar on the wall of my cell.
It had one thousand and ninety-five little squares representing one thousand and ninety-five days. One hundred
and sixty-six weeks! Each evening I marked one day off.
Sometimes I marked off a whole week—ten weeks down,
one hundred and fifty-six more to go.

Johnny went back to Arizona to stay with my family.
Brenda appeared faithfully at the prison gate every Sunday to visit me. Each time I saw her she looked more de-
jected. Her pretty face was pale and drawn. She smiled a
sad, forced little smile. She was becoming thin and nervous. Finally, her lovely skin developed blotches and
soon her face was covered with raw, red hives.

The hives progressed into a chronic rash, but she never
stopped coming. She appeared at the gate every Sunday
like a little wilted flower. Her skin became so encrusted
with rash that it would crack and bled every time she
tried to smile. My heart bled with it. As time went by, she
grew more ill. She was becoming a shadow of her former
self. Oh, what was happening to my beautiful baby? As I
looked at her sitting there covered with crusty blotches,
cracking, bleeding skin and swollen eyes, I hated Judge
Hall with a passion. I had never known what it was to really

hate a human being before. Now I knew! I felt a fiery, un-relenting hatred for the pompous man who was instru-mental in doing this thing to all of us.

My hatred didn't stop with Judge Hall. It included Laughlin Waters and the whole slimy political machine. I hated them all. My greatest contempt was for hypocrites like Robert Kennedy.

"Oh, Mom, I wish they'd lock me up so I could stay in your place. It would be easier that way than the way it is," Brenda said through her tears.

Then one Sunday she didn't appear at all. There was no letter of explanation. I was worried. Had she grown too ill to make the trip?

I overheard two inmates talking, "Ah hopes that poor lil' thing didn't just dry up and blow away or lay down and die of malnutrition," said one. "Or that dang rash didn't eat her up alive," said the other.

When I walked into the dining room, the girls were look-ing at a newspaper. A hush fell over the group. One of the girls ripped off a page of the paper and stuffed it into the wastebasket as I walked in. Was that page something they didn't want me to see? I rushed for the wastebasket. Two girls grabbed me and tried to hold me back. I slung them roughly aside. The girl nearest the wastebasket snatched the crumpled newspaper and started to tear it up. I grabbed her wrist and took the paper away from her. "Liz, it's best you don't see this," she cried. I uncrumpled the paper.

Headlines swam crazily before my eyes. *LIZ RENAY'S DAUGHTER BEATEN BY EX-MATE.* I scanned the ac-count of how fragile little Brenda was knocked through a screen door and down two flights of stairs by an angry, drunken ex-husband. Oh, my poor, poor baby! She was alone and defenseless. The type leaped from the page:

*GIRL SUFFERED A FRACTURED NECK, BROKEN
ARM, CUTS AND ABRASIONS, WAS RUSHED TO
EMERGENCY HOSPITAL, CONDITION IS SERIOUS.*
I rushed back to my quarters. "My God, I've got to go to
her. I've got to get out of here. I've got to see her. I've got
to be sure she's okay." Sure you do—sure—sure—sure,
echoed the gray resounding walls of my cell. "Ha, ha, ha,"
came the boisterous laugh of a passing inmate, as if to
write the finale to the futility of my desire. Those walls
knew I wasn't going anywhere—not even if she died.

Before long, Brenda was back at the gatehouse, her arm
in a sling, and a giant white neck brace stretching from
her pinched, blotchy little face to her frail shoulders. She
was always there—always forcing a smile, a smile that
cut deeper than a whip across my back.

Sometimes Johnny would come out from Arizona by
Greyhound bus. He'd come to the visiting room with
Brenda, sitting quietly with his head lowered, saying very
little. It was hard to tell what he was thinking. They tried
not to speak of their problems. Even if I had succeeded in
drawing them out, it would have been useless anyway.
My hands were tied. I couldn't help.

Then one day I abruptly came to my senses and began
to face facts. I guess that's part of the process known as
adjusting.

I sat down and had a good talk with myself. It went
something like this:

"Liz Renay, you're dead! As far as the free world is concerned, you're dead! Buried. You don't exist for the free
world and the free world doesn't exist for you. Fighting,
twisting, turning, fretting won't solve anything. You're
helpless. Accept it. Forget your obligations. Stop trying
to be a part of the outside world. Become a part of the
world you're living in. Look around you. Do something con-

structive with this time instead of wasting it by batting your brains out."

I said, "All right, that's logical. Let's see what I can do within the confines of these walls that makes any sense."

When Brenda appeared in the visiting room the next Sunday, I was a different person. I met her with a happy smile, a kiss, and a hug. "Darling," I said, "I've figured a way to outsmart Judge Hall after all. I'll turn the tables on him. I'm going to work like hell! I'll accomplish more in this three-year period than I would if I was outside."

Brenda's eyes lit up and her smile wasn't forced any more. "What do you plan to do?" she beamed.

"I'm going to paint. You can send me some art supplies. I'll walk out of this gate with a hundred oil paintings ready to exhibit. And what's more, I'll walk out with a book under my arm; I'll write. I'll make every hour, every minute, every second of this time count. They said they were giving me three years—all right, let them give them to me! This wasn't my idea, but if Uncle Sam wants to sponsor me while I work, I'll take advantage of it."

"Oh, Mama, that's great! What else can I do to help?"

"Main thing is to be happy, stop worrying, and get that face cleared up. Don't think of me as being in prison. Pretend it's a girls' school or a monastery, a place where I can work undistracted for three years and accomplish grand and glorious things. This will be my work period."

Within three days my art supplies arrived. That week I made my debut from the little gray cell at the Admissions and Orientation Building, where newcomers are locked for the first month until they've had their examinations and classifications. Then they are sent to one of the regular dormitories at the Palms or Sea Breeze areas.

The Sea Breeze dorm used to be called the honor cottage. Girls whose behavior was considered beyond reproach were sent there. No officer was on guard at night. That was before they discovered that several sailors from the Coast Guard station across the way had been coaxed across the fence and were in bed with the girls. It was a shocking experience for the honor cottage, especially when one of the girls turned up pregnant from the episode. After that, the honor cottage became just plain Sea Breeze, and an officer was posted on guard day and night. The inmates said it was comedian Lenny Bruce's ex-wife who initiated the romantic escapade.

The girls considered high security risks were automatically sent to Palms, the dormitory closest to the office where the warden and top prison staff were located. This office was known as "Control."

I was sent to Palms. Our building was locked at night, but the girls were allowed to roam the corridors pretty much as they pleased. A guard was posted in the lobby in case anything got out of hand.

Terminal Island was a country club, compared to the Los Angeles County Jail. There were clean, white sheets on the beds and crisp, starched curtains at the windows. The floors were mopped, waxed, and polished. The cells, or rooms as we preferred to call them, were kept more immaculately clean than most people's homes—regulations.

Some girls were assigned to the maintenance crew—others to the yard, the kitchen, and dining room. Those crews—they kept the place like a first-class hotel. The food was good, the place was neat and orderly and, what's more, we had our own flower gardens. I was classified to the sewing room, where inmate clothing was turned out. Later I was transferred to the education department to teach the oil painting class. It all came about like this:

One night, shortly after I checked in at the Palms dormitory, I heard the girl in the next cell crying herself to sleep. I went over to see if I could console her. "Oh, my baby, my baby," she cried, producing a tattered snapshot of a wistful-looking three-year-old girl. Then she burst into uncontrollable sobs. "My little girl, they won't let me see her. They've taken her away and are telling her awful things about me. She'll be eighteen when I get out of here."

I tried to comfort her, as great sobs racked her body. "There, there, maybe you'll make parole and be out of here in a little while. Maybe they aren't telling her bad things about you. Maybe they just don't want her to see you like this. She wouldn't understand why she couldn't be with you. Maybe they're doing what they think is best."

Slowly, the convulsive jerking of her body began to subside and she became almost limp. "You're a good, kind woman," she said. "God bless you for what you've said. I'll try to believe it."

I took the crumpled snapshot from her hand. She was so spent that she offered no resistance. "I'm going to fix this picture nice for you," I said. "You'll have it back tomorrow."

Next day I painted my first picture—the wistful life-sized face of that little girl! She was a beautiful child. Her beauty tugged at my heart and warmed my soul. My longing for my own children, my sadness and my compassion for the mother all poured into the canvas. When I finished and stood back to appraise my work, I was startled. The little girl looked like she could step out of the picture and climb upon my knee. Her sensitive little mouth seemed almost to tremble. She looked alive.

"Magnificent," cried a voice from behind. I whirled to see an officer admiring the painting. "You're a genius," she said. "What are you doing in a place like this?"

I thanked her for the compliment and hurried to put the

painting in Bertha's room before she returned from her work assignment.

When I returned from work, Bertha met me in the hall. She grabbed me, hugged me, kissed me, and danced me around the room. Tears of joy shone in her bright eyes.

"Honey, I can't tell you how much that painting means to me. It's the next best thing to having little Alice right here with me. I love you for it. I've got a present for you." She led me by the arm to her room, where she produced a half-finished afghan she was crocheting in bright, vivid colors. "That's yours, it's all yours as soon as I get it finished."

That's how it began—my art career at Terminal Island. Suddenly I found myself painting for everyone. Babies, husbands, lovers, mothers, and even grandmothers. One day soon after I had painted Bertha's little girl, a cute, chubby girl from the kitchen, named Ida, stood shyly in my doorway, clutching a picture of a bouncing, brown baby boy. He was adorable, with his big, animated smile and wide-open eyes.

"Will you paint 'im?" she asked. "I'll crochet you an afghan, too, or knit you something pretty if you'll just paint 'im up pretty like you did for Bertha."

I took the brown cherub's picture and was off to the races painting portraits for inmates. They gave me knitted or crocheted articles in exchange. When Brenda and Johnny came to visit, I always had presents for them: for Brenda, pretty hand-knit sweaters and stoles, and once a full-length coat; and for Johnny, ski sweaters and socks. I sent the afghans to my mother, sisters, and aunt for Christmas. After all the presents were taken care of, there were knit suits and dresses left for me and flashy, handmade jackets, gloves, and accessories.

I painted nearly a hundred portraits for the inmates and

forty canvases for my exhibit. I had intended to paint only for my exhibit, but who could resist such eager customers? They appreciated the paintings too much. Soon my art was scattered throughout the institution. I even painted portraits for officers and the prison dentists.

Soon a group of about fifty girls petitioned the warden for permission for me to teach an art class, and I was taken from my regular work assignments. I was assigned to the education department, and I taught social living and dramatics classes as well as the art class.

The art class was so popular that my class never ended. My students followed me home. Any time I was painting, seven or eight girls lined up on the floor to watch me, eagerly following every brush stroke. When we ran out of canvas, we used old window shades. We painted with anything, on everything—murals for the chapel, sets for plays, posters for coming events, and pictures, pictures, pictures.

We had several well-received art exhibits attended by outside visitors as well as the inmate population. I really got to know the girls through my classes.

In my spare moments, I worked on my book. I wrote it after "lights out" was sounded. Enough light filtered into my room from the light in the courtyard for me to make out the pages. It was a strain on my eyes, but I usually managed to keep with it for about half an hour each evening. Day by day the book was growing. I wrote it on tablets purchased at the prison commissary and kept it hidden under my mattress.

As the days stretched into weeks and the weeks into months, the book grew to enormous size. My roommate must have mentioned it to someone. Somehow a rumor started that I was writing a prison exposé. I was called to report to "Control" to see Miss Hollerand, acting warden of the women's division of Terminal Island.

"You are not allowed to write about the prison, the inmates, officers, or what goes on here. In fact, you are not even permitted to write about yourself while you're in this institution," she informed me. "Is that clearly understood?"

"Yes," I answered, glad I hadn't been pinned down and asked whether or not I had already written the book.

After I left, the warden issued an order for my cell to be shaken down and searched for the book.

"If there is a book, we'll confiscate it and send it to Washington," she said. "It may contain valuable information."

This order was overheard by inmates working as secretaries in the control office, and soon word was buzzing out over the grapevine that my book was about to be confiscated.

Before I could get back to my room, my friends searched the place, found the book, and took it to the incinerator.

Nancy greeted me in the hallway with a beaming smile. "Don't worry about a thing, Honey. It's all taken care of."

"What's taken care of?"

"The book—the book!" she laughed, jumping up and down. "They can't confiscate that book now unless they want to confiscate a pile of ashes."

"Oh, no," I cried. "You didn't." I was sick. Months and months straining my eyes under the light from the courtyard—pages and pages of effort—up in a puff of smoke.

"Gee, Liz, I was only trying to help. I was afraid you'd get in dutch."

"Thanks, Nancy, you did what you felt was right. Don't worry, the book isn't lost. It's still clear in my mind. I won't forget it. Some day I'll do it all over again."

I walked back to my bunk. I think I knew some of the reasons the prison authorities wanted to confiscate my book. There were certain things they were anxious to keep quiet.

The hospital for one. The hospital was a pathetic joke. The medical care, or rather the lack of it, was appalling.

Of course, they'd like to hush up the homosexual activities that were encouraged to flourish, too.

My book discussed prison policies, pro and con. I marveled that prison authorities could blissfully assume these things would never come to light. They were like ostriches with their heads stuck in the sand believing no one could see them.

Confiscating books couldn't bury the truth. They couldn't keep me here forever. I was scheduled to go before the parole board next month. Maybe what the man from the Davenport office had told me about a fix from Robert Kennedy's office wasn't true. Maybe the parole board would give me a fair shake and I'd be out in no time at all. The mystery man said I'd have to do every day of my time. Yet it was hard to believe anyone, even Robert Kennedy, could fix a federal parole board. Even if such a thing was true, I'd still be free in two years. Free to turn a glaring spotlight on Terminal Island.

Chapter 31

INSIDE TERMINAL ISLAND

I mentally reviewed my chapter on the hospital. Yes, I guess that chapter would be quite upsetting to the parties responsible. Inmates were assigned as nurses, inmates who had never worked in anything remotely connected with a hospital. They dashed about, giving shots like they were going out of style, vaccinating other inmates, and running the hospital. I was offered the job of playing nurse my-self when I first arrived. "I can't work in the hospital. I have absolutely no medical training," I said.

"Neither do any of the others," I was told.

It made me shudder.

One girl, who was a mental case under psychiatric care, was allowed to work as a nurse in the hospital. She caused a near-tragedy by giving a whole group of girls pellets that were supposed to be used to sterilize surgical instru-ments. The pills produced a churning action, much the same as Drano put into a clogged sink. They were harsh and poisonous enough to eat away the lining of the stom-ach. This mentally incompetent inmate nurse gave the pills to the girls when they reported for sick call. She told them they would cure their headaches.

The girls became violently ill, turned blue, and fell into comas. They were rushed back to the hospital, where more inmate nurses tended them through the night. The doctor phoned in instructions. The girls were given raw

356

eggs and milk to induce vomiting. The doctor didn't bother to pump their stomachs. Luckily, the horse-and-buggy remedy worked, and the girls vomited up the pill residue. If they hadn't, they'd no doubt have been dead by morning. The pills were lethal.

No investigation took place; no tests were run. The cause of their violent illness would not have been discovered if the doctor hadn't later noticed some of his pills missing when he prepared to sterilize his instruments. The kooky nurse laughed, and said, "Oh, those! That's what I gave the girls for their headaches when we ran out of aspirin, but it only made them sicker." She was punished briefly but soon was a familiar sight back at the hospital!

I felt sorry for the girls who were truly ill in a place like that. Several died. Poor Sarah used to beg and plead for them to send her out to a hospital for care. She had her feet operated on—*by the dentist*. (The doctor was unavailable that day, as usual.) Her feet didn't heal, and she hobbled around on crutches with her shoes cut open for months. She was in such pain that she often broke down and cried. She was not relieved from her work assignment. That would have brought attention to her faulty foot operation. As the months stretched on and Sarah's feet got worse instead of better, the doctor wouldn't listen. "She's just a hypochondriac trying to get attention like most of the rest of you," he said.

Poor Sarah tried hard to be cheerful. But she went from bad to worse until she was unable to leave her bed. I painted a bouquet of roses to hang on her wall, and the yard girls sneaked flowers into her room. She lingered there, sewing and stuffing little toy animals for the girls to send out to their babies and crocheting bedroom slippers for people in exchange for hot chocolate. We all looked after her as best we could. Then she was finally taken back to our so-called hospital, where she lay for several weeks.

At last, after all the long months of begging to be sent to an outside hospital, she got her wish. She was sent out for examinations and an emergency operation. It was too late. Maybe she could have been saved a few months earlier, but not now. They opened her up, sewed her together again, and sent her back to Terminal Island to die. She was eaten up with cancer. Nothing could be done.

I visited her at the hospital, and she squeezed my hand and said, "Liz, I'm dying. They told me. Please tell the people outside about this hospital—what they do to people in here."

I promised I would.

With 230 women huddled together in those squat, wooden buildings, there was bound to be someone who needed a doctor. What if a prisoner had a heart attack in the middle of the night? We didn't have a doctor on the premises or a registered nurse from the outside. The doctor dashed in for only a few hours on certain days of the week, and the outside nurse came in for just a few hours and left. Why? Surely enough taxpayers' money was appropriated to Terminal Island to allow the prisoners adequate medical care.

Another provocative question was that of homosexuality. Prison policy encouraged it to flourish. It wasn't surprising, considering that the women's warden, the captain, and the parole officer all were single women who had never been married and, according to the stories of the inmates, had no biological desire to marry. A good many of the officers looked so obviously butchy that it was hard to tell if they were male or female. Several of them carried on such brazen affairs with inmates that it was common knowledge all over the compound.

In exchange, the homosexual officers smuggled the girls' letters out, made phone calls for them, and sneaked in special cosmetics and other contraband items for their pleasure, including narcotics. According to the inmates, 90 percent of the dope smuggled into the institution was brought in by the lesbian prison-guard-lovers of the narcotics offenders.

There were two kinds of lesbians there, as I suppose there are elsewhere. The swaggering, he-man type who fancied themselves men—they were known as Butch Broads. Then there were the Femmes, who played the role of girl friend, or wife. They considered their Butch Broad girl friends men.

Terminal Island was a paradise for the Butch Broad. I believe many got themselves arrested again and again on purpose so they could go where the girls were. Some of them had been in and out five or six times and were considered habituals—and why shouldn't they be? Terminal Island was a homosexual haven. Uncle Sam supported them and their lovers. They were allowed to have their hair cut like a man's in the prison-sponsored beauty shop. They were allowed to wear government surplus combat boots, leftover fly-boy leather jackets, and khaki-colored army pants. They looked exactly like men. It was hard to think of them as anything else. If I was undressed, I instinctively covered myself when one of them swaggered down the hall.

When my family came to visit me from Arizona, my mother asked what those fellows were doing out there with all the girls.

Imagine the effect these male impersonators had on women who hadn't seen a man in, maybe, five years! Some average, red-blooded American females without a homosexual bone in their bodies found it hard to resist their masquerade. It would have been hard to entice normal women into homosexuality if women were obliged to look like women. But some of the love-starved females found it easy to stretch their imaginations to the point of thinking of these Butch Broads as men when they sauntered along in their mannish haircuts, combat boots, and leather jackets, cigarettes dangling from their mouths, with a "Hi ya, Baby, you're a doll."

I witnessed it several times. Women with children and husbands outside sometimes succumbed to Butch romances.

Prison attitude and policy strongly encouraged homosexuality. Women were punished severely, sent to the hole, given disciplinary reports and a loss of days earned if they so much as waved to a man across the fence. Yet they could sit in the lobby and neck with each other, and the officer would pretend she didn't notice. When girls were caught in bed together, the punishment was very mild—usually just a scolding or a day in solitary confinement.

If two lovers wanted to play house and live together, all they had to do was go to Control and request it. The request was always granted. The women running the prison seemed to be well-equipped to deal with homosexual love affairs, but if women came to them with serious problems about their families, they were at a loss for an answer. How could they know about husbands or children?

The affairs between prison guards and inmates were always the subject of gossip: Who was making it with whom was considered the latest news around the compound.

Miss Bowman, the warden in charge when I arrived at Terminal Island, was carrying on such an illustrious affair with her "private" inmate secretary that the whole thing got out of hand and caused tidal waves that reached to Washington. Miss Bowman used to take her inmate secretary home with her on "private" nightly assignments, returning her to the institution at late hours, hilariously high on God knew what. (The girl was there for narcotics addiction.)

The warden's private secretary flaunted all sorts of gifts when she returned from her trips—items that were contraband for other prisoners. She paraded down the hall in frilly contraband nighties, while the rest of the inmates wore clownlike outfits made of parachute material that looked like hell. Some of the inmates got jealous and started smuggling letters out to Washington through their homosexual officer friends. When Mr. Bennett, head of the Board of Prisons, visited Terminal Island, a group of girls passed complaining notes to him as he strolled across the compound.

Meantime, the secretary came up for parole. When it was denied, she threw a tantrum that brought the whole thing out into the open, screaming, "You lied to me! You promised I'd make parole! I've been prostituting myself all these months for nothing, you dirty bitch!"

More letters flooded Washington. Was Warden Bowman fired? Hell, no! She was transferred to a bigger and better prison in Alderson, Virginia, where she could practice her tactics on other inmates—next time possibly with more discretion.

I wondered why the Board of Prisons hired known lesbians with obvious mannish attributes. After all, homosexuals represented only 15 to 20 percent of the inmate population. It seemed that in a land where majority rules, they'd select women qualified to handle problems that concerned the (80 to 85 percent) normal average female. Couldn't they find women who had raised families to run places like Terminal Island? Most of the inmates were mothers of children of various ages.

If a woman like my mother got hold of a place like Terminal Island, she'd straighten it out in no time.

With open encouragement of homosexuality and so many officers involved, it was reassuring that only one in five engaged in homosexual practices. The larger portion of the inmate populace chose to remain women, dress as women, act as women, and have fantasies about men. They relieved themselves while looking at their lovers' pictures. It was a better way to hold on to their sanity. Among those who played the homosexual game, there were constant fusses, fights, and emotional outbursts. They fought over petty jealousies and imagined wrongs. They were caught in a conflict born of the fleeting nature of their Terminal Island love affairs, with all their shallow pretenses.

They knew that one day their lover would walk out the prison gate, leaving them behind—or vice versa. They were obsessedly possessive in their wild attempts to hang on.

The weaker females found solace and a kind of strength in the arms of someone who at least looked like a man. They clung to the swaggering bullies, allowing them to curse, beat, and take every conceivable advantage of them because they needed affection so desperately.

I felt sorry for them and sorry for the Butch Broads as well. They were victim of the illusions they created. One of them sauntered up to me and said, "Hey Baby, I'll bet I could show you the best time in bed you ever had."

"Sorry," I said, "but you weren't born with the right equipment for me." The Butch looked crushed and slunk silently away.

When I first arrived at Terminal Island, some of the Butch Broads made passes, offering to buy my commissary supplies if I'd be their girl. I used to joke with them. "Honey, it takes a lot more than $15 a month to keep me."

Fifteen dollars a month was all each girl was allowed. This broke down to $3.75 a week. If the Butches persisted, I'd say, "Look, Honey, if you gave me your big $3.75 a week, there'd still be a little something missing!" That usually stopped them.

Girls who weren't interested in homosexual affairs were called "Don't-Play Broads" by the lesbians. I was not offended by the title.

The climax to my approaches by Butch Broads came when Control moved a notorious 200-pound lesbian into my cell as a roommate, at her request. She had just transferred to Terminal Island from Alderson Prison. She soon became obnoxious in her advances. She grabbed my breasts one day, hurting them in her strong hands. I was furious. I shoved her through the swinging cell door and she landed, kaplop! in the hallway on her oversized rump. "Get out of my room and stay out," I yelled. "Every time you walk in this door, I'll shove you back through it."

The overstuffed lesbian looked stunned. She got up and waddled to Control as fast as her fat legs would carry her and asked to be moved at once. Her request was granted.

Word spread like wildfire across the compound. After that, the Butch Broads left me alone. The weak Butch Broads were afraid to risk the embarrassment the encounter might bring. The ones tough enough to handle me were afraid of my underworld connections. The position they chose was one of friendly detachment.

This was great—but, in the process of making my position clear to the Butches, I created a new problem. The Femmes started flirting with me. One of them undulated up with a little giggle. "Oh, Liz," she breathed, "you're so wonderful and brave. We always wondered why you didn't play with the Butch Broads—when all the time you were a Butch Broad yourself."

"My God, whatever gave you that idea?" I asked, in amazement.

"Oh, we could tell by the way you fought off the other Butch. Boy, you sure fixed her wagon!" she tittered. "Can I be your girl?"

Suddenly I was swamped with Femmes wanting to give up their lovers and live with me. Some of them said, "All you have to do is buy my commissary and I won't look at another Butch." Others said, "I'll be your girl and you won't even have to buy my commissary." Still others offered to reverse the procedure and buy my commissary.

One day I told a whole group of them that, even if I were a Femme or Butch, I wouldn't want any part of their game. I said, "With you girls, it's more than sex for the sake of sex. You make a big romance out of it. You become lovers. Then you get possessive and jealous and start beating each other over the head with lamps and irons and kicking the hell out of each other. Who needs that hassle and aggravation? Even if I was a lesbian, I'd remain celibate in here."

A week later there was a knock on my door in the quiet of the evening. There stood Rhonda, a tall, slinky, brown-skin girl with a seductive look in her eyes. A whimsical smile played at the corners of her full lips. She was wearing nothing but her robe. She opened it as she stepped into my room, revealing her magnificent golden-brown body.

She moved in close to me with a determined look on her face. "All right, Baby," she said, "what's your excuse now? I'm leaving tomorrow. Tomorrow I walk out that gate a free woman. You'll never see me again and I'll never see you. You won't have to worry about getting involved with headaches or hassles. Let's have fun tonight. Let's be together like there's no tomorrow, 'cause there is no tomorrow for us, see? Give me a nice send-off—a going-away present, Baby."

I looked at her in disbelief. I liked Rhonda. She was such a nice girl. She was too lovely to be so confused.

I reached out to her. I took the sashes of her robe in my hands and tied them together at her waist. "Rhonda," I said, "you're going out of here tomorrow into a world full of men. Go to bed thinking of the wonderful man you're going to meet out there—a man who will love you and take care of you—a real man, not a make-believe man like you've had in here. Walk out of here feeling like a woman, if you can. Give up this bullshit. You don't need it."

Rhonda burst into tears. She threw her arms around me. "I'm afraid, I'm afraid," she quivered. "Oh, Liz, I'm afraid to go out there and face men again. I've been locked up too long. Five years is too long."

"Don't worry, Honey. It'll all come back to you in five seconds when a real man takes you in his arms. You'll be all right. Now pull yourself together and go get some sleep."

Rhonda got up slowly, as if in a trance. When she reached the door, she stopped and looked back at me, a broad grin crossing her bronze face. "I guess that's the nicest way I ever got turned down in my life," she said.

This episode repeated itself many times in the months to come. One time the little fat girl from the kitchen came to see me and said, "Liz, I'm being released and I want to show you a good time before I go. I think you're nice—I just want to do it for you as a favor, no strings."

It was hard to convince some of these girls I didn't want their favors. I didn't dislike them or blame them. I felt sympathy for them. I hoped they could some day adjust to the normal way of life and discover the heterosexual joys they were missing. I soon became on good terms with them all, even the one I shoved out of my room. I learned to feel compassion for her and to be her friend.

I'm convinced that, if conscientious family women were running the prison, if homosexual officers were discouraged or not hired, if the inmates weren't allowed to dress and look like men, and if a different example was set, the rate of converts to homosexuality would be cut in half.

I'm not about to judge the pros and cons or rights and wrongs of the homosexual issue. One of my strongest beliefs is that every individual has a right to conduct his or her sex life in any way he damn pleases. It's no one's business what he does behind closed bedroom doors—as long as it doesn't hurt anyone. However, in a captive area like Terminal Island, where the inmate population is predominantly heterosexual, it is both unfair and unsuitable to run the place with officers who have never been married and have had no experience in dealing with the family problems of wives and mothers.

Chapter 32

AMONG THE NOTORIOUS

One day the institution was a-buzz with excitement. Pat Conway was being transferred to Terminal Island. "Wow! She's a real big-shot," beamed Nancy. "Next to you, she'll be the biggest wheel in the institution."

"Yeah, she's a big operator, all right," agreed Gail. "She just got fifteen years for shootin' some guy. She was the head of an international smuggling ring, a narcotics ring, and a prostitution set-up."

"How do you know?" I asked.

"Girl, it's been in all the papers for weeks. Don't you read any publicity but your own?"

"Did you say she killed a man?"

"No, she shot a couple of guys, but her aim was so bad that they lived. She shot the last son of a bitch in the ass."

"Yeah, they're flying her in from San Francisco. I'd like to get a peek at her," exclaimed Nancy.

Pat Conway arrived in a few days. She was tall and attractive, with flaming red hair and smoldering black eyes.

To my dismay, I learned they were moving her in with me. I suppose it was because we were both considered top security risks at Terminal Island. My cell was right next to the officers' desk, where they would have no trouble keeping an eye on me. This way, they could watch both of us at once.

I wanted nothing to do with Pat. This didn't bother her

367

one bit. She was quiet and sullen. But, as the weeks stretched on, we became friendly.

I learned that her word was her bond, once she had given it. When she said something, it was as good as done.

This was not too common a trait among the inmates at Terminal Island. With many of them, lying, cheating, and conning were second nature.

Terminal Island had a way of reducing people to their basic selves. Life was transparent in this human goldfish bowl. It stripped away all pretense and bared each girl's traits, character, and soul for easy viewing. Every girl was soon known to all for exactly what she was. Some girls had one thing, some another; and it didn't take long to find out.

Pat Conway had honesty, a sense of fair play, and a quiet integrity about her. She was intensely fascinated by my art work. She was too stand-offish to join my class, but I taught her to paint in spare moments in the evenings in our cell.

She also developed an interest in my social living class. She became part of my homework sessions, eagerly reading the briefs I prepared for class. I had books sent in and usually spent about an hour studying after dinner. Pat joined these study periods. If I decided to do something else, she was obviously let down.

She seemed to be such a nice person that I almost forgot about the publicity and the fantastic things I had heard of her background, though they remained somewhere in the back of my mind. I wondered whether the things I'd heard were true or just newspaper exaggerations like my publicity. My newspaper image was as black as hers— Gun Moll, Darling of the Underworld, Gangster's Girl Friday, etc., etc. Maybe she wondered about me, too.

One day I asked her, "Pat, is it true you ran an international vice ring and shot a couple of guys?"

She looked at me for a long moment and then she smiled. "Yeah, it's true and then some. I can be a mean bitch when somebody crosses or mistreats me, Liz. I'm sorry those two bastards I shot didn't die."

"How did you get mixed up in a life like that?" I asked.

"Well, I guess it could all be traced back to little 'Naked,'" she said.

"Who in the world is little Naked?"

Pat's smoldering eyes leaped with excitement. "Let me tell you about him," she said. "Little Naked was the only thing I really loved in my whole life except my dog and that madam. You know, Liz, that's why I shot that last son of a bitch. He was trying to kill my dog.

"When I was a kid we were very poor. We lived in a shack on a run-down farm outside of town. I didn't mind that part, but I couldn't understand why my father hated me and kicked me around the way he did. He was nice to the other five kids. My mother barely tolerated me and always acted guilty when she gave me a little hug or kiss, and she made sure Daddy didn't see her. Even the other kids treated me like an unwanted stepchild. I didn't get toys at Christmas like they did. They'd get new ones and I'd just get some old broken thing wrapped in Christmas paper.

"I felt like an outsider and misfit with my own family. My father wouldn't speak to me if he could avoid it, and when he got angry, he called me 'that damned little bastard.' I didn't know what the word meant, but I wondered why he never called the other kids bastards.

"Later I found out why. My mother had been raped by a Negro and I was the bi-product. That's why Daddy hated me. I didn't belong to him. I think it irked him that I was the prettiest kid of the lot, and he knew he couldn't take the credit.

"Anyway, during the days when I was being kicked around without knowing why, little 'Naked' came into my life. He was something to love that would love me back.

"It began one day when my mother threw a pan of scalding water out of the doorway. A chicken ran into the path of the boiling water. The poor thing flopped in pain and looked as though it would surely die. I ran to rescue it. I poured pans of cold water over its back to ease the pain. The poor thing seemed to know I meant to help it. It seemed grateful.

"When Daddy came home, Mother said, 'You'd better kill that chicken, Pa. I threw hot water on it, and it's going to get sick and die, anyway.'

"Daddy said, 'Looks to me like it's already sick. I don't want to eat no sick chicken. Wait and see if it gets well.'

"I ran forward with the chicken wrapped in my apron. 'Please,' I said, 'may I have him? If I nurse him back to health, can I have him for my own?'

" 'If you think you can make a dying chicken well, go ahead and try,' Daddy said, grudgingly.

"I was overjoyed. I ran into the yard and made a little bed of boards and straw. I put cold cloths on my chicken's back all day long. I brought him crumbs from the table and soon, to my delight, he recovered, but all his feathers fell out and he never grew any more.

"When he was able to get out of the box, all he had was one little fringe of feathers around his neck. The rest of his body was nude, so I named him 'Naked.'

"By the time he recovered, he was so in love with me he followed me around like a little puppy dog and never let me out of his sight except when I left for school.

"The moment I returned, I'd run into the yard behind the house, calling, 'Here Naked, here Naked.' He loved me as much as I loved him. Naked became my whole life. He belonged to me. He was my pet.

"When Daddy was planting corn, I kept Naked away so he wouldn't pick up any. I didn't want to give anyone an excuse not to like him.

"I was so happy with Naked. Then one day when I came home from school and ran into the yard calling for him, he didn't come. I ran around the yard and out in the fields searching for him. But, no Naked anywhere. I ran into the house. Mama was fixing dinner. The other kids were sitting around the kitchen, watching. 'Where's Naked?' I asked. 'Has anybody seen Naked?'

" 'Never mind about Naked, just wash up for dinner,' my mother answered.

" 'Yes, Ma'am,' I said, 'but does anyone know where Naked is?'

"The other children began to snicker and look toward Mama at the stove.

"I smelled chicken frying in the pan. Suddenly, an awful thought struck my brain that was too terrible to think about. No, it couldn't be. 'Is that Naked in that pan?' I cried.

" 'Shut up and get ready for your dinner,' my mother snapped. The other kids snickered louder.

"Good God, that just couldn't be Naked—not my little pal, Naked. I ran blindly from the room and around to the back of the house where the garbage bucket stood. I began rooting through the trash, afraid of what I might find. Suddenly, I saw it. There it was. Naked's little head with the fringe of straggly feathers around the neck. The only feathers he ever had since he got scalded with the water. I picked up his head and held it to my breast and cried out loud.

" 'Come in here and eat your dinner,' my mother called.

"I was horrified. I ran in the back way and up the rickety stairs and hid under my bed. They wouldn't get me down there to that table.

" 'Leave that damn kid alone,' I heard my father say. 'She'll come down if she gets hungry enough. Until she does, that's one less mouth to feed.'

"I stayed up there in the dark and brooded until the incident was so exaggerated in my mind I considered the whole family a bunch of murderers and cannibals and hated them all. Maybe this was the climax to a life of being kicked around—I don't know. Anyway, it was the last straw. Something seemed to snap in me. I hated them so much I decided to kill them all. I sneaked downstairs to the basement and got the kerosene lanterns. I sprinkled kerosene all around the house and set fire to the place while they were in the kitchen eating little Naked. Then I ran out into the woods to watch them burn.

"Well, Liz, you asked about my life in crime and how it got started. That's it. It goes back a long, long way."

"What happened to your family?" I asked, amazed at the incredibility of what I'd just been told. "Were they burned to death?"

"Oh, no," said Pat, a wry smile playing around her lips. "You can't kill people like them. They have escape hatches built under their skins. They all got out, put the fire out before much damage was done, and tracked me down in the woods. I don't have to tell you they beat the hell out of me. They damn near killed me. They kicked the hell out of me for weeks over that. Every time someone of the family brought up the subject, I was in for it again. The point isn't what I accomplished, it's what I attempted to do that counts. It's all the same, you know."

Pat was thoughtful for a moment. "You know, Liz," she

said, "I guess the good Lord looks after me. I've never killed anyone in my life, but I sure as hell tried a few times. It's no fault of mine that those damned fools are still alive."

A chill passed through me. Pat had so much pent-up bitterness, hatred, and despair in her that it was clear she was capable of murder with not too much provocation.

She continued, "At the age of twelve, I ran away from home and went to live with a married sister. My brother-in-law promptly raped me. When I ran to my sister in tears begging for protection, she beat me within an inch of my life for lying and then kicked me out of the house.

"I wandered the streets, sleeping in alleyways and raiding café garbage pails for scraps of food until a pimp discovered me, cleaned me up, and took me to the madam of the local whorehouse.

"You know something, Liz, this may sound funny to you, but that Madam was the closest thing to a mother I ever had. She was the first person who ever gave me any show of kindness. I grew to love and respect her. I was her pet. When she finally took ill and was confined to her bed, I took over and ran the house for her. She was bedridden for six months. I looked after her day and night. I really cared about the old biddy. When she died, she left everything she had to me. I went on running the whorehouse as usual. It nearly killed me to lose the only friend I'd ever known. I was just fifteen—the youngest Madam in history. I tried hard to follow in her footsteps and run things the way she'd have wanted it.

"I befriended many young strays the way she befriended me. I took in any girl who was desperate and needed help. They were free to go whenever they pleased. Live and let live was my policy. I never turned a girl away, no matter what she looked like, what color she was, or what her story was. Finally, I took in so many stray 'pussy

cats' that I had to open another house, and another, and
another. That's about it, Liz. I just kept expanding. Flesh-
peddling is the oldest business in the world. There will
always be customers. Businessmen, doctors, lawyers, and
judges like the ones who sent us here—they're all customers. I've even had ministers from time to time. When I
get out of here, I'll do it again. It's my profession, my way
of life. Do you understand that, Liz?"

"Yes, Pat, I guess I do," I said, thoughtfully.

Pat and I joined the Dale Carnegie public speaking class
offered at the institution. The classes progressed nicely
and were great fun. One night our instructor informed us
it was time for the "Breaking Out of Your Shell Session."

"Tonight you will all get up and make a speech about
the things you are most angry about. Will you start, Liz
Renay?"

"I can't think of anything I'm angry about just offhand."

"All right, we'll go on to someone else and come back to
you later. Now, just stop and think of the last time you
were really angry—furious—fighting mad—then make a
speech about the things you were angry about."

Speeches droned on and on as I tried to think of the
last time I was fighting mad. Then it hit me. How stupid
of me not to have thought of it at once! The time Judge
Hall sentenced me. Boy, I was fighting mad then, all right!

"Liz Renay, have you thought of a subject yet?"

"I sure have. I'm going to speak about crooked federal
judges and politicians." I got up and made a speech to end
all speeches, pouring forth all the pent-up fury I'd held
in my heart since the outrage took place.

The applause was deafening. The inmates whistled and
cheered and gave me a standing ovation. I was awarded
first prize as the best public speaker in the class and
awarded a golden pencil marked, "Best Speech."

Sandra came to visit me the next Sunday. "Guess what, Sandra," I laughed. "Would you believe I made a speech last week about crooked politicians and federal judges, and the institution awarded me first prize and gave me a gold pencil?"

"That's a good one," chuckled Sandra. "I'm going to tell that to Winchell."

Soon I was called to Control and confronted with the item from Winchell's column. It read:

> Mickey Cohen's one-time friend, Liz Renay, won first prize from the Dale Carnegie Institute for Public Speaking for a speech she gave in the prison to which a Federal judge sent her. The subject of her elocution was "Crooked Politicians and Federal Judges."

"You seem to have a direct pipeline to Walter Winchell. This time you've gone too far. You have embarrassed a federal judge," said the warden.

"I didn't mention any names. If the shoe fits, let him wear it."

"Well, here's some news you won't find so amusing, Miss Renay. As of now, I'm striking all visitors from your list except your immediate family, and they are suspended for two weeks."

Chapter 33

BRENDA BEATS THE BAY

A week later I received a puzzling letter from Brenda. "Dear Mom, Here is a little poem I wrote for you. I love to gather sea shells by the shore. Sunday, I'll gather some by the ocean's roar."

What an odd thing for her to write! Wait a minute— she must have been notified about my loss of visiting rights and was telling me to go to the sea wall.

Sunday, I sat by the sea wall with a group of my friends to wait and see what happened. Just as I was about to doze off in the warm sunshine, a voice shook me awake.

"Hi, Mom. They can't stop me from seeing you, come hell or high water, and this is high water!"

I blinked open my eyes, and there was trusty little Brenda in a tiny motor boat. My God, she must have rented the boat in Long Beach and piloted it all the way to the Terminal Island sea wall by herself. Poor, brave little angel. She looked so tiny, all alone in the big ocean. The wind was blowing, briskly rocking the small craft to and fro. "Careful, darling—don't stand up like that. The thing might tip over."

As she stood smiling and waving, the wind suddenly whipped her loose dress tightly around her frail body. My God! Brenda was pregnant, sure as hell.

As the wispy material flapped about her body in the wind, the outline of a tight little pod the size of a small pumpkin was clearly visible. Good heavens, why hadn't she told me?

Just then, the Coast Guard cutter roared into view. "Get back. No boats allowed within 100 yards of the fence," a voice announced over the loudspeaker, "under the penalty of fine or imprisonment, or both."

"I'd better get out of here," cried Brenda, in a panic. "I don't want to get you into trouble."

She got the boat going, forgetting the anchor was still down. The anchor rope got caught in the motor and she was going nowhere fast. A siren screamed. Brenda panicked. The boat rocked wildly from side to side, nearly capsizing in the lapping ocean waves. "Oh, Mom," she wailed, "what shall I do?"

Oh, God, what if that boat tipped over? Brenda was a lousy swimmer and, in her condition, she might drown. I rushed to the wire fence and began frantically climbing it.

"Come back," screamed an inmate, "climbing the fence is a five-year offense if you're caught!"

"Who cares? I have to save Brenda," I yelled, as I struggled to clear the electric wiring at the top.

Suddenly Brenda managed to free the anchor and speed away, throwing kisses as she went—her blonde hair blowing in the breeze. I watched with my heart in my mouth until the little boat became just a speck on the ocean that soon faded away into the purple mist. God, what a scare!

I couldn't wait to see Brenda when the two weeks' suspension was over. She appeared at the gate house in the same loose, billowy dress. It was easy to see how she had been able to conceal her condition from me. If the sea breezes hadn't betrayed her, I would never have guessed.

"Brenda, darling, don't you have something you'd like to tell me?" I said, looking her straight in the eye.

"Like what, Mother?" she said, avoiding my gaze.

"Like maybe I'm going to be a grandmother, Honey," I smiled. "That's too thrilling a secret to hide from me."

"Oh, Mom, you don't mind?" she exclaimed, relief registering in her weary eyes. "I—I—tried to keep it from you because I thought you'd worry. Next month you come up for parole and you'll be home. I was waiting till then. You'll be out before it's born."

"How far along are you?"

"It happened when I had that awful fight with Leo. He came back and just moved in on me. He forced his attentions on me."

"Well, Honey, he was your husband, you know."

"Yes, that's what he kept saying, but I had left him and was getting a divorce. Anyway, we had a terrible quarrel over it. I ordered him out of the house. He refused to leave. He kept hanging around and drinking. He started getting drunk—and—well, you know the rest."

"Yes, I guess I do. Well, darling, you're beautiful and Leo is a handsome young man. You'll probably have the most adorable baby you ever laid eyes on. I'm thrilled about it. What do you want, a boy or a girl?"

"I want a girl. It's already settled. I'm going to name her Liz Renay. I want the world to know I'm proud of the name Liz Renay."

"No, Honey, don't name your baby after me. The name Liz Renay has been dragged through the mud. It would take a lot of whitewash to get it clean again. No use starting the baby out with that. You don't have to prove you're proud of me. I know you are."

I returned to my cell full of new hopes and dreams. Soon I'd be out of this place, and what a ball I'd have with the precious new baby!

Mrs. Gilliland, the education supervisor, called me into

her office one day and said, "Liz, I was looking over the papers you filled out when you entered the institution. The employers you listed for the past three years were Warner Brothers, ABC, NBC, CBS, various theaters and night clubs. You list your occupation as actress and entertainer. You're the only girl at Terminal Island with a theatrical background. Would you consider taking over a little theater group and putting on plays?"

I was overjoyed. With my acting class, painting class, and social living class, I was spending no time at all at a regular work assignment.

Soon my little theater group became a consuming occupation. In addition to designing the costumes, there were the jobs of painting backdrop scenery for the stage, coaching the girls in their parts, and writing the special material and skits.

When Mrs. Gilliland found out I could write, she kept me busy writing articles for the prison paper too.

My art class students helped paint the stage backdrops and the sewing room girls helped with the costumes. My first endeavor was a variety show called Terminal Island Follies. I had open call. I rounded up every girl on the compound who could sing and dance. I gathered a group of the best dancers and organized a chorus line.

I designed short, frilly chorus girl costumes fashioned from worn-out bed sheet material, tinted a rosy pink with food coloring from the kitchen. I sprinkled them with a package of silver glitter I ran across in the art department. I designed a striking low-cut evening gown for myself from more of the worn-out sheeting. It fit me like a second skin. I painted it jet black with poster paint from the art class and sprinked the rest of the silver glitter over it in sunburst effects. The dress was a knockout.

I wrote comedy skits about the officers and prison au-

thorities and a good-natured spoof on prison life. The revue consisted of short scenes, black-out humor, and prison-
inspired parodies on old familiar songs. There were jokes
about our parachute nighties, and impersonations of the
prison staff.

We rehearsed for six weeks. My art class plastered the
compound with posters of high-kicking chorus girls and
announcements that the T.I. Follies were soon to be presented at the fabulous Island Inn, located in the heart of
California's most exclusive finishing school.

"Yeah, it's so exclusive they built a fence around it to
keep people from sneaking in," laughed an inmate.

I emceed the show, announcing the acts and doing a
running narration to tie the show together.

Soon the big night arrived. I walked out on stage in my
breathtaking black gown, a-glitter with silver splashes.

"Welcome to T.I. Follies," I smiled. Warden Smith, from
the men's side, was seated with our warden in the front
row. They were flanked on each side by prison staff members.

I went into a spiel of risqué comedy patter designed to
warm up the audience before getting on with the show.
Just as I was about to do my most seductive piece of material, a loud, resounding rip was heard! It seemed to have
come from the back of me. I don't have to tell you what it
sounded like—and a loud one at that! Peals of laughter
shook the room.

It was then that I noticed my glamorous gown had become nothing but a wide flat piece of material, held on by
two dangling straps. It had ripped all the way down the
back and was just hanging there.

My shocked reaction brought more peals of laughter,
as I frantically clutched the dress. It swished to one side,

revealing my half-clad body. I pulled it together behind me and held it behind my back.

I soon regained my composure. "Tsk, tsk, tsk. What an awful thing this is with Warden Smith sitting in the front row. If you think my dress fell apart because it was made of rotten sheets painted with poster paint, you're wrong. The whole thing was rigged. It was a sneaky way to get away with doing a strip." There were howls of laughter. Warden Smith laughed so hard he had to wipe his eyes.

When I went off stage, Mrs. Gilliland pinned my torn dress together with a row of giant safety pins, using the width of the pins to make the dress wider, exposing a strip of skin laced with safety pins down the back. "No one will see it," she comforted. "Just keep your back away from the audience."

The hell with it! When I went out to introduce the next act, I did a little dance, ending by striking an over-the-shoulder pose with my back to the audience. This revealed the row of safety pins stretched across my bare skin. The audience howled with glee. I could hear Mrs. Gilliland clearing her throat backstage. The show moved at a rapid pace and was a smashing success.

Warden Smith congratulated me. "This is the best entertainment we ever had here," he said.

When I went backstage to change clothes and congratulate my group on their performances, I was greeted by a loud "Surprise! Surprise!" A card table covered with crepe paper held cups of hot chocolate and a bowl of oatmeal cookies. Then I noticed a big white stork made of shredded crepe paper pinned to the wall. The stork carried a card in its bill with the words, "Congratulations, Brenda."

"The art class made him," beamed one of my students.

"We all pitched in on the cocoa and cookies," said another.

"This is a baby shower, in case you can't tell! We've been planning it as a surprise."

"Open the presents," said Nancy, gesturing toward another card table piled high with bootees, caps, sweaters, and baby dresses.

"There sho' has been a lotta crochetin' and knittin' goin' on 'round here the las' six weeks," smiled Ida. "I done made half a dozen things myself. Ain't nothin' too good fo' any baby that sweet lil ole Brenda tens on havin'."

I looked at the pile of tiny pink and blue garments, all daintily hand-made—enough for Brenda's layette, and then some. I knew the hours of tedious labor involved and the sacrificing necessary to purchase the yarn. I wanted to cry. So these were hard-hearted convicts. I wondered if my friends in the free world would be as thoughtful.

I looked around the room at my new friends. It was hard to realize these smiling faces belonged to thieves, murderers, and bank robbers.

I helped the girls with their make-up and hair when they were expecting visitors. I did what I could to make them look glamorous with our limited supplies. I smuggled water colors out of the art department and concocted flattering shades of eye shadow, rouge, and lip gloss by mixing the colors with vaseline. The girls were so grateful for these small favors that they wouldn't allow me to do my personal laundry or ironing. They took turns doing it for me. They mopped and waxed the floor of my cell, emptied my trash, and kept my place as neat as a pin. I couldn't do a thing for myself.

"I'll put it like this, Baby," said one of the students. "This is the onliest thing we kin do fo' you—the only way we kin do somethin' fo' you is to become a buncha chamba' maids."

One morning I was called from my art class and told to report to Control at once.

Two tall, well-dressed gentlemen were waiting in the warden's office. They introduced themselves as Mr. Knowland and Mr. Broady of the FBI. Mr. Knowland did most of the talking. "How'd you like to make parole, Miss Renay?"

"I expect to make it," I said.

"Oh? What makes you think you will?"

"I have every reason to make it. My parole is practically automatic."

"How do you figure that?"

"It's simple. One: My sentence was a first offense. I had no prior record. Two: My revocation was on the minor misdemeanor of disturbing the peace. Three: I have a perfect record in the institution. Everyone here says parole is inevitable for me."

"Please believe me when I tell you it isn't. If you'll co-operate with us and give us information that will help us nail Mickey Cohen or some of the people involved with him, things will be different. We'll put in strong recommendations that you make your parole."

"Look, I don't need your recommendations. My record speaks for itself. The decision to grant a prisoner parole is based on whether or not the parole board feels the individual is a safe risk to turn loose on society. If it's a dangerous criminal, they have to decide whether or not he's apt to go out and commit his former crime. In my case, it's not very risky. The only question they have to answer is: Is there a danger she may go out and disturb the peace again or tell a fib to someone? You know, that's not much of a risk, especially for someone who has been recommended for the Section Two. That's the highest honor a prisoner can receive."

"You don't get the picture, Liz. Unless you cooperate with us, you won't make parole and that's that."

"Who says so? I don't believe you. You can't tell me you can fix a federal parole board."

"You really are naïve, aren't you? Don't you realize all we have to do is write a letter stating you have an uncooperative attitude and aren't ready for parole. Looks like you'd smarten up after what happened to you in court."

"I have nothing to say to you. I wouldn't believe you on a stack of Bibles."

"Better think about it, Liz. You won't come up for parole again for another year. If you're going to cooperate, do it now. If you don't, you're not going to make parole this time or the next!"

I walked back to art class, my heart pounding.

I was scheduled to appear before the parole board with a long list of other girls. There was a girl serving time for first-degree murder. She was convicted of taking her husband's gun and blowing his brains out while he was asleep. I faced the board with her and several grand larcenists, embezzlers, forgers, dope addicts, and a gun smuggler. My disturbing-the-peace charge sure seemed puny in such fast company.

We all dressed our best, put our best foot forward, and appeared before the board, one by one. The sessions lasted through most of the day. When it was all over, we sat around discussing our opinions about making parole.

All the girls were convinced that I'd make it. But I felt a little uneasy because of the disinterested attitude the parole board representative exhibited toward me. I was before him less than a third of the time he spent with any of the other girls. He scarcely talked with me, and seemed totally uninterested in anything I had to say.

Time dragged by for the next few weeks, as we waited

for our answers to come back from Washington. One by one, they began to roll in at evening mail call.

"Whoopee, I made it! I'm going home!" shouted Mary, the murderess.

"Yea! If you can make it, there's a chance for me!" yelled Evelyn, the bank larcenist.

"I never thought they would grant parole to a gal serving twenty years for first-degree murder. You've only been here a year, Mary," exclaimed Jody.

"Yes," said Mary, "about a year and a half."

The next night the gun-runner got a letter. A look of sheer delight danced in her eyes as she looked at the piece of paper. "I got it! I got it! It's granted!" she cried, grabbing Mary and dancing around the room with her. "And look at the date here—I go home three days before you do!"

One by one, all the answers trickled in—all the answers but mine. Each evening I rushed to mail call and waited for my answer, but it never came. Every night my name was called. Every night my heart leaped with hopeful anticipation. Always, the letter the officer handed me was written on Brenda's familiar stationery.

I looked at every answer that came in. Even the denials. The denials were interesting. They were based largely on the prisoner's behavior after entering prison, with consideration given to the prior record and the nature of the offense. Some girls were denied parole because they had serious fights with other inmates or serious arguments with officers. Dope addicts were denied because they had been caught with smuggled-in narcotics. Thieves and embezzlers were denied because they'd been caught stealing things in prison. There were always logical reasons, causes, and explanations for denials.

One evening my name was called and I rushed forward.

The officer handed me two letters. The top one was from
Brenda. The other was from my mother. I went back to my
room to sit on my bunk and enjoy my mail. I opened Brenda's letter and my heart leaped. It read:

Oh, Mom. I'm so happy, so excited—I just knew you'd make
parole! What is the exact day you are scheduled to leave? The
one on your parole answer slip? Write and tell us the day and
the hour so we can pick you up. Your friends want to come with
me to get you, and the newspapers have been calling. The parole
officer came to visit Grandma. He told us you would make parole.
He said they'd have to grant it. I'll be out to see you Sunday. You
can tell me the time then. I can hardly wait. I love you.

> Brenda

I tore open my mother's letter with trembling hands.

Dear Liz—The parole officer was here. He says you're coming
home. We sure are happy about it. Your dad and I are making a
lot of plans for you. You are being paroled to us, you know.
Brenda and your friends will pick you up and bring you here. We
sure are glad you made it. We'll be waiting to see you. Love,

> Mom

I rushed out of my room. I bumped into Pat Conway on
her way in. "Pat! Pat!" I cried. "I'm going home! I'm going home!"

Pat looked stunned. "Really?" she said. She smiled, but
it was a sad smile. "I'm real happy for you, Liz," she said,
wiping a tear from her cheek.

"Do you always cry when you're happy?"

"Not always Liz. Only when I'm happy and sad at the
same time. I'm going to miss you a lot. I'm not meant to
have a friend, I guess. Any time I care about anything, it
gets snatched away from me."

"Stop that, Pat. Don't talk like that. I know you want to see me get out of here."

"Oh, Liz, of course I do!" she smiled, snapping out of her mixed mood. "Of course, I'm glad."

I raced out of the room to tell the other girls the good news.

Wednesday's mail call went by . . . Thursday . . . Friday. Saturday evening I stood at mail call with my heart in my mouth. Finally, my name was called. I rushed forward. The officer handed me a brown envelope.

"It's here! It's here!" I cried, ripping it open in delight. "Just in time for Brenda's visit tomorrow. Hooray!"

"Don't you think you should read it before you start shouting?" said the officer quietly.

"I've already made parole. I already know," I smiled. "I just want to see what time I'm leaving."

I withdrew the slip of paper. My name and prison identification number were on the top. Aside from that, there was only one word on the paper: *DENIED*. It was in the center of the page in parentheses.

I sat there staring at the paper in a stupor. The officer stepped forward. Her voice sounded hollow and dreamlike. "Liz, would you like a tranquilizer?" she asked.

"I don't need to be tranquilized," I said. "I'm already paralyzed." I rose and walked down the hall in a trance.

Pat Conway rushed to meet me. "Liz, what does it say? When are you going home?"

My throat was dry, with a lump too big to swallow. I didn't answer. I just handed Pat the paper, climbed into my bunk, and turned my face to the wall.

All through the night I kept waking up, thinking the whole thing was a nightmare. I was glad when morning finally came.

I dressed for breakfast like a sleepwalker. Pat and I walked to the dining room like robots, not uttering a word. My friends in the chow line greeted me with a simple, "Hi, Liz." No one mentioned my unhappy news.

Over oatmeal and toast, Pat finally spoke up. "The sooner you face it and talk about it, the better off you'll be. You can't change it by ignoring it, you know. What gets me is the way they gave you no explanation—no reasons. I never saw a denial like that. It's hard to understand."

"Yeah," I said. "Well, let me tell you something worse. Brenda will be here in an hour to find out what time to pick me up. What do I say? Come back in two years?"

I went back to my room and dressed for her visit. She soon arrived in a pert, pink and white maternity dress and saucy white hat. Her patent leather pumps clicked happily down the walk to the visitors' bungalow.

"Liz Renay—visitor," boomed the officer's voice.

I made my way slowly down the path to the visitors' area. I would have sooner taken a beating than break the news to Brenda. As I entered the door, she sprang to her feet, smiling eagerly. She practically ran to meet me, grabbing me around the neck and kissing me, jumping up and down with joy the way she did when she was a little girl.

"Oh, Mom! Oh, Mom! Just think—you're coming home!"

"My, you look pretty today," I stalled, avoiding the unpleasantness a little longer.

"Oh, thank you, Mom. This is my first real maternity dress."

"Brenda, I've got some disappointing news to tell you."

"Nothing could disappoint me now that I'm going to have my mother home again," she bubbled.

"That's just it, darling. I won't be coming home. My parole has been denied."

"Oh, but Mama, it couldn't be! It's a mistake. The parole officer said—"

"—It was the parole officer who made the mistake, Honey—a big mistake. He assumed I'd be treated fairly, but that's not the rule in this game."

Brenda's happy, smiling face changed to one of sober disillusionment as she grasped the significance of what I told her. I thought she would burst into tears. Instead, she suddenly smiled again. It was that old, strained, forced smile I hadn't seen for so long. She was making an effort to be brave for my sake.

"It's all right, Mom. Don't worry about anything. We'll file some new motions like those we filed before. I'll talk to your friends—we'll get a new lawyer—we'll get you out somehow!"

"Sure, Honey, we'll do whatever we can."

"Mama, how long will it be if—if—"

"Two years, Darling."

"I have to go now. You see, someone's waiting to drive me home," she lied, forcing the smile again. She threw her arms around my neck and hugged me tight, burying her blonde head against my shoulder. Then she quickly let go and rushed out the door without looking back.

I watched her from the visiting room window as she dejectedly walked to the gate house. Only the heaving of the shoulders told me she was sobbing.

When I got back to my cell, I wrote her a letter: "Darling, go home to your grandmother. Mama was expecting me. She'll be as hurt as you are about the denial. Don't have your baby here alone. Stay with Grandma until I get out."

"No, Mom," she answered. "I couldn't do that. I can't go where I'll be too far away to visit you. Two years is a long time. I can't leave you here alone."

"But you must go there until the baby is born," I wrote back.

"Okay, but I won't leave until a month before the baby is due. I'll stay till the last minute!" she replied.

She continued to write me every day and visit me every Sunday through the remaining months of her pregnancy—always full of encouragement.

I found myself thinking about Judge Hall again. How I detested that man! I couldn't hear his name without my blood boiling. I sat down in front of the mirror.

"Liz Renay," I said, "it's time you had another long talk with yourself. You have got to stop hating Judge Hall. You can't afford to waste any more time and energy thinking about him. He's an old man ready for the grave. He's to be pitied. He isn't worth more thought, time, or concern. You've spent a year hating him—that's long enough. You must forgive and forget right now—do you hear?"

I pulled out a sheet of my prison stationery and wrote him a letter telling him I held no ill will or hard feelings and mailed it before I could change my mind. As I dropped the letter in the box, I felt a weight drop from around my shoulders.

Chapter 34

WHO IS GOD?

"Mormon services are beginning," called the officer. I slipped on my sweater and hurried to Control. I was not a member of the Mormon Church, nor had I belonged to any church since the day I rebelled against the Assembly of God and ran off to the skating rink. But, having been brought up in the predominantly Mormon town of Mesa, Arizona, and attending Mormon services with my school friends, I developed a healthy respect for the Mormon people. I had always loved to go to the old Mezona, a dance hall owned and operated by the Mormon Church. It has stood on Mesa's Main Street for as long as I can remember.

When I heard that Mormon missionaries were conducting services inside the typing room every Sunday, I attended out of curiosity. I had been going six months now. The services were bright and cheerful and something to look forward to. It was uplifting and fun to see those lovely ladies fresh from the free world, wearing the latest fashions and smelling of perfume. It was an hour's escape from the drab, prison-garbed population. I could close my ears to the slang, curses, and vulgarity of prison life and glimpse the world I loved to remember.

The missionaries played records for us and showed films. I looked forward to them. They were showing a film today. I didn't want to miss it. I hurried to the classroom. The girls were seated, and the service about to begin. I looked around for a place to sit. Every seat was taken. Ruth slid over and allowed me to share hers.

When I first started going to Mormon services, the two Mormon girls in the institution were the only ones attending. Then one day I discussed a film I'd seen at church with my art class, and it aroused curiosity. The next Sunday three of my art students attended. Word spread. Now sixteen of my students and friends were attending. It was a good thing there weren't more of them or they'd never fit into the small room. Too bad the Mormon missionaries weren't allowed to conduct their services in the chapel, the way the Catholic priest and the Episcopal minister did. We opened our song books and began to sing. It always seemed strange singing without accompaniment.

Before the service ended, one of the missionaries spoke up, "Which one of you young ladies will volunteer to ask Miss Hollerand if we can conduct our services in the rehearsal room adjoining the chapel? Our group is growing so fast, this room is no longer adequate. There's an organ in the rehearsal room. We could bring an organist out to accompany you girls with your singing."

I raised my hand along with three other girls.

"Fine," said the missionary. "You girls see Warden Hollerand and discuss it."

"Why don't we ask if we can conduct the services in the chapel, like the others?" I asked.

"No, no, we know that is not possible. We were refused that request already, but perhaps Miss Hollerand won't mind if we move our services from the typing room to the rehearsal room."

I left the service puzzled, wondering why the Mormons weren't allowed to conduct their services in church.

Soon there was a knock at my door. It was Carole, one of the Mormon girls.

"May I come in?" she asked.

"Of course."

"Liz, there's something you ought to know. Miss Hollerand doesn't like Mormons. She did everything she could to stop the missionaries from coming out here. She couldn't stop them so she put us in the typing room for spite. She uses every excuse to give us a bad time. She's prejudiced against Mormons."

"Carole, perhaps you're imagining things. Why would Miss Hollerand dislike Mormons?"

"Well, for one thing, she's a religious fanatic—a bug on Catholicism. She'd like to convert the whole world if she could. To her, there is no religion but her own. The rest of the world is wrong."

"Look, Carole, what you're saying makes no sense. So she's a confirmed Catholic—so what? Lots of people get overzealous about their religion."

"Oh, it's more than that, Liz. Don't bring the subject up about the rehearsal room. She'll fight you on it and she may hold it against you. The best way to make points with Hollerand is to join her church! Everybody in the institution knows that. Why do you think all those girls are studying to become Catholics? Hollerand tries to cram Catholicism down everyone's throat!"

"Nonsense, she hasn't tried to cram it down my throat." I thought back to when she called me aside to suggest I could study to become a Catholic when I was ready. It was only a suggestion. She didn't push me.

"Stop and think, Liz. Who was the first person you were sent to see when you were ready to be classified?"

"Why, Father Riley, of course. We all were sent to him. There's nothing wrong in that."

"And how about every time you have a problem? Who are you sent to? Who sits in on every S.I.G. meeting and attends every affair at the institution, including the parole board meeting?"

"Carole, you're making a mountain out of a molehill. Sure, Father Riley shows up everywhere. What of it? I'm glad he does. I like him. When he shows up at my art class, he's more than welcome. After all, why shouldn't he attend every function? He's the only religious figure we have here."

"That's exactly what I mean. Don't you see? He's the only chaplain at Terminal Island. Miss Hollerand saw to that. She made life so miserable for the Protestant chaplain that the poor fellow quit right after she took over, and she never replaced him. She allows that Episcopal minister to come in for an hour or two on Sundays and she can't wait to get him out of here.

"This institution is violating prison regulations by not having a Protestant chaplain. She's also violating our constitutional rights and religious freedom. A prison is supposed to have a full-time Protestant minister and a Catholic priest in attendance and a Jewish rabbi on call. Any faith, no matter how small a minority, is allowed to send its representative to see imprisoned members. That's why Hollerand can't stop the Mormons from coming in. What she's doing is unfair. It makes me mad, but don't oppose her. It will only make things worse."

"Why don't you discuss this with the missionaries?"

"Are you kidding? Let's let well enough alone. I wouldn't want to make any waves. They might get discouraged and stop coming in altogether."

"Gee, maybe you're right. I'd sure hate to see them drop the classes. Still . . ."

Carole shrugged her shoulders and left the room. I sat down on my bunk to think. It hadn't occurred to me the institution was operating against prison regulations by not having a Protestant chaplain on staff. Was Miss Hollerand really a religious fanatic the way Carole said? There was one way to find out: Go see her as I had promised the missionaries. What we were asking was reasonable.

The next day Betty, Nancy, Gail, and I marched to Miss Hollerand's office to request the use of the rehearsal room. I was spokesman for the committee.

"Miss Hollerand, the Mormon missionaries would like your okay to conduct services in the rehearsal room next to the chapel, due to the way our group is growing."

Miss Hollerand looked like she'd blow a gasket. Her face turned florid and she sputtered angrily. "They'll do nothing of the kind. I told those—those people they weren't going near the chapel. I'm going to do everything within my power to stop them from coming in at all! Why, they aren't even a recognized religion!"

"Why do you want to stop them? They're not hurting anyone. And you're mistaken about Mormonism not being a recognized religion," I said.

"Roberta, come in here at once!"

"Yes, Miss Hollerand."

"Go get those books from the file again. I want to go over them more thoroughly. There must be some way to stop them. I've got to find a wedge to keep them out. Meantime, I'm issuing an order that no girl will be allowed to enter those services from now on unless she registered as a Mormon when she was booked into this institution."

"But, Miss Hollerand, how can you do that? You allow everyone to attend the other services. You encourage girls to become Catholics. Why can't we become Mormons?"

"That's about enough, Renay! The discussion is closed. Tell your friends that any unregistered Mormon attending those services will face disciplinary action and receive disciplinary reports against their records."

"One question, Miss Hollerand. I didn't sign in as a Mormon, but I didn't fill in any other religion, either. I left that space blank because I'm not a member of any church. Who's to say I'm not a Mormon by now? I've been attending for six months. You can become a convert in a lot less time than that."

"I have issued the order. Anyone who doesn't abide by it will be punished. I will hear no more! Go back to your rooms. You are dismissed," she snapped.

"Are you going to services?" Gail asked, when we were out of her office. "I'm undecided."

"My friends are sending a lawyer to see me tomorrow," I said. "We'll see what he has to say about it."

The next day I was called from art class to meet the lawyer. "Don't forget to ask about church," reminded half a dozen art students.

The attorney turned out to be a handsome young man in his late twenties with sandy brown hair and hazel eyes. "Hello," he said. "My name is Conrad Judd."

"How do you do, Mr. Judd. I know you came to discuss filing another motion. Tell my well-meaning friends it's a lost cause. If you don't mind, I'd like to discuss something else with you first."

"Of course." He smiled, and motioned for me to be seated.

"Mr. Judd, I have been attending Mormon services for six months. So have a lot of the other girls. Out of a clear sky, Miss Hollerand issued an order that if we attended the services we'd get disciplinary action. How can she stop us from going to church? Don't we have the right to attend the church of our choice?"

"You certainly do. This is still America. You don't lose your religious freedom by going to prison. Miss Hollerand has no authority to make a rule against attending church."

"Well, the girls say she's radical about religion—thinks hers is the only one and fights against anything that doesn't agree with it."

"Why do you want to attend these services? Are they really important to you?"

"I enjoy them, or I wouldn't have attended for the last six months. And another thing, I don't want anyone violating my rights. We don't have many rights left, so we'd like to hold on to the few we have."

"Liz, if it's important to you, go ahead and attend. Miss Hollerand is only bluffing. She can't take disciplinary action or write a disciplinary report against you. What could she write on the report—that Liz Renay attended church?"

"Okay, I'll go, but please keep in close touch in case I run into difficulty," I said. He agreed. We discussed the new motion, and he walked out of the Control building.

When I stepped out of the door, a group of the girls were waiting. "What did the lawyer say?" they asked. "Can we still go?"

"I'm going," I answered. "I don't have parole to worry about. Let me be the test case."

"That's a good idea," said Nancy. "Gail and I heard the order, so we'd better not chance it. But some of the others could go and say they hadn't heard the order yet."

"Yeah," said Evelyn. "All the rest of us can go. What did the lawyer say, Liz?"

"He thinks Miss Hollerand was bluffing. He said we are allowed to go to church and she hasn't the authority to rule against it. But don't count on it. Lawyers can be wrong, you know."

The next Sunday thirteen of us walked to Control when Mormon services were announced. As we reached the door, we saw an officer posted in front of it. She quickly admitted the two Mormon girls, then turned to the rest of us.

"I have an announcement to make," she said. "Disciplinary Court is now in session. Any girl proceeding through this door while Mormon services are being conducted will receive an automatic D.R. and will be brought before Disciplinary Court for punishment."

"I like the services, but no service is worth getting a Disciplinary Report over. I'm too close to parole time," said Jody, walking away.

"Me, too," said Vera. "I don't want anything to stand in the way of gettin' out of here. If Miss Hollerand wants me to be a Catholic, hell, I'll even do that!"

"I hate to let her get away with this," said Martha. "But I can't take the chance!"

"Let's go, Ruthie. Let her win her damn point. I'm not going to argue with a D.R. court," said Sally, pulling at Ruthie's arm.

As they walked away, Barbara followed them, calling back over her shoulder, "If you go as the test case like you said, let us know what happens."

"Oh, is that it? So you plan to act as a test case?" said the officer. "If that's it, walk right in. Miss Hollerand will make a test case out of you, all right. Look, girls, there's only five of you left. Why don't you go home? Quit while you're ahead."

"I'm going in," I said. "I have to see this to believe it. How can she punish anyone for going to church?"

I mounted the steps, with Pat, Wanda, Juanita, and Rosemary behind me. We took our places with the two Mormon girls in time to join in on the last hymn of the morning.

The missionaries smiled. "Good morning, girls, there are

only a few of us today, but the Lord says if only two are gathered together in His name, there He is, also. Liz, you were on the committee that saw Miss Hollerand about the rehearsal room. Do you have anything to report?"

"Yes. You can't use it. Her answer was no."

"I was afraid she would refuse. What a shame—but we have an alternative. If Miss Hollerand wants us in a typing room, perhaps we could use the regular typing room at the school building instead of this room that's set up to accommodate only a few office typists. We wouldn't be so crowded, and we could show movies on a large screen, instead of this tiny one."

"I suggest you cool it for a while," Pat said. "Miss Hollerand is reading every book on the compound, looking for a way to stop you from coming here at all."

"Yeah, we are here under threat of D.R. There's an officer posted outside. Hollerand issued an order against attending your meetings," explained Wanda.

"All but us two registered Mormons," admitted Carole.

"That's terrible! We don't wish to cause trouble for anyone."

"My attorney says she can't do it. We'll let you know next Sunday if he's right," I said.

We went on with the service. The officer stood at the door until we all filed out and she checked our names.

The next day, I was summoned to Disciplinary Court, along with Pat, Wanda, Juanita, and Rosemary. We were ushered into a quiet room with a big desk. The "gleesome threesome" were seated behind it: Miss Hollerand, Miss Clark, and Miss Circle—warden, captain, and parole officer.

Miss Hollerand stood as we walked in. "Renay, I warned you, personally, not to attend the services. I made it perfectly clear to you. I did not warn you other young ladies.

Therefore, I have no way of knowing whether you understood what you were doing. Pat, Wanda, Rosemary, and Juanita, this is my final warning. If you ever attend those services again, it will go hard with you. As for you, Liz Renay, you seem to be the ringleader of all this. I understand you set yourself up as a test case. I hope your punishment will serve as an example. I am hereby stripping you of the thirty days you earned for meritorious good time. Because you attended that service, you will remain in this institution thirty days longer. Tell me, is one Mormon service worth sacrificing thirty days in the free world?"

We sat in shocked silence. "Any questions?" she asked.

"Yes," I said. "How will my Disciplinary Report read? How can you explain taking thirty days from me just because I attended a church service?"

"I'll be happy to answer that, Liz," she smiled. "Your D.R. will say you openly defied the orders of an officer and broke a rule issued by the warden. That's all. We are under no obligation to explain details. Any further questions?"

We walked out of the room aghast. "Gee, I'm sorry," said Pat. "Not that I mind having you as a roomie for an extra thirty days."

"That woman is unbelievable," said Rosemary.

The next day my attorney greeted me with a big smile.

"One of the girls said they took away your thirty days," he laughed.

"And you find that amusing? It's not funny!"

"Relax, Liz. Like I told you, the old gal is bluffing. She had to make an example of you. You can bet your bottom dollar she didn't really take those thirty days or write that report. Wait and see, she'll figure out some way of restoring them to you before you leave the institution. She won't risk getting involved in a religious squabble and she couldn't cover up the facts. There are too many witnesses."

"You don't know Miss Hollerand, Conrad."

"Do you dislike her?"

"She's doing what she thinks is right. I guess she's just a misguided crusader for the Catholic church."

"Liz, maybe you should attend services next Sunday. Call her bluff. You'll find out she doesn't have a leg to stand on. If we make an issue of it, she'll have to pull in her horns and back away. If you have a problem getting those days restored, I'll write Washington myself and tell them why, and how, you lost them."

"Okay, I'll go. Keep in touch. I want to be allowed to go to church and have my days restored."

I told the girls what the lawyer had said.

"I'm going with you," announced Pat.

"Please, Pat, let me do this alone. It will make it easier."

"Okay, but I don't like it. I'd feel better if some of the rest of us went along."

"Hell, they're not going to bite me—what can they do?" I said. I walked to the service the next Sunday with the two Mormon girls. No officer was posted at the door this time. We sat down and began the meeting. When the service was about half over, an officer opened the typing room door and marched in.

"Come on, Liz," she said. "You're going to the hole. It's solitary confinement for you." She grabbed me by the arm and marched me out of the room while the missionaries looked stunned. A crowd quickly gathered as the officer led me across the compound to "Lock-Up." I had never been inside the hole. It was reserved for the most serious offenses in the institution. I had heard stories of the place —now I would see it.

I was led to a shower room, where my clothes were taken and I was given a nightie. They took everything away

—even the bobby pins were removed from my hair. I was led to a dingy, dark cell without windows. The room was empty except for a commode in one corner and a canvas cot in the other.

"This is it," said the officer. "In the hole you are allowed no privileges, not even a cigarette. You will see no one. Time goes by mighty slow staring at the ceiling. Miss Hollerand says to tell you you may have a Bible to read if you wish."

"Tell her I don't want the Bible, just send me the Book of Mormons," I said.

The door clanged shut, and the endless hours began ticking by. Soon I noticed the air was getting close. I could hardly breathe. It got worse. I felt like I was smothering. God! I had to have some air or I'd pass out. I looked around the windowless room with its tight metal door. This place was practically airless. I was suffocating. I noticed a small crack under the door. I lay on the floor breathing in the thin stream of air—I fell asleep.

Ka-wham! The officer who opened the door nearly knocked my nose off. It promptly started to bleed.

"Watch where you're stepping," I yelled.

"What are you doing there on that floor? Get up from there," snapped the officer. "Here's your dinner tray. Hey, your nose is bleeding! Lean over the commode until I get some cotton."

"There's no air in here," I gasped. "I can't breathe. I'm suffocating."

"Your sinus condition must be bothering you, that's all. Lots of girls have been in this hole, and no one has suffocated yet."

"You can't tell because you've got the door open." I sneezed loudly, splattering blood in every direction.

"I'll tell the hospital to send some antihistamine pills.

You've got hay fever," she said, and the metal door clanged shut for the night.

Thank God, she had managed to let a little air in! I felt faint. I placed my tray in front of the door so I could lie on my stomach and breathe while eating. There was a book on my tray. It was the Book of Mormons. I had only requested it to bug Hollerand. Damned if she hadn't sent it. I put it aside and surveyed the food in front of me.

The food wasn't bad, even in the hole. I guess I had been expecting bread and water. There was a big mound of potatoes with gravy, a bowl of salad, and some rice pudding for dessert. I tackled the mashed potatoes. Wait, what was this? This wasn't potatoes. It was nothing but a pile of cigarettes covered with a thin layer of potatoes and gravy. The girls in the kitchen were risking D.R.'s to smuggle me cigarettes. Hadn't anyone noticed I didn't smoke?

I dived into my salad and found the matches to go with the cigarettes. Chopped salad greens covered a bowl full of smuggled-in essentials. A glob of cold cream was wrapped in tin foil, a blob of make-up foundation in another foil ball, a scoop of face powder, a chunk of rouge, a dozen bobby pins, even a squirt of toothpaste and a piece of pencil. All this neatly hidden under what appeared to be a salad! I marveled at the ingenuity of the kitchen girls, but what good was make-up in the hole? Meantime, I was damned hungry. I hoped something on my tray was real.

I stuck my spoon into my rice pudding. Christ, it wasn't real, either. An inch of rice pudding covered a crumpled ball of paper. It was a letter from the girls. "Dear Liz: Don't worry about a thing. We'll keep you supplied with cigarettes. We sent make-up so you could look nice for your good-looking attorney. We got word to him through our Sunday visitors. Send your requests in notes hidden under the leftover food."

What leftover food? They must be kidding!

"The Mormon missionaries in San Pedro are holding a Liz Renay Day tomorrow. They are going to pray for you all day. Keep your chin up," the note continued.

I took the scrap of pencil and wrote on the back of the note, "Thanks for everything. I don't smoke—don't need any more supplies. No air in here, can't breathe." I covered the note with salad greens. I flushed the cigarettes down the commode. All that was left on my tray was a slice of bread and a glass of water. Hell, I guess it's bread and water after all!

Heels clicked down the hall, followed by the plopping sound of a kitchen girl's flats. "When I open this door, hand your tray to the kitchen girl," ordered the officer.

I wedged myself and the tray in the doorway. "Look, I've got to have some air. This place is stifling. You should furnish oxygen masks with this deal."

"Stop complaining! The hole isn't meant to be a picnic, you know. Here's your pills. No one ever complained about the ventilation before."

"What ventilation?" I asked, taking the pills and handing the tray to the winking kitchen girl. I slept with my nose to the crack at the bottom of the door again. I was shoved awake by an officer the next morning.

"Get off the floor," she said. "You'll catch your death of cold."

"Yeah, well, I'd rather die of pneumonia than suffocation."

"Here's your breakfast tray," she said with a puzzled look.

This time the only thing hidden under my food was a letter buried in the oatmeal.

"Liz, we have set up a continuous line of diggers. We are digging with nail files and scissors every hour of the day. We are gouging a hole through one of the concrete blocks to give you some air. Last night we took poster paint and marked swastikas all over the Control building. We wrote, 'Germany had Hitler. We have Hollerand.' We're raising hell. Hollerand is shook up, fears a riot, should let you out soon."

Next morning I was awakened by a whirring sound like an electric fan. The room was no longer stuffy. I could breathe again. The noise came from the gray metal box in the wall near the commode. I walked across the room to it. Air billowed out. "I'll be damned." It was a ventilator.

Just then an officer opened the door with my breakfast tray. It was that pleasant officer Mrs. Metz. "You poor child," she said. "I don't see how you were able to breathe. The officer who put you in here forgot to turn the ventilation on. It's been off for three days. Luckily I discovered it. Funny you didn't notice it."

"Didn't notice it? Didn't notice it? Good Lord, I've been smothering to death!"

"Why didn't you report it to someone, dear?"

I just looked at her. I couldn't think of an answer to that one.

"I'm not supposed to tell you your attorney's coming Friday, Liz, so I won't tell you. But if I were you, I'd expect him just the same," she smiled.

I thanked her for the information, though it was unnecessary, for under the oatmeal was the usual note. "Liz, Mail Room Grapevine advises your attorney is tied up till Thursday. He will see you Friday!"

I gave my finished tray to the kitchen girl, and I was alone again.

I heard an officer's heels clicking down the corridor toward my cell. Just then the nail-file brigade broke through the concrete.

"Can you hear me, Liz?" yelled a voice loud and clear. It was Pat. "Now we can talk through the wall. We won't have to send notes."

I put my mouth to the hole. "Run like hell, an officer's coming!" I yelled.

"Bye, now," cried Pat, as she scurried away from the wall. It was a good thing, for the visitor was Miss Holler-and. She opened the cell door and walked in. She looked weary and beat. "I'm sorry things turned out this way, Liz," she said. "However, you will have to learn my word is law in here. Your attorney will be here Friday. You will face D.R. Court Saturday. I suggest you consider the consequences before you follow any more of your attorney's brilliant suggestions. I understand it was his advice that influenced you to put yourself in this position. It's easy for him to advise you to oppose authority. He's not in here. You are! Remember that!"

I made no comment.

"I'll see you in D.R. Court," she said. "Oh, by the way, I'm sorry about the lack of ventilation. It was not intentional. We are not attempting to smother you."

Conrad Judd arrived as scheduled. "Things are getting out of hand," he said. "Warden May, of the men's side, had to either overrule Miss Hollerand's order or back her up by going along with it. Prison rules must apply to both sides. I guess he thought it simpler to go along with her. He issued an identical order, pulling over thirty men out of the Mormon services on the men's side, and now a riot is brewing. The girls write swastikas on the building as fast as the guards can wash them off. Now the men have taken it up, only instead of lipstick and poster paint they're using black enamel, which represents a bigger clean-up problem."

"I'm sorry to hear that. I hope none of them lose days or get in trouble."

"This thing is out of your hands now. It's gotten too big. You couldn't stop it if you tried. They're planning to let you out tomorrow. They've got more than they bargained for with your art class, theater group, and social living class raising havoc about their teacher being locked up—it's driving the authorities nuts. There's a line of protest all day long."

The next morning I was called into D.R. Court to face Miss Hollerand, Miss Circle, and Miss Clark.

"Perhaps you have learned your lesson by forfeiting thirty days' meritorious time and spending a week in the hole," she began. "I hope you have. In the event you haven't, I'm here to tell you that, if you defy me again by entering that service, you won't get off so easy next time. If you do it again, it will cost you more than you bargained for. I will strip all your statutory days from you."

"Now, wait a minute, Miss Hollerand. I have nine months in statutory days. Do you mean to say that, by going to church one Sunday, I could remain in prison nine months longer? Why, that's crazy! I don't believe it."

"If you don't believe it, just try me and see," she said, fixing me with eyes as cold as steel.

"No thanks, Miss Hollerand. I give you this round. I'll not attend those services again. I think you're bluffing but I'm not about to risk nine months in here to find out. I'll take this up the day I'm released. The newspapers will carry this story, coast to coast. You can answer to the public when the investigation starts."

Miss Hollerand's face registered concern. Miss Clark spoke up, "Oh, that's what every inmate says. They're all going to set the world on fire as soon as they walk out that

gate. But who listens to them? Who cares? Do you think
the press will print a prisoner's complaints about the
prison?"

"I'm releasing you from the hole today. You are free to
return to your quarters," said Miss Hollerand.

I was greeted by a throng of inmates. "Rah!" they
screamed. "It worked, she's out!"

"What worked?" I asked.

"Oh, we all wrote anonymous notes to Control last night
saying if you weren't released today, we'd start a riot tomorrow."

Soon the episode faded into the background in favor of
more current matters. But not before it set my mind to
thinking about God and religion. I was not a Mormon. I
didn't believe in Joseph Smith or his heavenly visions of angels and departed saints, any more than I believed in a
Christ Ambassador's narrow view of the world. Still, there
were many good teachings in both. I began to study religions. I studied the philosophy of China, Buddhism, Ju-
daism, Hinduism, Mohammedanism, Mormonism, Catholicism, and leading Protestant sects and beliefs.

At first, they were confusing, but gradually I came to see
the similarity in them all. After a thorough study of the
world's leading religions, I began asking myself what, or
who, is God? Is there really a God? From all accounts,
men have been believing in gods and worshiping them
since the beginning of time. The problem seemed to be in
defining God.

Gods and goddesses of the world had thousands of
names, fables, and myths surrounding them, but they all
had several basic things in common. They provided answers to the mystery of life and offered an explanation for
its purpose, beginning, and end. All but a few held out
promises of life hereafter. They offered strength and guid-

ance for meeting daily problems and set forth a pattern of conduct to live by—sort of a second conscience.

It was obvious man possessed the desire to worship a god and had woven his basic needs into questions answered by his gods. Primitive minds seemed unable to conceive of one god powerful enough to perform all things, so he had many gods, a god of fire, wind, rain, crops, etc., but, as the minds and imaginations of man progressed, the fewer gods he needed.

Soon he was able to realize one god so powerful as to be creator, sustainer, and protector of all.

The oldest religion still prominent in the world today, Hinduism, made its adjustment, not by ceasing to believe in its 330 million gods, but by recognizing them all as different forms of the one true god, Brahman, creator of all. Hinduism adjusted to include other religious concepts. It made room for Buddha and Jesus Christ by recognizing them as reincarnations of their ancient god, Vishnu. Of course, Vishnu was merely one of the 330 million forms taken by the one true god, Brahman.

It was clear that all religions had much in common—almost as if a composer had written several different arrangements of the same song. They all carried the same theme and led to the same goal. Eastern thought was introverted, Western concepts extroverted.

Eastern thought embraced asceticism, solitude, and meditation. The goal was eventual perfection after many rebirths, good deeds, and self-denial. Western thought looked on this life as the only preparatory period to get ready for the next world. These differences seemed the most significant ones. It was interesting to observe that, though the Bible was written hundreds of years after Hindu scriptures, there were striking similarities in the stories of both.

Manu, a Hindu holy man, performed much the same functions as Noah, Abraham, and Moses all rolled into one.

He was told to build a ship to escape the flood. Noah built an ark for the same purpose. He was asked to offer his only child as a sacrifice, the same as Abraham. He set forth laws to the people, the same as Moses. The commandment given Moses was "Thou Shalt Not Kill." Manu's law stated, "Wound Not Others." Hindu scriptures state, "As you think, so you become." The Bible states, "As a man thinketh, so is he."

The Hindu version was written over 4,000 years before the Bible. Did the men who wrote the Bible copy their ideas from the Hindus? Many say Jesus learned the wisdom of his teachings from the Hindus.

I came to the conclusion that it's foolish for man to attempt to pinpoint or define God. What human being has more knowledge as to who or what God is than any other human being? We all come into this world as guileless babies, knowing nothing of God. Unless some people are born with invisible antennas under their skin that work as receiving devices, tuning in on special messages from on high, I can't see how one innocent babe knows any more about who or what God is than any other. How is one human being better qualified to write a book about God than any other human being? I decided that, if I was going to trust anyone's revelations or hunches, I'd rather trust my own. If departed saints or angels started appearing to me, I'd go see the nearest psychiatrist.

It seems to me that God answers equally well to the name of Allah, Jehovah, Hari, or Brahman. What does it matter what name we call him as long as we're sincere? All religions strive to help people live better lives. So, it appears to me that the most foolish of all arguments is that of what god to worship, and what to call him.

Perhaps some day the world will stop trying to define God and recognize religion as a universal concept and alter their ideas concerning churches, the way the Hindus adjusted the concept of 330 million gods to be one and the same.

Maybe some day it will be recognized that all religions are basically the same and all churches only various forms of one church. Then religious bickering can cease.

Chapter 35

A ROSEBUD BLOOMS!

I was startled out of my reverie by a sharp knock at the door. "You have a telegram," announced the officer. "Report to Miss Hollerand's office at once."

"Oh, God, I hope it isn't bad news," I thought, as I rushed along behind her.

Miss Hollerand was smiling when I walked into her office. "This is the first good news I've ever had for you, so I called you here instead of letting you get the wire at mail call," she said, handing me a telegram.

It was from Arizona. I quickly opened the yellow envelope.

HI, GRANDMA, LIZ RENAY, JR. WAS BORN EARLY THIS MORNING. SHE WEIGHS SIX POUNDS. SHE'S BEAUTIFUL. WE'RE DOING FINE. PICTURES WILL FOLLOW. BRENDA

"Yippy!" I shouted. "Thanks, Miss Hollerand." I ran from Control. I had to tell every girl on the compound. A celebration was called for. This time I'd buy the cocoa.

Two weeks later Brenda appeared at the gate house with a teeny bundle in her arms.

"We took a plane as soon as the doctor would allow us to travel," she beamed. "I brought her bottle and timed it just right so you could feed her. I'm going to bring her to visit you every single week so you won't miss a thing!"

412

I pulled the blanket away from the tiny face and peeped in. Two of the biggest eyes I'd ever seen stared up at me. Brenda was right, little Liz sure was a beauty. I sat down on a bench in the visiting room, and Brenda placed the tiny pink and white bundle in my lap.

One of the officers took the bottle. "I'll take it to the lavatory and run some hot water over it to warm it," she said.

The officer squirted some milk on her arm to test the temperature.

I gave the warm bottle of milk to the tiny, heart-shaped face that was mostly eyes, and the wee rosebud mouth began sucking. As I watched, I felt something close around my pinky finger. I looked down—five tiny fingers were holding on for dear life. I kissed the tiny baby fingers. My —they were little. I had forgotten how small newborn babies could be. So this was little Liz Renay, Brenda's first-born. How perfect she was—how healthy—how beautifully formed. Yes, God was good to us. We had our share of problems, but this precious bundle sure helped balance the scale.

When I returned to my room, I painted a picture while little Liz lingered in my mind's eye. A tiny face, with enormous soulful eyes like a Walter Kean painting.

Not too many visitors' days later, Brenda came to see me with surprising news.

"Mom, I've met a swell guy named Mike Hanover. We have had several dates. He's crazy about Lizzy. It's getting serious fast with us. I'm going ahead with my divorce from Leo. I want to be free to marry Mike."

"Oh, darling, please don't be hasty. Think it over seriously."

"Mom, I'm tired. I'm all alone. You're going to be here for over a year more. I can't go on fighting with no one to help me. It wasn't so bad when it was just me. Now, it's me and Lizzy. I want to stay home and take care of my baby. We need someone to take care of us."

"Brenda, darling," I said, "I know how weary you must be. I know how tough it has been for you. But it's only for a little longer. Please don't marry Mike unless you think you can be happy—unless you really love him!"

"Of course I care for him or I wouldn't be marrying him, Mom. Don't ask me to wait. I can't hold out any longer—not with Lizzy to care for. It's too much."

I looked at her pale, tired face and her frail, dainty body. Her long blonde tresses looked like they needed combing. She wore no make-up. Lizzy was always as fresh and sweet as a breath of spring, but Brenda's own grooming was slipping badly. She was out there in a tiny furnished room, all alone except for the added responsibility of a baby to bathe, feed, and look after. She was working as a cigarette girl nights, taking care of a baby all day, driving thirty-five miles to visit her mother in a prison on her only day off. Sleeping only when the baby slept. No wonder she wanted an escape.

It reminded me of the treadmill I was on when she was a baby. I knew too well what she was going through, but there was nothing I could do. I was helpless. I buried my head in my hands.

"Don't worry, Mom, it's not as bad as all that. I care for Mike. He's a hell of a nice guy. Really he is. I'm sure we'll be happy together. It's not the end of the world, you know."

One evening I received a telegram from Las Vegas.

DEAR MOM, DIVORCE FROM LEO FINAL THIS MORNING. MIKE AND I WERE MARRIED THIS AFTERNOON. WE REGRET YOU COULDN'T BE HERE. LOVE,

BRENDA AND MIKE

I sat down and cried. If only I had been out there to take care of her! Now I had a son-in-law I hadn't even seen. I hoped he'd be kind to Brenda. God knows, she could stand a little kindness after all she'd been through.

Brenda brought Lizzy out to visit every Sunday as she promised. It was easier now. Mike drove her out and waited at the gate to drive her back. Meanwhile, he applied for visiting privileges.

I lived for those Sunday visits with my two little girls— my baby and my baby's baby. Brenda arranged the timing for her visit so I could give Lizzy her bottle each time. As the months stretched on, the tiny hands let go of my finger and grasped the milk bottle. Soon Lizzy was feeding herself, then sitting up, crawling, and finally one day she took her first faltering steps across the visiting room amidst the cheers of half a dozen smiling inmates who had adopted pretty Lizzy as their mascot months ago.

The federal prison wasn't exactly the place I had in mind for bringing up my grandchildren, but sometimes I almost forgot we were there. The visiting room group could have been almost any group of people out for a little Sunday socializing.

As time went by, Brenda began appearing at the visiting room in maternity smocks again and announced that a new baby was on its way.

"Why do you wait until it's impossible to hide it before you tell me?" I asked.

"Well, Mom, I know you'll worry and fret about not getting to be there when it's born, and I just figured the shorter time you had to know about it, the less time for fretting. I wish I didn't have to tell you until the day before it was born."

"How long will it be?"

"Not very long. I'm further along than I look. Nearly five months."

"No wonder it's impossible to hide it. Good heavens, don't tell me we're going to have another baby in just four months!"

"That's right, Mom. I scarcely show until I'm in my fifth month. Lizzy's brother or sister will be here before we know it."

"Dammit, I won't be out in time again. You'd think I would have managed to be out in time for the second one, at least!"

"Don't worry, Mom. It won't be long now. You'll be out right after it's born. It'll only be about three months old when they release you, in spite of the extra month you have to stay for going to church."

Old Mary Jane, the Island fortuneteller and soothsayer, overheard the conversation. Mary always eavesdropped for any scrap of information or news she came upon. Then she'd pretend she saw it in the cards. Her fortunes were as phony as three-dollar bills, and more transparent. The girls knew this, but Mary was harmless and good for a laugh or two. She'd tell a fortune at the drop of a hat for a candy bar.

I wasn't surprised when she showed up at my room that evening insisting on reading the cards for me. I wasn't surprised, either, when she said, "Oh, it says here your daughter is soon to become a mither again." But I was so surprised that I nearly fell over when she said, "Only this time it will be different. The cards say this time she is going to 'ave twins!"

Twins! I bolted upright before remembering Mary's fortunes were about as accurate as the sayings you get on a card when you step on a penny scale in the drugstore.

Chapter 36

ROSE PASSION COCKTAILS

"Don't you be a-laughin' at my perdictions—or a curse will be on ya," she warned.

Mary couldn't stand to be ridiculed about her fortune-telling. Once she got so mad at an inmate who teased her that she rushed into her cell and fashioned a makeshift voodoo doll from an unused Kotex and promptly began sticking pins into it. She was weird! She dabbled in all sorts of occult practices. She held séances and talked to the spirits. At times she gave us all the creeps. She constantly called up Albert Anastasia's spirit for my benefit, but always as he was about to divulge who murdered him, her connection would mysteriously cut off. I tried to tell her I really didn't want to know.

"Look, Mary, I'm not laughing at you! I'm just happy to hear the good news, that's all," I soothed, not wanting to ruffle her feathers.

I could hardly keep a straight face as I thought of what happened with her last prediction in the visiting room. She overheard Gail's father saying he was going to the race-track in a few days. Later that evening she pretended it was revealed to her in the cards that he should play number seven in the seventh race. Gail got word to him, and he followed Mary's advice. He bet the seventh horse in the seventh race, and the horse came in, all right. As a matter of fact, it came in seventh! Another time, Mary sold us

417

all on the story that the flowers of a certain tropical tree on the compound were intoxicating.

"Oh, my word," she cried as she passed the tree. "If the prison authorities knew what that tree is used for, they'd pluck it out by the roots tomorrow!"

"What do you mean?" we asked.

"Why, that is a Rose of Passion tree from the Tahitian Islands. Its blossoms are used to make one of the most powerfully intoxicating drinks you ever saw. They call them Rose Passion Cocktails and they won't sell more than one to a customer. That's all anyone could take and still walk out of the place!"

"Oh, come now, Mary. How could a flower be intoxicating?"

"Don't ask me, but the Islanders say the Rose of Passion is 90 percent natural alcohol. Why, it was the first intoxicant known to man. I'm surprised you girls never heard of the Rose of Passion trees in Tahiti!"

We all laughed it off, but before nightfall the tree had been stripped of its blossoms as though a flock of locusts had hit it. Gail and I were among the locusts doing the stripping. We returned to the room with our pockets, hands, and aprons full of rosy blossoms.

"How do the Islanders make the Rose Passion Cocktails?" we asked.

"All you do is mash the blossoms up and cover them with water. Allow them to stand for an hour or two, then drain off the juice."

We had a rather bad time with the flowers, which proved to be loaded with gnats and other insects. We strained the bugs out and pushed the flower pulp through a piece of cheesecloth into milk bottles we sneaked from the kitchen, and soon we were ready to test the brew.

"I don't see why the bugs don't get drunk and—by the

way—since when do bugs go for 90-proof alcohol?" ventured Gail.

The Rose Passion cocktails turned out the way most of Mary's predictions did. No one got drunk, but twenty inmates showed up for sick call next day complaining of diarrhea.

Mary wasn't the only colorful character that livened up our otherwise drab existence on the Island. There was the pretty little hula girl from Hawaii serving time for passing bad checks. She kept herself busy teaching the hula to interested inmates in exchange for services or commissary items. I painted a Hawaiian landscape on her window shade in payment for my hula lessons. A well-known vocal coach also graced our dorm. I studied with her twice a week and paid her with portraits of her husband and children. I did the same with an incarcerated drama teacher.

Girls from all walks of life were locked behind those walls. By exchanging services, a girl was able to accomplish many things.

There was time for reflection, contemplation, and evaluation. If prison serves a useful purpose, this must be it. There is time for deep thought and analysis. Conclusions are arrived at. Confusion has a way of clearing up, and people's souls are stripped naked for viewing. One is able to observe one's self as well as others in the glaring spotlight of reality. Prison life reduces people to their basic truth, stripping away all sham and pretense.

The Bible says, "By their works ye shall know them." This was never truer than within the confines of prison walls. There, no one can hide, no one can escape. Only what one can produce gauges one's bargaining power in prison. Only true talent prevails. It was interesting to note that almost every prisoner's life fell into much the same pattern inside as it did outside in the free world.

I compared life at Terminal Island with my life outside. On the outside I was occupied with painting, writing, and acting. In prison I was doing precisely the same thing! Within the framework of prison regulations, I lived my life much the same as I had lived it outside. I adjusted the prison to fit my needs, rather than adjusting to meet its regimentation. By painting, acting, holding exhibits, and putting on plays, my life was involved in the same goals and pursuits as it always had been.

The same was true with the other girls. Those who had been cooks and waitresses outside were usually found among the kitchen staff. Chambermaids in the free world were cleaning latrines in prison. Prostitutes on the outside were selling their favors to lesbians on the inside. Dancers found themselves in my T.I. chorus line. Singers found themselves in the prison choir. The smart continued to take advantage of the stupid. The strong rode over the weak. The kind remained kind—the cruel got crueler. The law of cause and effect prevailed, and life continued here as elsewhere.

Chapter 37

THE PSYCHIATRIST

There was a psychiatrist available once a month for inmates with problems.

No one took him very seriously. It was widely known that lazy girls who wanted to avoid work assignments would put on an act so that he would say they were mentally ill and not eligible for work.

One day I met him while going from the compound to the dining room. He took a long, appreciative look at me and then whistled softly under his breath.

"How did *you* ever get in here?" he said. "You're too beautiful to believe!"

"Oh, Doctor, I'll bet you tell that to all the girls," I kidded.

He stood still, silently staring at me. Then: "How come you haven't been in to see me?"

"Let me ask you a question. How come you are so easily fooled by those fakers who come to you to get out of work. Don't you know they're not sick?"

He laughed. "But they are sick, young lady," he said. "Any girl who'd rather pretend to be crazy than to work is obviously emotionally disturbed. They don't fool me. They fool themselves. They really are ill. Okay?"

"Well . . ."

"If you ever have any problems—"

"—You're so busy, nobody can get any time with you,"
I said.

"I'll make time for you any time," he smiled, with obvious admiration in his voice.

And so, a short time later, I found myself in his office,
pouring out the story of my life. He gave me a great deal of
his time. On top of that, he surprised me by reading up
on my newspaper publicity so that he knew about my public
image as well as my private life.

After a few months I found myself asking: "Why do I do
the awful things that make me feel so guilty?"

"What kinds of things?"

"Well, I guess I can sum it up with one word: men. I love
men. I thoroughly enjoy men, both in and out of bed.
Some men turn me on sexually and I just can't say no.
God, I must have slept with a hundred men!"

"Why should you feel guilty?" he asked. "You're a lucky
woman to be able to attract men the way you do and to
enjoy sex the way you do. You should be proud and happy,
not ashamed."

"Then why do all the authorities try to make me feel so
guilty about having sex? I'm here just because I went to a
motel with a man and was accused of having sex with him."

"Elizabeth, that isn't why you're here. You're here because you made a compact with the courts and you broke
it. Is the punishment just? Forget about justice. There is
no justice in this world. Accept that fact."

"Do you know," I said, suddenly changing the subject,
"I think I still feel guilty about the things I did with soldiers, sailors, and marines when I was a teen-ager."

"That's because you keep telling yourself that you've done
something wrong. Unless your act needlessly, definitely,
and deliberately harms another person, it is not morally

wrong. You brought pleasure to men. You certainly didn't harm them.

"You didn't force them or even induce them to have sex with you by lying or misrepresenting things, did you? They were responsible adults, capable of making decisions, weren't they? You didn't harm them and you didn't harm yourself. So who did you harm?"

"Maybe I was trying to harm someone."

"Who?"

There was a long period of silence. And then he suggested, "Are you punishing your parents?"

"I don't know."

"Liz, we don't have the time we really need to do a proper analysis with you. This prison psychiatry is something of a charade, and I suppose it's done more to placate do-gooders outside than to help prisoners. You're one of the brightest girls here, so you know that. I mention this because I have to telescope things . . . to tell you things that ordinarily we would develop in many months of daily sessions."

"Like what?"

"Liz, did you get enough love from your parents? Think about it before answering."

"No."

"Why do you say no?"

"I guess because when I think about it I realize that I have always felt full of love and I have wanted to love and be loved, but my mother—well, I guess I never felt deep inside that she loved me very much. She seemed to prefer my sister. I was her Jezebel. I did things to get attention. I tried to win affection but there wasn't much for me."

"What about your father?"

"I guess I feel that he loved me more than Mama did, but

he was careful not to show it because my mother would criticize him for favoring me."

"The fact is that both of your parents, because of their provincialism and their religious beliefs, could never accept what you've done. They could never give you the credit you deserve—and you do deserve credit. You're a spunky girl. You've stood on your own two feet with no support in the wings from your family. On the contrary, they've apparently disapproved of everything you did, even your success. You held out your arms to them, and they turned their backs on you."

He let that sink in. Then he continued: "You are full of warmth and affection. Now you must stop telling yourself that you're guilty of displeasing your folks. Forget about pleasing your mother. She doesn't control your life. Nor need you punish her for not loving you. It doesn't really matter any more. All you need do is recognize the effect your childhood has had. Even your desire to become a famous actress—and you apparently came very close to becoming just that—even that is your way to win public acclaim to compensate for the acclaim your mother refused to give you."

"Why am I obsessed with the idea of becoming a movie star?"

"Your beauty has something to do with it, of course. When a person is gifted with great physical beauty, many times that person feels an obligation toward it—wants to share it with the world—to display it for the world to see. It's another form of reaching out for love. Your desire for love is so great you reached out—not to one man, but to many men. Now you're reaching out to the world. You want to have a love affair with the world."

"A love affair with the whole world?" I laughed. "What an exciting idea!"

"Yes, you want to give yourself to the world. Nothing would better describe the way you feel. And that's fine . . . but only if you recognize the fact that the world can be a fickle and cruel lover and may not always appreciate you or give you kiss for kiss in return.

"Liz, your first obligation is to yourself. Not to the world or your mother or your father or even to your children. You must come first. And it's what you think of yourself that counts: not what others think. And if you don't think highly enough of yourself, it is because you're telling yourself the wrong things."

"And my guilt? Over my children and—"

"Forget it. It's self-defeating. You've done the best you could. You've done wonderfully well, considering circumstances."

I had a lot to think about until his next visit. But there was no next visit. He was transferred.

Weeks later, I received a book from him. It was *Sex Without Guilt* by Dr. Albert Ellis. It was inscribed: "To an end to guilt, and a new beginning!"

Chapter 38

TESTIFYING FOR MICKEY

Tammy rushed into the room. Tammy was a Hollywood starlet caught smoking marijuana during a narcotics raid. "Hey, guess what just came over the radio?" she yelled. "Marilyn Monroe is dead! You hear me, she's really dead, committed suicide!"

The words made me weak. "Tammy, if this is some kind of joke," I said, sitting down on a bench. "It's not very funny."

"Man, she's really dead, I'm telling you! Let's see if we can catch it on the TV newscast in the dining room."

Harriet ran up with the newspaper from Control. It was true, all right. Beautiful Marilyn was dead.

I felt sick. I went back into my cell and sat down on my bunk.

I remembered the vivacious, smiling Marilyn the way she looked when I was introduced to her shortly after I won the Marilyn Monroe Look-Alike Contest for 20th-Century-Fox. I had dreaded meeting her. I thought she'd be unfriendly, perhaps even contemptuous, toward anyone claiming a resemblance to her. I knew I didn't look much like Marilyn and was embarrassed to face her.

My apprehensions vanished the moment she turned her warm, radiant smile on me. The sincerity with which she said, "I'm so happy to meet you, Liz," was unmistakable.

She gave my hand a little squeeze and said, "You're beautiful, Liz. Some day they'll be having a Liz Renay Look-Alike Contest—wait and see!"

Then, with a swish of taffeta and a breath of haunting perfume, she was gone. I never saw her again, but I never forgot her kindness and encouragement.

There was a knock at my door. It was Tammy. "It sure is awful about poor Marilyn. I'm sure that jerk Robert Kennedy had something to do with this."

"Robert Kennedy? What on earth could he have to do with Marilyn Monroe?" I asked, amazed.

"Don't tell me you don't know. Everybody in Hollywood knows. You've been locked up too long! Well, anyway, Kennedy met her at a swimming party at Peter Lawford's place. You know Peter Lawford is Kennedy's brother-in-law. Poor Marilyn fell head over heels in love with the bastard, and they've been having one big love affair ever since. Everyone in Hollywood knows it. Peter Lawford was the go-between. The papers say Peter was the last one to talk to her before she committed suicide."

"Tammy, you're not making sense. Suppose she was having an affair with Kennedy as you say, what does that have to do with her killing herself?"

"What would you do if you were in love with a character like that? A married man with ten jillion kids putting on the goody-goody act of a righteous father and husband. Out to clean up all the sin and vice in the world while all the time he couldn't wait to sneak back to Hollywood and jump in bed with you? A back-street affair with a married jerk is depressing to any girl."

"How do you know what you're saying is true, Tammy? You can hear anything in Hollywood. How can you know what took place between those two?"

"Well, you can bet your life a hypocrite like Kennedy wasn't playing tiddlywinks with a girl like Monroe for nothing!"

"You sure hate Kennedy, don't you?"

"You're damned right, I do. I hate hypocrites! And there are too damned many in high places!"

Pat burst into laughter.

"What's so damned funny?" Tammy asked.

"Oh, I just can't help thinking of the irony of it all. If what you say is true, maybe Bobby was in bed with Marilyn when he picked up the phone and issued the order to toss Liz in jail for disturbing the peace. I understand Kennedy is due to visit Terminal Island soon," Pat said. "You should have a chance to meet the dear boy."

I decided to break the gloom by painting another picture. I'd paint the beautiful Marilyn Monroe as I remembered her, alive with warmth and vitality. The prison contained more than two hundred built-in art critics. When I was painting, there wasn't a girl or officer on the compound who could pass my cell without stopping to offer criticism, advice, praise, or comment.

"Hold it, I think the mouth should be a wee bit fuller." "Wait, Liz, that hair is not quite the right shade." "Hey, Liz, why not cut her neckline lower, show more cleavage?" And on and on.

I would miss all these interruptions when I was outside again painting in the solitude of my studio. Ha!

An officer knocked on my door. "Liz, report to Control immediately. You're wanted in Miss Hollerand's office," she said.

"Go ahead, I'll clean your brushes," Pat volunteered.

Soon I was seated in front of Miss Hollerand's desk.

"You are going out to court tomorrow," she said. "You

have been subpoenaed in Mickey Cohen's income tax evasion case. He's finally going to trial."

When I told the other girls, they were envious. "At least you'll get out for a breath of fresh air. You'll get to know how it feels to ride in a car again and look at something besides these damned walls for a change."

"Yeah, and you'll be with people in the courtroom."

"Yeah, and maybe you'll see some good-looking men."

"I hope so," I answered. "That would certainly break the monotony."

I found myself looking forward to the day's outing.

The next day a federal marshal and policewoman picked me up and drove me to Los Angeles.

I enjoyed the ride along the seacoast. What pleasant sights the outside world presented. I would certainly appreciate the simple pleasures of ordinary living when I returned to them again.

To my horror and amazement, the marshal's car stopped in front of the Los Angeles County Jail. "Oh no, not here again!" I cried.

"You may be here a week or more," said the marshal. "You have to be handy any time they get ready to put you on the stand, and the way this trial is going, no one can tell when that's going to be."

I was sick. Prison was no picnic, but this place was unbelievable. I had hoped I'd never see it again.

Back I went, back through the fingerprint routine, the bucket of DDT, the filthy canvas pad on the floor, and the rats and cockroaches.

They had made a halfhearted effort to clean the place up. They had slapped a coat of sickly, green paint over the walls since I last saw the jail. Cockroaches still skittered around, but at least they had a slicker surface to skitter on.

Early each morning the matron told me to get dressed for court. Each day I sat on my bunk anxiously waiting to be called. Each day I was told to get ready again the next morning. It was nerve-racking!

I slept on the floor as I had before. My cell was already occupied by two other prisoners. The girl on the top bunk spoke no English and made no attempt to communicate. Sometimes I forgot she was there. The other bunk was occupied by Clara, a big buxom woman in her sixties.

Clara was in jail for shoplifting. She chattered about her grandchildren and how she just couldn't resist picking up new toys for them every time she passed a store. She helped pass the lonely hours as I waited to be called to court. "I swear stealin' them dang toys is more risky than coppin' jewelry. They'll catch you every time," she confided.

One day I noticed the police matron marching a pretty blonde out to court from the cell beyond mine. As the blonde returned to her cell that evening, she paused by mine, briefly. She looked at me, sadly. "Poor baby," she said, "you didn't deserve any of this."

It was Candy Barr. She had been flown in from Texas to appear as a witness at Mickey's trial.

Big Clara looked me over. "My, you're a sight for sore eyes, child," she said. "How can you go to court in that filthy white dress?"

"I don't know what to do, Clara," I sighed. "I've been here for ten days, now. Every day I'm told to get dressed and stay ready. No one ever calls me, and who can keep a white dress clean for ten days in a filthy trap like this?"

"I know, I know, but you can't go out there lookin' like that. Why in tarnation did ya wear a white dress to jail in the first place?"

"I had no idea I was coming to jail, Clara. I thought I was getting dressed for a day's outing in court."

"You'll be leaving for court in one hour, Miss Renay," boomed a matron's voice. "Be ready."

"Hell, I've been ready for ten days. Is she kidding?"

Clara walked to the tiny tin closet, reached in and pulled out a big navy-blue taffeta dress with white polka dots.

"See this dress?" she smiled. "This is what you're wearin' to court. I ain't letting no roomie a mine walk outa here in that dirty rag."

I looked at the pretty polka-dotted silk taffeta. It was a nice dress with a wide flaring collar and pleated skirt, but it was huge. This dress was designed to fit 200-pound Clara. It would swallow me.

"Thanks a lot, Clara, but I can't wear your dress. It would never fit me."

"Try it on," she demanded. "If it won't work, it won't work, but at least try."

I slipped out of my dirty, white sheath and into the navy-blue tent just to satisfy Clara. It hung there like a huge sack. The sleeves were meant to be short, but they came down to my elbows. "See, Clara, are you satisfied?"

Clara studied the dress with a gleam in her eye. "I think it will be all right," she said. "I can make it work. It's not too long, right? The collar and neck are okay, right? So, presto—all we have to do is tie a belt around the middle to nip it in at the waist. Don't worry none about those sleeves. Who'll know they weren't made elbow-length?"

She dived into the closet and produced a belt, which she was able to wrap around me twice. She pinned it in place and, to my amazement, I looked smartly dressed in a crisp navy-blue, polka-dotted frock with bat-winged sleeves.

"Don't tell a soul you're wearing my dress. It's against the rules, and I could lose my privileges," she warned.

Before I could consider the idea further, the matron unlocked the cell door and motioned for me to step out. "The
marshal has come for you," she said.

Press photographers ran along the street, snapping
photos all the way. I was thankful for Clara's kindness. I
felt smart and elegant as I was paraded across the street
in the swirling, swishing taffeta.

Soon I was seated in the crowded courtroom between
the marshal and my attorney, Robert Herrmann. I saw
Mickey on the other side of the room with his attorney. He
looked beat and weary. His head was bowed.

I was called to the stand. I was asked the same questions
I had been asked by the Grand Jury. I gave the same answers. It seemed pointless to keep going over the same
things, but I suppose there was some technical reason for
having this read into the court record.

I felt sorry for Mickey. I knew he didn't stand a chance.
If Robert Kennedy could justify giving me three years
without parole just because I knew Mickey, what would
he do to Mickey?

Soon it was over, and the marshal was leading me
through the flash bulbs and floodlights into his waiting
car. "If we hurry, you'll be back at Terminal Island in time
to catch the newsreels," he said.

"Wait," I cried, "we can't go straight to Terminal Island.
I've got to go back to the jail. I'm wearing my cellmate's
dress."

After much arguing, I convinced the marshal to take me
back to the jail to exchange clothes.

"I may be able to wear Clara's dress," I said, "but it's a
cinch she can't get into mine."

We waited in the entrance room while an annoyed policewoman went to get my dress.

Soon she returned, pushing and shoving the protesting

Clara along in front of her. Clara's face was white, her lips tight. "I told you not to tell anybody, child. Now they're going to give me a week in solitary confinement and cut off my tobaccy privilege. Why'd you go tell them?"

"Clara, honey, I'm terribly sorry, but they were taking me straight back to Terminal Island in your dress. You couldn't get your big toe into mine, so what would you have worn out of here?"

Clara laughed. "I see your point, Dearie, but you needn't have worried about old Clara. When it comes time for me to go, I'd go, if I had to leave in my skivvy-drawers. Besides, don't forget I'm a shoplifter. They'd a been some other fat lady missin' a dress when I walked outa here!"

I thanked Clara again, bade goodbye to the Los Angeles County rat hole, and headed for Terminal Island.

"What did Mickey get? What did they do to him?" I was asked.

"It's not over yet." I answered.

We watched the papers for the outcome of Mickey's trial. Soon it was over and the verdict was in. Pat ran in with the papers. Mickey's verdict was splashed across the front page. "Look at this," she said, "that poor cat got fifteen years."

Tammy grabbed the paper. "Look," she cried, "it says, Attorney General Robert Kennedy sent his personal congratulations on the outcome of the case. Why, that dirty bastard!"

"May I see the paper?" I asked.

"Fifteen years for income tax evasion," echoed Pat, shaking her head in disbelief. "Why, no one was ever given a sentence like that on income tax evasion—not even Al Capone. He only got seven."

"I told you Robert Kennedy was a louse," said Tammy.

"Yeah?" said Pat. "Then why don't you cold-cock the

son-of-a-bitch when he comes out here on that visit. Then maybe you can shut up about him."

"As a matter of fact, the whole Kennedy clan gives me a pain in the ass!" Tammy said. "Look at this!" She held up a copy of *Photoplay* with Jackie Kennedy's face on the cover. "You can't pick up a movie book without this bitch's face on it," she continued. "Hell! She ain't no movie star!"

"What's the matter, Tammy? Jealous?"

"Jealous? Of what?" she said, her voice rising an octave. "What's she got to be jealous of? Her eyes are too far apart. She's got a flat nose and a big mouth. Beside that, she's flat-chested and bow-legged! She's a great big nothin'— a zero!"

"Well, Tammy," Pat said quietly, "she doesn't have to be beautiful. She's the First Lady—not a pin-up girl."

"Yeah, but *Photoplay* and the others keep callin' her beautiful, and that's what burns me. Beautiful compared to what? A dead herring? Maybe she's beautiful compared to Mamie Eisenhower. But she ain't no movie star."

I cut in. "Tammy, nobody is saying she's a movie star. Or comparing her to them, either."

"Bullshit! Then why do they keep plastering her panface on all the movie magazine covers? It makes me want to throw up!"

Another girl who had joined us said, "Say, did you know that Joe Kennedy made his millions bringing Scotch whiskey into America?"

"Well, hooray for him!" said Pat. "I sure wish I had a bottle of it now. I'd surely drink to the old bastard's health! For another bottle, I'd drink to Jackie's too!"

It wasn't long before Robert Kennedy appeared for his formal visit at Terminal Island.

Many of the girls planned to ask him for help.

One girl wrote a letter about the religious suppression Miss Hollerand practiced. Another wrote a note about the lack of medical care and the conditions of the hospital. Another wrote a complaint about a homosexual officer. They planned to slip the letters to him as he surveyed the compound.

But when he arrived, he was surrounded by an entourage of protective stooges, plus a bevy of camera-clicking photographers, and no one could get within twenty feet of him. He fairly danced through the institution, prancing and posing for the photographers and signing autographs for Miss Hollerand and other members of the prison staff.

"Gee, if he didn't have a reputation as a woman-chaser, I'd swear he was a fag, the way he swishes around," laughed Lottie Joe. "He looks like a fairy."

"Yeah, he sure thinks he's purty all right. Why, the way he carries on he mus' think he's a movie star or somethin'," laughed Lou Anna.

"Hey, aren't you gonna at least have a look at him, Tammy?" teased Pat.

"No, I'm afraid I'd vomit!"

"Well, I'm going to have a look," said Harriet, pushing through the little crowd. "I don't care what anybody says about him. I'm going to get his autograph."

"Yeah," teased Vera. "If I can get those cockamamie bastards away from him long enough, I'll offer him a piece of ass in exchange for his autograph—on a parole paper, that is!"

"Hell, I'd like to get that son-of-a-bitch in bed just once. He'd never go to bed with another girl if I did. I'd bite the damned thing off!" said Tammy.

"Ow-w!" winced Pat. "You are a mean little bitch, ain't cha?"

"Hey, look," said Nancy. "Harriet broke through the flunkies. I'll bet she gets his autograph. Hope she gets it—on a release paper!"

Soon Harriet was thrust away and she returned to the group all a-twitter. "Oh, I spoke to him; I talked to him and he spoke to me. Imagine that! He turned and spoke to me—the Attorney General of the United States spoke to me!"

"Harriet, you're stir-crazy," laughed Pat. "What did he say?"

"He said, 'I'm sorry, lady, I cannot converse with you.' Just think, he called me lady."

"Ay-yy-yy-yy-yy, they better turn you loose soon—you're crackin' up!" roared Pat.

Soon Robert Kennedy breezed out the gate and was gone. His visit was soon forgotten, and life went on as before.

One evening I received a letter from Brenda. "I'm leaving for the hospital," she said. "Next thing you receive will be a telegram announcing the arrival of your new grandchild."

I waited impatiently until a wire arrived the next day.

AMBER DAWN WAS BORN AT 3 P.M. SHE WEIGHS 5-1/2 POUNDS. MOTHER AND BABY ARE FINE. MIKE

I returned from Control and told the girls. Soon, I was hustled into the recreation room for another surprise party. Cocoa and cookies stood on the card table again, another stork was pinned to the wall, and another pile of baby clothes graced the card table.

"Surprise, surprise!" yelled the girls, dancing around the room with me. "What was it this time?"

"Another girl. Her name's Amber Dawn. Isn't that pretty?"

"Yeah," said Nancy. "Just like Forever Amber."

"Sounds like a movie star's name, or a stripper," said Lila. "But let me tell you one thing. You better stop havin' grandchildren so dang fast. You're wearin' our fingers to the bone a-fixin' up their layettes."

"Well, I've got news for you, girls. This is the last baby. It takes nine months to grow one, and I don't have that long left."

It was a nice party, and soon Brenda was back at the visiting room with two bundles. The biggest bundle toddled in front, while she carried the newest one.

"Mom, I brought Amber's bottle so you could feed her the way you did Lizzy," she said.

I pulled back the blanket to take a look. A beautiful pink and white face, as soft as peach down, nestled there, with a golden-brown wisp of hair curling from under the wee bonnet. She opened her almond eyes. They were golden-brown, too. I could see why Brenda named her Amber. She was amber. She had amber eyes and hair to match.

The last few months of my stay at Terminal Island dragged by, bit by bit. I painted, directed an inmate play, rushed to see Brenda and her rosy cherubs, played with Lizzy, gave Amber her bottles and then, suddenly, it was time to go home. I picked up a *Photoplay Movie Magazine* in the recreation room and read Walter Winchell's column:

A beautiful woman named Liz Renay will have paid her debt to society (as the saying goes) sometime this summer. She was sentenced to Terminal Island, a Federal prison for females, following her conviction in a trial involving Mickey Cohen, West Coast gang chief. She will have served three years.

I met Miss Renay before she got into trouble with the law over Cohen. She was applying for a role in the "Untouchables," ironically. She brought along some of her art, painted by herself. Quite a talent.

I have a letter from her teen-aged daughter about her mother's release from prison. In it she reminds me that her mother once was chosen as the girl who most looked like Marilyn Monroe. It was a national contest held by 20th Century-Fox. Liz and Marilyn were born the same year too.

The daughter says her mother will shortly have a book published. In it the author says, "I know what I did was wrong, but what else could I have done? Can you hurt a man who helped you when you needed it? Can you turn your back on him when you see him with his back to the wall? I was forced to choose the lesser of two evils. There was no way to win."

At the prison gates when Liz Renay comes out, she will be greeted by her daughter Brenda and husband and their babies, born while she was paying her debt of honor.

Walter's words made the whole thing come alive for me. I pictured Brenda, Mike, and the babies, and my friends waiting for me. I knew that at last the gates would swing open and there was nothing Judge Hall, the political machine, or even Robert Kennedy could do to stop them. I was going home.

Chapter 39

HELLO, FREE WORLD!

I called all my Terminal Island friends around me and gave away my books, my cosmetics, and my cherished art supplies.

It was a sad occasion. The girls cried—especially Pat. "What are we going to do without you?" sniffed Nancy. "We won't have no art teacher, no theater group, no nothin'."

"Nancy, no one is indispensable. You'll manage. If you really want an art class and a theater group, you will continue to have them. Someone will fill my place. Besides, if you don't have that, then you'll have something else to replace it. That's the way life is. Haven't you noticed?"

"Maybe I could take over the theater group," said Tammy. "I've had some acting experience."

"And, Pat, why don't you take over in the art class? You're coming along great with your painting. It would give you something to do," I suggested.

"Right now, I'm too blue to think about it," she sniffled.

When the morning of my departure arrived, I was escorted to the A & O Building, where I slipped into the lovely champagne-colored dress and matching picture hat Brenda had sent in for me. There were shoes, gloves, and handbag, and all my favorite brands of make-up. Brenda had thought of everything.

I enjoyed pulling the sheer nylon hose over my legs and

slipping into the frothy underthings. It had been such a long time.

"You can go into the dining room for breakfast and say goodbye to your friends, and then I'll escort you to the front gate," said the officer.

When I got to the dining room, the girls had set up a farewell party for me. Three long tables were pulled together. My closest friends were seated around the table, with a place at the head reserved for me.

The table had a bouquet of pansies from the yard. Crepe-paper streamers from the art class decorated the table. Everything looked festive, but the attempt to make this a happy occasion failed miserably. This was the saddest-looking group I had seen in many a day.

The girls dabbed at their eyes during the meal and, when it was time for me to go, they burst into tears and cried out loud. Pat was trying hard to smile through the tears streaming down her cheeks.

"I'm glad you're getting out, Liz, honest I am. You'll have to believe me. These danged old tears just won't stay back."

Oh dear, I had to get out of there before I started crying with them. What would people think if I stepped out the gate in tears? As the officer and I left the dining room, I looked out over the long, sprawling compound. I knew every inch of that ground, every sprig of grass, every tree, every flower. How often I had taken long walks from one end of it to the other, all alone. How often I had walked along this very path singing, "You've gotta walk through the lonesome valley, you've gotta go there by yourself."

How long and tedious this unending path had seemed. I had walked it for twenty-seven months, but now it was over. I would never walk it again. My eyes caressed each little primrose and lingered over every sunny pansy face. The flowers had been so comforting to me. I had picked them, painted them, and loved them. This was goodbye, Terminal Island—goodbye, flowers, friends, foes, woes, and heartaches. Hello, free world. I'm back!

When we reached Control, Miss Clark stepped out and joined us. I wondered why.

"I hope you still don't have any ideas about talking to the press about the Mormon Church issue," she said.

I laughed. "What are you worried about? You said they wouldn't listen to me! When I step through that gate, I'm a free woman. You can't tell me what to do. I'll never have to listen to your bullshit again. What you say will mean absolutely nothing. Irritating, isn't it?"

"You don't intend to go through with this foolishness, do you? You've nothing to gain. I urge you to forget it. It will only cause trouble."

"You should have thought of that before you took away my thirty days. You're damned right, it will cause trouble, but not for me. You won your round, Baby. The round coming up is mine."

"Do you think the press is really out there?" she asked, a worried look crossing her face.

"According to you, they won't be."

The gate opened, and Miss Clark's face turned white when she saw the crowd of newsreel cameramen and press photographers poised for action.

"Good Lord!" she gasped.

Brenda rushed up, throwing her arms around my neck and kissing me. "You're free! You're free!" she shouted. Flash bulbs exploded and newsreel cameras ground as we stood embracing. Then Johnny was beside me kissing my other cheek. "Oh, Mom, it's finally over," he sighed.

As the reporters closed in around me, I caught a glimpse of the frantic Miss Clark scurrying back through the gate, severing my last connection with Terminal Island.

I exposed the prison's religious suppression over every major network, coast to coast, and discussed the institution's attitude toward homosexuality and its pathetic medical care. Newspapers churned out stories. Magazines clamored for articles. Interview shows rushed to get me set for their TV schedules. Paul Coates and Tom Duggan did feature programs with me again. Always, I made sure my friends at Terminal Island were informed of the time and channel so they could watch the shows. One of the inmate's sisters managed to get the news in and out.

I'll bet Miss Hollerand rued the day she decided to remove religious freedom from the institution.

Finally, one of the networks put Warden May from the men's side on the air in answer to me. He couldn't deny I was sent to the hole for going to church. He hemmed and hawed and looked foolish in his attempts to evade the questions.

"Was Liz Renay really sent to the hole for going to church?" asked the commentator.

"Well, I don't like to call it a hole. You see, it's really just a segregation cell," he stammered.

"But was Miss Renay sent there for attending a church service?"

"Well, her report read: Defiance of an Officer."

"In what way did she defy an officer?"

"Well, the incident did arise out of something pertaining to Mormon Church services, but I can't give you the exact details. You see, it happened on the women's side. I was not present when the incident occurred."

Inevitably I was approached by a close friend of Cappy's. He had a package of money for me. A lot of money.

"This is for you, Liz," he said. "We know you've been a stand-up broad and you really went through a lot, and the boys want to make it up to you."

I was silent. I was touched, but the images of Brenda's tear-stained face and the anguish in Johnny's eyes when they led me away to prison were still too fresh in my mind.

I turned the money down. I explained that I had not changed in my feelings: I had affection for my old friends. But I had paid dues that money couldn't repay, and what I really wanted now was to be out of it.

And that's how it was left, with my "Give my love and kisses to Cappy and the boys and tell them I really appreciate the offering but the whole thing is a closed chapter and I'll make it somehow without the reward."

I did.

The *Saturday Evening Post* offered me $3,000 to do a ten-page story. I accepted and they flew a writer out from New York to work with me.

Knight magazine paid me $500 for a one-page article on Mickey Cohen as I had known him. I called it "Mickey and His Monster," referring to the newspaper image responsible for his downfall.

The *National Insider* paid me $1,500 to do a six-part article exposing the conditions at Terminal Island. I told the story of Sarah's death, the religious suppression, and the homosexuality between officers and inmates.

Millionaire magazine called me to do a story on art. I wrote one, based on my experience teaching the Terminal Island art class. They paid me $1,000 for it.

I was becoming a widely published writer! Miss Clark was a bad prophet when she had predicted the papers wouldn't be interested in what I had to say!

Chapter 40

STRANGE INTERLUDE

Brenda and her new husband, Mike Hanover, and I stopped by a neighborhood bar, and Mike bought drinks to celebrate my homecoming. What a kick to taste Scotch on the rocks again! All the old familiar pleasures were so new and fresh to me.

And then the greatest pleasure of all: a beautiful man. Read Morgan, a handsome 6′5″ actor I'd met before my imprisonment. He was six years younger than I and had a fabulous physique. I guess he looked even better to me because I hadn't known a man romantically for twenty-seven months.

We made a date and he took me to a beach party. We went for each other in a big way.

He was great! He did everything he could to help me adjust to my new freedom. He paid the storage bills that had piled up against my possessions so I could reclaim them. He helped me get settled in a new apartment, hanging mirrors and paintings and making himself useful in every way he could.

It was great fun, and we were together constantly. He was sweet and encouraging. Within a month, he proposed to me. He assured me that the six-year age difference made no difference at all.

"Hell, you look younger than I do," he said.

444

Just as our wedding plans were firmed up, President Kennedy was assassinated. Although we both felt bad, even that didn't delay our plan to get married.

We drove to Las Vegas, and were married the same day President Kennedy was buried. Las Vegas was the place to be that day. Nothing could dampen the spirits of "action city" for long. The Kennedy burial was observed by the casinos draping the craps and blackjack tables with white bedsheets. It was too much bother to obtain black ones. The sheets remained in place for one hour, and then the cards were dealt, the wheels were spun, and the dice were flung again.

Read bought us a beautiful house on Acre Street in Northridge, a town just north of Hollywood. It was a cheerful yellow house with white shutters, surrounded by orange trees.

For a while I lived a happy life, waking to the birds singing in the orange trees. Read was right: the age difference didn't matter. Unfortunately, there was something else that did.

My husband insisted that we keep our marriage a secret. He didn't want any publicity. He was afraid my notoriety would hurt his career.

His career had its ups and downs. He had appeared in a television series with Henry Fonda called "The Deputy" for a year, and had done cameo roles on many other television shows and in several movies. His position as an actor wasn't strong enough as yet to allow him to feel secure. And so, no one could know about our marriage.

At first, this didn't bother me. However, as time passed, the situation became harder to live with. If a friend or producer dropped me off from the studio, I couldn't invite him in and yet I couldn't explain why. I couldn't even give anyone my phone number.

On one occasion, a movie director drove me to my door. As he pulled up in the driveway, he said, "Liz, I hope you don't mind. I'd like to use your phone. I just remembered an important phone call that I have to make."

I was so embarrassed I didn't know how to reply. I almost couldn't refuse him this simple request, but then I imagined Read running around the house in his shorts or, more probably, in the nude. I mumbled something about my phone being out of order.

My friends began to wonder. I kept myself apart from people. I turned down party invitations. I invited no one to my home. I felt like a mystery woman, and it really got to me. Finally, one day, I decided I'd had it.

We had a bitter argument. Read had been out of work for some time and nevertheless was telling me that if we didn't keep our marriage a secret it would hurt his career.

"*What* career?" I asked.

This was a blow that left him speechless.

Like a healthy pregnancy, our marriage lasted nine months. Then I couldn't stand the "secret" nature of things any more.

"Read, darling," I said, "it's time to split."

"Oh, no," he said, "I'm not letting you go, Beautiful. I'm not giving you any divorce. And that's final."

It was final until I replied: "My love, if you don't agree to get a quick, quiet divorce, I'm going to announce our marriage in full-page ads in the *Hollywood Reporter* and *Daily Variety*!"

He quickly reversed his position. We drove to Tijuana, Mexico, and had a ball. We celebrated our divorce more, both in and out of bed, than we had celebrated our wedding.

After the divorce we continued to date, for our mutual

strong physical attraction continued. We were and have remained good friends. I continued my post-divorce court-ship with my fifth ex-husband until Tom Freeman came on the scene.

Chapter 41

ENTER: TOM FREEMAN

I met Tom Freeman at the roulette table of the Desert Inn in Las Vegas.

We struck up a winning conversation while playing a series of losing numbers.

Tom asked me to join him in the cocktail lounge for a drink, and before long I was having a more private drink at the bar in his penthouse suite upstairs.

Tom Freeman and I clicked right from the start. He was an attractive businessman with dark curly hair and wore Steve Allen-type glasses. He owned a nationwide trucking company and was also in the mining business.

He had been around long enough to have his own firm convictions about life and how to live it. His maturity was a refreshing change. More, he didn't give a damn about my past, my publicity/notoriety, or what anyone thought about it. He thought I was great.

His courtship reflected his generosity. Expensive gifts to me included a Cadillac convertible, a $12,000 diamond ring, two mink coats, and a $750-a-month Hollywood penthouse. He jetted in from the East to see me every weekend.

One day I telephoned his office. His secretary put me on hold. I hung on quite a while before he took the call. When he did, I said, "Honey, don't leave me on hold like that.

If you're too busy to talk, say so and call me back when you have a chance."

"Darling," he said, "I'd like to put you on hold for about twenty years."

"What's that supposed to mean?" I asked.

"Liz, I want to marry you. I'm asking you to be my wife."

All I could think of to say was: "After five marriages, don't you think I'm a bad risk?"

"I'll take that risk. The rest of them just didn't know how to handle you. I think I do. I'll outlast them all."

"And just how do you plan to do that?" I asked.

"Easy. By letting you do anything you want to do. You want to paint? To write? To make movies? I know you're a maverick and a hellion, but that's one of the many reasons I love you. I like your spirit. I want you wild and wonderful—just as you are."

"Tom, no man has ever been able to keep me on a leash for long—"

"—And no man should," he interrupted. "Listen to me, Liz. I know that you've been busy cutting leashes all your life. I'm on your side. I won't try to block you. Maybe it has something to do with your alabaster skin and your big speckled green eyes." He paused. "Honey, we can't miss! How about it?"

"Well, it's the best offer I've had today," I kidded. "How can I say no? Yes, Tom, if you're game, I'll marry you."

Tom rented the large ballroom at the Ambassador Hotel in Los Angeles. He hired two orchestras and a half dozen vocalists. The wedding banquet had some of the echoes of a Roman orgy. The champagne and liquor flowed from 7:00 P.M. until 3:00 A.M.

As with everything I did, my sixth marriage was grist for the news mills. Newspapers, magazines, television newscasts all covered the affair. Even *Confidential* did an article on it. None of this bothered Tom. Rather, it amused him.

There were three hundred guests. Brenda was my matron of honor, and her two little girls were my flower girls. Tom flew my mother, sister, and nephew from Arizona and his mother from Oregon.

Sandra Lane was there. So were two of my long-time fans and friends from New York: Rita Schoeller and Dick Stanzioni.

Then we took off for our honeymoon in Las Vegas and Hawaii.

Five years have flown by. Tom's optimism was justified. Our marriage has lasted longer than all my other marriages combined.

We have had some hectic scenes, wild jealousies, and ups and downs, but we've survived together through all of them. Tom is the only man I ever married who really understands me.

Due to his busy schedule and constant travel, we see each other only on weekends. I feel like a legalized mistress waiting for her out-of-town John to come in.

Our relationship is never dull, never routine. We don't see enough of each other to get into a rut or take each other for granted.

Often, we fly to meet in strange, exciting places. Our marriage has been a continuing romance.

Chapter 42

COMEBACK

Dame Fortune seemed to be smiling at me again.

Jobs came looking for me. I starred in three movies, one after another. I did a cameo role opposite George Peppard for CBS; I did two more for MGM, one opposite Hank Williams, Jr., and one with Jean Simmons and Dana Andrews. Acting parts in independent movies became plentiful. None were important roles in "A" films. None would make me the superstar I once dreamed that I would be. I was cast as Poker Kate in a historical Western, a movie star's wife in a suspense thriller, a foreign undercover agent in a spy comedy, a society woman in a dope addiction film, the girl friend of the leader of a motorcycle gang, and an oversexed psychiatric patient.

Brenda and I and Little Lizzie shot a mother, daughter, granddaughter television commercial for Ivory soap, and were flown to New York to do a magazine layout. Stan Siedan, the producer of *Good Night, Ladies,* gave me the starring role in another play, *Baby Doll,* with Brenda co-starring as my daughter. It was a delight having my real-life daughter play my stage daughter.

I flew to New York for a major art exhibit of my paintings. Paula Insel handled it. It featured eighty-seven paintings—all done at Terminal Island.

Before we got the pictures hung, photographers, reporters, and newsreel cameramen swarmed over the place

451

photographing, interviewing, and writing feature stories. The Huntley-Brinkley news report covered my exhibit coast to coast, and NBC and CBS gave running accounts of the affair nationally.

The day after the opening, a huge picture of me posed against my Cleopatra canvas appeared in the paper, with an article about my art and my comeback. An article and picture appeared in another paper, captioned LIZ RENAY VS. PICASSO. Nice to be mentioned in the same breath with one of the truly great artists of our time! Papers as far away as London wrote about my exhibit.

The *Saturday Evening Post* hit the newsstands with its ten-page story. It featured a half-page reproduction of my biggest mural, a six-foot-long painting of a Grecian paradise with satyrs chasing wood nymphs across an enchanted forest. Paula displayed the *Post* article next to the painting.

The exhibit glittered with celebrities and press. The publicity soon attracted the eye of a committee in charge of conducting the National Arts Festival, an affair conducted annually in Madison Square Garden. They sent their representative to see me. He invited me to enter under their sponsorship. I entered, and to my amazement won first prize. This brought a feature story and center spread in the *New York News,* and John Carr contacted me for information so he could list me in his *National Directory of American Artists and Sculptors.*

Things were going my way again. I appeared in a stage play at the Alcazar Theater in San Francisco and then in one at the Huntington Hartford, Hollywood's most honored theater.

"Everyone should have goals and interests," Tom Freeman said. "Life would be static without them. We humans aren't happy unless we're striving toward something."

"Tom," I said, "I want to be a good actress, paint good

paintings, and write good books. I even want to produce movies and—guess what—I want to write the scripts."

Meanwhile, fate continues to pen a most unusual script for my life. Many of the men who participated in the charades that cost me so dearly are now dead and nearly forgotten.

Robert Kennedy is dead, and gossip about his affair with Marilyn Monroe has faded from the scandal-monger repertoires. Friendly Judge Martin is dead. Attorney Augustus Mack, who so eloquently defended me before him, is dead. Pierson Hall, the cruel and unfeeling judge who nearly wrecked my life, is no longer on the bench. He retired in 1968. He has had his own bad luck and heartaches. Shortly after I was released from Terminal Island, I read in the papers that his third wife Gertrude Hall had died mysteriously. Her gentleman friend was being held as a suspect due to conflicting stories he had given police. Seventy-year-old Judge Hall was also suspected by many since his ex-wife had obtained her divorce from him on the grounds of cruelty and desertion. Also Judge Hall had reputedly been very bitter over the settlement which gave Gertrude $700.00 a month in alimony and their $30,000.00 home, the car and the stocks and bonds. She was fifteen years his junior.

The television commentators who followed my story have floated into the oblivion of dust and memory. Paul Coates, Tom Duggan, and Joe Pyne are all dead. So too is Dorothy Kilgallen, who traced my activities in her nationally syndicated columns. Her husband, Dick Kollmar, one of my ardent admirers, is also dead.

At this writing, my friend, Walter Winchell, has recovered from a serious illness. They say the tragic suicide of his son caused him to lose heart and he stopped writing his autobiography.

Newspaper editor Agnes Underwood, a friend of Mickey Cohen's and the one largely responsible for creating the image that I was Mickey's girl, has retired from newspaper work.

Mike Hanover, the man who rescued my Brenda by marrying her while I was in Terminal Island, is dead. Brenda no longer lives in my shadow: She has gone out to make her own mistakes and create her own heaven or hell.

My Johnny married his childhood sweetheart and brought forth three beautiful children—two girls and a boy.

Cappy was nabbed at a New York airport attempting to board a plane for Rome. He was carrying a million and a half dollars' worth of negotiable stocks and bonds. Unfortunately, they happened to be part of the loot stolen in a Brink's armored-car robbery. He was given a three-year prison sentence.

Tony Bender, who gave me a Bon Voyage party at the Gold Key Club, when I won the Marilyn Monroe lookalike contest, has vanished, and the underworld scuttlebutt is that he was murdered. Little Augie Carfano was murdered, along with an innocent girl friend who just happened to be in the car when two men raised up from the back seat with .45-caliber pistols.

Itchy Mendell, the bodyguard Mickey Cohen used to send to meet me at the airport when I'd arrive in Los Angeles, is dead. As I write this, Mickey sits in a wheelchair, unable to walk, as he finishes serving the fifteen-year prison sentence he received for income tax evasion. He was crippled for life when an inmate from a mental hospital was placed in the cell with him and a lead pipe was somehow available to the inmate, who promptly bashed him over the skull with it.

Ed Davenport, the city attorney who reduced my resorting charge to disturbing the peace, has progressed to the position of a judge. He has become my friend and has been quite helpful with advice and guidance.

U.S. Attorney Tom Sheridan, who prosecuted me, is now in private practice. I recently enlisted his services to help straighten out the mess he helped create. He sent to Washington for the papers and I filed for a Presidential pardon.

Chapter 43

AFTERTHOUGHT

Today my life is filled with fun and frolic, parties, first-class seats in zooming jets, leisurely yachts, race tracks, roulette wheels, laughter, and exciting, creative people and things.

In the last eight weeks, for example, I have been to New York, Las Vegas, Frankfurt, Rome, and Jamaica, W.I. Newspapers in Europe described me as "the sensation of the Frankfurt Book Fair," and the book publishers' trade journal, *Publishers' Weekly,* in reporting the Book Fair, said that "Leslie Fiedler was the outstanding American, second of course to Liz Renay."

At the Vatican, I was taken to see the Pope's "private treasure," and the Sistine Chapel was opened and lit up just for me. I sat there for an hour devouring the beauty of Michelangelo's masterpiece.

Once, I had everything going for me. Once, I had every reason to believe I would skyrocket into film stardom. I was so close I could taste it.

Que sera, sera. Whatever will be, will be.

I've painted and written and sung and danced and joked. I've gamboled and gambled and won and lost—but I've never engaged in the wasteful game of feeling sorry for myself more than momentarily.

I've tasted the bitter tea of defeat only fleetingly—and then tried again.

Life for me begins with every sunrise. Each day is a new day. Beautiful. Promising. Exciting. Delicious. I live every hour and love every minute. I've come a long way from Mesa, Arizona. A long long way.

I'm Liz Renay and I'm proud of it. And conscious, too, that we are all playing roles in a human comedy of errors. I play mine with love.